SAGE was founded in 1965 by Sara Miller McCune to support the dissemination of usable knowledge by publishing innovative and high-quality research and teaching content. Today, we publish over 900 journals, including those of more than 400 learned societies, more than 800 new books per year, and a growing range of library products including archives, data, case studies, reports, and video. SAGE remains majority-owned by our founder, and after Sara's lifetime will become owned by a charitable trust that secures our continued independence.

Los Angeles | London | New Delhi | Singapore | Washington DC | Melbourne

STATE VS. SOCIETY IN NORTHEAST INDIA

Thank you for choosing a SAGE product!
If you have any comment, observation or feedback,
I would like to personally hear from you.

Please write to me at **contactceo@sagepub.in**

Vivek Mehra, Managing Director and CEO, SAGE India.

Bulk Sales

SAGE India offers special discounts
for purchase of books in bulk.
We also make available special imprints
and excerpts from our books on demand.

For orders and enquiries, write to us at

Marketing Department
SAGE Publications India Pvt Ltd
B1/I-1, Mohan Cooperative Industrial Area
Mathura Road, Post Bag 7
New Delhi 110044, India

E-mail us at **marketing@sagepub.in**

Subscribe to our mailing list
Write to **marketing@sagepub.in**

This book is also available as an e-book.

STATE VS. SOCIETY IN NORTHEAST INDIA
History, Politics and the Everyday

SAGE STUDIES ON INDIA'S NORTH EAST

Editor
G. Amarjit Sharma

Los Angeles | London | New Delhi
Singapore | Washington DC | Melbourne

Copyright © G. Amarjit Sharma, 2021

All rights reserved. No part of this book may be reproduced or utilised in any form or by any means, electronic or mechanical, including photocopying, recording, or by any information storage or retrieval system, without permission in writing from the publisher.

First published in 2021 by

SAGE Publications India Pvt Ltd
B1/I-1 Mohan Cooperative Industrial Area
Mathura Road, New Delhi 110 044, India
www.sagepub.in

SAGE Publications Inc
2455 Teller Road
Thousand Oaks, California 91320, USA

SAGE Publications Ltd
1 Oliver's Yard, 55 City Road
London EC1Y 1SP, United Kingdom

SAGE Publications Asia-Pacific Pte Ltd
18 Cross Street #10-10/11/12
China Square Central
Singapore 048423

Published by Vivek Mehra for SAGE Publications India Pvt Ltd and typeset in 10.5/13 pt Adobe Caslon Pro by AG Infographics, Delhi.

Library of Congress Control Number: 2021941154

ISBN: 978-93-91370-37-4 (HB)

SAGE Team: Amrita Dutta, Syed Husain Naqvi, Sonam Rana and Rajinder Kaur

Contents

List of Illustrations vii
List of Abbreviations ix
Acknowledgements xiii
Introduction xv

Part I: State, Region and Border

1. Social Imaginaries, Minorities and the Postcolonial
   History of a Region 3
   Anup Shekhar Chakraborty

2. Colonial State and Annexation of Cachar in a Strategic
   Frontier of British Bengal 25
   Santosh Hasnu

3. Spatializing Nation at the Border District of
   Arunachal Pradesh 48
   Sherin Ajin

Part II: Memory, Ethnicity and Civil Society

4. Public Spaces and the Politics of Remembering
   in Northeast India 71
   Jangkhomang Guite

5. The Socio-spatial Politics of 'Tribal' and 'Non-tribal'
   in Meghalaya 100
   Oyindrila Chattopadhyay

6. Interrogating the 'Civil Society' in Naga Society 124
   Rashi Bhargava

Part III: Security, Emergency Laws and Protest

7. Politics of Counter-insurgency and the Expansion of Security Bureaucracy 149
   M. Amarjeet Singh and R. K. Sanayaima

8. Emergency Law in Nagaland and State's Classification of People as Suspect 172
   Chubatila

9. Encountering the State in Manipur: A Political History of Women in Public Space 197
   L. Basanti Devi

Part IV: Development, Trans-nationality and Accessibility

10. The Trajectory of 'Development' in a Resource Frontier 223
    G. Amarjit Sharma

11. Development Schemes and How People Engage with the State in Manipur 248
    Tanmoy Das

12. Informal Political Networks, *Dalals* and Local Governance in Assam 275
    Amiya Kumar Das

About the Editor and the Contributors 295
Index 300

List of Illustrations

Figures

4.1	Assam: Assam Movement, Battle of Saraighat and Shraddhanjali, Guwahati	78
4.2	Manipur: Anglo-Manipur War Memorials, Imphal and Khongjom	80
4.3	Meghalaya: Old Monolith, Martyr Pillar, Memorials of Tirot Sing and Kiang Nangbah	81
4.4	Mizoram: Memorial of Laldenga and Martyr Cemetery in Aizawl and Sesawng	83
4.5	Nagaland: Khonoma Fort and Memorials of A. Z. Phizo and K. Seyie	84
4.6	Assam: Bodofa U. N. Brahma (Bodo), Bhasa Sahid Memorial (Bengali), Gen Chilarai (Koch-Rajbongshi), Semson Sing Ingti (Karbi)	90
4.7	Assam: Sambhudhan Phonglo (Dimasa), Rani Gaidinliu (Naga), Chengjapao Doungel (Kuki), Paona Brajabashi (Manipuri)	91
4.8	Rabindranath Tagore (Bengali), Haipou Jadonang Park (Zeliangrong), Anglo-Kuki War Monolith and Tintong (Kuki)	93

Tables

7.1	Major Operations against Insurgents by the Security Forces	158
7.2	Major Violent Incidents Causing Death and Injury to the Civilian Population	159
7.3	Assistance under Security-related Expenditure (in ₹ crore)	164

7.4	Funds Released to Army/Central Armed Police Forces Deployed in the Northeast under the Civic Action Programme (in ₹ Lakhs)	166
7.5	Strength of State Police Force	167
7.6	The Armed Forces (Special Powers) Act in Northeast India	168
11.1	Composition of the Sample Population	250
11.2	Overview of Mahatma Gandhi National Rural Employment Guarantee Act in Tamenglong Headquarters and Nungba Subdivisions	254
11.3	Number of Houses Completed under PMAY-G till 2018 (Tamenglong, Block Wise)	256
11.4	Physical Progress of the Housing Scheme under Pradhan Mantri Gramin Awaas Yojana till 2018 (Tamenglong)	257

List of Abbreviations

AASU	All Assam Students' Union
ADB	Asian Development Bank
AFD	Agence Française de Développement
AFSPA	Armed Forces (Special Powers) Act
AGP	Asom Gana Parishad
AMSU	All Meghalaya Students' Union
AOGs	Armed opposition groups
ASEAN	Association of Southeast Asian Nations
AYO	Angami Youth Organization
BADP	Border Area Development Programme
BDO	Block development officer
CAG	Comptroller and Auditor General
CAP	Civic Action Programme
CAPFs	Central Armed Police Forces
CEC	Central Executive Committee
CHC	Community health centre
CMA	Chakhesang Mothers' Association
CMO	Chief medical officer
CRAM	Centre for Research and Advocacy, Manipur
CRPF	Central Reserve Police Force
CSO	civil society organizations
CSR	Corporate social responsibility
DAC	Development Assistant Committee
DBT	Direct benefit transfer
DC	Deputy commissioner
DEC	District Executive Committee
DEG	German Development Bank
DFIs	Development finance institutions
DoKAA	Department of Karmik and Adhyatmik Affairs
DoNER	Development of the North Eastern Region

DRDA	Department of Rural Development Agency
EIB	European Investment Bank
EIC	British East India Company
ENPO	Eastern Nagaland People's Organization
ENSF	Eastern Naga Students' Federation
ENWO	Eastern Nagaland Women Organisation
FIR	First Information Rreport
FKJGP	Federation of Khasi, Jaintia and Garo People
GDP	Gross domestic product
GEC	General Executive Council
GoI	Government of India
IAY	Indira Awaas Yojana
IDB	Islamic Development Bank
IFC	International Finance Corporation
ILP	Inner Line Permit
INA	Indian National Army
IO	Investigating Officer
IPC	Indian Penal Code
JICA	Japan International Cooperation Agency
KCP	Kangleipak Communist Party
KHADC	Khasi Hills Autonomous District Council
KSU	Khasi Students' Union
KYKL	Kanglei Yawol Kanna Lup
LPG	liberalization, privatization and globalization
MCC	Manipur Chamber of Commerce
MDM	Mid-day Meal Scheme
MEA	Ministry of External Affairs
MGNREGA	Mahatma Gandhi National Rural Employment Guarantee Act
MNF	Mizo National Front
MoU	Memorandum of understanding
MRRSA	Meghalaya Residents Safety and Security Act
MSU	Meghalaya Students' Union
NBCC	Naga Baptist Church Council
NCAP	National Centre for Agricultural Economics and Policy Research

List of Abbreviations xi

NEC	North Eastern Council
NEFA	North-East Frontier Agency
NEHU	North Eastern Hill University
NGO	Non-governmental organization
NGT	National Green Tribunal
NHPC	National Hydro Power Corporation
NHTDC	Naga Hills District Tribal Council
NMA	Naga Mothers' Association
NNC	Naga National Council
NOC	No Objection Certificate
NPC	National Planning Committee
NPM	Naga Peace Mission
NPMHR	Naga Peoples Movement for Human Rights
NREGA	National Rural Employment Guarantee Act
NSA	National Security Act
NSCN	National Socialist Council of Nagaland
NSCN-K	National Socialist Council of Nagaland-Khaplang
NSF	Naga Students' Federation
NTC	Naga Tribal Council
NYA	Nungba Youth Association
OALP	Open Acreage Licensing Policy
OBC	Other Backward Classes
OIL	Oil India Limited
PANMYL	Pan Manipur Youth League
PDS	Public distribution system
PLA	People's Liberation Army
PMAY	Pradhan Mantri Awaas Yojana
POTO	Prevention of Terrorism Ordinance
PREPAK	People's Revolutionary Party of Kangleipak
PRI	Panchayati Raj Institution
SASEC	South Asia Sub-regional Economic Cooperation
SC	Scheduled Castes
SHG	Self-help group
SIB	Special Investigation Branch
SMRF	Save Mon Region Federation
ST	Scheduled Tribe

STF	Special Task Force
UCIL	Uranium Corporation of India Limited
UCM	United Committee Manipur
ULFA	United Liberation Front of Asom
UNLF	United National Liberation Front
VC	Village council
VDB	Village development board

Acknowledgements

The book's initial idea had emerged during the conference on state and society held in 2014 and organized by North East India Studies Programme (now Special Centre for the Study of North East India), Jawaharlal Nehru University, Delhi, India. Since then, the attempt has been to bring out a critical volume of works on the state, in a space like Northeast India, by scholars belonging to diverse disciplinary backgrounds. This book has been possible because of the commitment and cooperation of the contributors. They have shown high endurance in working on their chapters through several rounds of online and offline discussions.

I want to acknowledge the valuable time I spent with my colleagues at the Special Centre for the Study of North East India, Jawaharlal Nehru University, Delhi. Discussions among us on numerous academic platforms of the Centre on the emerging disciplinary approaches in social sciences and their relevance for the region also enabled me to conceptualize the book's core idea. The book can be understood as a result of the series of discussions at the Centre to initiate a critical study series on Northeast India.

I would also like to acknowledge Professor Tiplut Nongbri, with whom I began to associate academically in 2009. As a research associate under her directorship of the then North East India Studies Programme, I had the initial opportunity to engage with the submitted MPhil and PhD works on Northeast India in Jawaharlal Nehru University, Delhi, and understand the evolving Northeast India studies. I would also like to thank my doctoral student, Tanmoy Das, for going through some of the book's chapters and providing his critical feedback. Finally, I would like to thank the book's anonymous referee for the critical comments and suggestions and the SAGE team for the consent and cooperation in publishing the book.

Introduction
G. Amarjit Sharma

Let me begin with a brief prefatory statement on how the plan of writing this book began. The initial spark for this book began in February 2014 at a conference in Jawaharlal Nehru University, New Delhi. It was organized under the theme 'State and Society in North East India'. Scholars from various disciplinary backgrounds, who were teaching and doing research in various states of India and outside India on Northeast India, were gathered to discuss the above theme. Few of the contributors in this book were part of the conference. Significantly, contributors in this book are mostly located outside what we call 'Northeast India'. Their works are intensely based on the archival and literary sources on the region and ethnographic fieldwork which has been carried out in Northeast India. They are historians, political scientists, anthropologists and sociologists. Interdisciplinary approaches are broadly followed throughout the chapters of this book. Their location outside Northeast India, yet engaging with the latter, is an interesting academic position that bears mark on their research work. The position of 'outside' appears to me not just as coming out of anxiety of necessity to continue connection with the region but also as a position that allows us to rethink and question the region and the experience that bears on us.

The journey of this volume, although long taken, to date is significant for two reasons. One is an epistemic reason. This reason should be interpreted as the reason that has evolved through a series of daily discussions that I had with my colleagues at my department at Jawaharlal Nehru University and people with whom I interact in a platform like the above conference. Conference on state and society was held after the first base of faculty, including me, joined the then newly established North East India Studies Programme at Jawaharlal Nehru University. The idea behind such gathering was not merely to make our presence felt as academics but to initiate critical engagement with what has been studied on (state and society in) Northeast India and to rethink what looks like an emerging area of study: Northeast India studies. To be critical, to some of us, is to cultivate a practice of engagement (and rethinking wherever it is possible) with what has been conventionally understood about Northeast India, although it is an idea and area of study with which (and through which) our sense of location as academics is officially defined.

One such area of investigation that was immediately in our mind was the idea of Northeast India. The study on Northeast India is presumably, and mostly to many sections of observers, about policies that can deal directly and accurately with the emerging political development, movements and law and order, for instance, from the lens that can only be handled by the national security or policy experts. This was evident in the interaction, at the beginning, with the scholars who applied for their doctoral research in the programme. The scholars partially or completely dwelled on assumption that Northeast India is mostly about national security and policy. Scholars would hardly come with social science conceptual and theoretical preparedness while applying for doctoral research. However, one cannot blame them, as this was an issue seriously felt to introspect on why, despite years of social science research on Northeast India in universities and institutes, such an impression and foundation are made.

We feel, as a result, certain practice of problematizing and questioning history, politics and culture of the people and society in the region requires an urgent attention. Our effort was left, therefore, to re-teach ourselves the social science approaches of dealing with the facts, practices and experiences of the people in Northeast India. Our primary job was to ensure that social science disciplinary passage, which each of us passed through before we selected Northeast India as an area of study, is given prime importance. In brief, the perception of Northeast India as an area less dealt by the disciplinary strength of the social scientists to an area that can be effectively dealt with by the latter is being emphasized. Hence, the importance of an interdisciplinary approach is emphasized and put into practice while formulating ideas and thoughts on Northeast India.

Another reason that comes with a hope of change is the time in which we study societies and politics of Northeast India, which I feel is evolving and challenging (both the time in which one lives and the direction in which research is carried out). This is the time not merely limited to the immediate places of our work, thanks to increasing academic mobility through conferences, seminars, workshops and fieldwork. Judging by the time in which we live, studies on Northeast India could be considered as evolving because of two further reasons.

One, it is felt that studies on Northeast India have taken a new direction made possible by the generation of scholars exposed to new theories and concepts in social sciences. Interestingly, in many of the conversations with my colleagues and scholars working on Northeast India in academic platforms, it was concluded that a primary driving force of this new direction is the opening up of multiple ways of looking at history, polity and society and the usage of multidisciplinary frames to analyse long-struggling or marginalized societies. One major strand of this direction is the scepticism of any homogenizing tendency. This tendency is found in both the nation-building projects of India and the counter-nationalist projects, primarily known, in the studies of Northeast India, as the politics of ethnonationalism or subnationalism or the insurgency movement. I wish to say that most of the earlier works on Northeast India in the 1980s and the 1990s were particularly on insurgency and ethnonationalism. In one of my earlier unpublished works that reviewed the doctoral thesis and pre-doctoral dissertations submitted to Jawaharlal Nehru University (from 1980 to 2006), it was found that majority of the studies had been on insurgency, ethnicity and nationalism that hardly acknowledge or sense that homogenizing tendency of the state could be equally found in certain responses to the same state. However, researchers now, being exposed to the postmodernist theorization, have started questioning homogenizing concepts and categories. Issues on gender, marginality within marginality, the assertion of smaller communities against majoritarian ethnic identity projects, etc., could be cited as new areas of study. The second reason why I say evolving is that there have emerged new scholars who choose to look beyond the national and continental frames while looking at an area like Northeast India. Partly shaped by the connection that nation states are looking beyond the border for economic relationships and partly by the social and cultural histories of connections and political dynamics less guided by nationalist histories and politics, Northeast India becomes an area to be less understood through national history and more by looking at both sides of the national border.

This book covers varied experiences of living with and within the state in Northeast India and explores layers of political practices. The volume looks closely at how society encounters state, on the one hand, and how state shapes and is shaped by society, on the other. The chapters of the book discuss the expansion of state in colonial and postcolonial times, fluidity of border, boundaries and community, ethnicity and the politics of history, memory and space making, everyday legal discourse and classificatory practices of state, cases of women and state encounters, everyday forms of informal networking with the authority of state through the developmental projects and the trajectory of development in a transnational space like Northeast India.

The chapters of the book focus on five states—Nagaland, Manipur, Assam, Meghalaya and Arunachal Pradesh—which continue to throw up challenging context-specific facts and experiences. These states continue to be societies where mechanisms like asymmetric federalism (that seeks to accommodate multiple political demands, within the fold of Indian nationhood) require more innovative strategies because of various autonomy demands. The historical and present political experiences of these states throw up conceptual, theoretical and methodological challenges for social scientists, and the book engages with these. The content of the book is organized at two levels: some of the chapters discuss Northeast India in general and other chapters focus on specific states/communities and cases.

However, all the states of Northeast India could not be covered in this volume. States of Nagaland and Manipur continue to be societies that contest the state of India. Demands range from autonomy within the state of India to self-determination. Nevertheless, this book also highlights the fact that the state is looked upon as an object of hope and solution for contested issues of identities and ethnic boundaries (in Meghalaya, Nagaland and Manipur). Whether one likes it or not, the state assumes the role of an anchor around which issues of identities, territoriality, rights and justice are sought to be resolved. The states of Manipur and Meghalaya continue to be states where notions of tribe, non-tribe and territories are debated and contested. The state of Assam also continues to be a deeply troubled state (cross-border migration, inter-group relationship and questions of citizenship). Historically and presently, Arunachal Pradesh is a politically sensitive border state because of sensitive Indo-China boundary disputes. Its history of becoming a part of India through developmental initiatives has received attention but needs to be debated and discussed further. Moreover, owing to its strategic location, Arunachal Pradesh bordering China continues to be the site and space of contesting border.

Having given this brief background, let me discuss in the following section the critical framework, which may help readers to understand the chapters in this volume on society and state.

State in Society: A Critical Framework from the Margin

The broad objective of this edited volume is to understand the society in Northeast India, which does not lie strictly within the sovereign boundary of the nation state of India (for there are evidence of people connecting across the border both as lived experience and as a part of the identity assertion), yet in spite of its trans-border historical and cultural experiences and connections, it has also been manifesting developments that contest for the recognition of identities within the state. One may argue that Northeast India has experienced a 'post-nation -state' kind of situation due to trans-border historical and political connections, but there has equally been an argument that no such situation has arrived in the region (Menon 2009). This is because although the major movements (meaning insurgency movements) in the region reject the nation state of India, they still talk of a nation state. It is a fact that despite the social and political formations that transcend the boundary of the state, people in the border region also exhibit tendency to belong to the state of India. Nevertheless, once we move beyond the study on insurgency or major political movements to an everyday analysis of the society at the border, one will encounter several narratives of connections already established or continue to establish across the border of the nation state; this implies a relationship that is not necessarily dependent on the nation state. We assume that under such condition, the state (India) has a different history of shaping itself or being shaped by such formations. The critical question, then, is how does the inwardly experience of belongingness of the people, as legal citizens of India, work in a region, which is also marked by social and political formations that precede as well as exist in parallel with the nation state. Our argument is that such experiences do not necessarily contradict each other.

Hence, in Northeast India, there is cohabitation of two forms of identity: one that transcends the state and the other that seeks recognition within the state. To discuss this type of cohabitation, one has to broaden the geographical and historical area that includes broadly the present Northeast India and its neighbouring areas. Perhaps this will allow us to not only see the historical geography of the region but also see how this broader historical geography acts as the constitutive outside of politics of identity within the state of India. The outside could be represented either as a space of ethnic origin of people living inside the state of India or as a shared historical and political consciousness of belongingness in a bigger imagined ethnic homeland. The former could be present in demand for the Scheduled Tribe (ST) status while authenticating themselves as the old tribal group of people. The latter could be present in the form of larger or greater homeland demands, which could be states within the union of India or a separate sovereign state. Both the aspirations work on relatively similar connected history. Hence, when such senses of outside determine the political orientation of the communities to existing state, the content of their identities and the politics of cultural differences cannot be seen as something strictly produced within the settings of the nation state. Such ethnic settings imply that the state as a constitutional and legal entity requires a different treatment. While the state shapes politics in the region, the society shapes the state. Although not in the strict sense, this broader concern is a major area that can be understood as a shared issue among all the chapters of this volume.

In looking at people who experience border space of Northeast India, it is, however, pertinent to engage with relevant and existing normative and theoretical frameworks on society and state in India. Let me now engage with these frameworks. Among literature on trans-border connections, one may, for instance, cite the recent works of Stuart Blackburn (2007) on Apatanis in central Arunachal Pradesh and the work of Robbins Burling (2007) on the Garos of Meghalaya to illustrate a point. The folklore of the Apatanis, to Blackburn, indicates a cultural connection with people in the Eastern Himalayan region. However, the Apatanis' politics of identity perceives threat from their southern neighbours such as the people in Assam and, therefore, they traced their origin to the southern Tibetan areas. As a result, there has been a politicization of origin to counter the imagination of the pan-Naga homeland that includes parts of Arunachal Pradesh, Assam and Manipur. For a folklorist like Blackburn, the 'cultural connection' (folklorist accounts and linguistic anthropology of people) is different from the 'political connection'. Such duality of connection can be seen equally in the work of Robbin Burling when he engages with the meaning of the term 'tribe' in the context of the Garos' origin myth. To him, one can make sense of the duality of the everyday life of people. Tribe to the people in the region, to Burling, is both a legal and ethnic. Although people use tribe in legal sense (as Scheduled Tribe under the Constitution of India) to relate with the state, in everyday life the meaning of tribe is less legal and used more like an 'imagined community'.

In short, while there is a distinction between 'cultural' and 'politics' in the case of Apatanis (Blackburn), there is a distinction between 'legal' and 'ethnic' in the case of Garos (Burling). In both the cases, there is an equal emphasis that there is a notion called 'political only' when it comes to one's orientation to the state (either for the politics of recognition or legal recognition). The problem with such argument is not merely with their seeming assumption of something called apolitical cultural connection and imagined community but also with the dichotomous ways of understanding culture and politics, on the one hand, and legal and ethnic, on the other. There can be an equal argument that culture could be very much a part of the politics and ethnic as it is a part of the legal sense of community or tribe. However, it is true that the politics of culture and community is not necessarily dictated by the state, although such politics occurs within the state. Such condition (of identity and politics not necessarily dictated by the state) is also possible for the people in present Northeast India not merely because they live in a historical space much larger than the present one but also because they carry an identity that does not necessarily orient to the state as a way of life. It is important to make sense of this bigger space in the contemporary readings of society and state. This is the reason why we begin the book with the chapters that are placed in a larger historical and geographical canvas beyond the existing idea of Northeast India as a region.

With regard to historical geography of the people living in the present Northeast India, an important work of David Ludden may be brought in briefly. David Ludden (2003) argues that there is a relationship between mobility and territorialism. It means that the nation's map does not necessarily determine the territoriality of the people; instead, it is the mobility that determines the territoriality of the people. In the process, territoriality itself changes along with mobility. Also, the idea of the border was in a much looser sense than the modern legal and political meaning of sovereign boundary. A significant contribution of Ludden's work is that state sovereignty was not based on fixed territory; instead, it was dependent on people's mobility, for instance, if one looks for the idea of the sovereignty of the Khasi and Jaintia states in the 17th century, one would find that it extends up to the Sylhet areas. Ludden's (2003) work on Sylhet has given us sufficient information and discussion on the connected histories among the Khasi, Jaintis, Cacharis, Manipuris, Tripuris and the kingdoms (Afghans and Mughals) established around the plain of Sylhet. In fact, William van Schendel's study (2004), to cite a study, has shown how 'Bengal borderland' includes a large part of the present Northeast India.

The problem with much of the existing works on state and society in India, however, is that such larger historical space (of fluidity, mobility and territoriality) is a matter of less concern. To address this concern, let us look at the political, sociological and anthropological studies on state and society in India under two broad distinctions: one view talks of state as the aggregate of societies, thereby meaning diverse segments of the society oriented towards the state, and the other talks of the split between state and society. To the first kind of studies, one may cite the work of Sugata Bose and Ayesha Jalal (2014). Sugata Bose and Ayesha Jalal (2014, 6–7) observe that what South Asia lacks in historical depth, it makes up for in political neutrality. As a result, South Asia (and its people) is being characterized as a picture of diversity in unity and as a picture of immense diversity within the broader contour of unity. To them, twin dialectics of centralism and regionalism, and nationalism and communitarianism give a meaningful framework for considering history of modern South Asia, without ignoring historically shifting definitions of and relationships between centre, region, nation and community. To them, this is of essence if we are to establish the contours of both the idea and the structure of India (or South Asia) by an analysis of the relationship of its constituent parts with the whole. It is through this framework that this cited work tends to view issues of power relationship along class and gender lines, and the alterations in the social relationship within the subcontinent are also understood as a result of the increasing linkage of the parts and whole of South Asia, and India relates with the world since the early 19th century. Furthermore, alterations are understood to occur along class, social and cultural relationships, community, gender and generation.

One can also think of the work on the imperial state by Rudolph and Rudolph (2010). To them, India's concepts of stateness and collective representations of the political universe featured an imperial state. This means that, on the one hand, it aggregated diverse territorial, cultural and functional communities, on the other, it featured a symbolic and institutional state domain (Rudolph and Rudolph 2010, 557). This continental and imperial view of the state, however, dwells on an order in which the constituent parts orient towards the state. The problem of this type is equally found in the work of Sunil Khilnani (2004). To Sunil (2004, 3), the arrival of modern Indian state is a historical fact that marks a shift from a society where authority was secured by diverse methods to one where it is located in a single sovereign agency. The problem with such approach is that it understands state as the aggregation of diverse things, thereby giving less space for thinking of the state, as that entity not merely shapes the society but has also been shaped continuously by the society.

For the second type of studies, one may cite the works of what Pranab Bardhan (2012) called the 'anarcho-communitarians', which include scholars such as Partha Chatterjee, Sudipta Kaviraj, Ashis Nandy and Ranajit Guha. While I am not going into the details of each of their works, let me present some of the key points that can be discussed. One aspect, which is common to these scholars, is that state in India is an elitist project and, as a result, there has been a gap between the state and vernacular society. This gap is being understood as something that can explain much of the contemporary crisis in India. Another commonality among these scholars is their understanding of the trajectory of Indian state that postcolonial state in India inherits a colonial state that is uniform in two senses: administrative and cultural.

Fundamentally, the problem with the above understanding is the understanding of state and corresponding assumption of a stable and autonomous society. One line of argument is that although, legally and constitutionally, the state denotes a territorially and legally defined and bounded space, in reality, people's relationship with the state does not always work in such legal and constitutional space. Partha Chatterjee (2009, 38) argues that most of the inhabitants of India are tenuously right-bearing citizens in the sense imagined by the Constitution. Largely, people operate in the languages, which are not formal and legal, and they are not actually the members of civil society. Yet, to Chatterjee, they are a part of state, not outside, and relate to the state through a political relationship that cannot be defined under the formal and legal languages of politics. Basically, he means, people do orient themselves to the state through various networks and relationships, which can only be defined under the concept of political society. However, it is also an empirical reality that laws of the state are not merely binding to but also constitute and set the terms of engagements between the state and society. People look up to the state for legal reforms and for defence of their political and economic rights. Not only there are cases of people using legal channels like National Green Tribunal to stop developmental projects that result to displacement and dispossession of land, the same people also conduct legal awareness campaigns to assert their rights over land and resources. Scholars like Sivaramakrishnan (2011) have shown that new state spaces have emerged since the 1980s, which are 'hybrid spaces' formed not just between court (oversight) and political executives (accountability) but also between state and civil society on the matters of environmental protection to protect the right to life of the people affected by various developmental state projects. Also, the phenomenon of legalization also occurred among the environmental civil society groups and environmentally concerned and protesting non-governmental organizations (NGOs). This gives a sense of necessity of legal awareness on the part of people to claim what is entitled and due to them when the state fails to respect the rights of the people over environment. This is also equally true in the context of Northeast India where multiple developmental projects, such as hydel power projects and road infrastructure, have encouraged various concerned organizations have compelled concerned civil society organizations in Manipur, Assam, Sikkim and Arunachal Pradesh to initiate civic campaigns to assert the people's self-determined rights over land and resources. This led to a series of cases filed against the developmental projects in National Green Tribunal (NGT) of India.

Now let us go back to the social and political phenomena of people who locate within the state as legal citizens, yet they have transnational cultural and ethnical linkages with societies beyond the state. It is a familiar political phenomenon that the actual content of identity of the people, such as Kuki-Chin and Nagas, consists of cultural and symbolic materials and motifs that are not strictly limited to the boundary of the nation state, even though they live as members of the states within India. It is not a new fact that the politics of recognition as STs or as tribes who demand autonomy within the state would seek to claim themselves as old and not new people, with a longer history across and earlier than the modern states. Yet they use such statements of identity as basis of claiming exceptional status within the state. Culturally and politically, identity consciousness is not necessarily limited to the state. It is not merely the orientation and legal and constitutional linkages with the state that one should look at but also the content of identity and politics. The politics of Kuki state demanded by Kuki National Organisation, based in Manipur and Mizoram, is to equally demand two broad states, namely the Eastern Kuki-Chin and Western Kuki-Chin, but these states are claimed to be within the nation states of India and Myanmar.

This phenomenon brings us to the question of thinking beyond or within the nation. To Partha Chatterjee (1997), the question of thinking beyond the nation (state) is problematic because first, it involves risks of violating the geostrategic boundary of the state and second, a lot is happening within the nation which needs to be theorized. It is in this context that the idea of political society is supposed to be conceptualized and visualized. However, our argument is hinting at the limits of political society as well as the juridical-political state as conceptual categories while understanding certain kinds of historical and contemporary developments of state and society in Northeast India. Nevertheless, in our context, one can locate two understandings of the state: one, it is a juridical-political entity, a formal, legal and constitutional structure of power; the other understanding is that of the state which is not a fixed but a daily experience. The state is also a historical experience that lives not just as our present experience but also as an entity that has lived with us through historical times in various forms of personality, symbols, policy, territory making, frontier making and so on. In our context, we feel it is important to historicize the state and society.

When it comes to the history of the present Northeast India, it is incomplete to see the state only as a centre-oriented structure of power. If one looks at the work of Wouters (2012), the state was also an object of constant aspiration for the surrounding people. His work, using historical data of Assam, is a critic to James Scott's popular work on people living in upland Zomiain Southeast Asia. However, it is also widely argued that the historical state was an object from which hill people evade deliberately. Recent work of Guite (2019) explores statelessness and resistance of the people in the upland areas of Northeast

India against state making in the lowland areas. Statelessness, however, is not merely a theoretical position (following Scott's work) but a deliberate political position that hill people take which is stated with clarity in Scott's work (Scott 2014). But there is the third position that one can see in the political history of the state. If one looks at the work of David Ludden (2003), there is a focus on the fluidity of state and people's interaction with it because of the mobility of the people and state. This I feel gives an understanding of a larger political formation beyond the frame of hills and valleys (upland and lowland).

Precolonial states of the present Northeast India either had the organic model of state and society or the model of the state where society evades state making or remains autonomous from the state. Comprising the state-making experiences in both hills and valleys, while the organic model involved a system of clans and chiefs' representation in state making, in the latter model, state making was achieved through military expeditions, labour mobilization, classification of people, etc. These models of state–society were historically coexistent. However, under the colonial regime, the state–society relations were reframed to construct the empire's frontier and territorial enclaves. The new nation state of India then further reconstructs these polities and societies in new frames of state–society relations.

A state–society analytical framework that recognizes both the looseness of the state and cohabitation of legal citizenship within nation state and cultural identities beyond nation state in society will help to historically understand the location of the state as a political unit and practices in what we now understand as Northeast India. This also very importantly opens the scope to investigate state in our parts of the world as either an entity representing society as its integral part or an entity which the society resists and carves out autonomous spaces. This framework could help us to re-read how we understand society historically. The state exists in our past, among us and with us through our long historical times as what we generally understood as the precolonial state, colonial state and postcolonial state. Throughout these states, what could be interesting is not actually the distinction between the state as a juridical-political entity and daily experience, but the existence of two such forms of state simultaneously. Then, how do we understand a state that has its defined structure of power and legitimacy, yet also prevalent among us and in the past and present of Northeast in particular, as forms of daily powers.

This is where one also needs to think about what we called society. There could be, and there are historical debates on whether society includes state or state includes society, but what is important in our mind and context is not the exclusion or inclusion of each other; rather, it is the notion that society, as an idea and practice, gives one a field of inquiry to explore how the state operates in various forms beyond its juridical political structure and how, through the experiences of people, a state is understood and expanded. The very distinction between the state and society is taken as the defining characteristic of modern political power. The expansion of state, particularly in a space like Northeast is an interesting field of inquiry; here, it is not just viewed as a state that exercises a system of power but as a state that has been resisted, but this is still a very modernist kind of explanation or exploration. We do feel that the state existed and expanded in our past, but then, is this past state something we should differentiate from present or something that should be treated as a continuum. In many of our debates, the old state appears to be organic and, hence, is differentiated from modern, but this old state is found to be problematic once we know there is a large scholarship of how people in old times resisted state making and various responses have led to various ecological, social and economic formations.

One of the areas that can locate these new frames could be found in the political shift from government to governance. This shift is being perceived as a sign of the state mediating between the compulsion of developing marginal areas and societies and the art of mediating differences among the communities. One thing is clear that not just in academic research but also among policymakers, analysts, security experts, NGOs, etc., there has been an increasing adoption of the term governance. Two things may be mentioned here to understand such adoption: one, there is a visible shift (both at the national and international settings) from the rational-legal institutional focus to process aspects of government; two, there is involvement of relatively non-formal actors such as civil society groups and customary institutions in the management of the social and economic resources.

These changes reflect post-Cold War developments, particularly in the Third-World countries when these countries open up their economies and shift from a centralized state system of government to a relatively loose form of government. However, this shift does not completely give up the formal institutional control and leverage in the management of the social, political and economic resources. One area that could be discussed is the nature and degree of involvement of what is being termed as 'non-formal' actors in the process of governance and the factors that decide such involvement in a multi-ethnic society like Northeast India. The issue of managing and inclusion of differences emerges in this context. The difference could be located in diverse ethnic identities, indigenous knowledge, polities, customary laws and institutions. The process of involving non-formal aspects and actors is being understood as a form of managing social and economic resources for bringing the certainly defined notion of development. This leads to a further extension of the meaning of government to the practices of accommodating differences.

It is suggested that perhaps the above issues could be best debated by bringing in 'society'. While there could be a sense, a vision or a map of society from the perspective of state (as above), there could be another sense of community emerged while people in everyday life approach state and its institutions. One could say that the latter is the sociological or anthropological understanding of everyday governance. In multi-ethnic societies like Northeast India, this perspective needs further exploration. On the one hand, this is needed because of the location of the customary laws and institutions (for which much of the north-eastern societies are known for) in the formal definition of government, as exceptions to the national laws and institutions, on the other, there are emerging spheres of civil society groups, where there is people's mobilization on various issues of identity, rights and justice.

One could identify the spheres of customary and civil society (although they are not strictly compartmentalized) as the informal space of people through which much of the access to formal institutions and process is being negotiated. However, one could problematize the relationship between ethnic politics and the process of governance. We do not mean that all the social actions are necessary parts of governance, but how society and social institutions are part and parcel of governance could be discussed. Furthermore, the relationship between the mobilization of ethnic groups (includes electoral politics) and governance could be discussed. One can say that there are two types of politics: first, the type of politics that questions government instead of forming parts of; second, those politics of identities that claim state recognition. There could be a transformation from the first type to the second.

Let me now engage with some of the recently emerged borderland perspectives. There have been an increasing number of scholars from the West doing research on Northeast India with newer methodologies and perspectives. We may cite the first Asian Borderland Research Network Conference at Guwahati at the beginning of 2007, in which I participated, where I encountered a new perspective of studying Northeast India, something that has been known as the borderland studies. Also, I want to cite the later publications by a group of scholars, who follow borderland theory, which were published in December 2007 in the *Journal of South Asian Studies*. As an idea and approach, borderland gives a way out for many of the scholars who, on the one, hand strongly criticize the nationalized history and polity, on the other, are trying to make sense of the ethnic ties across the national territory. It is true that such an approach has enabled, to an extent, what we think of Northeast India for one begins to problematize multiple ethnic connections and histories across the rigid national boundary. However, to cross the border or consider both sides of the border as the major approach to find an alternative way (questioning national history and politics) of studying social and political dynamics of people at the periphery is still limited. For the developments within the nation boundary have equally opened the possibility for newer ways of understanding state and society. Let me engage with the borderland theory for some time.

The borderland theory questions the state-centric approach to study people at the territorial border of nation state. It questions the political constructions of the modern state border, but it argues that in spite of the rigidity of official boundary, lives of the people at the border are less dictated by it. People cross it whenever it suits them, and they use it to their advantages for social, economic and cultural activities in ways that are not intended and anticipated by the creators of the border. Because of this, border regions have their social dynamics and historical development (Baud and van Schendel 1997, 211–212). To study, therefore, such dynamics and development of people at the border regions, one needs to relate to people on both sides of the nation states' border. I will not go into the details, but this theory or approach is brought in particularly for the reason that it seeks to evolve a new approach by questioning the state-centric approach to study the social dynamics and historical transformation of people of the border regions whose ways of life in fact are not obliged to be restricted within the official mapping of territory and societies.

While the borderland approach enables to study certain dynamics of people at the border regions, what I think equally necessary to debate is whether one needs to cross the nation for archival or ethnographic field trips to analyse the dynamics of people on one side of the border. Baud and van Schendel's (1997, 241) basic argument is that by emphasis on the geographical, legal and political aspects of the creations and consequences of borders, the researchers reinforced the 'national history', and even those historians, they argued, who have distanced themselves from the state and axioms of national history, have done this by retreating from the state to a 'civil society' that is still seen as contained within the state territory. So, in brief, the approach is the one which does not begin in one side of the border but by looking both sides of the border. In another study, this sense of going beyond national history is seen in one of Sanjib Baruah's works. Sanjib Baruah (2007) argues that to break away from its troubled past and present (which he means the 'post-frontier'), a new policy vision for Northeast India must also be post-national. To Baruah, Look East Policy (now Act East Policy) is the opportunity that gives a broader space for the recognition of the identities as well as the economic benefits to the people in the region. Like Buad and van Schendel, Baruah is also sceptic about the nation state that Northeast India cannot be entrapped by the national security manager's narrow imaginary of the nation state.

In the above-cited *Journal of South Asian Studies*, Northeast India is defined as part of the cultural area formed by people at the margins of South Asia, South East Asia and East Asia. This area is understood as the extension of Eastern Himalayas, sharing certain similar traits of swidden cultivation, migration stories, myths of creations, etc. Given the history, society and politics of people in Northeast India that spread over a larger geographical area outside the existing national boundary, this approach enables to understand various social and cultural dynamics of people in this region. One can detect two ways of crossing the border in the Northeast: one, social and cultural histories, that is, migration and creation myths; two, crossing the border to imagine a greater homeland. Both the ways of crossing the border can be understood either as a way of life for social and cultural connection or as larger identity assertion. But I do agree with what is argued in earlier works that one cannot treat both social and cultural linkages and identity as the same. Stuart Blackburn (2007) has argued there is a difference between migration myths and identity assertion. Migration does not necessarily mean a collective group consciousness, but identity assertion would construct a linear history of a collective group identity.

Although there are merits of this approach, I do not think stories of people within the border are not necessarily determined and fixed by the state. The experience of the people conveys the fact that people also shape the way a state should be. I argue this for two reasons: one relates to our understanding of state in the border and the other, the empirical reality of the people in Northeast India. In the border, state may not be what Baud and van Schendel (1997) referred to as the 'central state'. For in this term, they give the impression of the state as that which is located physically at a geographical centre and reaches out to people at the border. The way in which the state has expanded and reproduced into different actors and lived in the daily life of people is an important area of study, which has barely been touched upon so far in the studies on Northeast India. In that case, the idea of margin (as used by Deborah Poole and Vena Das) is considered significant, for instance, how state legitimatizes its own illegitimate actions at the border or how state actors cross the line between lawfulness and unlawfulness of its own making to make its presence felt in the daily lives of people. This can be understood briefly for our purpose in two ways: one is the productiveness of state power and the other is the creativity of people to engage with or become a part of it. In this book, Chapter 8 has brought in this aspect of state power by arguing that military discourse (classification and gradation of detenue under the Armed Forces Special Powers Act [AFSPA]) normalized as the practices under the constitutional laws and the procedural intricacies involved in the process through the analysis of an extraordinarily laws in the state of Nagaland.

Hence, the understanding of border, as inhabited by the triangular relationship among the central state, regional elites and people at the border (that Baud and van Schendel argued), limits one from understanding the production and diffusion of power (e.g., the normalization of military laws as constitutional laws in Chapter 8). The state is not distantly present in the sense of 'central state' but lives with people. Reproduction of state power and creative contestation of state practices through various agencies are areas that are yet to be uncovered in the studies on Northeast India. The idea of civil society comes into picture here to discuss whether the social and political dynamics of people could be solely understood by thinking of the state and civil society. My point is contrary to what Baud and van Schendel (1997, 241) have argued that while there are attempts to retreat from the state (meaning from the state-centric approach) to 'civil society', the latter is still seen as contained within the state territory. There are social and political spaces of articulations and actions that should not be reduced completely to state space, even though they are seen inside the territorial border of the state (e.g., chapters in this book, particularly Chapter 4, can be seen to elaborate this point).

However, this, of course, needs prior problematization of what we called civil society as the space of social and political actions. There have been quite a few good studies in this regard. Civil society as space of political actions, at least in Northeast India, has been intensely associated with the state and non-state actors' armed conflict; hence, the meaning of civil society groups is understood as right-based bodies. In this context, civil society emerged more as a space of engaging with the state forces, questioning the principles on which forces of violence are used in a democratic society. This, however, does not rule out civil society groups, which also become stakeholders in the projects of the state: projects of town planning, development programmes, etc. Neera Chandhoke (2007, 607–608) observes that from a context of autocratic states (referring to Stalinist states in the then Eastern and Central Europe), the concept of civil society came to signify a set of social and political practices that sought to engage with state power. The idea is that it was through civil society that individuals and groups set out to challenge 'unresponsive and authoritarian' states through peaceful and non-violent methods, for example, protest and demonstrations. As result, she feels, two aspects on the argument of civil society appear tremendously significant: one, there is sustained demand for political rights, and, more particularly, civil rights—the right to freedom of all kinds, that is, from freedom of expression to freedom to form associations; two, there is complete disenchantment with the vocabularies that spoke of taking over state power through revolutionary means—smashing the state or transforming the state.

However, one needs further discussion on the notion of civil society, as it exists on the ground. For the language of civil society may be differently accessed and articulated, not just too limited language of civil and constitutional rights. Partha Chatterjee (2004, 38–39) has talked about how larger sections of society in India are tenuously connected with the formal sense of civil society. He states that in terms of the formal structure of the state, as given by the Constitution and the laws, all of society is civil society; everyone is a citizen with equal rights and, therefore, needs to be regarded as a member of civil society. The political process is one where the organs of the state interact with members of civil society in their capacities or as members of associations. Nevertheless, he argues that this is not how things work. For most of the inhabitants of India are only tenuously, and even then ambiguously and contextually, right-bearing citizens in a sense imagined by the Constitution. They are not, therefore, proper members of civil society and are not regarded as such by the institutions of the state, but to Chatterjee, they are not outside the reach of the state and not even excluded from the domain of politics. As populations within the territorial jurisdiction of the state, they have to be looked after and controlled by various government agencies. However, even if these activities bring these populations into a certain relationship with the state, this relationship does not always conform to what is envisaged in the constitutional depiction of the relation between the state and members of civil society.

Without proceeding to his notion of political society (the term which, he feels, explains the non-formal domain of politics of people in India), for the moment, we can bring this understanding that people are tenuously related to the formal sense of civil society to the understanding of the domain of politics in Northeast India. In contrast to Partha Chatterjee's notion, my understanding is that in Northeast India, both the formal sense of civil society and non-formal domain of politics are either operated simultaneously or coexist. The formal sense of civil society is retained to question the state using the language of constitutional rights of the individuals or the moral rights of the people through a global civil society network, or national and state alliances, which many of the rights-based civil society groups have used effectively to question morally the human rights violation at the hands of security personnel or the employment of extraordinary laws or the trial of extrajudicial killing and fake encounter killings in the region. Some of these bodies have approached the Supreme Court of India and the Central Bureau of Investigation (CBI) to get justice for the victims or victims' families, but this, of course, needs to be engaged with the other non-formal domains of politics that involve religions, culture, language, ethnicity, etc. In this book, Chapter 8 is concerned to some extent with the formal sense of civil society. Chapter 4, for instance, could be brought in for the discussion on the non-formal domain of politics. What is equally worth looking at is the connection between the two domains of politics. Let me also problematize this connection in the following paragraphs.

Sanjib Baruah (2010, 10–11) has talked about the existing civil society in Northeast India while discussing politics of subnationalism in Assam, in particular. He locates politics of subnationalism in the civil society to denote a collective will that can bridge the cultural, religious and linguistic rifts, while, at the same, it can confront the state. Speaking about the subnational protests in Assam, civil society is considered as the domain of 'non-political' and higher order for the life of the nationality. The organizations that lead such protest consider their concerns different from and of higher order from the politicians (assuming the 'political' to be the domain of the politicians and not of the protests). Further, he observed that organizations and individuals who led such protests belong to a cultural domain. To him, this notion of civil society as the higher order can build Assamese nationality irrespective of their lower-order engagements, which the membership of political party or civil service cannot, and this competes with the obligations of national citizenship. Baruah's concern, however, is the capacity of subnational to sustain autonomous visions and agendas because subnationalist mobilizations have often been settled through negotiations, which can obscure such autonomy.

Indeed, civil society in Northeast India came to be questioned on two grounds: one, presence of ethnically particularistic identities and their contestation; two, the civil society is mixed with insurgency, but the distinction between what is civil and what is not is problematic. To argue for civil society as the civil space impacted by bodies that are by nature 'non-civil' would fail to locate the theoretical implications of a non-formal sense of politics. Likewise, Sanjib Baruah's sense of civil society as an autonomous domain where visions are collectively shaped on nationality question fails to understand the other kinds of perceptions on the sense of civil society as either the carrier of homogenizing collective national or as speaker of the dominant community language (as discussed in Chapter 4 of this book). It is true that on many occasions, civil society has become a strong space of state criticism in Northeast India. It is also true that there is nothing completely civil about it. Such formal sense of civil society, at times, because of the populist politics or state appropriation, becomes a space of ethnic bias and exclusion or a space used, directly or indirectly, as a springboard for joining electoral politics or members of state institutions.

Nevertheless, both the above-mentioned ways of looking at Northeast India (on the one hand, looking at the social and political dynamics of people in both sides of the national border and looking at the developments within the national boundary to search for a non-national or non-state-centric study, on the other), however, give the impression that we still have not questioned the idea of Northeast India. Although borderland theory allows us to understand people beyond the national boundary, it has not effectively enabled us to question what we think of as living in Northeast India.

About the Chapters

The book is divided broadly into four parts. Part I consists of three chapters, by Anup Shekhar Chakraborty, Santosh Hasnu and Sherin Ajin, which could be understood as providing a broader historical and anthropological frame that locates state and its border in a fluid political and social dynamics of the margin.

Chapter 1, by Anup Shekhar Chakraborty, questions whether the colonial subject (and also the category of native) is a homogenous category. To probe into this question, he probes the colonial state-making process and the creation of boundaries in the region. He argues that the lack of a single unifying strand of the region's history makes the process of flipping through the pages of time even more necessary. As a space, the region is hemmed, and the fringe areas of it have remained a cartographic challenge. Where does the 'Northeast' begin? Does the territorial map correspond to the social imaginaries working among the myriad tribal groups and communities? Why is the region a cartographic challenge? While addressing the first question, he says, one realizes that it is indeed very challenging to demarcate the beginning and the end of the region. Coming to the second question, one realizes that there is no straight answer to this highly webbed question. He stresses that though geopolitically closer to the 'Northeast', the region of North Bengal, which serves as the gateway to the Northeast through the 'Siliguri–Cooch Behar corridor', has not been combined with the Northeast, but the desire to be included within the region remains strong among some people.

Chapter 2, by Santosh Hasnu, studies the process of colonial expansion in the principality of Cachar and its formal annexation into the British East India Company's dominion in the early 19th century. A part of the principality of Cachar was within the greater Sylhet region before the Partition of India, now mostly in Bangladesh. In post-Partition India, Cachar has become an administrative district of Assam consisting of two subdivisions, Silchar and Lakhimpur. In the beginning of the 19th century, Cachar was a region of political interest to the neighbouring state of Manipur, Burma and the valley-based Dimasa Raja and hill chief Tula Ram (within Cachar). Colonial conceptions of customary precedents and initiating the process of assessing lands under cultivation, which were intended to be fiscally attractive, served to legitimize the annexation of this strategic territory that was key to the security of British Bengal. This chapter discusses the specific nature of how the Company Raj employed its ideological and diplomatic resources to annex Cachar and will provide readers with insight into the nature of how a colonial state actually behaved in a 'strategic borderland'.

Chapter 3, by Sherin Ajin, argues that in reality, nation as an 'imagined community' is rarely congruent with the geometry of state, thus making the nomenclature of nation state more of an abstraction. This, she observes, is very much true in the context of Tawang, the border district of Arunachal Pradesh at the Indo-China border. Owing to its strategic significance, the space of Tawang is a perpetual theatre of the relentless pursuit of materialization of the nation state of India. This chapter intends to capture the unravelling of spatial politics in the Eastern Himalayan geography of Tawang. Employing ethnographic mode of inquiry, this chapter also attempts to explore the interface of contending spatial narratives, from both above and below.

Part II, which consists of three chapters by Jangkhomang Guite, Oyindrila Chattopadhyay and Rashi Bhargava, concerns with the official public spaces such as museums, monuments and memorials, and the non-official history, memory and space making as tribe and ethnic group. Also, the chapters are concerned with how the state shaped such non-official space-making politics to a large extent.

Chapter 4, by Jangkhomang Guite, examines how the collective official and non-official memories are produced, sustained and responded in postcolonial Northeast India. In other words, it is concerned with how the past events are represented in public spaces such as museums, monuments and memorials and how these not only reflect the historical imagination of the state but also shaped/animated social and ethnic relation in the region. It explores new possibilities for further investigation, partly, in the scholarship of memory studies, and partly, in understanding the problems of ethnicity in the region. It will be observed that the emerging states in the region have deliberately favoured the historical imagination of a politically dominant community within the state and remained persistently insensitive to the imagination of the marginal 'others' in the state. This generated virtually two sets of social relation. First, it encouraged the dominant community to assimilate around such shared past. Second, it generated a sense of 'neglect' and 'invisibility' to the less dominant and minorities who responded with 'vernacular' memorials to embody their historical imagination and likewise encouraged their assimilation, often against the dominant community. There was, thus, a parallel rise to prominence of two or more competing nationalisms within the state/region, which often produced a violent form of contestation imbued with the fissiparous tendency.

Chapter 5, by Oyindrila Chattopadhyay, observes that the notion of tribe is very much a spatial category, not merely a politicized social, legal and constitutional category. When we speak of spatial category, we take tribe as part of the governing practices of state in a geographical area. Tribe spatially refers to a geographical space, not just the traits of culture, society, religion and economy of group of people. In a similar manner, to the Khasi civil society, tribe is not a mere social and cultural category but a spatial category that denotes a group of people in a geographical area. It is within this context that we can understand the category of tribe and non-tribe, as the corresponding politics of divide. The difference between the official and civil society meaning of tribe lies in the fact that the latter requires more stringent distinction between the Khasi–Jaintia–Garo tribe and non-tribe.

Chapter 6, by Rashi Bhargava, explores the space of civil society in the state of Nagaland tracing the origin of the term 'civil society/ies' and deconstructing it to unravel its numerous understandings in contemporary times, especially in relation to that of the state. It puts forth the contention that state–society relations in Nagaland are of a specific nature, given its sociocultural organization and its political history, which can only be laid bare by interrogating the sphere of civil society in Nagaland. In doing so, it emerges that contemporary structure of what is referred to as civil societ(ies) in Nagaland draws from the traditional social organization of the Naga society, thereby according them a certain degree of 'social power'. This social power emerges from a combination of horizontal and vertical alliances and can be found to be located within the cultural bases of collective life of the Nagas.

Part III consists of chapters by M. Amarjeet Singh and R. K. Sanayaima, Chubatila and L. Basanti Devi. These chapters are concerned with the politics of counterinsurgency measures, everyday forms of classification of people under the extraordinary militaristic laws and the women's protest against the extraordinary laws and human right violations.

Chapter 7, by M. Amarjeet Singh and R. K. Sanayaima, observes that for the last several decades in Northeast India, insurgency and counterinsurgency responses have killed and injured people, destroyed public and private properties, caused population displacement and created fear and insecurity. They affect the state's ability to provide public goods and guarantee rule of law and security to its citizens. The state response to the crisis has tended to be centred round use of force, political reconciliation and the promise of development. The counterinsurgency strategies also included the use of divisive tactics to split insurgent groups and use them against one another. This chapter studies these policy responses and shows how they have been only partially successful. In reality, the policy of counterinsurgency, with the use of vast government resources, has largely succeeded to expand the security bureaucracy of the state.

Chapter 8, by Chubatila, addresses the classification of 'suspect' population by the state in Nagaland, enabled through the usage of emergency law (AFSPA). Such practice allows a military discourse to get normalized as a routine practice in constitutional law without explicitly naming it as an emergency procedure. The study unpacks categories to show the continuities between the discourse of war and the everyday legal discourse. At the same time, it focuses primarily on the impact of the emergency law of AFSPA on the everyday life of the people in Nagaland through analysis of judgements on illegal detention, torture and custodial deaths. She argues that classification and classificatory practices remain crucial for any governance regime in making body populations legible, easier to be located and treated as subjects and in simplifying the task of governing. It addresses the classification of 'suspect' population by the state, enabled through the usage of emergency law (AFSPA in this case).

Chapter 9, by L. Basanti Devi, focuses on the political history of state versus women encounters in Manipur. In the context of Manipur, the women and the state have been engaged not as legitimate adversaries; there has been the state that claims to exercise monopoly over legitimate use of violence, on the one hand, and women who challenge the laws and actions of the state, on the other. For the state, the category of women who are involved in protest movement has been stereotyped as ones 'linked with insurgents'. However, to the women, their movement has been a legitimate exercise that is compelled upon them to bring forth a state of society free from torture, equality and state's violence.

Part IV consists of chapters by G. Amarjit Sharma, Tanmoy Das and Amiya Kumar Das. Their chapters deal with the issue of 'development' in transnational local spaces in Northeast India and the 'development schemes' that involved complex local manifestations of power and authority involving local stakeholders and networking among the people, institutions and civic bodies.

Chapter 10, by G. Amarjit Sharma, enquires what does 'developing' a region in a transnational space mean. India's Northeast has been re-imagined officially in recent times as the 'engine of growth' for India. In this context, this chapter looks at the imagination and production of Northeast as a developmental object, particularly since the year 2000. However, the study will broadly cover the times since the beginning of planning for the Northeast as a region of postcolonial India in the 1970s till the contemporary post-Planning Commission era in which state actively collaborates with international financial institutions. The chapter argues that the state's objective of developing the region is not merely confined to 'state-making' or 'nation-making' paradigm (which prominently has been the core focus of several studies of development in recent times); instead, it is now also actively involved in making and governing the region as the vital geopolitical and economic space in a resource frontier.

Chapter 11, by Tanmoy Das, studies the role of postcolonial India in planning and implementation of developmental schemes for improvement of the life of citizens. This chapter focuses on the actual working of the developmental state on the ground with particular focus on the relationship between the district official authorities and local stakeholders (community elites and political leaders, local youth organizations and insurgent organizations), drawing data from the author's research in the Tamenglong district of Manipur. Centrally sponsored schemes are largely influenced by the politics of the key stakeholders who have access to the authorities of the autonomous district council and district administration. The common villagers use various strategies to reach out to some of the stakeholders to receive the benefits of the schemes.

Chapter 12, by Amiya Kumar Das, studies the informal ways people employ to reach out to the local authorities or departments of the government in the Sonitpur district of Assam. Establishing community based linkages and seeking help of the 'intermediaries' are important mechanisms people use to procure the welfare benefits entitled to them. Informal connection with the authorities in local Gram Panchayat office is important for the people to get the benefits. Even through petty corruption that includes payment to the 'intermediaries', people attempt to get access to the local authorities. However, he argues that the network is established around religion, ethnicity or community allegiance. This chapter draws field data from the author's research conducted in the Sonitpur district of Assam.

References

Bardhan, Pranab. 2012. 'The State against Society: The Great Divide in Indian Social Science Discourse.' In *Nationalism, Democracy and Development: State and Politics in India*, edited by Sugato Bose and Ayesha Jalal, 184–195. Delhi: Oxford University Press.
Baruah, Sanjib. 2007. *Durable Disorder: Understanding the Politics of Northeast India*. Delhi: Oxford University Press.
———. 2010. *India against Itself: Assam and the Politics of Nationality*. Delhi: Oxford University Press.

Baud, Michiel, and William van Schendel. 1997. 'Toward a Comparative History of Borderlands.' *Journal of World History* 8, no. 2 (Fall): 211–242.
Blackburn, Stuart. 2007. 'Oral Stories and Cultural Areas from Northeast India to Southwest China.' *Journal of South Asian Studies* XXX, no. 3: 419–438.
Bose, Sugata, and Ayesha Jalal. 2014. *Modern South Asia: History, Culture, Political Economy*. Delhi: Oxford University Press.
Burling, Robbins. 2007, December. 'Language, Ethnicity and Migration in North-Eastern India.' *Journal of South Asian Studies* XXX, no. 3: 391–404.
Chandhoke, Neera. 2007, August. 'Civil Society.' *Development in Practice*, 17, no. 4/5: 607–614.
Chatterjee, Partha. 1997, 4 January. 'Beyond the Nation or Within.' *Economic & Political Weekly* 32, no. 1–2: 30–34.
———. (2004) 2009. *The Politics of the Governed: Reflections on Popular Politics in Most of the World*. Delhi and Ranikhet: Permanent Black.
Guite, Jangkhomang. 2019. *Against State, Against History: Freedom, Resistance, and Statelessness in Upland Northeast India*. Delhi: Oxford University Press.
Khilnani, Sunil. 2004. *The Idea of India*. Delhi: Penguin.
Ludden, David. 2003, 29 November. 'Investing in Nature around Sylhet: An Excursion into Geographical History.' *Economic & Political Weekly* 38, no. 48: 5080–5088.
Menon, Nivedita. 2009, 7 March. 'Thinking through the Postnation.' *Economic & Political Weekly* 44, no. 10: 70–77.
Rudolph, Lloyd I., and Susanne Hoeber Rudolph. 2010, November. 'Federalism as State Formation in India: A Theory of Shared and Negotiated Sovereignty.' *International Political Science Review* 31, no. 5: 553–572.
Scott, James C. 2014. *The Art of Not Being Governed: An Anarchist History of Upland Southeast Asia*. Delhi: Orient Blackswan.
Sivaramakrishnan, K. 2011, November. 'Environment, Law and Democracy in India.' *The Journal of Asian Studies* 70, no. 4: 905–928.
Van Schendel, William. 2004. *The Bengal Borderland: Beyond State and Nation in South Asia*. London and New York, NY: Anthem Press.
Wouters, Jelle J. P. 2012. 'Keeping the Hill Tribes at Bay: A Critique from India's Northeast of James C. Scott's Paradigm of State Evasion.' *European Bulletin of Himalayan Research* 39: 41–65.

Part I

State, Region and Border

CHAPTER 1

Social Imaginaries, Minorities and the Postcolonial History of a Region

Anup Shekhar Chakraborty

Vexed Histories: The Colonial State and Subjectification

Northeast India and its complex precolonial, colonial and postcolonial history(ies) remind one of the layered challenges and contestations (Hussain 2004, 292) involved in attempting to fit the region's 'histories' into the nationalist narratives of Indian history (Barooah 1970; Baruah, 2005; Dubey 1978; Guha 1977, 1991).

F. S. Downs argued that until the coming of the British rule in the early 19th century, the entire region was never linked politically with any major Indian political power (Downs 1992, 2). The British had initially maintained a policy of non-interference towards the tribes in the Northeast. By the middle of the 18th century AD, the Ahom Dynasty and other prominent kingdoms such as Manipur and Tripura were gradually declining under multiple internal and external pressures. The Burmese aggression (Barpujari 1977, 4) and migration of several other tribes into the territory threatened the very existence of the 'Ahom-Sanskritic culture' of the Brahmaputra Valley and Barak Valley and the 'Vaishnavite culture' of Manipur Valley and the Kingdom of Tripura.

All these kingdoms felt threatened by the Burmese and the flow of other tribes into the territory. Left with no other options, they invited the British forces for external protection and military assistance at different times. However, it was at the behest of the successive rulers of the Ahom Dynasty that the British agreed to adopt a new policy of direct/partial interference, which later took the form of the annexation of Assam and, eventually, the whole of the Northeast region (Singh 2004, 53–78). The British ousted the Burmese from Assam in 1826 and steadily consolidated and expanded their presence in the Northeast (Verghese 1996, 3).

The British acknowledged the strategic significance of the North-Eastern Frontier and subjugated these tribes, not with an interest in its tribal people alone but with their land which had natural resources in plenty and was of strategic geopolitical importance for the British Raj, that is, better protection of Bengal, as argued by Captain Welsh (Singh 2004, 66). The British were attracted by the promising commercial possibilities of the land in terms of tea plantations, timber and the possibility of creating a buffer against French Indo-China and China (Baruah 2004).

'Northeast' itself is 'a colonial construct or more so a residue of colonial existence', as argued by scholars like Ranabir Samaddar (2001), S. K. Chaube (1973, 1985) and others. Trans-border strife on ethnic lines has continued to persist in Northeast India just as it did in ancient times and had, over the years, led to the fragmentation of the region in the name of federal politics. Before the annexation of Assam in 1826 by the East India Company, the hill tribes of the region had regular exchanges with plains people, as is evident from the development of pidgin languages like Nagamese among the Nagas. The Tripuri tribes were influenced by Bengali culture, and the Zo/Mizo tribes spoke the Sylhet–Cachar Bengali (Chatterjee 1985; 1990, 6, 16, 149, 166). Punitive British expeditions led to the annexation of the Naga Hills in 1878, the Mizo (Lushai) Hills in 1890 and the present Arunachal Pradesh. From 1947 onwards, the tribes in Northeast India have been coalescing politically under generic identities.

An interesting question that crosses one's mind while traversing these vexed histories is 'Was the colonial subject (and also the category of the native) a homogenous one?' To probe into this question, it is necessary to glean into the colonial state-making process and the creation of boundaries in the region. Tracing through the historical backdrop of Assam and the Northeast down the ages helps as a useful reference point for having 'a bird's eye view' and at the same time 'a worm's eye view' of the complex, layered trajectories of 'Politics in the North-East'.

As elsewhere, the colonial state and the creation of new borders by erecting buffers and barriers failed to prevent cross-migration, primarily due to the escalation in the demand of the colonial state for labour, soldiers, farmers, etc. This produced problems of identity and raised issues of citizenship and created fears of statelessness unfurled in the form of National Register of Citizens of India (NRC) in the entire North Eastern Region in postcolonial India. The history of the colonial expansion and the treaties that followed continued to eclipse the state-building process and the issue of citizenship. Independent India inherited a territorial boundary that had been fixed by the exigencies of an alien imperialistic administration and inevitably cut across many ethnic consolidations. Myron Weiner (1978, 84–87) discussed how British control of Assam also implied frequent alteration of boundaries and map. In 1826, it was made part of Bengal, but it separated from Bengal in 1874. It was redesigned as a part of separate Muslim Bengali province in 1905 and then reconstituted again in 1912. In 1947, Assam lost the district of Sylhet to Pakistan. Later on, the formation of states within the Union of India such as Nagaland, Meghalaya, Arunachal and Mizoram substantially altered the map of the state.

The Northeast has not been free from boundary disputes in spite of the reorganization of states and other specific schedules, which is why it is being called 'Cosmetic Federalism' (Baruah 2005); for instance, a section of the Zo/Mizo tribes have been demanding that all areas inhabited by the Mizos, now lying in different states such as Assam,

Manipur, Tripura and beyond the international borders, should be integrated into it (Chakraborty 2013a, 1–14). The emerging historiography of the region attempts to restructure the relationship between the Northeast and 'mainland India' with an overriding emphasis on establishing its coveted place in the emerging idea of 'India'. Chaube (1973) mentions that the problem has been intensified by a 'diffusionist modernizing' wave that had practically no relation with the prevailing mode of production and was bound to create a cultural crisis. The colonial administrators had encouraged the idea of allowing selective access to land in the frontier region. Subsequently, the Line System allowed for limited colonization of lands by settlers. Areas that were dominated by indigenous groups were marked off as 'Out of bounds' for settlement. The postcolonial administration in the Northeast inherited this structure. Though at the outset it seems to be a strategy aimed at fending off areas, it also contained the initial kernel of plural legal regimes of land use, property, ownership and control over resources (Barbora 2006).

The Northeast, in general, has been experiencing the need for redrawing the boundaries into North-eastern territorial zones and spaces (Chakraborty 2008a; 2008b; 2008c; 2009; 2012), that is, remarking the geopolitics based on the logic of traditional game land (Chakraborty 2008a; 2008b; 2008c; 2009; 2012; 2013a) that the people had lost due to the British and other external forces. The people of Northeast India, especially the tribal people, differ from the plains people of India in respect of culture, customary behaviour, faith and race. What Ananda Bhagabati calls the distinctive 'geo-ethnic character' (Bhagabati 1982, 218) of the Northeast helps clarify the multicultural nature and the cultural differences between the people. About three-quarters of the region is covered by hilly terrain, and one-quarter is made up of the four plain areas of Assam's Brahmaputra and Barak valleys, the Tripura plains and the Manipur plateau. Those in the thinly populated hill areas are the people we now call 'tribals', and in the fertile plains and plateau are mainly the 'non-tribal' people who comprise more than 80 per cent of the total population. In recognizing the cultural distinctiveness of the 'tribal' people of the hill regions, we should bear in mind that the Sanskritization of the plain areas has been going on for centuries. The anxiety that looms large over tribal people of the Northeast as elsewhere has been 'how to preserve their culture and pristine identity(ies)'.

Ostensible Homogeneities and Variegated Heterogeneities

The Northeast of India is marked by ostensible homogeneities amidst variegated heterogeneities, coupled with the ethno-religio-linguistic diversities in its population, rural–urban disparity, social difference and uneven human development across the states in the region, which are quite significant.

Underdevelopment is the often-cited unifier of the region and the reason for the persistence of violence in the region (Barbora 2006). The economy of the region is dependent on the primary sector, even though there is no dearth of educated persons available for secondary and tertiary sectors of the economy (Fernandes 2004, 4609–4611). The underdevelopment of the region and the underuse of the potential resources of the region evoke a sense of being neglected and treated as stepchildren and not belonging to either of the two categories 'India' or 'Bharat'. The federal asymmetries that run vertically and horizontally have resulted in creating disparities and an artificial rift between the people; for instance, the developmental activities in the fields of agriculture, communication, trade, education, etc. initiated by the Centre to counter the insurgency in that state made the Mizo leaders conscious of their wretched plight (Verghese and Thanzawna 1997, 6). The beneficiaries of the policies of the governments, both Centre and the State, and the North East Council (NEC; Maheshwari [1968] 2002, 424–442) side the leaders (traditional as well as new), while the fence sitters and the marginalized rely on alternative leadership, opposition leaders or traditional leaders/clannish heads or even the guerrilla or self-styled Maoist forces who claim to wage a people's war. In other words, the tradition–modernity antitheses were rooted deep in a conflict of interests between traditional elites and also the modern/new elites themselves.

The everyday images that the region, in general, evokes in the minds of the mainland Indians at large are that of tribes who have been converted to Christianity and, as a result, consider themselves to be different and distinct from mainland India. In other words, Christianity is considered to be an essential marker of tribal 'Identity' and the sole reason for the secessionist and anti-nationalist overtones in the region. Though Christianity in South Asia predated the colonial advent and St. Thomas had reached the Malabar Coast immediately after the death of Christ (Fuchs 1973; Moares 1964; Soares 1964), the wave of proselytization was stronger in the Northeast. The most crucial factor that contributed to the popularity of Christianity among tribes of the Northeast, such as the Zo tribes, was the psychological emancipation that it promised. The missionaries were successful in winning the confidence of the tribes of the region. The Khasis were the first among the tribes of the region to have converted to Christianity way back in 1812–1813, and the missionary activities were initiated in the Naga Hills in the 1840s and the Zo/Mizo/Lushai Hills in in 1894–1895 (Fuchs 1973). In this sense of time frame, the Zos/Mizos were a late arrival to the Evangelical missions. However, the success rate in the Zo Hills has been the maximum in terms of mass proselytization.

Awakening to a new sense of identity, political consciousness, proto-nationalism and ethnic consolidation within larger kinship groups, the tribal communities sought to differentiate themselves from the new sovereignties being asserted by the heartlanders. Ethnicity, an amalgam of race and culture, including language, religion and the tribal way of life, came to define 'we' and 'they'. Situated athwart international frontiers, and with historical memories and kin-groups straddling them, the effort by these border peoples to resist 'national integration' through differentiation appeared separatist or secessionist to the rest of people in India, while plausibly offering such an option to these border people (Verghese 1996, 3).

The discussions in this section accentuate the attempt at gross overgeneralization of the use of the term 'Northeast' and the tendency of most scholars to pass off region or state-specific studies, mostly in this case the study of Assam, to be reflective of all the other states in the region. The studies conducted by prominent scholars who have been frequently referred to as 'Northeast Experts' suffer from such a tendency. Often these writers tend to undermine the fact that the region and the terminology 'Northeast' are very much contested in nature and need to be re-evaluated. The monolith that the term intends to carry or convey lacks the united face, especially when juxtaposed against the bittersweet ground realities of the region; for instance, in her article 'Where is this North-east?' (in Sen 2006, 177) Patricia Mukhim makes a sweeping generalization that the Northeasterners feel like aliens in the big Indian cities. Apparently, the statement fails to explore the other side of the argument. The construction of Northeast as a singular political and racial experience fails to notice the politics of otherization operating inside the region at multiple levels. A non-tribal from Cachar is reportedly treated as much the other as anyone else from mainland India in the hill states of the region. Also, a Meitei is allegedly exposed to the experience of other in Southern Mizoram among ethnic groups of the Lai and the Mara. This otherization within the region works, however, differently in the case of Sikkim where anyone and everyone from any part of India are bracketed as 'Indian' (with a pejorative, racial overtone). At the same time, residents, including the domiciled of the state, are treated as locals, that is, Sikkimese, with a sense of foreignness and superiority and not necessarily feeling to be a part of India, or what I call a reluctant Indian.

Us and the Others: Locational, Positional and Situational Ambiguities

Now turning our attention to how migration across the new frontiers facilitated by the colonial state resulted in demographic changes and 'fear of the other', it is interesting to note that the migrant communities much later faced situations of 'fei-ization that questioned their citizenship (Nag 2003, 184). Nag (2003) argues that although the Nepalis are an integral part of the history of the region, they are treated as 'migrants' and not as 'people', thereby denying them any history. He points out that the growing literature on the history and society of the region hardly gives space to these 'migrants'. This history also excludes the Bengalis, Marwaris, Sikhs and ex-tea garden workers, as they are considered non-indigenous to the Northeast (Nag 2003, 184). The Nepali presence in the Northeast has a long history, and their role in the development of the region has been crucial.

The politics of Northeast India has been deeply influenced by the influx of people from other regions. The most striking development has been in Tripura.

Over the years, due to the migration of the Bengali Hindu population from East Bengal, the tribal autochthones were outnumbered. The tribal population dropped from 64 per cent in 1874 to 29 per cent in 1971. The Bengali population became 68 per cent of the total population in 1971. From all available accounts, the Bengali percentage is now 70. The result has been that political and administrative power passed from the hands of indigenous tribals to immigrant Bengalis. The transfer of land from the tribal population to the Bengali migrants proved to be the most critical factor in deteriorating social relations, and a flashpoint occurred in June 1980 at Mandia leading to a carnage, initiated by the tribals with Bengalis taking retaliatory measures, in which several hundred people lost their lives and 300,000 were rendered homeless. There is a widespread apprehension in the minds of the Assamese caste Hindus that, shortly, they will lose political power in favour of numerous migrants. The other states of the region also share the Assamese fears. In a democratic framework of one-man-one-vote, the role played by demographic factors remains crucial in bringing about spectacular changes in power politics (Singh 1987, 257–282). The fear of Tripurization continues to haunt states in the Northeast, and such fear is echoed by North East Students Organization when it says: 'the entire region has been smothered by aliens migrating from other parts of India...the native population is on the verge of being smothered' (Hazarika 1992; *Statesman* 1997).

The history of the permanent settlement of the Gorkha in Mizoram began in the year 1891. However, they had been active in the region throughout the initial encounters between the British and the 'Kuki-Chin-Lushai tribes'. The expansion of territories by the Kuki, Chin-Lushais towards south and south-west from Hakka and towards eastern Mizoram from Tiddim Falam region of Burma (Myanmar) in the beginning of the 19th century and the gradual extension of the British Frontiers towards the Northeast led to the confrontation between the 'wild tribes' and the 'colonial world'. The British developed the ingenious method of protecting the frontier by establishing 'fortified posts in the hills'. Such a move would call for the import of human resources, and the experience in Darjeeling and elsewhere made the Gorkhas the chosen workforce. T. H. Lewin (1912) summed up the reasons for the migrations of the Gorkhas into the Zo Hills as follows: 'I had formed a high opinion of the little *Gorkha*, who under Col. Macpherson, had done the fighting of the expedition, and I obtained permission to send to Nepal and get immigrants from there to colonize my frontier wastes'.

The British employed similar tactics even in the Zo Hills. Thus *Gallawalahs* were used to convince and assure the Gorkha of 'security and prosperity'. The Zo Hills were projected as the land of ample opportunities and attractive incentives where the Gorkha would get the best. Such projections were further solidified by sayings such as *Doodh le moohdhunu* (mouthwash with milk), *Pathakosikar rah pakwah* (lots of mutton and gizzards), and ample opportunity for *Ladaikhelnu* (to play battle, for in the Gorkha tradition, a battle is to be played not fought), etc. (Chakraborty 2008c).

The expansion work at Aizawl and Lunglei, as well as the setting up of administrative machinery, required the increase in the inflow of immigrants, that is, 'the trusted Gorkhas', as mentioned by O. A. Chambers ([1899] 2005) and Col E. B. Elly ([1893] 1978). The colonial system of administration required human resources as *dak-*runners, chowkidars, peons, cart drivers, traders, masons, etc., and since such work was unknown to the local people, it was felt advisable to introduce migrant labour. The migrant Gorkhas resembled the natives to an extent, and the factor of external beauty/attractive physical features and fair skin made them more acceptable to the 'native wild tribes' or *garkholas* ('arse flaunters') as the Gorkhas called them. Though the Gorkhas were not allowed to settle outside the allotted areas, many Lushai chiefs were eager to have them in their villages. They even entreated the Superintendent of Lushai Hills to permit the Gorkhas to reside in their villages (Shakespeare 1923). Accordingly, a few Gorkhas were given permission to settle in some of the Lushai villages. The settlement of the Gorkhas and the *Santhals* (*Midum* (Blacks)) led to the beginning of wet rice cultivation in the plains of Champhai (Pachuau 1990, also cited in Sunar et al. 2000).

The terms of the Chin Hills Regulations, 1896, and the Inner Line Permit (ILP; Sangkima 1995; 2004a; 2004b) were twisted and flouted, as reflected in the rapid increase in the flow of outsiders in and around Aizawl during the early part of the 20th century. A large number of these outsiders were the descendants of the discharged military policemen and colonial staff. As had happened with the indentured labour of the sugar plantations in the Caribbean Islands, many ex-servicemen were lured by the colonial administration to remain in Mizoram and were allotted plots and privileges at par with the Lushai chiefs with hereditary right of succession (McCall [1939] 1980); for instance, Dhojbir Rai was awarded the whole area of Survey Tillah (now Dinthar-II); Sriman Rai, the whole area of Sriman Tillah (now Zotlang); Singbir Rai with holdings in Chawnchhim (Champhai); Lalsing Lama was made the chief of Hrangmual (area around present-day Synod Book Room, Aizawl); and Joy Bahadur in Tuisenhnar Leilet (paddy field) settlement (Chawngbuanga 1990, also cited in Sinha and Subba 2003, 298). The Gorkhas were in the majority in Aizawl town during the colonial days, and naturally, the names of places were in Nepali/Gorkhali. It was only later in the course of the evolution of identity consciousness among the Zo/Mizo tribes that these names were changed in keeping with Zo/Mizo nomenclature (Singh et al. 1995, 54).

Culturally, the Gorkhas have, to an extent, successfully assimilated the local customs and practices (Bareh 2001; Singh et al. 1995) while retaining their distinct cultural identity. The Gorkhas in Mizoram have succeeded at crossing the threshold of the stigmas of the boundaries faced by the *Vai* or *the Burma mi* (*Poi*, Burmese) community.[1] The recognition of the Gorkha as 'Denizens' in Mizoram reflects well through the common conversational phrases used for denoting their historicity *Sap hunlai* (from the colonial times) and their assimilation into the Zo/Mizo world *Mizo angchiah* (just like the Mizo), *Zorilru an pu* (they think and feel like the Mizo), etc. (Chakraborty 2013c).

The settler communities began to be perceived as a threat by the host societies from the 1970s, in particular. The status of the Nepalis in the region was questioned. Were they Indian nationals or foreigners residing in India? The treaty of 1950 did not help because it allowed immigration into India as well as emigration to Nepal. The 1950 treaty allows the former to come, live and work in India, but this jeopardizes the position of the Indian Nepalis. To prevent this difficulty, R. K Sharma had suggested that the Indian Nepalis may be called the Gorkhas.

In contrast, Subba has coined the term 'Nepamul' to connote such people (Subba 2003, 62). The problem faced by the Nepalis has also been faced by many Bengalis, particularly Bengali Muslims, especially after the creation of Bangladesh. Such people are called illegal immigrants, but to draw a line between legal citizens and illegal migrants is often almost impossible. The real situation, as T. B. Subba puts, is: 'there are many "Nepalese"—in the sense of being of and from Nepal—who must be differentiated from the Indian Nepalis, born in India and probably living here for a few generations'.

The Nepalis in the region have been time and again made targets as illegal immigrants or the final 'Others' in the Northeast; for instance, in 1967, 800 Nepalis were driven out of Mizoram; in 1978, 200 houses of Nepalis were burnt in Nagaland; about 2,000 Nepalis fled Manipur in 1980; and large numbers of Nepalis were deported from Assam in 1979 and from Meghalaya in 1987 (Sinha 1982, 91–92; Subba 1992, 115–116; Sinha 2003). The political aspirations of the Nepalis in Northeast India are, therefore, woven around the struggle for equal economic and political rights as other Indian citizens. The terms of the 1950 treaty are categorical, yet ambiguities about the recognition of the Nepalese as citizens persist, transforming it into a political-legal problem (Chakraborty and Chakraborty 2016). The consequence is making many of these Nepalis, particularly those who had lived in parts of the Northeast for generations, as the 'Other'.

Constricting Spaces: 'Us' and the 'Others'

The intruders are leaving, but others will come. Sometimes we'll sense them. Other times, we won't.[2]

Following the ethnic clashes between the Nepali/Gorkha and the predominant local populations in the states of Assam and Meghalaya through the mid-1970s, the Nepali/Gorkha found themselves labelled as 'foreigners'. Although initially, the Assam movement, spearheaded by AASU (All Assam Students' Union) during 1979–1985 on the issue of 'foreigners', was directed against the Bangladeshis, eventually, the Nepali/Gorkha too could not escape the test of citizenship resulting in their large-scale displacement and experience of statelessness. Consequently, during the intensive revision of electoral rolls before the 1985 General Elections in Assam, thousands of Nepali names were unceremoniously struck off (Chhetry 2012, 475–487). All this led to a decline in the 'degree of citizenship' and increase in the 'degree of statelessness' of the Nepali/Gorkha in the region. The harrowing experience and trauma inflicted on the Nepali/Gorkha in Assam were replicated even in the Bodo agitation. Like AASU, the All Bodo Students' Union (ABSU), to prove the majority of the Bodos, started an ethnic cleansing operation following which the Nepali/Gorkha in the interior of the districts of Kokrajhar, Bongaigaon, Nalbari and Darrang were victimized (Chhetry 2012, 475–487).

It would be perhaps not wrong to say that the Assam movement was the precursor of similar agitations in other states of Northeast India in which Nepali/Gorkha were the principal targets. In 1980, Nepali/Gorkhas, who were accorded domiciled status as back as 1947 in Manipur, became targets of attack compelling them to flee for safety. Similarly, during 1987, violence erupted in Meghalaya, and Nepalis/Gorkhas living in Shillong, Jowai and other parts of the state became the targets. The Khasi Students' Union (KSU) and the government of Meghalaya together deported about 7,000–10,000 Nepalis in February–March 1987 (Chhetry 2012, 475–487). Post-1990s, almost all Nepali/Gorkha settlers were categorized as 'foreigners' in Meghalaya. Similar moves were systematically directed in Nagaland, Mizoram and elsewhere in the Northeast to brand all Nepali-speaking population in the region as foreigners residing there illegally. In Nagaland, for instance, in the 1980s, extortion was used as a means to terrorize the Nepali/Gorkha who had settled in the state before 1940 and were treated as indigenous non-Naga residents. In the Merapani region located on the border of Wokha of Nagaland and Sibsagar district of Assam, about 200 Nepalis lost their lives in clashes. Consequently, they were forced to resort to distress sale of their property and seek shelter in the hills of Dehradun, Nainital (in now Uttarakhand) and Darjeeling, Mirik and Siliguri (in West Bengal).

During the 1970s and the 1980s, many Gorkhas left Mizoram to resettle in Dehradun and other hill areas of Uttar Pradesh as well as Darjeeling. During this period, the Mizoram Gorkha Sangh requested the Mizoram (Union Territory) government for the first time to recognize the Gorkhas of Mizoram as one of the tribes of Mizoram, but this was not accepted. Later in the year 1984, a renewed demand for inclusion of the Gorkha community in the Mizoram Official Handbook to prove their recognized citizenship in India and residence in Mizoram was made to Lalthanhawla's Congress Government. The Congress leaders showed some muted support for the issues and concerns of the Gorkhas in Mizoram.

With the attainment of statehood and the change in power positions in the form of the rise of the Mizo National Front (MNF), the Gorkhas openly declared their total support for MNF and publicly made statements that pinched the Congress; for instance, several Gorkhas working for Congress switched sides, thinking the tide would be in their favour. With the re-entry of Congress (I) in the second State Assembly Elections, the Gorkhas realized their political mistake and once more switched sides. This time, under the Gorkha, workers within the Congress (I) such as N. S. Chettri, J. P. Thapa, M. K. Limbu, B. K. Thapa and others demanded the 'Conferment of Equal Facilities to the Permanent Gorkha Settlers of Mizoram'. The congress now did not want to lose its traditional minority vote bank and decided to accord certain facilities and decided that there should be a fresh census with the co-operation of the Gorkha community residing in Mizoram as on 26 January 1950 and the direct descendants of those people. The Cabinet Meeting of 20 December 1991 resolved to extend certain facilities to the Gorkhas of Mizoram who have been residing in Mizoram before 26 January 1950. Lalthanhawla announced the decision before a large crowd in the Gorkha School premises in Khatla, Aizawl. The facilities extended included granting of Post-Matric Scholarships, an extension of facilities in the matters of education, land settlement certificates including the transfer of ownership, employment and trade, and commerce on par with the Mizos and the issue of Permanent Residential Certificates. The Students' Joint Action Committee vehemently criticized the government and forced the government to review its decision to grant facilities to the Gorkhas 'on par' with the Mizos.

The second tension between the *Vai* and the Mizo/Zo in the 1990s did not spare even the Gorkhas. Several shops and small businesses owned by the Gorkha community were burnt, including the shop of Kapur Chand Thakuri, the political face of the Gorkhas in Mizoram. The Mizo Zirlai Pawl (MZP), the largest students' representative in Mizoram, forced many Gorkhas to roll down the shutters and move out of business. To counter the trimming mission of the agencies, the Gorkha conveyed full support to the actions of MZP to move out the *Vai* from Mizoram. The Gorkha youths and students' union came out with pamphlets supporting the cause of MZP and the agencies of the *Nexus*, even though it meant that the Gorkhas were also affected. They declared all losses were for the greater glory of both the communities, which have been living in peace since times immemorial. The tensions were followed by the strategy of mass conversions. In the 1998 elections, the MNF Party promised to grant Other Backward Class (OBC) status to the Gorkhas under the constitutional provisions of the Mandal Commission Report (Engineer 1991; Maheshwari 1995) if they acted as their vote bank (Zoramthanga 1998). The government of Mizoram accepted 4,453 as the figure of the permanent Gorkhas settled in Mizoram before 26 January 1950 and approved the issue of Land Settlement Certificate (LSC)/passes in respect of land traditionally held by them.

From the 1980s onwards, the Gorkhas have faced serious challenges (Pradhan 2009, 225–236) to their existence in Mizoram, owing to the unchecked flow of migrants from Nepal. After the Peace Accord the government clubbed both the categories as 'Foreigners', as they were unable to distinguish between the 'old settlers' and the 'new migrants'. Such a move triggered the need to consolidate the permanent Gorkhas and make their positions clear in terms of 'genuine citizenship'.[3] traced back to the colonial times. The Mizoram Gorkha Youth Association (MGYA) and other Gorkha organizations have been pursuing (by submitting memoranda) different governments from 2002 onwards 'to push forward their demand of being granted and recognized as

OBCs in Mizoram' Mizoram' (MGYA 2002, 2004a, 2004b, 2004c, 2005, 2006a, 2006b). To substantiate their arguments for OBC status, they appended documentation from other states and regions where the Gorkhas have been recognized as OBCs such as Meghalaya, Nagaland, Assam, Haryana, Punjab, and the Mandal Commission Report which listed the Gorkhas as one of the Backward Classes in Mizoram.

Historically speaking, even though the Gorkhas are a later migrant population, and they have succeeded in camouflaging their identity with the majority Zo/Mizo identity. For instance, the Gorkha organizations in Mizoram like the MGYA formed in 1976 on the lines of the Young Mizo Association (YMA) aim at cultural assimilation with the majority Zo/Mizo culture while maintaining its distinct Gorkha flavour, further substantiating the argument that migrations do not imply a complete break from the past; rather, the migrant must be understood as inhabiting two worlds simultaneously (Thapan 2005, 15).

Many of the *Vai* (Bengali Muslims) from Cachar and Karimganj, who come to Mizoram as menial labour, often do not possess legal documents, or their documents have expired, making them illegal migrants. The vanguards of the Ideal Zo Christian state target this group of people and exploit them for selfish ends, including physical assaults. Of late, the *Vais* have been regulating their presence by emulating the twin model of YMA and MGYA to chisel out their space within the ambit of the Ideal Zo Christian state in Mizoram. The predominantly Muslim *Vai* people formed the 'Mizoram Muslim Welfare Society' (MMWS) in 2001 to consolidate their voices and have attempted to work in collaboration with YMA (Chakraborty 2013b, 150–159). However, YMA continues to set the terms of negotiation during conflicts between the *Vai* and the Mizo/Zo; for instance, in case of assaults or manhandling of the *Vai* by MZP or YMA or Kristian Thalai Pawl (KTP), the first step that the victim of mob rule has to do is 'non-reporting', that is, the victim should not report to the police or legal agencies; instead, the victim should bring the case to the notice of the Central YMA and the Church. Failure to do so makes the case unfit for discussion at the negotiation table, and the victim has to face the music.[4]

The Gorkhaland movement, which has been relentlessly mustering efforts to bring all the diaspora Nepali/Gorkha communities (Bhattarai

2009; Chhetri 2011; Khati 1994; Lama 1996; Rawat 1996) under a common platform, thus, has become an attractive option for the Nepali-speaking community in the Northeast in general. No doubt, the Gorkhas in Mizoram have continually supported the idea of creation of Gorkhaland in and around Darjeeling, be it under Subash Ghising in the 1980s or under the aegis of Bimal Gurung post-2007. However, a word of caution is that the creation of a new state named after a particular community in the region around Darjeeling Hills would naturally have a rippling effect on the marginal communities in North Bengal and boost similar contending/contesting demands. There is undoubtedly a strong yearning to define 'a native', 'an immigrant' and 'an insider', and to substantiate the same, and there is a strong tendency to prove original inhabitancy. In other words, the competing communities unleash a wave of contesting historiographies.

Post-1986, the intensity of identity consciousness among the non-Gorkha in Darjeeling hills has reflected the embattledness of identity politics, eventually affecting their degrees of citizenship. The 'later non-Gorkha immigrants' such as Bihari, Punjabi and Rajasthani have strong discomfort with the *Madheshiya* and *Bhaiyaji* tag given to them by the Gorkha. As a response, these 'immigrants' employed survival strategies of camouflaging their identities in tune with the Gorkhey Identity; for instance, newer and more convenient forms of defining community identities in synchrony with the overarching 'Gorkhey Identity' have been sought by most immigrants in the region. Gorkhey-Bihari, Gorkhey-Punjabi, Gorkhey-Rajasthani, Gorkha-Muslim, etc., are the hybridized identities that have evolved and are displayed in public in contemporary times among inmigrants, especially the younger generations born and raised in the region and who typically are multilingual and conversant in Nepali/Gorkhali language. Among most inmigrants, the older generation tends to display, both publicly and privately, more conservative responses; for instance, privately, they stick to their identities as Bihari, Punjabi, Rajasthani, Bihari-Muslim, etc., while conveniently referring to themselves as Bihari-Gorkhey, Punjabi-Gorkhey, Rajasthani-Gorkhey, etc., when it comes to the public. Likewise, the ostensible styling of the self-defined identity among the Muslims in Darjeeling hills, as 'Gorkha-Muslim' or 'Gorkhey Muslim' rather than 'Bihari-Muslim',

'Bengali Muslim' and the like, substantiates and unfolds a bewildering diversity of Muslim communities and multiple manifestations of their identity. Gleaned from the above case, one can understand 'otherization' to be a complex web of bracketing people or communities into boxes of convenient categories.

To conclude, we would like to state the following: The notion of citizenship in the 'Northeast' is braided in the notion of the 'other' vis-à-vis the 'self'.[5] Through the politics of camouflaging, the minorities bargain their existence in the ethnically fisted territories. The politics of camouflaging may or may not solve the complex problem of acceptance in the battle of identities; for instance, migrants employ the tactics of marrying local women. While it has helped the *Poi* and the Gorkha, it hardly acts as a full proof strategy for the *Vai*. The *Vai* continue to be a 'permanent pariah', fit only to serve the realms of the economy. All this reaffirms Horowitz's (1985) formulation that 'though ethnicity is commonly tied to territory changes in territorial boundaries can lead to significant changes in ethnic identities'. Individuals may also regard each other as ethnic strangers in one place but as ethnic kin in another where they may discover both common cultural commitments and common material interests in the face of competitors from radically different cultures. Ethnic identity can be shifted upwards or downwards to more inclusive or narrower levels to meet situational exigencies. Ethnic and national groups can similarly fuse or split apart. Such processes may combine 'primordial' sentiments and strategic calculations.

Notes

1. However, this does not mean that the Gorkha has been accepted unconditionally. The diaspora Mizo/Zo or the *Zohnahthlak* from Tripura, Manipur and elsewhere has been voicing concerns over the issue of accepting the Gorkha as Denizens, while they remain at the threshold.
2. Mrs Mills in Nicole Kidman starrer *The Others* (Amenabar 2001).
3. In this study, 'genuine citizenship' refers to those with proper documents. In the case of Mizoram, any colonial document mentioning the names of the individual's forefathers. The Gorkhas in the state of Mizoram underwent this drive of styling themselves as 'genuine citizens' as a class apart from the later entrants from Nepal and elsewhere who came to Mizoram taking the benefits

of the 1950's provision between the two countries. The 'genuine citizens' are the first movers in terms of historical time frame among the migrant Nepali-speaking population in Mizoram (ASC)
4. Personal interviews in 2008 (17 February) and 2010 (20–21 March) with Mamon Mazumdar.
5. Interestingly, the usage of the term 'self' in a tribal context is itself debatable. Here, the individual gains his/her identity through the collective and historical identity of the tribe, which has been preserved and transferred through generations. Hence, the notion of 'self' transcends to that of collective good and rights rather than individual benefit (ASC).

References

Amenabar, Alejandro. 2001. *The Others*. New York, NY: Dimension Films & Warner Bros.
Barbora, Sanjay. (2006). Rethinking India's Counter-Insurgency campaign in the North-East. *Economic & Political Weekly*. September 2-8, pp. 3805–3812.
Bareh, H. M. 2001. *Encyclopaedia of North-East India, Mizoram*. Vol. V. New Delhi: Mittal Publications.
Barooah, N. K. 1970. *David Scott in North-East India 1802–1813: A Study in British Paternalism*. Delhi: Munshiram Manoharlal.
Barpujari, H.K. (1977). *Political History: 1826–1919*. Guwahati: Govt. of Assam.
Baruah, Sanjib. (2004). *Between South and Southeast Asia: North-East India and the Look East Policy*. Guwahati: CENISEAS
Baruah, Sanjib. 2005. Preface. *Durable Disorder-Understanding the Politics of North East India*, vii. New Delhi: Oxford University Press..
Bhagabati, Ananda C. 1982. 'Emergent Tribal Identity in North-East India.' In *Tribal Development in India: Problems and Prospects*, edited by B. Chaudhuri, 218. Delhi: Inter-India Publications.
Bhattarai. Ganga Prasad. (2009). *Ragat Le Lekheko Itihaas*, Siliguri: Shivakoti Printing Press.
Chakraborty, Anup Shekhar. (2008a). Emergence of Women from 'Private' to 'Public': A Narrative of Power Politics from Mizoram. *Journal of International Women's Studies*. Bridgewater, Vol. No. 9. 3 May.
———. (2008b). Manufacturing of Spaces: The 'Others' in Zo/Mizo Politics. *South Asian Journal of Socio-Political Studies (SAJOSPS)*. Vol. 9 No. 1, July–December.
———. (2008c). Mustering Empowerment experiences from Mizoram: A Leap from 'Private' to 'Public' Living Spaces. *Global South SEPHIS e-magazine*. Vol. 4 No. 4 July.
———. 2009, 18 February. 'Regulating Citizenship: Politics of "Check-In" and "Check-Out" in Mizoram, India.' Refugee Watch Online (A Co-Publication of Refugee Watch).

Chakraborty, Anup Shekhar. 2012. 'Construing and Gleaning the Vexing Notion of the "Outsider" in Mizoram: Pre-Statehood to Post-Statehood Times.' *QUEST: The Journal of UGC-HRDC* 6, no. 2: 297–304.
———. 2013a. 'Identity and Virtual Spaces among the Zo Hnahthlak: Emergent Zo Cyberpolitics.' In *The Virtual Transformation of the Public Sphere: Knowledge, Politics, Identity*, edited by Gaurav Desai, 169–193. New Delhi/ London: Routledge Publications.
———. 2013b. 'Regulating People, Consolidating Voices: Mizoram Muslim Welfare Society and the Positional Order of Things in the Zo/Mizo Cosmology.' In *Dissenting Voices, Collective Voices, And Politics of Assertions: A Pan-Indian Perspective*, edited by Pradip Kumar Sengupta and Manas Chakrabarty, 150–159. Kolkata: Levant Books.
———. 2013c. 'Elementary Aspects of "Otherness" in Mizoram: An Enquiry into the Nature and Processes of Social Inclusion and Exclusion in a North-East Indian State' (Occasional Paper VII). Department of Sociology, University of North Bengal, Siliguri.
Chakraborty, Anup Shekhar, and Subhas Ranjan Chakraborty. 2016. 'Ambiguous Identities: Statelessness of Gorkhas in North-East India.' In *The State of Being Stateless: An Account of South Asia*, edited by Paula Banerjee, Anasua Basu Ray Chaudhury, and Atig Ghosh, 207–245. New Delhi: Orient Black Swan Pvt. Ltd.
Chambers, O. A. (1899) 2005. *Hand Book of The Lushai Country*. Reprint, Kolkata: Firma KLM/Aizawl: Tribal Research Institute.
Chatterjee, Suhas. (1985). *Mizoram Under the British Rule*. Delhi: Mittal Publications
Chatterjee, Suhas. 1990. *Mizoram Encyclopaedia*, Vol. I. Bombay: Jaico Publishing House.
Chaube, S. K. (1973). *Hill Politics in Northeast India*. Patna: Orient Longman.
Chaube, S. K. 1985. *Electoral Politics in Northeast India*. Madras: Universities Press.
Chawngbuanga, C. 1990. 'Champhai Chanchin.' In *Champhai Centenary Souvenir*. Champhai: The Souvenir Department, YMA Champhai.
Chhetri, Hira. 2011. *Bharathya Nepali Patra Patrika Ko Shatapdi 1887–1986*. Kalimpong: Impression Printing.
Chhetry, D. B. 2012. 'Nepalis and Bangladeshis in Assam: Comparative Historical Analysis of Migration, Identity and Citizenship.' In *Politics of Culture, Identity, and Protest in North-east India*, edited by Padam Nepal and Anup Shekhar Chakraborty, Vol 2, pp. 475–487. New Delhi: Authors Press.
Downs, Fredrick S. 1992. *Northeast India in the Nineteenth and Twentieth Centuries: History of Christianity in India*, Vol. 5, Part 5, 6. Bangalore: The Church History Association of India.
Dubey, S.M. (Ed.). (1978). *North-East India: A Sociological Study*. New Delhi: Concept Publishing Company.
Elly, E. B. (1893) 1978. *Military Report on The Chin-Lushai Country*. Calcutta: Firma KLM Private Ltd.

Engineer, Asgharali. 1991. *Mandal Commission Controversy.* New Delhi: Ajanta Publications.
Fernandes, Walter. (2004). Limits of Law and Order Approach to the North-East. *Economic and Political Weekly,* 39(42), 4609–4611.
Fuchs, Stephen. 1973. *The Aboriginal Tribes of India.* London/Madras: The Macmillan Press Ltd.
Guha, Amalendu. 1977. *Planter Raj to Swaraj: Freedom Struggle and Electoral Politics in Assam 1826–1947.* New Delhi: Indian Council of Historical Research.
———. 1991. *Medieval & Early Colonial Assam-Society, Polity, Economy.* Calcutta: K. P. Bagchi & Company/CSSS.
Hazarika, Sanjoy. 1992, 6 February. 'Bangladeshisation of India.' *Telegraph,* Calcutta.
Horowitz, Donald. L. 1985. *Ethnic Groups in Conflict.* Berkeley, CA: University of California Press.
Hussain, Manirul. 2004. 'Nationalities, Ethnic Processes, and Violence in India's Northeast.' In *Peace Studies: An Introduction to the Concepts, Scope, and Theme,* edited by Ranabir Samaddar. New Delhi: SAGE Publications.
Khati, Tika. 1994. *Nepali Bhasha Manyata Andolan Ka Pratham Senani: Anand Singh Thapa.* Darjeeling: Darjeeling Printing House.
Lama, Mahendra P. 1996. *Gorkhaland Movement: Quest for an Identity.* New Delhi: Department of Information & Cultural Affairs, DGHC.
Lewin, T. H. (1912) 1977. *A Fly on the Wheel.* Calcutta: Firma KLM on behalf of Aizawl. Aizawl: Tribal Research Institute.
Maheshwari, S. R. 1995. *Mandal Commission Revisited: Reservation Bureaucracy in India.* New Delhi: Jawahar Publishers & Distributors.
———. (1968) 2002. 'North-Eastern Council.' In *Indian Administration,* 6th ed., 424–442. New Delhi: Orient Longman Pvt. Ltd.
McCall, A. G. (1939) 1980. *The Lushai Hills: District Cover.* Aizawl: Tribal Research Institute.
Mizoram Gorkha Youth Association. 2002, 28 November. 'To the Honourable Home Minister, Government of Mizoram.' Letter No. MGYA(C)/OBC/2002–03/02. Aizawl.
———. 2004a, 15 February. 'To the Honourable Home Minister, Government of Mizoram.' Letter No. MGYA(C)/OBC/2003–04/1. Aizawl.
———. 2004b, 30 April. 'To the Secretary, Home Department, Government of Mizoram.' Letter No. MGYA(C)/OBC/2003–04/3. Aizawl.
———. 2004c, 10 December. 'To the Honourable Home Minister, Government of Mizoram.' Letter No. MGYA(C)/OBC/2004–2005. Aizawl.
———. 2005, 11 January. 'To the Honourable Home Minister, Government of Mizoram.' Letter No. MGYA(C) 1/2005/A/1. Aizawl.
———. 2006a, 16 January. 'To the Honourable Chief Minister, Government of Mizoram.' Letter No. MGYA(C)/OBC/2004–2005. Aizawl.

Mizoram Gorkha Youth Association. 2006b, 11 January. 'To the Honourable Home Minister, Government of Mizoram.' Letter No. MGYA(C)/OBC/2004–2005. Aizawl.

Moares, George Mark. 1964. *A History of Christianity in India: From Early Times to St. Francis Xavier A.D 52–1542*, Vol. I. Bombay: P. C. Manaktala & Sons Private Ltd.

Nag, Sajal. 2003. 'Fei-ization of the Nepalis of North-east India.' In *The Nepalis in Northeast India: A Community in Search of Indian Identity*, edited by A. C. Sinha and T. B. Subba, 184. New Delhi: Indus Publishing Company.

Pachuau, Thangvunga. 1990. 'Champhai Zawl Leilet Chanchin.' In *Champhai Centenary Souvenir*. Champhai: The Souvenir Department, YMA Champhai.

Pradhan, K. L. 2009. 'Mizoram *Gorkha*s: Issues & Problems.' In *Indian Nepalis: Issues & Perspectives*, edited by T. B. Subba, A. C. Sinha, G. S. Nepal, and D. R. Nepal, 225–236. New Delhi: Concept Publishing Company.

Rawat, Bhagirath. 1996. *Baans Salki Rahe Cha*. Darjeeling: Information & Cultural Department, GHC.

Samaddar, Ranabir. 2001. *A Biography of the Indian Nation, 1947–1997*. New Delhi: SAGE Publications.

Sangkima. 1995. 'Cachar-Mizo relation (AD 1832–1890).' *Proceedings of North East India History Association*, XVI Session, Agartala.

———, ed. 2004a. *Cross-border Migration Mizoram*. New Delhi: Shipra Publications.

———. 2004b. 'The Coming and Settlement of Myanmarese in Mizoram Since the Beginning of the Twentieth Century A.D to the Present.' In *Essays on the History of the Mizos*, edited by Sangkima, 283–294. Guwahati: Spectrum Publications.

Sen, Geeti, ed. 2006. *Where the Sun Rises When Shadows Fall: The North-East*. New Delhi: Oxford University Press.

Shakespeare, J. 1923. 'The Superintendent of Lushai Hills Order No. 31 of 1922.' *Mizo leh Vai Chanchinbu*, 33.

Singh, B. P. 1987. 'North-East, India: Demography, Culture, and Identity Crisis.' *Modern Asian Studies* 21, no. 2: 257–282.

Singh, Chandrika. 2004. *North-East India*. New Delhi: Manas Publications.

Singh, K. S., B. B. Goswami, C. Nunthara, and N. N. Sengupta, ed. 1995. *People of India: Mizoram*, Vol. XXXIII. Anthropological Survey of India. Calcutta: Seagull Books.

Sinha, A. C. 1982. 'The Nepalese in North-East India: Ethnicity and Resource Appropriation.' In *Social Tension in North-East India*, edited by J. B. Bhattacharjee, 91–92. Calcutta: Research India Publications.

———. 2003. 'The Indian Northeast Frontier and the Nepali Immigrants.' In *The Nepalis in Northeast India: A Community in Search of Indian Identity*, edited by A. C. Sinha and T. B. Subba, 42. New Delhi: Indus Publishing Company.

Sinha, A. C., and T. B. Subba, ed. 2003. *The Nepalis in Northeast India: A Community in Search of Indian Identity*. New Delhi: Indus Publishing Company.

Soares, Aloysius. 1964. *The Catholic Church in India: A Historical Sketch*. Nagpur: Maharashtra State Government Press & Book Depot.
Statesman. 1997, 22 February. 'Fear of the Foreigner.' Statesman, Calcutta.
Subba, T. B. 1992. *Ethnicity, State and Development: A Case Study of Gorkhaland Movement in Darjeeling*, 115–116. New Delhi: Vikas.
———. 2003. 'The Nepalis in Northeast India: Political Aspirations and Ethnicity.' In *The Nepalis in Northeast India: A Community in Search of Indian Identity*, edited by A. C. Sinha and T. B. Subba, 62. New Delhi: Indus Publishing Company.
Sunar, Pradip, Jeevan Kawar, and I. K. Subba. 2000. *The Gorkhas of Mizoram*, Vol. I. Aizawl: Mizoram Gorkha Students' Union (MGSU).
Thapan, Meenakshi, ed. 2005. *Women and Migration in Asia-Transnational Migration and the Politics of Identity*, 15, Vol. I. New Delhi: SAGE Publications.
Verghese, B. G. 1996. *India's Northeast Resurgent: Ethnicity, Insurgency, Governance, Development*, 3. New Delhi: Konark Publishers Pvt. Ltd.
Verghese, C. G., and R. L. Thanzawna. 1997. *A History of the Mizos*, Vols. I and II, 54. New Delhi: Vikas.
Weiner, Myron. 1978. *Sons of the Soil: Migration & Ethnic Conflict in India*. New Delhi: Oxford University Press.
Zoramthanga. 1998, 14 October. *Mizoram Chhunga Nepali/Gorkhali Awmhlun Mipuite Laka MNF Party Intiam Kamna*. Aizawl: MNF General Headquarter.

CHAPTER 2

Colonial State and Annexation of Cachar in a Strategic Frontier of British Bengal

Santosh Hasnu

This chapter looks at the process of colonial expansion in the principality of Cachar and its formal annexation into the Company's dominion. With the beginning of the Burmese westward expansion, the state of Cachar started to assume importance for the security of the Company's territories in Bengal. This war led to the signing of a treaty between the British East India Company (EIC) and the Cachar state in 1824, which turned Cachar into a protectorate state. This chapter also looks at how the British EIC engaged with notions of indigenous custom and 'tradition' as a pretext and context for its intervention in royal succession disputes in Cachar. Colonial investigation and conceptions of customary precedents also served to legitimize the annexation of this strategic territory that was key to the security of British Bengal. The desired opportunity offered itself when the Cachar Raja, Govind Chandra, died in April 1830 leaving no male heir to the throne. In the absence of any clear law of primogeniture, several candidates advanced conflicting interpretations of local custom and usages to support their claims to the vacant throne of Cachar. There were three strong contenders, namely Govind Chandra's widow, Indraprabha; the hill Cachar Chief Tula Ram who claimed the support of the 'forty *sengphongs*'[1]; and the Manipuri ruler Gambhir Singh.

As part of an exercise in intelligence gathering, the Company Raj had investigated the local usages and customs practised in precolonial Cachar. While enquiring into the pre-existing patterns and laws of primogeniture, the British officials reported that the destruction of all written records has rendered in the inquiry of ancient laws of Cachar. They, therefore, resorted to verbal interrogation of the local elites, especially gentry of the earlier regime. Though the British professed respect for tribal customs, they questioned the authenticity of their informants and their practicability under colonial conditions. The process of investigation was not just a depiction of pre-existing political institutions, but it also mirrored a series of rationalized bureaucratic processes that were marked different from preceding strategies of rule. The technologies of rule harnessed by the British colonial state distinguished it from earlier political regimes that sought to control the various populations of Cachar. The British Raj in India, through a century of existence, had forged a functional repertoire of administrative practices, but these practices were honed over many years through the governance of the Indian subcontinent. These may have served as examples of how best an empire should be organized, but how would these well-founded, time-honoured practices play out in borderland Cachar? The specific nature of how the Company Raj employed to annex Cachar can provide us with insight into the nature of how a modern colonial state actually behaved in a strategic frontier of British Bengal.

Contested Cachar

In this section, we will discuss the precolonial political condition of Cachar. This will help to understand the nature of expansion of colonial state in 19th century. Located to the south of Assam, present-day Cachar has a dual identity: it is ethnically half Bengali and half tribal and, topographically, half plains and half hills. For the first time, the Cachar valley area acquired a distinct political identity in the mid-18th century. Prior to that period, the area had been the colonial outpost of Koch Behar kingdom, ruled by a branch of the Koch royal family with its capital at Khaspur. The Koch rulers had inflicted a serious threat to the Dimasa rulers. The Dimasa hill state of Maibang and the Koch colony in the valley merged Cachar state in c. 1750s.[2] From the beginning of the early 19th century, Cachar was always an area of interest to its expansive neighbours such as Manipur and Burma. There was stiff contest for political power among at least five important players: the valley-based Dimasa Raja, the hill-based Chief Tula Ram within the domain of Cachar and outside players such as the neighbouring princely Manipur and expansionist Konbaung Burma coming from the porous southern borders. Therefore, the westward expansion carried out by Burmese rulers reached the very borders of British Bengal. Two historical events or contingencies offered the needed alibi for British expansion into Cachar: (a) the end of the First Anglo-Burmese War in 1826 and (b) the demise of Dimasa Raja without a male heir in 1830. On the first occasion, the British employed Burmese 'threat' to turn Cachar into a 'protectorate'. The second occasion provided a good excuse for the British to claim the Cachar throne, as its 'legitimate' heir premised on colonial knowledge of local customs related to succession disputes and confirming royal pedigrees. Pitched against the oral testimonies of the 'forty *sengphongs*' of Cachar Hills and other rival claimants, British conveniently concluded that the right of conquest had the backing of Dimasa customary law.

Before the outbreak of the First Anglo-Burmese War (1826), the struggle for dominion over Cachar was contested between three important Manipuri brothers: Chourjeet Singh, Marjeet Singh and Gambhir Singh. The former was the dethroned Raja of Manipur and was exiled by his own brother, Marjeet Singh; the latter was a Manipuri in the service of the Cachar Raja Govind Chandra. With the death of the previous Raja of Cachar, Krishna Chandra in 1813, the princes of Manipur had been anxiously waiting to advance into Cachar. This was further cemented by various facts. First, Chourjeet Singh had been making efforts to procure assistance from Jaintia; second, Govind Chandra's subjects in Dharampur were refusing to remain his tributaries; third, Govind Chandra's own *sirdars* or *gunnims* (official post) had sided with Chourjeet Singh; and fourth, letters of correspondence between Chourjeet and Marjeet intercepted by Govind Chandra show that though Marjeet Singh might not have be part of this impending campaign, he was very much aware of his brother's intentions (NAI 1830, Document No. 60). When the Cachar Raja became aware of these occurrences and suspecting his subjects will not side with him in case of an attempt of attack upon his country, he requested the British Magistrate of Sylhet to allow him 10 sepoys to enable him to keep his own subjects in subordination and prevent them from rising in case of an invasion.

Finally, when Marjeet Singh of Manipur was driven out from his throne in 1817 by the advancing armies of the Burmese, he fled into Cachar with 5,000 of his followers. Surprisingly, he met with little or no opposition from the troops of the Raja of Cachar, Govind Chandra. Thomas Fisher, a British survey officer engaged in surveying territories neighbouring Sylhet, opined that this lack of resistance to the Manipuri Raja caused the troops of Cachar to become 'disheartened' by the 'cowardice of their chief'.[3] However, at the frontier of Sylhet, the troops of the Cachar kingdom finally repelled the onward advance of Marjeet Singh, and perhaps, such a repulse might have caused him to retreat if it were not for the betrayal to the Raja of Cachar by Gambhir Singh, the brother of Marjeet Singh who commanded a small corps in the service of the Raja of Cachar. With this betrayal, the Raja of Cachar was forced to flee into British-held territories in neighbouring Sylhet.[4] Gambhir Singh, thus, unwittingly managed to draw British presence into this regional conflict by forcing the Raja of Cachar to flee into British-held territories. This event was not caused by any previous dissensions with the new Raja, Govind Chandra, but it was the consequence of the occupation of Manipur by the Burmese, which compelled Marjeet to seek an establishment in Cachar with a large body of followers (Anonymous 1827).

In a strange twist of circumstances, Chourjeet Singh, the long ousted former Raja of Manipur entered the fray. Chourjeet Singh, by virtue of living in exile in Sylhet at the time, made his way into Jaintia with a few followers and proclaimed that the British had advanced to the frontier and they were in the process of supporting Chourjeet's claims. Perhaps considering the reality of British presence in Sylhet and that they had advanced right to the frontier regions of Cachar which bordered the area, Chourjeet's bluff managed to bring under his control the combined troops of his brothers, Marjeet and Gambhir Singh. He then delegated to his brothers limited authority over certain tracts of Cachar and proclaimed himself the Raja of Cachar. However, Chourjeet Singh's reign over Cachar was short-lived. In the early part of 1823, with internal dissension on one hand and the threat of Burmese attacks on the other, Chourjeet Singh decided to concede the rights over Cachar to the British. The British accepted his offer, but before a treaty for the purpose could take place, Chourjeet Singh was overthrown by his own brother, Gambhir Singh. According to Thomas Fisher, under these two Manipuri rulers, the people of Cachar suffered greatly and fled to the neighbouring areas of Sylhet, Jyntea and Tipperah (NAI 1830, Document No. 59).

Cachar as British Protectorate

During the reign of his brother Marjeet Singh in Manipur, Gambhir Singh was forced to flee into Cachar. During the contest between Chourjeet Singh and Marjeet Singh, Gambhir Singh was made *senapati* (chief) of the military forces of Cachar by Cachar Raja, Govind Chandra. However, when Cachar was being attacked by the other two Manipuri brothers, Gambhir Singh deserted Govind Chandra and, siding with his brothers, assisted them in appropriating by far the greater part of Cachar.

In this context, the Burmese troops, which had retained permanent possession of Manipur since 1817, were now preparing to advance to Cachar. The Burmese declared that the excuse for invading Cachar was not one of self-interest or expansion but rather the desire to re-install the 'rightful' Dimasa ruler, Govind Chandra, to the throne of Cachar (from which he was ousted by the Manipuri princes).

These instances alarmed the Company Government (EIC) at Calcutta about a probable Burmese invasion into these territories. The Calcutta officials instructed the Magistrate of Sylhet to enter into negotiations either with Gambhir Singh or any other chiefs who might have established their power independently in Cachar (Anonymous 1827). Cachar had acted as a buffer between the two empires—the British EIC and the expansionist Konbaung Burma. According to Thant Myint-U, the British became worried about losing this 'buffer zone', which was important in their expansionist design. Therefore, he observed, they unilaterally declared Cachar as protectorate and sent a force to halt the Burmese advance (Myint-U 2001, 18). Coupled with a worsening situation along the disputed Arakan border, it eventually resulted in the British declaration of war on 5 March 1824 against the Kingdom of Ava, which led to a confrontation between the two armies in Cachar.

In the aftermath of the First Anglo-Burmese war, the British EIC restored the rulers to their rightful place—Govind Chandra reinstated as the Raja of Cachar and Gambhir Singh as the Raja of Manipur. It also led to the signing of the Treaty of Badarpur, concluded between David Scott (Agent to the Governor-General, North Eastern Frontier) and Raja Govind Chandra on 6 March 1824. According to the terms of the treaty, the Company undertook to protect Cachar from external aggressions and to arbitrate any difference that may arise between the Raja and the other states. It was also agreed that the internal administration of the country shall be conducted by the Raja, and the jurisdiction of the British Court of Justice shall not extend there, but the Raja agreed to attend at all times to the advice of the Governor-General in Council.[5] As a strategy of imperial control, the 1824 Treaty effectively placed Cachar under British's 'indirect rule'.

Focusing on early colonial expansion into northeast Bengal in the 1820s, Gunnel Cederlöf (2009) argues that the Badarpur Treaty became the base on which the Company exercised control of the Cachari territories (Cederlöf 2009). Cachar was in ruins after the war and in no state to pay tribute. In this condition, the Company used the treaty to achieve other ends; for example, instead of paying tribute in 1827, Cachar Raja constructed a road from Cachar to Manipur facilitating easy communication with Sylhet. Cederlöf observes that, on the one hand, the Badarpur Treaty is a sign of the Company's lack of actual capacity to interfere with internal politics, on the other, it is a sign of British determination to control frontier states nested within a larger political and economic context (Cederlöf 2009). However, the

Anglo-Burmese war was not the only experience that the Cachar state was going through. The state faced internal troubles by rebel Chief Tula Ram, who having allegiance of the Dimasas in the hill Cachar and of the Dimasa tribal institution called 'forty *sengphongs*', challenged the authority of Govind Chandra as the lawful Raja of Cachar.

The Manipuri ruler Gambhir Singh added a new dimension to the rivalry between the Cachar Raja and rebel hill Chief Tula Ram. By early 1830, the Raja of Cachar reported to the colonial authorities that he suspected Gambhir Singh (reinstated by the British at the Manipuri throne after Burmese war) of scheming to take possession of his country in alliance with Tula Ram (who held the northern Cachar hilly tract; NAI 1830, Document No. 84). However, to this complaint by Cachar Raja, the Commissioner of Sylhet, Furquard refused to interfere as he was convinced that Gambhir Singh would not act foolishly (NAI 1830, Document No. 84). On 24 April 1830, the Raja Govind Chandra was murdered through the machinations of Gambhir Singh. On receiving a report of the murder of the Raja, David Scott wrote to the Calcutta government that this was the right moment for the Company to hasten the pace for complete conquest instead of indirect rule (NAI 1830, Document No. 84). Since the Cachar Raja died leaving without an heir, it offered an opportunity for the Company to interfere effectually in the internal affairs of Cachar in the name of suppressing perceived disturbances. The opportunity was given by much of the local conflicts stemmed from the aspirations of rival Rajas for territorial expansion even as they faced larger threats from imperial British and Burma. After the death of Raja Govind Chandra, the kingdom was accordingly placed under the charge of Lieutenant Thomas Fisher in June 1830. Then on survey duties in Sylhet, Fisher assumed the powers of a magistrate and a collector (Bhattacharjee 1977, 53). However, EIC was still struggling to legitimize their rule.

Raj Ideology and the Laws of Succession

Cachar was a protectorate—not a colony—of the British Raj according to the terms of the Treaty of Badarpur, 1824. There arose rival claimants to the throne of Cachar, which had lain vacant since the death of the Raja Govind Chandra in April 1830. Whereas the claim of Tula Ram was based on customary law, the claim of Indraprabha (the Rani) was based on Hindu law of succession. Gambhir Singh did not directly claim the *gaddi* (throne); instead, he claimed the Cachar domain to be annexed to his own Manipuri throne as a land grant. To begin, the British EIC acted as a judge for these three claimants, but the Company state itself became a claimant in the end. The British found a legal loophole in the Treaty of Badarpur (1824) to stake claim to the throne of Cachar.

Thomas R. Metcalf argues that as the British extended their rule during the late 18th and early 19th centuries, the British had to confront the problem of how to govern this far-flung dependency, and more importantly, how to justify this governance to themselves (Metcalf 1998). Thus, by late 18th century, the British had put together a fundamental set of governing principles, most of its part being drawn from their own society, which included the security of private property, the rule of law and the idea of 'improvement'.[6] In the 19th century, these principles had become so deeply embedded in the shaping of ideology of the Raj that to question them would have been to challenge the very purpose of the Raj itself. What constitutes legal or illegal in the context of Cachar flows directly from this ideology of the Raj. However, the issue of legality is not simple as the colonial state encountered customary laws and practices with regard to the throne of Cachar. In the following discussion, we are dealing with this aspect of legality vis-à-vis the customary laws and practices prevalent under the Cachar kingdom.

The existence of various claimants to the Cachar throne led the colonial authorities to enquire into the situation from what it perceived as the legal, according to the above-mentioned British principles evolved in the 18th century. However, once the enquiries concluded, the British began to realize the complexities and contradictions between the oral narratives of their informants and the available written records they had collected. Thomas Fisher commented at this juncture that 'the destruction of all records has rendered inquiry into the ancient laws a matter of uncertainty and judging from the diversity of opinions on the subject among the Cacharees'.[7] Consequently, these enquiries inevitably led the colonial state to complex issues of customary practices and written records related to royal successions.

The British was intrigued by the alleged existence of the forty *Sengphongs*, who were elderly electors of the throne according to one version of the local custom.[8] A Cachari [Dimasa] informant called Kanoo Ram maintained that 'if the Raj left no heirs the right to choose a new prince lay in the muntaries forty sempongs, their choice however being confined to the Hassooncha tribe [sengphong/clan]'.[9] Aged around 60–70 years, Kanoo Ram held a responsible office under Raja Govind Chandra and belonged to the sengphong 'Hassooncha'. Kartic Ram, another informant about the same age as Kanoo Ram, upheld that the right of nominating a new prince was vested in the *muntaries* (official post) alone, although the election was said to be made by the forty *Sengphongs* (NAI 1832, Document No. 100).

The Company official sought references to the *Sengphong* traditions (to validate verbal claims) in written Bengali records such as the *Cheitharol Kumbaba* (royal chronicle of Manipur). It was argued that the Manipuri Chronicles made no mention of such a Cachari institution, although there were several other references of connectivity between Cachar Princes and Manipuri Chiefs through matrimonial alliances (NAI 1832, Document No. 100). Lieutenant Gordon, the political agent stationed at Manipur, wrote to Fisher that the Manipuri records trace the origin of the present family to an equally remote period, and although they give no precedent, they afford abundant materials for inferring what would have been the course pursued in the establishment of a new Raja. In the case of the royal line being extinct, the most powerful chief, like any most powerful prince has ever done, possessed himself of the throne by violence without any consideration of right whatsoever and would then have exacted submission by force and terror (NAI 1832, Document No. 100). Thus, the Company Raj concluded that the alleged right of the forty *Sengphongs* to elect a new Raja was dubious claim, and should it ever exist, it was said to be obsolete (NAI 1832, Document No. 98) due to disuse.

Such interpretation of tradition (forty *Sengphongs)* as dubious and obsolete reflects the operation colonial logic of power. To elaborate this logic, Neeladri Bhattacharya argues that while a dialogue with native informants was seen as essential to the production of authentic knowledge, such kind of extreme dependence (in our context, on forty

Sengphongs) was experienced by the British as a form of disempowerment (compromise the need for externality of colonial power to local tradition to govern the native). Furthermore, such less dependence (externality of power) was a result of colonial logic of sovereign power that the colonial rulers had to transcend their crippling reliance on native knowledge brokers and claim their superior right to represent local tradition (Bhattacharya 1996). Superiority of the colonial state comes only when sovereign power is preserved as external or alien to the native. It was within such logic of power over traditions that colonial writings of the early 20th century on the Cacharis also referred to the dearth of written records.

After the conclusion of his enquiries, Thomas Fisher suggested three possible ways of interpreting the institution of the forty *Sengphongs* in precolonial Cachar:

1. First, the royal line had never gone extinct until now and no occasion arose for the election of a new ruler.
2. second, only in later years did the law of primogeniture came into being, but in the past, succession was decided by a Chief of the royal clan who was strong enough to seize the throne probably by force and exact an acknowledgement of his title from the *muntaries* and *sengphongs* (patrilineal clans).
3. third, in the history of Dimasa rule, a free and fair election had never been the means by which a prince asserted his right over the throne (NAI 1832, Document No. 100).

Thomas Fisher had derived the above interpretations on the basis of evidence that the former office bearers of old Dimasa kingdom gave their obedience to the new king on the condition that he belonged to the royal line. To him, had it been a customary practice of choosing of a new king by an assembly of the *muntaries* and the *sengphongs*, this practice of choosing on the royal line would have been discontinued. In addition, the practice of electing king by the above assembly could not be revived due to the fact that there were no longer *muntaries* of rank and the *sengphongs* appeared to have been scattered; it would be impossible to collect the needed 'thousand families', some of whom had retreated to the mountains under Tula Ram's rule (NAI 1832, Document No. 100).

Hence, the petition of the 'forty *Sengphongs*' for reviving the custom can be seen as a confrontation and contestation of the Company's claim to superiority. The justification provided by the colonial ruler for their intervention was that 'the revival of this particular custom is not likely to be attended with any benefit'; it was considered that this could be a source of intermediate civil war, fought with probable danger with the colonial ruler as well. The Company further contended that internal or external commotion (meaning civil war) would ensure that no power was paramount. The only way to ensure their supremacy would be to form an administration best suited to encourage cultivation of the lands and the commerce and civilization of its inhabitants (NAI 1832, Document No. 98). Colonial authorities reported that 'Cachar under a better rule would become the granary of the surrounding regions' and was understood that 'Cachar under good management would in the course of ten to twelve years yield revenue equal to that of prospering Sylhet' (NAI 1832, Document No. 84). Thus, epitomizing the best values of British governance and economic development, the Raj felt that the British paramountcy in Cachar would be established gradually through a process of 'civilising mission' (reinterpretation of native's customs and laws to control Cachar as per the need of colonial state). To establish such mission, the Company Government (EIC) advised Thomas Fisher to remain in-charge of Cachar with powers of a political agent, civil, criminal and financial, subject to the Commissioner of the Division. As per the above principle of 'better rule' (of colonial state), Fisher was directed to draw up such local rules, as his experience may suggest, for the purpose of collecting revenue. However, such task of dealing with local rules consists of tactics of appropriating local tradition/rules wherever these facilitated the colonial administration. This is seen in the case of revenue collection. Though the British Raj denied the legitimacy of local customs and institutions, it was willing to adopt former land revenue collection, system since it was more convenient for them to use local intermediaries in the newly acquired revenue-producing territory. This colonial strategy was not specifically meant for ruling Cachar only.

According to Thomas Metcalfe, there were primarily two areas that concerned the British Raj when it came to governing their various colonies: the first belief was the establishment of British imperial rule through the implementation of rule of law to lend legitimacy to its military power. The second area of concern was how to appease the indigenous populace and to what extent their local customs and traditions could play a role in the British administration (Metcalf 2007). However, reinterpretation of customs was not a one-way process: colonial to native subjects. It also allowed the natives to negotiate with colonial authority. Apparently, the diverse claimants to the throne of Dimasa state after Govind Chandra's death were also structured by the new interpretations of Dimasa custom, and such interpretation was not completely a legal-rational process.

Moreover, interpretation was not just a matter of looking for justifiable or provable evidences (in records, chronicles, etc.), but it was more of a process of deciding which interests or which claimants served the colonial rule. Tula Ram's claim to the vacant throne was favourably considered by the colonial authorities on grounds of expediency rather than those of hereditary right, although he pretended that he descended from a royal lineage. However, the government left him with an undisputed possession of the mountainous region (North Cachar Hills) by the treaty of 1829.[10] This territory included nearly all that his supposed ancestor ever possessed. Though he claimed descent from royalty, the plains people of Cachar (Bengali inhabitants) dismissed his claim, and they remembered him being a lowly minister under Raja Krishna Chandra (brother of Govind Chandra). Flatly contradicting his claims of royal blood, colonial enquiries allegedly revealed Tula Ram to be the son of an ordinary Manipuri slave girl. Moreover, the British Raj felt that if somehow they were to recognize Tula Ram's claims, it would lead to further problems, as several other contenders such as Govind Ram (cousin of Tula Ram), all claiming royal heritage, would seek to claim the vacant throne. The Bengali inhabitants themselves believed that Tula Ram had played a major role in the murder of their Raja Govind Chandra, and this accusation reduced the eligibility of his claim to the throne.[11]

Tula Ram's claim of customary law was rejected by the British who insisted that Dimasa custom of succession was not 'clearly established'.[12] Local allegiance to customary law was divided between residents of Cachar hills and Cachar valley. The British EIC stuck to the status quo by rejecting Tula Ram's claim to the throne of Cachar, but he was allowed to retain his position of the hill Cachar (the EIC formally acknowledged his possession by concluding a treaty with Tula Ram in October 1834).

Unlike Tula Ram's claim on the basis of Dimasa customary law, Indraprabha (widow of Raja Govind Chandra) staked her claim based on the Hindu law of succession, known as 'the Dayabhaga school of Hindu law that prevailed in Bengal' (Chatterjee 2013). Under this law, a widow had inheritance 'rights in the joint family property'[13] in the absence of male heirs (Chatterjee 2013, 149). According to Thomas Fisher, the marriage of Indraprabha to Govind Chandra was not conducted according to proper Hindu practice. Indraprabha was originally married to Raja Krishna Chandra, the elder brother of Govind Chandra. Her second marriage was scandalized, and Fisher reported that this second marriage was 'inconsistent both with the Hindoo law and the custom of the country' (NAI 1830, Document No. 99). Even though her claim to the throne was dismissed, the British compensated her with zamindari grant 'with a life tenure' (NAI 1830, Document No. 99). Fisher remarked that 'the Ranee being advanced in years it is not probable that any very long period would elapsed before the estate would again escheat to Government' (NAI 1830, Document No. 99).

The British EIC, for one reason or another, demolished all legal claims to the throne of Cachar. As a matter of fact, EIC never applied the doctrine of lapse in present day of Northeast India (at a time when, in the rest of the country, EIC was using the doctrine of lapse when kings did not leave behind a legal heir) to acquire any of the native princely states, including Ahom state, Jaintia, Cachar, Manipur and Tripura. The doctrine of lapse was more suited for heirless thrones which were in the sphere of Mughal power. The inability to connect the local princes in Northeast India to Mughal source of authority makes the doctrine weak in the region. The complex legal process followed by the Company appeared more transparent and legitimate then the direct application of the doctrine of lapse. Consequently, EIC claimed the Cachar throne for itself, and the Treaty of Badarpur (1824) provided a legal instrument 'to occupy and attach in perpetuity'[14] the territory of the Cachar Raja. The Company was cautious in its annexation of Cachar, and it sought to gain legitimacy by using high-sounding moral pretext. EIC claimed that the Cachar country was disturbed and asserted that 'Government which is consequently morally responsible for the welfare of the inhabitants' (of Cachar; NAI 1830, Document No. 99).

Investing in Cachar: Rent and Revenue

After the Anglo-Burmese war, the British EIC felt the need for establishing a military store under the control of Gambhir Singh between Sylhet and Manipur to secure their frontiers and to prevent any future attacks. The Raja of Cachar objected to this proposal and strongly opposed to concede part of his territory to Gambhir Singh. The Company Government was aware that as a matter of right, Gambhir Singh was not entitled to hold any portion of Cachar's territory. The Calcutta Government instructed David Scott to find an agreeable solution to assign or grant a small tract of land in Cachar to Gambhir Singh, which could also be used to settle few of his followers, with a view to establish the safe custody of military stores between Sylhet and Manipur. The Calcutta Government further authorized David Scott to negotiate an arrangement to this effect with Raja Govind Chandra if the latter would be willing to accede to the proposal (NAI 1832, Document No. 84). David Scott came out with a proposal that the Cachar Raja should provide any portion of required land in lease for 15 years (NAI 1832, Document No. 87). Replying to David Scott's, the Raja of Cachar wrote:

> ...at the request of yours for the purpose of erecting a Government magazine in my territory, I cede, to the East of the boundary of Banskandee north of the Benbakra river at Chunderpore fifty kookahs of land for 15 years.[15]

However, the Sylhet Commissioner's office was of the opinion that the ground granted at Chunderpore to Gambhir Singh was a great source of oppression towards the subjects of Cachar, as the Raja had already demanded assistance of 100 sepoys to oppose the force of Gambhir Singh (NAI 1830, Document No. 84). Believing that Gambhir Singh would not commit such folly, the Company Government denied assistance to the Raja, but the Raja of Cachar was murdered in 1830, leaving without a legitimate heir that led to the various claimants to the throne. Besides, Tula Ram and the widow of late Cachar Raja, Gambhir Singh raised his claim to farm the entire Cachar state. Supporting his claim, Captain Grant, the political agent in Manipur, informed the Company Government that the Raja of Manipur was anxious to hold the country of Cachar on lease for a term of 20 years at a rent of ₹15,000 per annum (NAI 1832, Document No. 87).

Most reports by British officers, however, felt that Gambhir Singh wished to possess Cachar merely for the purpose of extracting the largest possible amount of immediate revenue to support his extravagance and to acquire labour to cultivate his own land in Manipur; at the end of the lease, the Company Raj would find Cachar drained both of inhabitants and wealth. The colonial authorities also felt that incase when Gambhir Singh failed to pay the rent punctually would lead to unpleasant relations with the Company Government. And if needed to expel Gambhir Singh, he will ultimately fall into the hands of the Burmese court. It was also uncertain that Gambhir Singh's court would continue to reside at Manipur. The colonial authorities apparently loathed continual interference with Gambhir by preventing him, and then, removing from Cachar, for which he has an avowed predilection. The colonial authorities further disagree with Captain Grant who saw the probability of the expectations of Gambhir's collections adding to the happiness and prosperity of his *ryots* (tenant farmers). W. Cracraft, Officiating Agent to Governor-General (Political Agent's office) remarked that Captain Grant's proposal of exacting an agreement from Gambhir Singh seemed 'replete with inconvenience and the project contains seeds of perpetual bickering and interference that could end only in annulling the farm'.[16]

W. Cracraft further drew the attention of the government about their experiences of Mysore, Oudh and in fact of almost every native prince whom policy or necessity have induced the British Government to have in possession of a territory over which the government have retained some charge of influence and interference (NAI 1832, Document No. 98). It led him to believe that the Company could not let Gambhir Singh continue in possession of Cachar, either in terms of justice to its inhabitants, or benefit to government, or the Raja himself, and that the Company's interference must increase continually till a necessity of annulling the lease would arise. It was, therefore, better to assume, openly and immediately, the Government of Cachar, than to wait till it be reduced by letting the Raja rack it for a petty sum of ₹15,000 rupees per annum. In fact, he thought it would be better to present Gambhir with aa sum of ₹15,000 per annum than admit him (NAI 1832, Document No. 98).

The Company Government consulted both R. B. Pemberton and Francis Jenkins (who were on survey duty) about their views on the question of Captain Grant's support to the Raja of Manipur's claim to the lease of Cachar for a term of 20 years at a rent of ₹15000 per annum. R. B. Pemberton learnt from the Officer-in-Charge of Cachar, Lieutenant Thomas Fisher that the actual present revenue was worth ₹39,007, and the expenditure amounted to ₹15,876. It carried a surplus balance of ₹23,131 or half as much again as the offer of Gambhir Singh. Pemberton added that the revenue earned from the district of Cachar not only covered its administration cost but would be adequate to cover the administration costs of even Manipur, seeing as there was the potential for improving revenue and harnessing the greater capabilities that Cachar had to offer. Pemberton felt that if the lease of Cachar was granted to Gambhir Singh, it would cause subject people such as the Manipuris, Bengalis and Cacharis already settled in Cachar to return back to Sylhet despite having extended cultivation and having improved the landscape to ensure profitable returns.[17]

Furthermore, R. B. Pemberton observed that the current Raja of Manipur owed his security to the British—they protected him from not only external aggression but also internal dissensions. Even after the Burmese War, it was the British who reinstated Gambhir Singh and provided protection to him and the people of Manipur. Therefore, even if they were to reject Gambhir Singh's request for the lease of Cachar, the British were well aware that considering how much protection the people and their king receive from them, they would not protest the decision (NAI 1832, Document No. 109).

Pemberton also felt that Captain Grant had no clear idea of the exact value of the revenue capability of Cachar. Therefore, his opinion that Gambhir Singh should hold the lease of Cachar holds no basis for the government to grant or agree to it; instead, he felt that the government would earn greater revenue by keeping Cachar to themselves rather than being paid the lease amount by Gambhir Singh (NAI (1832, Document No. 109). The reason underlying this opinion was that the capabilities of the Cachar country were generally considered so great by the wealthy zamindars of the Sylhet district that many were, at this moment, anxious to invest their capital in it and to form it at a rent considerably beyond ₹15,000 per annum.

Pemberton endeavoured to point out what appeared to him erroneous or partial views of the question of Raja Gambhir Singh farming Cachar in lease:

1. The Company Government can realize larger revenue by retaining Cachar than what was offered by the Raja of Manipur, Gambhir Singh.
2. The then military establishments of Manipur secured the Raja's position and thereby augmented his revenue from a far greater proportion of Nagas than any of his predecessors ever enjoyed, and that as he neither paid, fed nor equipped his troops, they can add but little to his expenditure.
3. The sepoys though enrolled were not altogether drawn from a participation in civil duties but were called out in times of need in their characters of citizens as well as soldiers.
4. Judging from former experiences, there was very little probability that the revenue derived from Cachar would be employed in objects considered to improve the country of Manipur.
5. The number of troops now in the Levy[18] cannot be augmented in the present reduced state of the population, grievously adding up to the burden of the remainder.
6. The use of the term 'restore' in endeavouring to establish the claim of previous possession in favour of the Raja of Manipur to Cachar was inapplicable and inadmissible.
7. The policy would appear rather to suggest the propriety of uniting Cachar permanently to Sylhet with whose people it was almost

identical in every respect than to annex it to Manipur from which it was cut off by cultural barriers and the total dissimilarity of their respective inhabitants in appearance customs and language.
8. By giving the Raja as far as the Madura Nullah, there was great reason to fear he would endeavour to increase the inhabitants and revenue of that portion of his territory at the expense of Manipur.[19]

Francis Jenkins agreed with Pemberton's objection to granting the lease to Gambhir Singh, fearing that it would drive out the majority of the population who objected to being under Manipuri rule. He argued that even Manipuris who then resided and worked in Cachar would not subject themselves to the Raja for fear of being put under the system of personal labour and arbitrary rule. Jenkins added that the Bengali population of Cachar would also object to being under Manipuri rule, as it would mean the loss of their right as landowners, thus becoming *ryots*. Jenkins further admitted that Cachar was extremely fertile, and in case of any future war, its abundant resources would be valuable. He noted that there was already growth of cultivation in the area which would be threatened by the sudden decision to hand over the lease of Cachar to Gambhir Singh. In Jenkins' own words, 'the experiment proposed to the Government appears to me in every way hazardous, impolitic and unjust'.[20] Therefore, both Jenkins and Pemberton agreed that giving the lease of Cachar to Gambhir Singh would be a policy blunder.

As a fiscal measure, Gambhir Singh's offer was not attractive enough for British Assam Government. Moreover, the demographic profile of Cachar plains was not favourable because Bengalis easily outnumbered the Meitei population, and both the Bengalis and Meiteis of Cachar preferred direct British rule rather than overlordship to Gambhir Singh of Manipur kingdom.

The Company Raj finally declared that Cachar plains should be annexed to the dominion of the Company, and the administration of the tract was entrusted with the Agent to the Governor-General, North East Frontier, at Cherrapunji (Bhattacharjee 1977, 53). Lieutenant Thomas Fisher was made the first Superintendent of Cachar, and later when the district was annexed to the commissionership of Dacca in 1836, the title of the officer in-charge was subsequently changed from Superintendent to Deputy Commissioner. This officer was to exercise the powers of a magistrate, collector and a civil judge under the supervision of the Agent to the Governor-General. In addition, he was to exercise political authority over the hill tribes on the Cachar frontiers on behalf of the Government of India (Hunter 1879).

Conclusion

An enquiry into past imperial policies and discourses allows for a close scrutiny of the strategies of colonial expansion and 'indirect rule' formulated in a borderland state. The Burmese annexation of Manipur in 1817 dislodged the Manipuri princes who, in turn, ousted the Raja of Cachar who sought British protection. Thus, a chain of causation linked Burma, Manipur, Cachar and British Bengal in a connected political drama during the early 19th century. The foundation of the indirect rule of the Company in Cachar began with the conclusion of the 1824 Treaty with Govind Chandra (the Raja of Cachar) made under duress. The murder of the Raja in 1830 left the kingdom with no male heir to the throne. This led to the rise of various claimants to the vacant throne, including the widow of Raja and the hill Chief Tula Ram. Manipuri Raja Gambhir Singh entered the fray by requesting the British to farm out Cachar in lease.

In the legal domain, the colonial contact resulted in an encounter between notions of the 'rule of law' and indigenous customs. Karuna Mantena's recent work (2010) discusses Henry Maine's theory of legal modernity and how imperial rule had forced a direct confrontation between modern and traditional institutions—a confrontation that seemed to necessitate the dissolution of native society (Mantena 2010). In the case of Cachar, the royal succession disputes opened the door for colonial interference in the internal affairs of Cachar by seducing local rajas and chiefs to conclude strategic treaties. To enrich their repertoires of rule, the British continually expanded their pool of local knowledge through official enquiries. Acting on their new knowledge of the Cachar country, the Company officials ridiculed the internal confusion and the inability of their informants to agree on what the traditional custom was, that is, whether it was the law of primogeniture or the democratic election by the forty *Sengphongs*.

Neeladri Bhattacharya rightly observes that enquiries into custom opened up space for negotiation and conflict over the truth of practice (Bhattacharya 1996). The British managed to dismiss with ease any claim to the vacant throne of Cachar either as illegitimate or baseless. Predictably, the Company Raj advanced its own claim to be the 'legitimate' ruler of Cachar through indirect mechanism of control. This was seen in their references to Hindu law as to whether the widowed Rani's candidature to the throne was legitimate.

M. Galanter (1968) argues that it was fundamental and persistent British policy that in matters of family law, inheritance, caste and religion Hindus and Muslims were to be governed by their personal law, that is, the law of their religious group. To him, this policy had become a medium for the uneven application of some indigenous laws and for the importation, sometimes uncritical, of a great deal of English law (Galanter 1968, 68). The exhaustive investigations of Company officials into local practices, as seen in the enquiries and investigations made by Thomas Fisher and the various exchanges between him and David Scott, reflected their attempts at establishing 'colonial legality' in the arbitration of Cachari succession dispute.

However, as Neeladri observes, the discourse on custom reveals a dialogue between masters and natives. The native voice (of Cachar, in our discussion) was inscribed within imperial discourse, but it was constrained, regulated and, ultimately, appropriated. He further argues that colonial relationship with native tradition was more complex, ambiguous and varied— spatially and temporally. Not all native voices could be easily accommodated within the imperial discourse on customary law, nor all the evidence was always recognized (Bhattacharya 1996). Thus, in our context, colonial knowledge and enquiry into local political institutions and customs for royal succession helped the Company Raj in advancing their own claims of legitimacy to rule colonial Cachar. Finally, the economic imperatives of the colonial state and in their process for bringing more land under cultivation dictated in turning down the request of Gambhir Singh to farm out Cachar in lease. Since Cachar plains were perceived to be fertile and well-endowed, the Company expected to earn higher profit by annexing it rather than leasing it to the Manipur prince. But the colonial fiscal state showed little interest in occupying Hill Cachar that had no fiscally unattractive. The logic behind the separation of plains Cachar from hills Cachar, in the words of Gunnel Cederlöf (2014), was 'a means of administratively containing unruly people and nature' (Cederlöf 2014, 240). In 1834, the British fixed a territorial boundary with Tula Ram, the hill chief. They did the same with the Raja of Manipur in 1835.

Notes

1. *Sengphongs* are patrilineal clans of the Dimasa community. The number of clans was fixed at 40. The Dimasa people became historically visible with the establishment of *Hachengsa* dynasty in Maibang during the 16th century AD. The 40 clans claimed allegiance to the *Hachengsa* dynasty. During the colonial period, the Dimasa community was politically divided between the hill Cachar chief Tula Ram and Cachar plains Raja, Govind Chandra. In post-independence era, the hill Cachar is renamed Dima Hasao district of the state of Assam.
2. In 1745, a Dimasa prince Lakshmichandra married Kanchani, a Koch princess and the only daughter of Bhim Singha, the last ruler of Koch dynasty. As a result of this matrimonial alliance, the Dimasa state shifted its capital to Khaspur in Cachar valley. For a study on the precolonial Dimasa/Cachar state and relations with neighbouring kingdom, see Khersa (2000).
3. NAI (1830, Document No. 59). Extract from Lieutenant Thomas Fisher Memoir in Cachar dated 24 November 1824.
4. NAI (1830, Document No. 59). Extract from Lieutenant Thomas Fisher Memoir in Cachar, dated 24 November 1824.
5. NAI (1829, Document No. 85). From David Scott (Agent to the Governor-General, North-Eastern Frontier) to Chief Secretary to the Government, Calcutta.
6. The principles of private property and improvement are Lockean ideas that prevailed in the aftermath of the English Revolution of 1688 (Locke 1970). The principle of rule of law was an old idea, but the phrase 'rule of law' came from Albert Venn Dicey's *The Law of Constitution* (1885). Rule of Law is often contrasted with the arbitrary rule of humans over other humans. Therefore, rule of law implies that humans are their own masters, and they do not have to obey anyone accept the written law.
7. NAI (1832, Document No. 100). To the Agent to the Governor-General, North-East Frontier from Lieutenant Thomas Fisher, dated 27 September 1830.
8. This can also be corroborated from the Arzee of Forty Sempongs to the Agent of the Governor-General, NAI (1832, Document No. 82).

9. Kanoo Ram further informed Thomas Fisher that 'he cannot say how the sense of the sempongs was ascertained but denies positive that representatives were chosen by the different tribes to make the election.' NAI (1832, Document No. 100).
10. Through the mediation of David Scott, an arrangement for fixing territorial limits satisfactory to both Raja Govind Chandra and Tula Ram was reached in 1829. By this agreement, Raja Govind Chandra recognized Tula Ram's possession of hill Cachar.
11. NAI (1832, Document No. 100). Enquiry report by Lieutenant Fisher (In-charge of Cachar Affairs) to the David Scott, Agent to the Governor-General, N. E. Frontier, dated 27 September 1830.
12. NAI (1832, Document No. 99). David Scott submitting his findings to G. Lwinton, Chief Secretary to Government, Fort William, dated 13 October 1830 (based on two reports received from Thomas Fisher on the subject of the succession of the Raj of Cachar).
13. NAI (1832, Document No. 99). David Scott submitting his findings to G. Lwinton, Chief Secretary to Government, Fort William, dated 13 October 1830 (based on two reports received from Thomas Fisher on the subject of the succession of the Raj of Cachar), p. 149.
14. Article V of Treaty of Badarpur (1824). Aitchison (1892, 216).
15. NAI (1832, Document No. 87). Letter from Raja Govind Chandra to David Scott, Political Agent's Office, N.E. Frontier, Sylhet.
16. NAI (1832, Document No. 98). Letter to Chief Secretary to Government, Fort William (Calcutta) from W. Cracraft (Officiating Agent to Governor General, Political Agents Office, N.E. Frontier) dated 22 March 1832.
17. NAI (1832, Document No. 109). Report sent by R. P. Pemberton (Officer on special Survey Duty) to Chief Secretary to Government, Fort William on 6 April 1832.
18. According to *Shorter Oxford English Dictionary*, a levy means the 'enrolling or conscription of men for war.' The word was traced back to the seventeenth century.
19. NAI (1832, Document No. 109). Report by R. P. Pemberton (On special Survey Duty), 6 April 1832.
20. NAI (1832, Document No. 110). Letter from Francis Jenkins to Chief Secretary to Government, Calcutta, 21 April 1832.

References

Aitchison, C. U. 1892. *A Collection of Treaties, Engagements and Sanads Relating to India and Neighbouring Countries*, Vol. I. Calcutta: Office of the Superintendent of Government Printing.

Anonymous. 1827. 'The Burmese War: Memoirs of Operations on the Silhet Frontier in the Year 1824.' *Asiatic Journal and Monthly Register* 24 (September): 319–325.

Bhattacharjee, J. B. 1977. *Cachar under British Rule in North East India*. Delhi: Radiant Publishers.

Bhattacharya, N. 1996. 'Remaking Custom: The Discourse and Practice of Colonial Codification'. In *Tradition, Dissent and Ideology: Essays in Honour of Romila Thapar*, edited by R. Champakalakshmi and S. Gopal, 20–51. New Delhi: Oxford University Press.

Cederlöf, G. 2009. 'Fixed Boundaries, Fluid Landscapes: British Expansion into Northern East Bengal in the 1820s'. *The Indian Economic and Social History Review* 46, no. 4: 513–540.

———. 2014. *Founding an Empire on India's North-Eastern Frontiers 1790–1840, Climate, Commerce, Polity*. New Delhi: Oxford University Press.

Chatterjee, I. 2013. *Forgotten Friends: Monks, Marriages, and Memories of Northeast India*. New Delhi: Oxford University Press.

Galanter, M. 1968. 'The Displacement of Traditional Law in Modern India'. *Journal of Social Issues* XXIV, no. 4: 68.

Hunter, W. W. 1879. *Statistical Account of Assam*, Vol. II. London: Trubner.

Khersa, Jolly. 2000. 'Dimasa State: A Study of Its Evolution and State' (MPhil diss., unpublished). Centre for Historical Studies, School of Social Sciences, Jawaharlal Nehru University, New Delhi.

Locke, J. 1970. *Two Treaties of Government*. Cambridge: Cambridge University Press.

Mantena, K. 2010. *Alibis of Empire: Henry Maine and the Ends of Liberal Imperialism*. Princeton, NJ: Princeton University Press.

Metcalf, T. R. 1998. *Ideologies of the Raj*. New Delhi: Cambridge University Press.

———. 2007. *Imperial Connections: India in the Indian Ocean Arena, 1860–1920*. New Delhi: Permanent Black.

Myint-U, T. 2001. *The Making of Modern Burma*. Cambridge: Cambridge University Press.

NAI (National Archives of India). 1829, 19 June. New Delhi: NAI Correspondence between David Scott, Agent to the Governor-General, North-Eastern Frontier and Chief Secretary to the Government, Fort William, Calcutta.

———. 1830, 28 May. New Delhi: NAI. Copies of correspondence between Sylhet Commissioner's Office and Agent to the Governor-General, North-Eastern Frontier relative to the land at Chunderpore and the application of Raja Govind Chandra of Cachar for military aid.

———. 1830, 18 June. New Delhi: NAI. Extracts from Felix Carey's letters to J. Ewing, the Magistrate of Sylhet; W.B. Bayley Chief Secretary to Government, Fort William and to Reverend William Carey of Serampore Extracts from Felix Carey's letters to J. Ewing, the Magistrate of Sylhet; W.B. Bayley Chief Secretary to Government, Fort William and to Reverend William Carey of Serampore.

———. 1832, 7–21 May. *Foreign Political Proceedings*. New Delhi: NAI.

CHAPTER 3

Spatializing Nation at the Border District of Arunachal Pradesh

Sherin Ajin

The frontispiece of the 1651 edition of Thomas Hobbes' *Leviathan* is one of the thought-stimulating frontal art expressions of all times, offering a fine visual summary of the central theme of the work. Wielding an ecclesiastical staff in the left arm and a sword denoting civil powers in the right (Bosse, 1995), Hobbesian sovereign king emerges as an amalgamation of abstract individuals. Ideated by Hobbes, this frontispiece serves as a window to the anarchic perils of the medieval European history, highlighting the necessity of mitigation, if not redemption. If the violent episode of the 1572 St. Bartholomew's Day massacre in Paris triggered Jean Bodin's pursuit of order and subsequent engagement with the idea of absolute sovereignty, Hobbesian treatise on sovereignty was largely a sequel to the 1648 Peace of Westphalia. In other words, triggered by 'the exhaustion and cynicism' (Kissinger 2014) inflicted by protracted periods of wars, the truce at Westphalia was not merely a resolution of a specific politico-temporal contingency; rather, it was a realist, existential quest for ordering a turbulent political world.

This project of ordering involved taming of the amorphous space into a regimented one whose boundedness was guarded by the stamp of border. The idea of sovereignty, that is, both internal and external sovereignty, was to seal the inviolability of the border and the territory it circumscribed. In other words, in this now naturalized scheme of world order, border was the 'imagined projection of territorial power' (Baud and Schendel 1997) and modern cartography a power-permeated art and science of knowledge production, its static coordinates binding the chaos of ambiguously defined geopolitical spaces. Border became the critical site of defining the contours of belonging, producing the community of citizens and, thereby, controlling the access to resources. More than any other part of the geo-body of the state, grafting the ideas of nation and state proved imperative at the border, acting as a psychological bulwark in containing external threats that might corrupt the loyalty of its border population. Thus, creation of the nation-state dyad assumed paramount significance, particularly in borders with competing claims of ownership of territory.

However, beyond the checkerboard of geopolitics, borders are infused with the cadence of everyday life. Mental representation of border gets manifested through the engineering of space, regulation of movement and in the human embodiments (Donnan and Wilson 1999) such as herders, traders and smugglers who live, traverse and sometimes even transgress the edges of the state. Conclusion of Cold War and the onset of globalization have marked a significant shift in engaging with the idea of border. Far from the static idioms of cold war such as iron and bamboo curtains (Baud and Schendel 1997), borders are now increasingly perceived as 'multi-perspectival…multi-scalar social constructions' (Laine 2016) whose spatial, discursive and everyday constitution are not prescribed by the state alone. Bypassing the monologue of Westphalian rationality, border dwells on an estuary of memories, bio-local narratives, folklores and imaginaries which are rarely linear. Border population are not always passive recipients of a highly securitized imagination of the space they inhabit; rather, they are participants of a constant dialogue with multiple scales of belonging, particularly state.

Structured around the conversation between these two strands of spatial imaginations, this chapter intends to explore the processes of routinising nation state in the Tawang district of Arunachal Pradesh. Based on ethnographic data collected from 2017 to 2019, this exercise is largely located within the framework of Ferguson and Gupta's definition of spatialization as 'specific sets of metaphors and practices through which states represent themselves as reified entities with particular spatial properties' (Ferguson and Gupta 2002).

Tawang: A Spatial Polysemy

Abutted by China in the north and *Druk yul* (Bhutan) in the south-west, an otherwise discreet Eastern Himalayan frontier of Tawang garnered international limelight as a witness to one of the dramatic episodes of the Cold War, the exile of the 14th Dalai Lama to India in 1959. Three years later, Tawang erupted into a battle ground between India and China. Then a part of the North-East Frontier Agency (NEFA), the district was besieged by the Chinese army before it announced unilateral ceasefire and retreat. Post splintering of the *Hindi-Chini bhai bhai* (Indians and Chinese are brothers) camaraderie and China's claim of Tawang (and the entire Arunachal Pradesh), as southern part of its Tibet Autonomous Region, Tawang has been mothballed into a highly sensitive border. Through what has now become a selective rendering of space through the prism of national security, Tawang has become a ritualistic annotation in the diplomatic and national media repertoire, especially during times of heightened Sino-Indian tensions.

With an area spanning 2,172 km², 70 per cent[1] of the district's population comprises of Monpas who are one of the few Tibetan Buddhism-practising STs in the state of Arunachal Pradesh. As much as Tawang is entrenched in the trope of security, this Himalayan borderland is shrouded in Lamaic mysticism, the spiritual citadel of Tawang monastery forming its visage. The ethnic nomenclature of Monpa has its genesis in the Tibetan imagination of space where the term 'Mon' refers to the low-lying, southern periphery of Tibet. Hence, in the Tibetan cosmology, Monpas constituted people who lived at the margins of both geography and civilization. Until Tawang was integrated into the Indian state in 1951, it remained under the partial administration of the Ganden Phodrang. An extended arena of sectarian rivalry in Tibet, particularly during the reign of the fifth Dalai Lama, the very name Tawang[2] is associated with the preponderance and proselytization of the *gelug*[3] sect in the region. The fortress-like design of the Tawang monastery and a cryptic painting of the Mongolian Khoshut Tenzin Choegyal Güshi Khan[4] adorning the wall of monastery's *dukhang*[5] are reminders of this historic episode.

Opposite to the *dukhang* of Tawang monastery stands a double-storeyed museum housing relics and artefacts in the possession of the monastery. The ground floor of the museum is largely curated as a leam into the sacral scape of Tawang, displaying personal belongings of the sixth Dalai Lama[6] his mother Tsewang Lhamo, Merag Lama Lodre Gyatso,[7] etc. Amidst the collection of wooden block prints, old ceremonial *chham*[8] masks and weaponry belonging to the king Kala Wangpo, a panoply of photographs capturing the visit of the Indian political dignitaries to the monastery forms the centrepiece of museum's display in the first floor. In other words, this museum inaugurated by the 14th Dalai Lama in 2009 is a carefully constructed visual site, offering an imbricated time travel of the sociopolitical transitions of Tawang.

While the museum's choice and presentation of exhibits naturalize the co-option of a hitherto Buddhist haven, which was under the rule of Tibet into the secular folds of the Indian state, what remains opaque is the pre-Buddhist history of Tawang. One of the prized possessions of the museum is a golden lettered *gye tongpa*[9] gifted to the monastery by the fifth Dalai Lama as 'a mark of the foundation of the Buddhist doctrine'[10] in the region. Interestingly, *gye tongpa* is encased in a pair of elephant tusks discovered by the mother of Khandro Drowa Zangmo, wife of the king Kalawangpo. In the Monpa folklore, queen Drowa Zangmo was the human embodiment of 'wisdom *dakini*' (Norbu 2016) who liberated the region from its barbaric way of living, instructing people to follow the Buddhist path of enlightenment. In the museum, Kala Wangpo represented an exemplar who was pious enough to acknowledge the sublimity of Buddhism, renouncing the 'less meritorious' Bon order.[11] Advent of Buddhism in the region involved creation of hierarchies, pushing lesser-known traditions like Bon to the lower pedestal. *Yul Mandrelgang*, name of the legendary kingdom of Kala Wangpo, is now a less remembered one, sanitized by the more Buddhist toponym of Tawang. Toponymical digressions such as this get eclipsed in the rhetoric of the border dispute, projecting the semantic politics solely along the binaries of the competing states.

Driven by the calculus of profit, the colonial hill–plain distinction and its manifestations such as Inner Line Permit (ILP) and *posa* were carefully orchestrated to surpass the inconveniences caused by the 'barbaric' hill tribes. This self-conferred exemption from the White man's burden meant frontier tracts such as Balipara[12] and Sadiya were placed under the spatial category of Excluded Areas, created by the Government of India Act of 1935. British interest in the remote frontier north of Ze La was primarily triggered by the imperatives of the Great Game and its proximity to Tibet. A forbidden land for foreigners, surveying Tibet for the colonial knowledge production involved incognito missions conducted by Survey of India's prodigies like Pundit Nain Singh Rawat. Rawat was arrested and imprisoned in Tawang for espionage and incursion. However, it was the arrest of the British botanist Frank Kingdon Ward in 1935 that kindled British political interest and caution in Tawang. Internally weakened by the cumulative effects of the World Wars, British were not in a position to substantially invest, politically or economically, in the de facto execution of the McMahon Line (Ajin 2020).

Postcolonial spatial imaginations of Tawang did not mark a significant departure from the colonial past and in fact, orbited around the colonial spatial frameworks such as Inner Line Permit. The last familiar station for the national elite in Northeast was Assam (Das 2012) and for the centre, the rest of the region resembled a babel of ethnic diversity. The perplexity of encountering differences and ambiguities in devising ways to navigate the complex mosaic got reflected in the shifting administrative nomenclatures from North-East Frontier Tract to NEFA, to Union Territory of Arunachal Pradesh, to the granting of statehood in 1987. In other words, arriving at the certitude (Schendel 1997) of border from the fuzziness of frontier involved an exhaustive political detour.

One of the blind spots of methodological territorialism is the myopic conceptualization of space, discounting the significance of the biotic web, which is intimately interweaved into the being of a place. An integral part of the Indo-Burma biodiversity hotspot, Tawang is a rich treasure trove of floral and faunal diversity housing variegated specimens of rhododendrons, primulas, orchids, red pandas, gorals, etc. Geographically contiguous to Tibet, which is metaphorically known as the 'third pole', 'roof of the world', etc, Tawang is stitched into the global risk discourse of climate change, transcending the conventional boundaries set up by the nation states.

However, entangled in the complexities of the border discord, this polysemic matrix of Tawang is camouflaged and many a times subsumed by the grand project of competitive state-making. The following sections of the chapter would briefly chart the trajectory of spatialization of nation state at Tawang through the intersecting discourses of security and development.

Production of a Nationalist Visual Regime

> *Seeing comes before words... It is seeing which establishes our place in the surrounding world; we explain that world with words, but words can never undo the fact that we are surrounded by relation between what we see and what we know is never settled...every image embodies a way of seeing.*
>
> —John Berger

> *What matters in aesthetics is not art but this whole project of reconstructing the human subject from the inside, informing its subtlest affections and bodily responses....*
>
> —Terry Eagleton

Dissolving the mould of a theocentric ordering of the world where the spectator constituted a passive recipient of the given, Enlightenment heralded a novel way of seeing in which 'the world was understood as that which could be seen' (Heidegger 1977). Production of image, thus, ceased to be a process solely 'mechanical' (Berger 1972). The very act of 'selecting one sight from an infinity of other possible sights' (Berger 1972) became a power permeated exercise where each image encased a 'compressed performance' (Pinney 2004). Though every image involves an element of selective representation and, thus, a guided dialogue with the spectator, few stark examples of visual engineering could be the socialist realist paintings and architecture produced in the Stalinist Soviet Union, anti-Semitic posters made in Hitler's Germany, propaganda posters of world wars, September 18 museum kindling memories of national humiliation in China, etc. Embedding a nation on the canvas of space, particularly at the margins of the state, involves sensorial mediation, importantly sight.

Ever since the 1962 Indo-China war, the Indian state has maintained its omnipresence in the region with its paraphernalia of military forces and technologies of surveillance. The visual tapestry of Tawang is interestingly interspersed with Buddhist *gompas* and prayer wheels alongside infrastructural reminders of Indian army such as army barracks, firing grounds and moss-laden bunkers of the 1962 war. The photo frame offered by the howitzer displayed at the Tawang War memorial capturing Tawang monastery comprises a unique snapshot of this border visual ensemble. Imprinting the hills of Eastern Himalayas with the acronyms of defence organizations in white paint, even nature in Tawang bears the hues of a militarized geography.

Apart from the machismo display of its defensive prowess, the state ingeniously employs army in instilling patriotic sentiments among its border population. One of the immediate responses of the 1962 war was the invocation of the loyalty of the border population through pictorial representations. Themes of posters created in the aftermath of the war included affective gestures such as the nursing of the wounded Indian soldiers by the indigenous population of NEFA (Guyot-Réchard 2017). A territory once briefly occupied by the Chinese army, legitimising its presence and claiming political obligation from its population required the state to invent ways of engineering the visual field, in consonance with the cultural sentiments of the region. Museumization of the sacrifices made by the Indian army during the 1962 battle, thus, became an effective trope in creating an intersubjectivity of threat, constantly reminding of an enemy across the border and, importantly, sacrifices made by the Indian army in defending its territory and people from the Chinese aggression.

Along the serpentine curves of the Bhalukpong–Bomdila road are stones erected in memory of the soldiers who laid down their lives in the 1962 Indo-China war. Recreating the trajectory of a perilous flight, these stones act as prelude to the altars of patriotism, awaiting to meet the traveller beyond the Ze La. On the way to Tawang, the first war memorial is that of Nyukmadong. Located in the Dirang *tehsil* of the West Kameng district, the memorial is built in the form of a terraced garden with a *chorten*[13] forming the centre of the monument. Festooned with Buddhist prayer flags, the *chorten* is flanked by granite and marble plaques of the army personnel who lost their lives during the Chinese aggression at Nyukmadong on 18 November 1962. After the 'fall of Tawang' (Prasad 1981) into the Chinese hands, the 62 Infantry Brigade who were the 'guardians of Se La'[14] were officially instructed to retreat to Dirang on 17 November 1962. However, the transit route from Ze La to Dirang was already besieged by the Chinese army, and the withdrawing army men under the aegis of Brigadier Hoshiar Singh were met with an ambush at Nyukmadong, resulting in heavy casualty. Situated at a distance of 24 km away from the Dirang town, the memorial is not presented as an aberration of a picturesque landscape, rekindling the memories of an unsettling defeat; rather, the architectural style of the memorial is in perfect congruence with the Buddhist ethos of the place, placing the martyrdom at the service of the nation in the refuge of Buddha.

Around 45 km from Nyukmadong, stands Jaswantgarh. Built in the memory of Jaswant Singh Rawat of the 4th Garhwal Rifles and his colleagues who lost their lives in the 1962 battle of Nuranang, Jaswantgarh is the centrepiece of the military hagiography of the 1962 war. Believed to have relentlessly fought the Chinese army for 72 h, *smrithi sthal* houses a tree stump upon which the severed head of Rawat was allegedly displayed by the jubilant Chinese army. Posthumously honoured with Maha Vir Chakra, Rawat continued to be in the service roster of the Indian army and was duly accorded with promotions till his retirement. The sanctorum of the memorial has Rawat's bust adorned with garlands where army personnel and visitors offer money and incense sticks to the 1962 war hero.

An altruistic tribute to the rifleman Rawat, a modest canteen is run by the Indian army in the vicinity of the memorial. A singular stopover for recess post climbing a 13,700-feet high Ze La, at the canteen, along with piping cup of teas, travellers are served with stories of the hovering spirit of Jaswant Singh Rawat. Akin to the Nathu La hero Captain Harbhajan Singh, Jaswant Singh is revered as a *baba* (patron saint) by army personnel who are posted at Nuranang. Enveloped by a litany of army slogans glorifying death on battlefield, Jaswantgarh offers a rare alchemy of religion and nation, a visual reification of the sacrality of nation to the spectator, both civilian and military.

Similar to Nyukmadong War Memorial, Jaswantgarh co-opts elements of Buddhist architecture but in a more elaborate way. The entrance to the memorial is constructed in the form of a Buddhist *kakaling*,[15] and prominent Buddhist icons of enlightenment such as yoghurt, mirror, coral branch, etc. and the six symbols of longevity are displayed as embossed frescoes on the entrance wall. Interestingly, one of the plaques installed at Jaswantgarh War Memorial states that the architectural style is not a serendipity, rather a deliberate choice. It reads,

> The War Memorial has been specifically and purposefully designed to respect the local religious sentiments and be in harmony with the beliefs of the people. The traditional gate and the main memorial sanctorum are a tribute to the local population who had contributed immensely to the war effort in the 1962 war and reflects the unflinching bond that the Indian army shares with the locals and their beliefs.

In other words, underlying the confluence of military and local Buddhist architectural styles is the intended interpenetration of 'structures of politics' (Eagleton 1988) and 'structures of feelings' (Eagleton 1988), producing an edifice of a 'successful social hegemony' (Eagleton 1988).

In synchrony with the visual sequence of the Nyukmadong and Jaswantgarh memorials, built in honour of the martyrs of the 1962 war, Tawang war memorial is conceived around the sacred aesthetics of Tibetan Buddhism, particularly *chorten*. Each morning, a deputed monk from the Tawang monastery visits the memorial to replenish the *yongchap*[16] placed in front of the *chorten*. Around the same time, in consonance with the solemn call of the bugle, an army officer unfurls the national tricolour on a flag staff abutting the *chorten*. Concurrence of these two events, an everyday Buddhist ritual and the display of banal nationalism (Billig 1995), produces a 'heterotopic'(Foucault 1986) spectacle, entrenching nation in the affective realm of religion.

One of the intriguing items of display at the memorial are earthen urns containing the blood-laced soil of the battle grounds of Jaswantgarh, Bum La, Topeng La and Zemithang. Representatives of a pensive battle field, these urns cache two archetypal symbols of belonging, that is, soil and blood. Next to the war memorial stands a sheltered amphitheatre. As the dusk descends, the light and sound show transmutes it into the battleground of the 1962 war. Along with the heroic figures of the war, the script of the show carefully places the legend of two Monpa girls Sela and Nura[17] who are believed to have helped Jaswant Singh Rawat in fighting the Chinese in the battle of Nuranang. With popular Bollywood patriotic songs playing in the background, the climax of the theatrical show highlights the army–civilian camaraderie in the district like snapshots from annual Maitree Diwas and charity initiatives of the army like Vidyashree school.

As a destination, Tawang meanders through multivalent geographies of anticipation. For a trekking enthusiast, Bailey's trail leading to Tawang offers the thrills of a Himalayan sojourn. For a devout Buddhist, Tawang is a sacred *beyul-kyimo-jong*,[18] braided with numerous sites of pilgrimage. In the nationalist geography, apart from being an international border, Tawang is a critical pedagogic site where the lessons of nation and martyrdom are intimately felt and seen. Interspersing the road to Tawang with memorial stones and war memorials such as those of Nyukmadong, Jaswantgarh, Tawang and Bum La are mimetic of a Himalayan pilgrimage where the sacred geography and deities emerge from the nationalist pantheon. However, this is not to arrive at a reductionist interpretation of the curated visual tropes where the role of the spectator gets diminished into that of a consumer alone. As in the case with the legend of Sela and Nura, there is an often subterranean process of filtering and reflection of the imageries produced, determining the efficacy of the intersubjectivity of an idea visually represented.

Development as Defence

In a postcolonial temporal framework, seeding of nation state invariably demanded identification of the territorial corpus of state. Although the political enterprise of integration under the stewardship of Sardar Patel forms one of the popular episodes of post-independence Indian history, the Nehruvian integrationist strategy was not keen enough to cajole or coerce the contested terrain of Tawang (Arpi 2016) till the unravelling of a political emergency in its Himalayan courtyard.

The onset of the 1950 Korean war deepening the fissures between the two antagonistic power blocks, coupled with political turmoil in Tibet, induced India to search for an answer for a fairly elusive dilemma, 'exactly what China is'[19] (Das, 1971). With 'a Communist China which has definite ambitions and aims and which does not, in any way, seem friendly disposed towards'[20] India, the age-old assurance of the 'impenetrable barrier of Himalayas'[21] suddenly started looking like an ossified myth. The unique nature of 'Chinese irredentism and imperialism'[22] conjoined with the internal challenges of 'the undefined state of the frontier and the existence ... of a population with its affinities to Tibetans or Chinese'[23], feeble network of communication, absence of defensive lines, 'unlimited scope of infiltration'[24] and understaffed outposts seemed like a lethal concoction, making North East Frontier India's Achille's heel.

Against this backdrop, it was the political expediency of the then Assam Governor Jairamdas Daulatram (Arpi 2016) backed by the efforts of Major Bob Khathing and his men of Assam Rifles that eventually led to the successful incorporation of Tawang into the Indian Union in 1951. The 'twin shocks' (Guyot-Rèchard 2017) of the Great Assam earthquake of 1950 and the Chinese occupation of Tibet pitched a perfect entry point for Major Khathing and his team to Tawang. Meanwhile, the recommendations of the high-level North and North-East Border Defence Committee, also known as Himmatsinghji Committee, tabled on April 1951, became an added stimulus to the relief and developmental activities undertaken in Tawang. Proposals put forth by the Committee included a significant makeover of the administrative apparatus and divisions of NEFA and, importantly, marshalling of a wide array of developmental activities such as establishment of hospitals, educational institutions, improvement of the agrarian scenario by the introduction of high-yielding seeds, and expansion of communication networks (Mullick 1972). Conceiving development as defence, recommendations of Himmatsinghji Committee enshrined foundational philosophy of statist development oeuvre in Northeastern border areas, which in principle is followed till date.

Post integration, a formidable challenge before the Indian state was to decide upon the strategy and quantum of development in Tawang to keep the newly integrated frontier loyal and engaged. As was the case with the rest of NEFA, the chasm of differences posed ontological dilemmas on the very idea of progress and casted 'doubts' on 'how far the *normal* idea of progress was beneficial for these people and ... whether this was progress at all in any real sense of the word'[25]. The question of 'dealing'[26] with NEFA stirred up intense debates resulting in the creation of camps advocating antithetical suggestions of isolation and integration. A self-proclaimed 'missionary of Prime Minister's gospel' (Elwin 2009) and Nehruvian confidante, Verrier Elwin was entrusted with the task of charting the contours of development in NEFA.

As emotional integration forms the corner stone of Indian state's policies in NEFA, the trajectory of development was carefully aligned with the sensitivities of this guiding tenet. First published in 1957, Elwin's work 'A Philosophy for NEFA' was nothing short of a primer, initiating the rest of India, especially officers posted at NEFA, to the intricacies of the land and its people. In 1956, along with his wife Lila, Elwin embarked on what he calls a 'Pilgrimage to Tawang' (Elwin 2008). The climax of the journey which took them to Tawang's Galden Namgyal Lhatse monastery on the day of Buddha Poornima was an experience that left a lasting impression in his mind. Elwin treasured the miniature idol of Buddha gifted to him by the abbot of the monastery till his death (Guha 1999). As opposed to encountering the corrosive impact of 'atomic age on a stone age people' (Elwin 2009) in large parts of NEFA, at Tawang, Elwin noticed an exception. According to him, people of Tawang were 'great gentlemen, whose way of life is higher than the majority of our staff' (Elwin 2009).

In his 'A Philosophy for NEFA', Elwin expresses his deep-seated concern for the Tibetan officers' sensitivity to Mon culture, reflected in their adoption of Mon sartorial appearance and architectural styles. To counter this benign, yet significant threat to India's influence in the region, Elwin had proposed officers to acclimatize to the local Monpa lifestyle, learning their local language and dialect. He also underscored the necessity of familiarising with 'Buddhism so that they will not make mistakes out of ignorance' (Elwin 2009). As was experimented in Buddhist pockets of 'Sikkim, Ceylon and Thailand' (Elwin 2009), Elwin, a seminarian turned anthropologist, proposed the syncretism of traditional *gompa*-centric education system with its modern, secular counterpart. Elwin's larger philosophy of interweaving development with the local sensibilities essentially aimed at advertising the desirability of a 'colourful and rich India' (Elwin 2009), thus buttressing the vulnerable loyalty of people who live in border areas like Tawang.

India's defeat in the 1962 war meant Elwin's developmental vision for NEFA was short-lived. If civilian frontier officials (Guyot-Rèchard 2017) were the conduits between Indian state and NEFA, conclusion of the war inaugurated a new era of development in Tawang, mediated by the Indian army. As a result, works like A Philosophy for NEFA, which formed an integral part of the training curriculum of the Indian Frontier Administrative Service officers, were gradually supplemented and replaced with brochures offering a synoptic view of the cultural geography of NEFA (Guyot-Rèchard 2017) to the newly appointed army officers in the region. Policy of insulating NEFA from the influx of outsiders was reversed. Marching in of military personnel in large numbers systemically altered the spatial and demographic constitution of Tawang.

To date, Tawang is intimately dependent upon Indian army and paramilitary forces in the development and maintenance of its basic infrastructures like roads and hospitals. In his 80s, one of the vivid memories shared by Brigadier Lakshman Singh[27] during his tenure in Tawang in the early 1960s was the fascination of local Monpas with the army medical facilities and movie projectors. On a lighter vein, Brigadier Singh recollected Monpa women's fascination with the adhesive medical plasters, which many of them enthusiastically experimented by plastering it on to their faces. Army also conducts free medical camps for the local people, particularly for the villagers in the far-flung areas.

A border district with scanty avenues for higher education, Indian army is a significant employment provider for youth in Tawang. One of the popular designations kept open for the local recruitment is that of the porters. A highly ad-hoc job with a tenure of 6 months, local porters are recruited by the Indian army in consultation with the state's Labour Department. Familiar with the challenging Himalayan weather and terrain from birth, local porters provide critical services to the Indian army, particularly in the manual transportation of heavy artilleries and other equipment. Interestingly, one of the common denominators that unites the diverse politico-temporal trajectory of Tawang are porters. Be it the case of Tibetan or Indian rule, these porters constitute the critical ground army facilitating movement in a tricky Himalayan terrain. Dexterously interweaving the discourses of security and development, Tawang represents a border landscape of *militarized development* (Aggarwal and Bhan 2009).

Sharing international borders with China, Bhutan and Myanmar, exceptionalism and federal asymmetry have been grafted into the heart of Arunachal Pradesh. From early 1970s onwards, there has been an active proliferation of the idea of a distinct Northeast region corporealized through a plethora of institutional frameworks such as North Eastern Council, Ministry of Development of North Eastern Region, and NITI Forum for North East. Instituted in the 1993–1994 time period as a centrally sponsored scheme catering the Western borders of the country,[28] Border Area Development Programme (BADP) has evolved as one of the significant capillaries of development schemes in Tawang. Placed under the aegis of the Department of Border Management, one of the nodal missions of BADP is demographic engineering of the border through the incentive of development.

Arunachal Pradesh remained a haven for the timber extraction lobby till the judgement of *T. N. Godavarman Thirumulkpad v. Union of India & Ors* case in December 1996. However, resource curse of the region found new in-roads into the state through a slew of dam construction projects. A 2003 appraisal by the Central Electricity Authority identified an estimated hydropower potential of 57,000 MW in Arunachal Pradesh, making it a promised land of surplus power generation. Out of the 142 memoranda of understanding (MoUs) signed for dam construction in the state, 13 were in Tawang. If dams like Bhakra Nangal signalled India's tryst with modernity through multi-purpose river valley projects, inauguration of hydro rush in Arunachal Pradesh beckoned the dawn of market-centric, single-purpose hydropower projects (Baruah 2012).

The state's pursuit of hydro dream in Tawang hemmed around three major reasons. The first and obvious reason was tapping of the commercial benefits accruing from the hydropower projects. As a special category state that is heavily dependent upon the centre for meeting its expenditure, sanctioning of hydropower projects and the subsequent sale of electricity was projected as a lucrative model of revenue generation for Arunachal Pradesh. Akin to National Hydro Power Corporation's (NHPC) Gurez model (Bhan 2014) of employing corporate social responsibility (CSR) as a channel of bringing border population closer to the nation state, 'corporate morality' (Bhan 2014) of the hydropower harvesting companies was contemplated as a medium for qualitatively intervening border people's life. Second, a non-polluting, zero fossil fuel-dependent source of power production, hydropower was projected as an ecologically responsible way of addressing the acute power shortage elsewhere in the country. Exporting electricity produced in a sensitive border land for meeting the energy demands of other regions of the country in itself constituted a symbolic act of asserting state's sovereign claim over its territory.

Finally, with China aggressively damming and diverting the transboundary river of Yarlung Tsangpo, India's attempt to tap the hydropower potential of Tawang was portrayed as a political exercise of competitive resource extraction.

Of Soliloquies and Dialogues

National and regional newspapers dated 3 May 2016 carried an unusual report of a firing incident in Tawang on 2 May, killing two locals, Nyima Wangdi and Tsering Tenpa. In few newspapers, photo accompanying the news report depicted a Monpa lay man and a Buddhist monk lying in a pool of blood. The police firing incident culminating in the death of two was in fact climax of a peaceful local protest condemning the collapse of the Mukto-Shakang Chhu mini hydel project in the district. Now, at the entrance of the Tawang monastery stands a memorial commemorating the victims of the violent incident.

Ever since state government's signing of MOU with 13 hydropower companies, Tawang has been a site of Foucauldian counter-conduct.[29] In 2011, it was two Monpa *geshes*,[30] Lobsang Sherab and Lobsang Choedar, living in the Mysore Tibetan Settlement who initiated discussions on the detrimental effects of dam construction in the sacred Buddhist geography of Tawang. With deliberations on dam gathering momentum, District Commissioner had ordered both the *geshes* to leave the district. It was during the 2012 Kalachakra initiation ceremony held at Bodh Gaya, that Lama Lobsang Gyatso, popularly known as Anna Lama, was chosen to spearhead the movement.

Forging connections with environmental activists from Assam, Maharashtra and Delhi, monks familiarized themselves with the legal lexicon of ecological conservation. Organising themselves into Save Mon Region Federation (SMRF), monks under the leadership of Anna Lama travelled across the villages of Tawang, educating people about the public hearing procedures for land acquisition. Simultaneously, within the functional scope of Department of Karmik and Adhyatmik Affairs (DoKAA),[31] *geshe* Lobsang Choeder published monographs educating the laity on the numerous sacred sites of Tawang. As STs inhabiting the borderland, the identity of Monpas stands doubly blinded by the statist conception and categorization of land. Welding a local, sacred geographic conception of land with global spatial categories of conservation such as biodiversity hotspots, monks at SMRF successfully crafted an alternate risk discourse.

In 2012, representing the Tawang Monpa community, SMRF challenged the environmental clearance given to the Nyamjang Chhu hydropower project at the National Green Tribunal. Citing concealment of dam construction site as the wintering stretch of the sacred black necked crane[32] and non-disclosure of downstream impact of the dam in Bhutan, SMRF demanded the roll back of clearance. In 2016, NGT suspended the environmental clearance given to Bhilwara Energy Ltd. Citing the inability to verify the address of many of the dam construction companies, in 2019, Arunachal Chief Minister Pema Khandu revoked the license of 22 hydropower projects in the state. The specificities of the scrapped projects remain ambiguous and the future of these dams is left for speculation.

Placing the fury in context, anti-dam agitations in Tawang do not represent a schism breeding rebellion. Tawang is power strained. Owing to substandard maintenance, 15 mini, micro and small hydel stations with an installed capacity of 17.41 MW[33] fail to provide district's modest power requirement of 6 MW. With power cuts part of the quotidian, for an average Monpa, the idea of harnessing region's hydropower potential for exporting electricity to other parts of the country is anything, but an irony. Also, participants of the anti-dam agitation are not a homogenous group. When it comes to electoral politics, candidature of Buddhist monks for furthering the ecological and cultural causes of the region is many a times identified with materialist quest for power.

Most of the tourist and pilgrim sites in Tawang exhibit twin name boards; for instance, a few metres away from the entrance of Jaswantgarh is a freshly painted green board displaying the name Saateng. A similar green board written Ogyenling invites visitors to the birthplace of the sixth Dalai Lama. Substantial presence of Indian army for a considerably long period of time had resulted in the Hindiization (Gohain 2020) of the local names, and these nameboards are a mirror to their ethnic anxieties. Through a notification of DoKAA dated 10 July 2017, the Governor of Arunachal Pradesh assented the restoration of 506 place names in Tawang and West Kameng districts.

In short, by defining the normative content and limits of the idea of development, the state anchors itself in the fragilities of the border. However, this statist rendering of development as a medium of moral improvement (Werner 2015) is often an unquiet site that sprouts counter-narratives of being and becoming. Along the interstices of what looks like a spatial repartee between the state and its border subject run striations of inter-ethnic tensions and resource competition. Tawang sits at the cusp of palimpsestic memories and lived realities. Between the rigidities of the Sino-Indian rivalries lies the borderless abode of Himalayan life. In other words, compass of the nation state alone fails to navigate the elusive space of Tawang.

Notes

1. According to the 2011 Census data, 69.87 per cent of Tawang's population comprises Buddhists.
2. There exist two interpretations of the genesis of the place name Tawang. According to the popular legend, which is recorded by historians like Niranjan Sarkar, Tawang refers to the place chosen by the horse (*ta* meaning horse and *wang* chosen) of Merak Lama indicating the site for the construction of Tawang monastery. However, Monpa historians like Tsewang Norbu are of the opinion that Tawang got its name from the Tamdrin initiation performed by the Bhutanese terton Pema Lingpa in the 15th century (*ta* as an abbreviated reference to Tamdrin or Hayagriva and *wang* referring to ritualistic initiation).
3. Sartorially identified by the characteristic yellow hat, *gelug* refers to the reformist Tibetan Buddhist sect founded by Je Tsongkhapa.
4. As told to the author by the caretaker monk of Tawang monastery during fieldwork conducted in 2019. Though there exists a contesting account that the painting refers to the Mongolian (Sokpo) army commander Jomkhar, who is believed to have aided the subjugation of Nyingmapa sect in Tawang, details of the mural refer to the possibility of it being the Mongolian Dharmaraja Güshi Khan.
5. *Dukhang* refers to the assembly hall for congregating to conduct daily prayers and other religious ceremonies.
6. Sixth Dalai Lama Tsangyang Gyatso was born in the Ogyenling (Urgyelling) village of Tawang.
7. The fourth Merak lama Lodre Gyatso founded Galden Namgyal Lhatse, also known as Tawang monastery under the guidance of the fifth Dalai Lama.
8. Monastic ritual dance.
9. Sacred text containing 8,000 verses of Prajna Paramita.
10. As written in the accompanying display description.
11. Though Tibetan Buddhism has elements borrowed from Bon religion such as the multi-hued prayer flags, sand mandalas, torma, etc., hierarchy is maintained between the two.

12. Balipara Frontier Agency, which was bifurcated into Sela and Subansiri sub-agencies in 1919, constituted the Western section of NEFA including the present-day district of Tawang.
13. A Buddhist memorial shrine.
14. As written in the memorial plaque at Nyukmadong War Memorial.
15. Kakaling is a *square hut like structure with its lateral walls made of stone and the roof of wooden shingles, bamboo mats or flat thin stone slabs. The ceiling and the top of walls are decorated with the paintings of Buddhist divinities and saints* (Sarkar 1980). With the advent of modern construction techniques, new *kakalings* erected in Tawang are concretized, including this one.
16. Sacred water bowls offered to Buddha and other deities.
17. During the course of her fieldwork, author could not verify the veracity of the local names Sela and Nura.
18. A hidden valley of pleasure.
19. In Nehru's letter to Sardar Patel dated 9 July 1950.
20. In Sardar Patel's letter addressing Nehru, dated 7 November 1950.
21. Ibid.
22. Ibid.
23. Ibid.
24. Ibid.
25. In Nehru's foreword to Verrier Elwin's *A Philosophy for NEFA*.
26. In Nehru's foreword to Verrier Elwin's *A Philosophy for NEFA*.
27. As told to the author by Brigadier Lakshman Singh in an interview dated 9 February 2019.
28. *Evaluation Study on Border Area Development Programme*, 2015, NITI Aayog.
29. In his 1977–1978 lectures at the Collège De France, Michel Foucault employs the term counter-conduct as a 'struggle against the processes implemented for conducting others'.
30. A monk conferred with the highest, Tibetan Buddhist scholastic degree.
31. DoKAA was constituted in 2009 for the protection and preservation of Buddhist cultural heritage in the districts of Tawang and West Kameng.
32. Listed by IUCN as vulnerable, Monpas consider the migratory black-necked cranes as the reincarnation of the sixth Dalai Lama.
33. See https://tawang.nic.in/department-of-hydro-power-development-division-i/

References

Aggarwal, Ravina, and Mona Bhan. 2009. '"Disarming Violence": Development, Democracy, and Security on the Borders of India.' *The Journal of Asian Studies* 68, no. 2 (May): 519–542.

Ajin, Sherin. 2020. 'Situating the Sino-Indian Border of Tawang in the Border Studies Discourse'. In *Tawang, Monpas and Tibetan Buddhism in Transition;*

Life and Society along the India-China Borderland, edited by M. Mayilvaganan, Nasima Khatoon, and Sourina Bej, 13–27. Singapore: Springer.

Arpi, Claude. 2016, 24 March. *Jawaharlal: Did He Want Tawang or Not?* Available at http://claudearpi.blogspot.in/2014/11/jawaharlal-did-he-want-tawang-or-not.html (accessed 25 January 2017).

Baruah, Sanjib. 2012, 21 July. 'Whose River Is It Anyway: Political Economy of Hydropower in the Eastern Himalayas'. *Economic & Political Weekly*: 41–52.

Baud, Michiel, and Willem Van Schendel. 1997. 'Toward a Comparative History of Borderlands.' *Journal of World History* 8, no. 2: 211–242. Available at http://www.jstor.org/stable/20068594 (accessed 3 December 2020).

Berger, John. 1972. *Ways of Seeing*. London: British Broadcasting Corporation and Penguin Books.

Bhan, Mona. 2014. 'Morality and Martyrdom: Dams, Dharma, and the Cultural Politics of Work in Indian-occupied Kashmir'. *Biography* (Winter) 37, no. 1: 191–224.

Billig, Michael. 1995. *Banal Nationalism*. Los Angeles, CA: SAGE Publications.

Bosse, Abraham. 1651. 'Frontispiece of Thomas Hobbes' Leviathan, with Creative Input from Thomas Hobbes.' Available at https://www.college.columbia.edu/core/content/frontispiece-thomas-hobbes%E2%80%99-leviathan-abraham-bosse-creative-input-thomas-hobbes-1651 (accessed 21 January 2020).

Das, Durga, ed. 1971. *Sardar Patel's Correspondence 1945–50*, Vol. X. Ahmedabad: Navajivan Publishing House.

Das, Gurudas. 2012. *Security and Development in India's North-East*. New Delhi: Oxford University Press.

Donnan, Hastings, and Wilson M. Thomas. 1999. *Borders: Frontiers of Identity, Nation and State*. Oxford: Berg.

Eagleton, Terry. 1988. 'The Ideology of the Aesthetic.' *Poetics Today* 9, no. 2: 327–338.

Elwin, Verrier. 2008. *The Oxford India Elwin*. Oxford: Oxford University Press.
———. 2009. *A Philosophy for NEFA*. New Delhi: Isha Books.

Ferguson, James, and Akhil Gupta. 2002. 'Spatializing States: Toward an Ethnography of Neoliberal Governmentality.' *American Ethnologist* 29, no. 4: 981–1002.

Foucault, Michel. 1986. 'Of Other Spaces'. *Diacritics* no. 16: 22–27.

Gohain, Swargajyoti. 2020. *Imagined Geographies in the Indo-Tibetan Borderlands; Culture, Politics, Place*. Amsterdam: Amsterdam University Press.

Guha, Ramachandra. 1999. *Savaging the Civilised; Verrier Elwin, His Tribals, and India*. New Delhi: Oxford University Press.

Guyot-Réchard, Bérénice. 2017. *Shadow States: India, China and the Himalayas, 1910–1962*. Cambridge: Cambridge University Press.

Heidegger, Martin. 1977. *The Question Concerning Technology and Other Essays*. New York, NY: Harper Perennial.

Kissinger, Henry. 2014. *World Order*. London: Penguin Books Limited.

Laine, Jussi P. 2016. 'The Multi-scalar Production of Borders'. *Geopolitics* 21, no. 3: 465–482. Available at https://doi.org/10.1080/14650045.2016.11951 32 (accessed 1 December 2020).

Mullick, B. N. 1972. *My Years with Nehru, 1948–1964*. London: Allied Publishers.

Norbu, Tsewang. 2016. *Tawang Monastery, The Spiritual Wonder of India*. Itanagar: Department of Cultural Affairs, Directorate of Research, Government of Arunachal Pradesh.

Pinney, Christopher. 2004. *Photos of the God; The Printed Image and Political Struggle in India*. Chicago, IL: The University of Chicago Press.

Prasad, Niranjan. 1981. *The Fall of Towang*. New Delhi: Palit & Palit Publishers.

Sarkar, Niranjan. 1980. *Buddhism Among the Monpas and Sherdukpens*. Itanagar: Directorate of Research, Government of Arunachal Pradesh.

Werner, Anna. 2015. *The Politics of Dams: Developmental Perspectives and Social Critique in Modern India*. New Delhi: Oxford University Press.

Part II

Memory, Ethnicity and Civil Society

CHAPTER 4

Public Spaces and the Politics of Remembering in Northeast India

Jangkhomang Guite

The study of memory in social sciences has expanded from collective memory to politics of remembering, forgetting and silence.[1] Misztal divided scholars working on memory into four groups. Thus, we have a group of studies which felt that memory is always 'socially framed', and it functions only within a particular social context which remembers collectively and selectively.[2] It has also been pointed out that collective memory is largely invented by the elitist state for the purpose of legitimizing authority, socializing the populations in a common culture and for establishing social cohesion.[3] In rejecting the idea of wholesale 'invention', there are also studies concerning popular memory, which felt that people tend to reject any vision of the past, which contradicts their recollection and sense of truth. It envisages that there are a spectrum of recollections and representations of the past in every society which make memory not only dynamic, conflictual, fluid and unstable.[4] Still another group of scholars felt that collective memory is an ongoing process of negotiation, and hence, remembering is a processual action in which people constantly transform their recollections and representations of the past.[5] Thus, memory is not only instrumental and social, but it is also dynamic, processual, fluid, conflictual and even political.

This chapter examines the politics of remembering in Northeast India and how it shaped ethnic relation in the region. The conclusion arrived at here is largely tentative and suggestive. My interest is twofold. First, this chapter intends to contribute to the scholarship of memory studies. Second, it intends to diagnose the ongoing contested ethnic relations in the region differently. On the one hand, it concerns with the construction of commemorative spaces by the various postcolonial 'States' in the region and how different sections of the population responded to such state-sponsored public spaces, while[6] on the other, this chapter examines the dialectical relationship and the tension it has generated between the dominant public memory and the 'vernacular'/'popular' memory and how this not only reflects but also shapes ethnic relations. This study is, therefore, an investigation into the politics of memory in Northeast India. In other words, it looks into the production of 'official' memories in state-sponsored public spaces (such as museums, monuments and memorials)[7] and how they have been responded by the multi-ethnic, multicultural societies in the region.[8]

Postcolonial Moment: Commemorating Defeat, Celebrating the Gallant

One of the most interesting aspects of remembering in postcolonial period in the ex-colonies was the dominant position the anti-colonial movement had assumed. Many of these events or persons commemorated were those that may be categorized as 'defeat'. History largely commemorated victory but not defeat. Yet, despite defeat, the fact that such resistance amounts to anti-colonial movements for their freedom had ranked high in the memory of the freed population in postcolonial period. To the freed people, such event of defeat does not seem defeat per se but a moment in the process that finally gave them victory and freedom. Thus, despite defeat, it was a moment of bravery and heroism to face colonial brutal suppression and, hence, worthy of highest honour.

Besides, there are other factors worthy of note. In many ex-colonies, colonialism provided the common ground for reminiscing. This is particularly so in multicultural, multi-ethnic countries like India. Colonialism offers, for one, a shared past to all sections of the population that anchored divergent, and often conflicting, memories. In their call on the multi-ethnic, multicultural societies to marshal a new nation, many of the emerging postcolonial societies found a common ground of reminiscing in colonialism itself. Thus, the staying on mode of colonialism as presenter's shared memory has become pervasive and effervescence. The reason for this is that the new nation, thus, formed has been, in most cases, founded on the pretext, and in the context, of colonial geography and its sociocultural and institutional apparatuses.

The failure of colonial, and the nationalist's, social reconstruction process and the failure to produce an all-pervasive alternative narrative in postcolonial society make the colonial presence even more profound. Reminiscing colonialism or, more specifically, the anti-colonial movements as an instrument of legitimizing the new authority, establishing stability and social order and socializing the diverse population to a common national project have become the most viable option before the new nation. Colonialism, therefore, stays firm as a reference point to mobilize the freed people around the new social reconstruction project.

The process in which memorialization proceeded is another interesting aspect of remembering altogether. The series of anti-colonial events were taken in a spontaneous whole within a single chain of change. The chain was episodic in character, yet in a series of defeat into victory, one enforcing the next in chain. Sometimes, the 'glorious' precolonial pasts emerged insofar as they helped the new state to legitimize its position. Quite often the memories of colonial armies (as in Malaysia), colonial institutions, maps and ideas (as in most ex-colonies) were used as a rallying point. It has become a shared memory to negotiate with, to mobilize, to organize the freed people and even to yoke them towards a totalizing national reconstruction project. The fallen 'rebels' become 'patriots' and 'freedom fighters', and the defeated 'rebellions', 'wars of independence'. They dominate the commemorative monuments and memorials.

While the romance of anti-colonial moments constituted the core of remembering, it took on three different turns. If certain anti-colonial events were 'overly remembered', others were either forgotten or silenced. The politics of remembering, based on party, class, caste, creed, gender, and ethnicity, are clearly at play here. In the process, events and persons belonging to the marginal sections were generally forgotten or silenced. They have become invisible in state-sponsored public spaces. They lived at the border of remembering and tend to fade away in time. Second, such official acts of remembering and forgetting were responded with 'counter-memory' or 'unofficial' memorials by some marginalized groups or communities with the same purpose of commemorating and to anchor the group's or community's shared memories. Third, there were also groups who remained silent for different strategic reasons. I intend to show here how remembering in state-sponsored public spaces (official memorials) not only reflects but also shapes ethnic relations in multi-ethnic, multicultural societies of Northeast India.

The situation in Northeast India is rather interesting in many ways. Like in other postcolonial societies, the historical imagination of the emerging postcolonial 'States' (hereafter, state) in the region mainly rests on two grounds: colonial and postcolonial events. In certain cases, the precolonial past also emerged significant but only to serve the purpose of the other two dominant formations. Most states begin with the precolonial period (visible in state museum) to show the indigenous origin of the community. However, such ancient nostalgia was soon overshadowed by the attention given to either colonial or postcolonial pasts as a reference point to anchor their identity and to marshal the society into a new 'nation'. Yet, such memorialization process involved the ghostly politics of ethnicity that not only reflected but also shaped ethnic relations. I intend to proceed on how official memorials came up in different states and then how the ethnic minorities in the state responded to them.

Northeast India: Official Memory, Hegemonic Order

The 'official' form of remembrance in public spaces in all the states of Northeast India draws our attention first. What becomes profound here is the dominance of historical imagination of the politically dominant community in each state. While some states commemorated the anti-colonial events, others gave emphasis to postcolonial events, and in certain cases, we see a mixture of precolonial, colonial and postcolonial events. They are largely selective, elitist, masculine and ethnocentric in character. On the other hand, the states remain persistently silent on, and/or deliberately forget, the historical visions shared by ethnic minorities and subaltern classes in the state. The reason for this is that the belief that the new state, thus, formed was due to the dominant community, and that it was the fruit of their resistance movement.

Regardless of the emphasis given, each state begins with their precolonial history, often with 'time immemorial', assumed to be the 'golden age', only to anchor the indigenous identity of the community. Archaeological artefacts, such as ethno-archaeological objects, inscriptions, manuscripts, coinage, pottery, terracotta, weapons, utensils, instruments of husbandry and ornaments, displayed in the museums speak volume for the 'golden age'. They typify the glorious hours of the community in question. The story goes like this. This community arose from the scratch, the primitive and, eventually, emerged glorious before colonialism consumed its hard-earned history. In states where non-tribals dominated, the tribalogy (the dominant idea of 'tribe') was displayed in a separate gallery ('ethnological gallery') as contained identities and, in many cases, 'misrepresented' as static, timeless and backward society of the state. In tribal states, however, the tribalogy assumed a pre-eminent position in the state museum, although they are equally influenced by the dominant civilizational discourse on the 'tribes'. To them, their present existence as 'indigenous people' is anchored by this 'glorious' root of being tribe; for instance, head-hunting, which represents primitivism in non-tribal state museums, is assumed as the lost tradition of the community's 'golden age' which is visibly displayed in Nagaland and Mizoram state museums.

As regards 'misrepresentation' of the tribes in non-tribal states, the representations in Assam state museum are explicit. Apart from showing their 'creative art', the tribes of Assam were, for instance, shown to possess certain 'prevailing' customs like marriage and religion. The 'prevailing marriage' among some tribes is, for instance, described as 'polygamy', which is 'not practiced by all' or among other tribes 'monogamy' although 'there is no bar to polygamy'. Their religions are variously described to be 'animism', 'super naturalism', 'traditional religion' or 'influenced by Hindu religion'. Overall, the tribal past is described to be an insignificant appendage to the 'Great tradition', which the museum is glowingly magnifying. Interestingly, such a narrative also somehow influenced the museums in tribal state, but here its magnification took on glorifying the disdained. What has become clear from the museum representations is the story of a linear rise of the politically dominant community in each state to power, be it tribal or non-tribal.

Museum's story does not end with tribalogy. It goes on narrating the story of anti-colonial movements, and in some states, the postcolonial movements. Assam has a separate gallery for 'freedom fighters' and martyrs. The main gallery in Meghalaya is adorned by large portraits of three leaders ('patriots') of anti-colonial movements: Tirot Sing, Kiang Nangbah and Togan Sangma. The only colonial event in Nagaland museum is represented by the pictures of some official buildings and the Second World War's Kohima battle. The small bronze statue and personal belongings of Dr Imkongliba Ao, President of Naga People's Council, who led in the formation of Nagaland state and was assassinated in 1961, represents the postcolonial case. The case of Mizoram draws particular interest. While it is silent on any anti-colonial event, the representations (through photographs) glorify the 'civilizing' process under colonialism and missionaries—Christianity, education, print culture, and so on. It goes on to narrate the story of MNF movement (e.g., telephone/telegraph post splintered with multiple bullet marks) until the signing of Mizo Accord in 1986.[9]

What happens outside the museum? Here, the story of their final triumph over 'opposition forces', such as colonial or postcolonial states, as the case may be, becomes clear. In Assam, Manipur, Tripura and Meghalaya, the historical imagination of the state to marshal the new 'nation' is built on colonialism. In other words, the anti-colonial movements dominated their vision of the past in public spaces; for instance, the leaders who led such anti-colonial resistance movements and those who were killed during the movement, especially occupied a special place. They are the 'patriots', 'freedom fighters' and 'martyrs' for the new 'nation'. Assam also has museums displaying precolonial Ahom's movements and the postcolonial anti-immigration movement. The state-sponsored public spaces in Mizoram and Nagaland are, respectively, dominated by the postcolonial anti-India movements under MNF and Naga National Council (NNC). Besides, monuments and memorials in public spaces, state also used other instruments to spread their official vision of the past in naming roads, public buildings, stamps, calendars, information technology, mass media, educational system and civil court of law.

The transition of different forms of memory in Assam is interesting. The early version of collective memory in public spaces was dominated by the anti-illegal immigration events or 'Assam Movement'. Symbolized by the great fist *Joi Ai Asom* and other celebrated lines like 'Dead is like an art', the movement was propagated through several 'Martyrs' Memorial Pillars' across the Brahmaputra valley that commemorated the 'Assam Movement' (1979–1985). Every year, 10 December is commemorated as 'Martyr's Day' in the state. It was during this movement that people found inspiration from not only the range of cultural icons of Assam but also from the famous medieval event of Ahom's victory at the 'Battle of Saraighat' against the Mughal's army. The moving line of General Lachit Barphookan, 'My uncle is not greater than my country', is sufficient to steer people to a particular direction. Defending the motherland at all cost from the illegal immigrants, or invaders in medieval sense, has, thus, created agitation in the minds of the people.

On the sidelines of this dominant memory of the movement were memories depicting the gradual emergence of anti-colonial movements in the state. This was particularly with the changing regime under Congress since the 1990s, which found the narrative of the movement threatening its very foundation in the state. The monuments of anti-colonial freedom fighters, public leaders, martyrs and Assamese cultural icons gradually occupied prime place in state-sponsored public spaces. Sankerdev Park, Shradhanjali Park and Nehru Park in Guwahati are few of such memorial parks dedicated to the freedom fighters of Assam. This new memorialization process under Congress

Figure 4.1 Assam: Assam Movement, Battle of Saraighat and Shraddhanjali, Guwahati
Source: Author.

government also shows its concern for cultural integration in the face of agitated minority communities in the state who felt marginalized by the Assam Movement; for instance, the Bodo nationalist icon Rupnath Brahma and the Koch-Rajbongsi national icon General Chilarai were also gradually included among the glitters of Assam's past in public space.

Similar to Assam, the official version of remembering in Manipur is also dominated by anti-colonial events—the Anglo-Manipur War 1891, Nupi Lan (1939) and the Indian National Army (INA) Movement. Soon after Manipur got statehood in 1972, Khongjom War Memorial Park was created at Khongjom with one monument (obelisk structure) at the top of the hill. A statue of Major Paona Brajabashi, an auditorium, an open-air theatre and a majestic gateway were added subsequently (since 1990s). Similarly, the foundation of a 'Martyr Pillar' was laid in the same year near the Pologround where Bir Tikendrajit and Thangal General were publicly hanged. Likewise, memorials and statues related to the war were also erected in different towns of the valley. To this was added later the memory of Nupi Lan and the iconic communist leader Hijam Irabot. The INA Martyr's Memorial Complex was also built at Moirang where the Tricolour was first hoisted on Indian soil. It housed INA Museum, memorial hall, library, Netaji Statue and the replica of INA Memorial in Singapore.[10]

In Meghalaya, anti-colonial movements that took place under the three dominant communities—Khasis, Jaintias and Garos—again dominate the official vision of the past in public space. While the state took great care to preserve the old monoliths that commemorate 'great occasion', memorials of the Anglo-Khasi War 1829–1833, Jaintia Uprising 1860–1862 and Anglo-Garo War 1872–1873 dominated public spaces and commemorations. A huge Martyr Pillar was erected in front of the state museum to commemorate these three events and to honour the three leaders U. Tirot Sing (Khasi), U. Kiang Nangbah (Jaintia) and Pa Togan Sangma (Garos). Separate memorials were also established at U. Kiang Nangbah Memorial Park (Jowai), Tirot Sing Memorial (Mairang) and Togan Sangma Memorial Park (Tura).

Figure 4.2 Manipur: Anglo-Manipur War Memorials, Imphal and Khongjom

Source: Author.

Figure 4.3 Meghalaya: Old Monolith, Martyr Pillar, Memorials of Tirot Sing and Kiang Nangbah

Source: Author.

In the public spaces of Mizoram and Nagaland, the official vision of the past is dominated by the postcolonial events such as homeland movements under MNF and NNC. In Mizoram (see Figure 4.4), there is a monument of Pu Laldenga, the 'Father of Mizo Nation', standing alongside the British war memorials at Aizawl. Besides, there are two 'Martyrs' memorial 'cemeteries' at Aizawl and Sesawng. In Nagaland (see Figure 4.5), the state erected a memorial in the memory of A. Z. Phizo, the 'Father of the [Naga] Nation' at Phizo Hills, in front of the new Secretariat in Kohima. The same memory resonated in monoliths in different parts of Nagaland. The only memory of colonialism in Nagaland was the preservation of historic Khonoma Fort as 'Our Pride Fort'. A monolith was erected in 2017 to commemorate the centenary of Naga Labour Corps who went to France in 1917.[11]

In selecting the past events for representations in state-sponsored public spaces, it is evident that the various states in the region were informed by the contemporary concern of promoting the rise to prominence of the dominant community in the state. It was not only ethnocentric but also masculine and elitist in character. While Assamese past dominated the historical imagination of Assam state, the historical vision of Meitei, Naga, Mizo and Khasi-Garo communities dominated state-sponsored public spaces in Manipur, Nagaland, Mizoram and Meghalaya, respectively. Each state government and, for that matter, each dominant community in the state, was evidently informed by, and guided towards, what George Orwell has noted of the agency which controls historical experience, 'those who control the past, control the future'.[12] In their effort to control the past and the future, each state wanted to avoid the parallel rise to power of two or more communities in the state and, hence, harped on 'seeing' the rise to prominence of only the dominant community. In other words, 'not to see' the 'others', the minority communities in the state were a part of the stated policy of the new social reconstruction process which would 'see' only the linear rise to power of the politically dominant community.

Seeing only the pasts of dominant community is not only an effort to assimilate, homogenize and solidify the diverse social realities in each state but also to legitimize and socialize the authority of the

Figure 4.4 Mizoram: Memorial of Laldenga and Martyr Cemetery in Aizawl and Sesawng

Source: Author.

Figure 4.5 *Nagaland: Khonoma Fort and Memorials of A. Z. Phizo and K. Seyie*

Source: Author.

dominant community. In this sense, memory is an instrument, or an ideological tool, in the hands of the elitist state, which strives for 'integration' of diverse social formation. In this context, such official commemoration is, partly, a positive action for integration of society for social stability and harmony, and partly, a negative action of conscious action of selection, omission and forgetting. This is the ghostly politics of remembering, which is governed by, and/or reflecting, contested ethnic relations in the state. Thus, behind the making of every project of public commemoration was an active form of what I would call 'kinship activism', the point I shall now discuss.

The Responses: Kinship Activism, Counter-memory and Silence

If official commemorative memory favours only the historical vision of the dominant community in the state, then the shared memory of the politically marginalized communities would remain ignored and invisible. We have noted that the minority tribes were largely 'misrepresented' in state museums. Some state minorities were completely absent in the state museum; for instance, the Muslims of Assam and Manipur, the Kukis and Kacharis in Nagaland, the Chakmas and Reangs in Mizoram, the Bengalis in Meghalaya and so on, are virtually invisible in state representations. Such absence was particularly profound in the state-sponsored public spaces outside the museums. Here, the shared memories of the minority communities are virtually absent as non-being. While favouring only the historical imagination of a politically dominant community, it remains insensitive to the marginal 'others' whose memories are invisible, unsaid and forgotten.

This 'official' vision of the past is responded broadly in three ways. First, it promoted a sense of belongingness and solidarity among the members of the dominant community who had assimilated around the official vision of the past. Second, it has generated a sense of neglect among the members of ethnic minorities who responded in two ways. The first group, who constituted a substantial population and who wanted to represent themselves in their own vernacular, responded with 'unofficial monuments' to embody and anchor their identity through the shared past. The second group, who constituted the third form of response, responded with silence. Due to their insignificant numbers, some others who constituted a substantial population remained silent for strategic reasons. They formed the 'silent' populations of the region, which each state has substantial population. I shall briefly discuss each of these responses separately.

Response I: Kinship Memory, Kinship Activism

The politically dominant community of the state responded to the official version of the past with favour, as it represents their shared memory. In so doing, such memory has become what I call the 'kinship memory' of the dominant community. In other words, the kinship memory, the 'official' vision of the past, is merely the reflection of collective memory shared by the dominant community; for instance, during the Anglo-Manipur War in 1891, a large number of Manipuri populations in the valley supported Tikendrajit Singh. Once the war was declared, the whole valley revolted, but they were soon suppressed. When Tikendrajit and Thangal General were hanged in public, thousands of white-clothed women (said to be around 8,000) gathered there to pay their last homage to them. However, this sense of mourning remained silent, suppressed and poetic under the intimidating gaze of the colonial power.

Yet, once Manipur got independence and the real power came under its control in 1972, this silenced memory came to the fore. As Meitei 'nationalism' grew from oblivion, such vision of the past shared by the community gradually became visible and significant to anchor their identity. Now more events were added upon the original frame. The memorialization process, thus, formed under the new state, dominated by the Meitei community, was just a reflection of the growing consciousness over their identity, thus, noted. Therefore, the 'identity-conscious' phenomenon or the self-conceived politics was instrumental and decisive in the process of memory construction in public spaces. The same process is true in all the states in Northeast India: Assam for Assamese, Nagaland for Nagas, Mizoram for Mizos, Meghalaya for Khasi–Jaintia–Garos and so on.

Once the state government took over the community's narrative for official commemoration and put up in the sacrosanct public spaces, it gave a new lease of life on its own. This was especially evident when it was transformed into a bodily practice with gazette holiday and annual commemoration when the ranks and files of the government offices and the mass participated in the bodily performed ceremonial event. Once an event is given an official sanction for bodily performance, such event has to turn into an occasion where people are taught and fed a lesson of patriotism, nationalism and whatnot. It is also an occasion where the state socializes its citizens to a common vision of the past and the future and legitimizes its authority. The year-round visit to such memorial sites by public enables the continuing dissemination of the message of patriotism to the people.

In such official commemorations, active participants were members of the dominant community who felt honoured by the promotion of their past in public spaces. As a result, it produced a stronger sense of belongingness among them and helped them to assimilate around the official commemorative memory. Being regularly fed with patriotism from the past, the growing sense of togetherness may transform into a sense of 'kinship' among them. The result was what I call 'kinship activism'. In the context of Northeast states, it was kinship of the real kind, not a mere 'fictive kinship', as we see in other cases. In other words, this resulted in 'nationalism' among the members of dominant community. It was they who had benefited most from such official memory. They came together, negotiated with each other, felt and imagined together and, eventually, assimilated around such collective memory as active kinship group. Active nationalism is the consequence of such kinship activism, the case we see in most states in the region.

Response II: Counter-memory, Subordinated Voices

We have noted that the memorialization process in state-sponsored public spaces in the region had forgotten the shared pasts of marginalized and minority communities in the state. Their memories remain invisible and unsaid even after they insisted. They may have participated in the official commemoration, but it was difficult for them to imbibe the message being served. The reason for this is that such official vision of the past contradicts their vision of the past and the truth of their recollections. They have always remained passive participants in state commemorations. Their presence there was a mere 'official protocol' and more of 'tactical' than political; it was to appease the political boss. In other words, they have their own vision of the past, which they expressed in 'vernacular/unofficial' memorials or in silence.

The sense of neglect, forgetfulness and invisibility in the official commemoration generated a moment of serious reflection, of an active reminiscing, to most ethnic minorities in the state. To them, an official act of remembering turned out to be an emotively charged social domain that often brought an endless saga of recollections. It provided them the occasion to explore the terrain of social landscape and helped them discover not only the subtle politics of remembering in the process but also reconfigure their forgotten past. In other words, the official act of remembering punctured the balloon of silence. The realization that something is missing in the picture helped them to initiate a new process of commemorating the forgotten. This is particularly so, when the state continues to maintain silence, despite knowing. In the process, there was a dialectical tension between the process of remembering and forgetting.

The tension was a reflection of, and being exacerbated by, the ongoing contested ethnic relations among different groups in the region. The tension became more open and even confrontational in a state where certain minority communities were asserting for their separation from the state or autonomy within it. To them, the state neglect of their shared memory was not only a point of reference for their marginality but also a point to begin with their own memorials to anchor their history and identity. Thus, the dialectical tension between the ethnocentric approach of official memorialization process and forgetting generated several 'vernacular' monuments and memorials from some minority groups in the state. They chose to see the past in their own vernacular against official act of forgetting.

Since such vernacular memorials are born out of the dialectical tension between official and vernacular memories, they are in a mode of competition, contestation and opposition to each other.

In this context, such vernacular memorials represent what came to be known as 'counter-memory', 'oppositional memory' or 'dissident discourse'. Interestingly, such tension is also reflected in the landscape of remembrance where the official memories were invisible in the area dominated by the minority communities who rejected such memory just as the 'unofficial' memory found its existence invisible beyond the community's ethnic boundary. Thus, the official version of commemorative history in Assam is invisible in Barak valley, Dima Haosa, Karbi Anglong and Bodoland just as Manipur's official vision of the past is invisible in the hills of the state dominated by the tribes.

The rise of 'vernacular' or 'unofficial' monuments in some states such as Assam, Manipur and Meghalaya is instructive. In Assam, ethnic minorities such as Bengalis, Bodos (Boros), Karbis, Dimasas, Koch-Rajbongsis and Manipuris responded to the official act of forgetting with their 'vernacular' monuments. To Bodos, the 'martyrs' of 'Bodo Movement' against Assam state emerged significant. Their statues and memorial parks came up in different places within Bodoland. To Bengalis, besides few Bengali nationalists and reformers, the *Bhasa Sahid* (language martyrs) of 19 May 1961 emerged significant for commemoration. Apart from some monuments and memorial sites at three district headquarters, at every street corner in towns and villages, 19 May is annually commemorated as 'Language Martyrs Day' or 'Bhasa Sahid Divas' across the Barak valley of Assam.

Similarly, the Koch-Rajbongsi community of Assam also commemorates the might of Chilarai, the medieval general of the Koch kingdom, as the community's memory par excellence. Chilarai parks were established in Dhubri and Guwahati. The Karbis found their heroes in those who led them for the Karbi Anglong autonomous district, of which Semsonsing Ingti and Khorsing Terang became significant. The Dimasas chose Veer Sambhudhan Phonglo, who fought the British colonialism during 1881–1882, as their patriot and martyr. The Zeme Nagas commemorated Rani Gaidinliu as their freedom fighter. The Kukis and Manipuris of Assam, in tune with their kinsmen in Manipur, found their patriots in Chengjapao Doungel (of Anglo-Kuki War), Bir Tikendrajit Singh and Paona Brajabasi (of Anglo-Manipur War) and Hijam Irawat, the communist leader.

Figure 4.6 Assam: Bodofa U. N. Brahma (Bodo), Bhasa Sahid Memorial (Bengali), Gen Chilarai (Koch-Rajbongshi), Semson Sing Ingti (Karbi)

Source: Author.

Figure 4.7 Assam: Sambhudhan Phonglo (Dimasa), Rani Gaidinliu (Naga), Chengjapao Doungel (Kuki), Paona Brajabashi (Manipuri)

Source: Author.

In Meghalaya, the Bengalis, the largest ethnic minority in the state, established memorials of Bengali nationalist figures such as Netaji Subhas Chandra Bose, Vivekananda and Rabindranath Tagore. In Manipur, ethnic minorities like Zaliengrong Nagas and the Kukis responded to such official remembering with their own memorials. To the former, Haipou Jadonang, and his follower Rani Gaidinliu, became significant as their patriots. To the Kukis, the Anglo-Kuki War 1917–1919 was considered important for commemoration. The Kukis celebrate the event on 17 October every year and have erected memorials and monuments of the war in different parts of the districts inhabited by them in the state.

If the landscape of memory is separated into official and vernacular spaces, the latter represents the site of dissident discourse. Just as the dominant community members gathered and assimilated around the official memory, we can also see a similar process of reminiscing around the unofficial monuments by members of respective ethnic minority. In the process, they also similarly learnt, internalized and imbibed the message of patriotism from their past. It was a process that not only promoted belongingness and anchored and moulded their identity in their distant past, but it also taught its members 'not to see' other's past for reminiscing. This resulted in another set of active kinship group and, hence, another kinship activism. Hence, the growing numbers of vernacular memorials not only reflect the existing tension between official and unofficial memories, between dominant community and minorities, but they also largely shaped the competing ethnic relations and contesting ethnic nationalisms.

Response III: Silence, Unsayable, the Subterranean World

We also come across many more communities in different states of Northeast India who felt ignored by the official act of remembering but who continue to remain silent. To them, silence could be 'many things' that 'still speak'.[13] Some of them remain silent as a form of active avoidance, others due to socially/politically sanctioned silence, still others for different reasons. They are the silent communities living quietly under the shadow of power in a subterranean world. As a social

Figure 4.8 Rabindranath Tagore (Bengali), Haipou Jadonang Park (Zeliangrong), Anglo-Kuki War Monolith and Tintong (Kuki)

Source: Author.

process, silence has manifested in many ways depending on the social and political circumstances of the state. Assam has the largest numbers of silent population. The Muslims of Assam, for instance, constitute more than 30 per cent of the state's population but continue to remain silent insofar as social commemoration of their past is concerned. Their silence may be understood both as repressive and strategic.

Large numbers of Muslim populations had been living there for centuries and had already been part of the dominant Assamese society. Yet, the growing number of their populations, especially after partition, threatened others, which resulted in labelling them as 'refugees', 'immigrants' and 'foreigners'. Once they were seen as 'dangerous', the fact that they emerged powerfully during the anti-illegal immigration movement or 'Assam Movement' 1979–1985, there was no way they could go back to their past for commemoration purposes. It was under such 'repressive' social and political environment that such silence remains discreet. It leads to a condition of 'repressive memory', a memory that can neither be spoken in public nor to fellow friends and community members. To many of them, Assam was a terrifying landscape that silence has becomes their saviour and safety.

Such silence was also considered 'political' or 'strategic' in order to suspend, postpone or truncate open conflict over the meaning of their past. Breaking the silence is likely to call attention to their 'unwanted' presence. In this sense, it can be considered as what Winter refers to as a 'banned speech'. Instead, they chose to adopt a 'polite' conversation with others, and also when they asserted their identity, through the less contested site like 'traditions' (both social and religious). This 'moment of inarticulacy', to use Vitebsky apt term, reduced them into living in a subterranean world and quietly lead a shadow-filled life with uncertainties. Being unable to dialogue with their past in the open may have troubled them deeply as non-being, but it continues to provide them space for negotiation with the state and the dominant political community in the state.

Similarly, many silent communities in the region took shelter in the more 'polite' culture and traditions to anchor their identity. The 'tea tribes' of Barak Valley, Assam, for instance, get together annually to celebrate the festival of Bara Baba at the temple of Bara Baba, Silcoorie

Tea Estate, Silchar. The occasion was used both as annual religious festival as to social and market fairs. The majority of the minority communities in the region seek to anchor their identity in such less combative 'traditions'. The Meitei Pangals (Muslims), Nepalis and some tribal communities in Manipur; the Rabhas, Koches, Karbis, Nepalis, Assamese, etc. in Meghalaya; the Chakmas and Reangs in Mizoram; and the Kukis, Dimasas, Karbis, etc. in Nagaland continue to remain the silent communities under this category. Very often, some groups of silent communities join hands to form what Jay Winter has called 'fictive kinship group' (Winter 2006). They are a unified group bonded not by blood ties but by experiences of indignity under a dominant community in the state. The case of Tripura's tribes against the dominant Bengali community is one good case in point (Chakravarti 2001).

Contested Memories, Memories of Contestation

What we can see from the evidences of monuments and memorials, and that of silence, in Northeast India is that memory constituted a site of conflict and contestation between different ethnic groups in the region. If the state commemorated the historical vision of the dominant community and persistently ignored the collective memory of the minority ethnic groups in each state, such official acts of forgetting were responded in at least three important ways. While the dominant community in the state responded by collaborating with the state to exert their memory of the past, some ethnic minorities encountered with their 'vernacular' monuments, whereas others remained silent.

We have noted that the 'official' vision of the past not only encouraged the dominant community to assimilate but also generated a sense of belongingness as active kinship group and, hence, produced kinship activism, or what in commonly known as, 'ethnonationalism or subnationalism' among them. Similarly, the 'vernacular' or 'unofficial' memories encouraged members of ethnic minorities to come together as another set of active kinship group, often oppose to other kinship groups and, hence, the formation of kinship activism. We have also seen that silence is not a mere complacency; it is simply another way of contesting the official act of forgetting. There was then a parallel rise to prominence of two or more competing memories, of kinship activisms, of 'official' and 'vernacular', hegemonic and subordinated voices and state-sponsored and community-based memories. This eventually produced a competing historical imagination and, hence, competing identities in the region in general and within each state in particular.

This parallel rise to eminence of two or more competing kinship memories, imbued with violent past, has thereby produced violent forms of conflict and contestation among different ethnic communities that often witnessed fissiparous tendencies. Violent nationalism, it may be added, was largely the result of the masculine representations of the past, both in official and vernacular monuments. If violent resistance movements against either colonial or postcolonial states formed the central theme of memorialization process in the region, then it is easy to concur that the violent character of ethnic contestation and ethno-nationalism in the region owes much from this process of remembering.

The role of memory in shaping community's identity and that of tension should not be, however, overstated. The existing social order that willy-nilly drew its reference point in colonial mania of classificatory order is perhaps the main dossier to this particular set of contested ethnic relations. We have seen that ethnic consciousness has been built up during the colonial period, well into the formation of many 'national' organizations even before India's independence. Yet, the fact remains that instead of putting a stop to this progressive trend of ethnic nationalism with some sense of adjustment and accommodation (as in the prevailing notion of 'inclusive politics'), no matter how slippery such ethnic landscape was, the emerging states in the region ignore them altogether.

We have seen that most states in the region instead swim themselves dangerously in the endless flood of 'nationalisms' by a dialectical process of remembering and forgetting sensitivities. No sooner than such ghostly politics of remembering, of the ethnocentric one-track approach, took its stroll in the official mind and on the street, it soon witnessed its opposites, challenging its hegemony. It resulted in the parallel rise to eminence of two or more kinship activisms within the state which are competing with each other. Thus, while each of these communities found their reference point of existential order in the colonial mania of classification, the present official representations in public spaces harden such ethnic conviction.

Therefore, the contested memorialization process in the region not only reflected the existing social realities, largely in the form of colonial hangover, but it also greatly contributed to its growth, especially towards the shaping and production of violent nationalism in the region. It was within such competing visions of the past, of the dialectical tension between the dominant and subordinated voices, that one may locate the ongoing animated violence and ethnic contestations in the region. In other words, contested memory reflects contested social relationship and contestation over memory, which, in turn, fashions contested social relationship in a big way.

Concluding Remarks

From the facts drawn from above discussion such as the form, character and nature of memory, one can come to the conclusion that memory is not only instrumental and social, but it is also dynamic, processual, fluid, conflictual and even political. Memory can also be coherent and incoherent, hegemonic and subordinated and open and silent. Part of a particular memory could be permanent and consistent whereas other parts are always invented and temporal in dimensions. Collective memory, which we are concerned about, is, therefore, an ongoing process of negotiation between several memories, and hence, remembering is a processual action in which people constantly transform their recollections and representations of the past over the time. The dynamics of this collective memory changed over time from colonial to postcolonial period and from early independent era to the present time, with new forms of recollections emerging daily with the changing circumstances. Lastly, collective memory is not just a reflection, a signifier, of social relations, but it also shapes, largely refashions and reframes social relations, while it is also ever changing in time and space.

Acknowledgements

This chapter is part of my ICHR Research Project. I am grateful to ICHR for the generous support for the project.

Notes

1. See, for instance, Misztal (2003); Rossington and Whitehead (2007); Hodgkin and Radstone (2005); Ricouer (2004); Connerton (2008); Winter (2006); Young (1993); Ben-zeer et al. (2010).
2. See especially Halbwachs ([1926] 1992); Schwartz (1982).
3. Important contribution in this respect is Hobsbawm and Ranger (1983).
4. See particularly Johnson et al. (1982); Szacka (1997); Fentress and Wickham (1992); Debouzy (1986).
5. See for instance, Connerton (1989); Schudson (1997); Schudson (1989); Schudson (1992); Schwartz (2000); Zelizer (1995).
6. 'State' here refers to the various states (or provinces) of India in Northeastern region such as Assam, Meghalaya, Mizoram, Manipur and Nagaland.
7. Here, the terms museum, monument and memorial are understood from its literal dictionary meaning and do not concern with the technical aspect of them. While museum is a familiar case, we use monument in term of any structure or building that honours or commemorates a notable person, group, or event.
8. On the same line of argument, I have investigated the case of Manipur earlier. See Guite (2011).
9. Unfortunately, I was not able to access the state museums of Manipur, Tripura and Arunachal Pradesh during my fieldwork and hence not included here.
10. For detail discussion on Manipur see Guite (2011).
11. My study on public memorials in Tripura and Arunachal Pradesh is not sufficient to provide a broad picture for analysis here. Tripura could have provided an interesting case post-facto this research on how regime change could mark a change in public memory as was often the case in many places.
12. As quoted in John Petrovato's 'Producing National Identity: Museums, Memory and Collective Thought in Israel'. https://zcomm.org/znetarticle/producing-national-identity-museums-memory-and-collective-thought-in-israel-by-john-petrovato
13. For discussion on silence, see Winter (2010) in Ben-zeer, Ginio, and Winter (2010, 3–31).

References

Ben-zeer, E., R. Ginio, and Jay Winter. 2010. *Shadow of War: A Social History of Silence in the Twentieth Century*. Cambridge: Cambridge University Press.

Chakravarti, M. 2001, 23–29 June. 'Insurgency in Tripura: Some Trends'. *EPW* 36, no. 25: 2229–2231. Available at http://www.jstor.org (accessed 6 March 2014).

Connerton, P. 1989. *How Societies Remember*. Cambridge: Cambridge University Press.

———. 2008. 'Seven Types of Forgetting.' *Memory Studies* 1: 59–71.

Debouzy, M. 1986. 'In Search of Working-class Memory.' *History and Anthropology* 2: 261–282.
Fentress, J., and C. Wickham. 1992. *Social Memory*. Oxford: Blackwell.
Guite, J. 2011, 8 February. 'Monuments, Memory and Forgetting in Postcolonial North-East India.' *Economic & Political Weekly* XLVI, no. 8: 56–64.
Halbwachs, M. [1926] 1992. *On Collective Memory*. Chicago, IL: Chicago University Press.
Hobsbawm, E., and T. Ranger, eds. 1983. *The Invention of Tradition*. New York, NY: Cambridge University Press.
Hodgkin, K., and S. Radstone, eds. 2005. *The Politics of Memory: Contested Pasts*. Piscataway, NJ: Transaction Publishers.
Johnson, R., G. Mclennan, B. Schwarz, and D. Sutton, eds. 1982. *Making Histories: Studies in History Making and Politics*. London: Hutchinson.
Misztal, B. 2003. *Theories of Social Remembering*. Maidenhead: Open University Press.
Ricouer, P. 2004. *History, Memory, Forgetting*, trans. K. Blamey and D. Pellauer. Chicago, IL: University of Chicago Press.
Rossington, M., and A. Whitehead, eds. 2007. *Theories of Memory: A Reader*. Edinburgh: Edinburgh University Press.
Schudson, M. 1997. 'Lives, Laws and Language: Commemorative Versus Noncommemorative Forms of Effective Public Memory.' *The Communication Review* 2, no. 1: 3–17.
———. 1989. 'The Present in the Past Versus the Past in the Present.' *Communication* 11: 105–113.
———. 1992. *Watergate in American Memory*. New York, NY: Basic Books.
Schwartz, B. 1982. 'The Social Context of Commemoration: A Study in Collective Memory.' *Social Forces* 61, no. 2: 374–402.
———. 2000. *Abraham Lincoln and the Forge of National Memory*. Chicago, IL: Chicago University Press.
Szacka, B. 1997. 'Systematic Transformation and Memory of the Past.' *Polish Sociological Review* 118, no. 2: 119–132.
Winter, J. 2006. 'War Memorials: A Social Agency Interpretation.' *Remembering War: The Great War between Memory and History in the Twentieth Century*. New Haven, CT: Yale University Press.
———. 2010. 'Thinking About Silence.' In *Shadows of War: A Social History of Silence in the Twentieth Century*, edited by Efrat Ben-Ze'ev, Ruth Ginio and Jay Winter, 3–31. Cambridge: Cambridge University Press.
Young, James E. 1993. *The Texture of Memory: Holocaust Memorials and Meaning*. New Haven, CT and London: Yale University Press.
Zelizer, B. 1995. 'Reading the Past against the Grain.' *Critical Studies in Mass Communication* 12: 214–239.

CHAPTER 5

The Socio-spatial Politics of 'Tribal' and 'Non-tribal' in Meghalaya

Oyindrila Chattopadhyay

Identity Politics, Who Is a Tribe?

Identity politics is considered to be one of the most dominant political discourses in the context of north-east of India. The region has been witnessing violent retribution of identity politics. Identity politics is usually interpreted, as a 'political orientation built around a (pre-existing) social identity' (Ford 2005). This politicization of social identity (Tajfel 1981) is more about recognition of social groups based on certain markers such as ethnicity, tribe, caste, and gender.

In the case of Northeast India, tribe, in general, is used to signify a group whose primitive trait attributes a distinct identity to it. These traits could be a product of colonial administration. According to Virginia Xaxa, 'the use of the category "tribe" to describe people so heterogeneous from each other in respect of physical and linguistic traits, demographic size, ecological conditions of living, regions inhabited, or stages of social formation and level of acculturation and development was put forward by the colonial administration' (Xaxa 2005). This category of tribe, however, has become more significant in the post-independence era under the positive discrimination laws of the state that accorded special status in certain areas of the Northeast under special provisions of the Constitution of India, for example, Fifth and Sixth Schedules,.

In Meghalaya, the discourse of tribal (and non-tribal) started with the inception of the state in 1972. The concept of *Dhkar*, an identity given to (or synonymous with) the 'non-tribals' in the state has been very much prevalent in Meghalaya. Due to this identity of *Dhkar*, the Khasi tribal community often targets the non-tribal community (such as Bengalis, Nepalese, Beharis and people of the plains). This is because the Khasi community believes that the state of Meghalaya only belongs to the tribes of the state, a view stemmed from the notion of ethnicity. When they say tribes, it means the tribes in Meghalaya such as Garo and Jaintia. Ethnicity refers to the idea of common descent, race, territory, language and kinship bond, which is unduly related to identity politics. Here, tribe becomes an ethnic tribal identity that is based on shared bonding among the three tribes in the state. Such identity formed the basis of state formation as well as identity formation vis-à-vis the migrant population.

The north-east of India, an ethnically diverse region which shares international territory with Bangladesh, Myanmar and Tibet, witnessed a huge inflow of migrants from other parts of British colonies, brought in by the colonial rulers for building this economically vested region. As a result, over time, the ethnically oriented region has also received large number of migrants.[1]

Meghalaya too became a destination of mass migration from across the border of Bangladesh. The fear of being reduced to a minority (as happened reportedly with the tribals in Tripura) led the tribal population, especially the Khasis, to launch a protest against all the non-tribals. Ethnocentrism[2] took shape in the minds of the tribals. As a result, soon after the creation of Meghalaya, along with the migrants from the international border, the migrants from rest of India who were settled in the region for generations also came to be categorized as illegal migrants and became privy to violent identity politics.

Identity politics, a dominant discourse in contemporary politics has been layered by the various discourses prevalent in the context of north-east of India. As articulated by psychologists like Erikson,[3] identity has been the ignition point of identity theory. His idea of identity formation emerging from the various crises in life cycle was expanded in Tajfel's (1979) theory of social identity, which highlighted self-recognition through the membership of a group. As interpreted by sociologists like Halls, these social groups accord to cultural identity, which has its basis in common history and ancestry (Hall 1990). Undoubtedly, this is applicable in the context of the tribes of the north-east of India who were initially perceived as savage, exotic and primitive by the British (McDuie-Ra 2009). This distinct nature led the colonial administrators to produce bounded categories of 'tribe' versus 'plains' and 'tribes' versus 'hill tribes' in the hills (McDuie-Ra 2009) that later became the basis of the British policy of 'Partially Excluded and Excluded of 1874' areas that segregated the hills from the plains (Meetei 2014). As a result, the differentiation of governance within the hill tribes[4] in due course sowed the seeds of ethnic identities in the region even within the tribes. Ethnic boundaries defined psychologically, culturally, socially or politically have attributed to socially exclusionary identity conflicts in north-east of India (Baruah 2003). This politics has also fundamentally raised a serious question on the nature of citizenship. The categories of tribe and non-tribe have almost become a distinction between citizens and non-citizens in a context like Meghalaya.

Given the above backdrop, this chapter attempts to understand the socio-spatial politics of 'tribe' and 'non-tribe' in Meghalaya. The categories of tribe and non-tribe are the derivatives of governing technology of state, not a mere product of primordial affiliation and connectivity. They have emerged as a result of various legislations on land, property and trade. Legislation could be understood partly as the result of affirmative policy of the state (to bring at par with a relatively advanced group of people) for the historically and socially 'backward' groups and, partly, as the political intervention to integrate people who inhabited the formerly governed British northeast frontier. However, once these categories become part of the everyday ethnic civil society politics, rigidity of such categories is felt and contested among the diverse social groups.

The chapter looks at how the Khasi, Jaintia and Garo civil society groups employ spatially the categories of tribe and non-tribe at various stages and how the so-called non-tribe respond to their politics.

Laws of State and Tribe as the Politico-spatial Category

The notion of tribe is very much a spatial category, not merely a politicized social, legal and constitutional category. When we speak of spatial category, we take tribe as part of the governing practices of state in a geographical area. Tribe spatially refers to a geographical space, not just the traits of culture, society, religion and economy of group of people. The Scheduled Districts Act and the Extent of Local Laws Act of 1874 were the first of prominent colonial laws that created distinction between hill populace and the plain settlers based on the perception of backwardness of the former. The Garo Hills Regulation of 1876 (extended to Khasi and Jaintia Hills) restricted exploitation of the forest resources of the hill populace by plain settlers. However, the Government of India Act, 1935 gave a more specific spatial definition of the geography where tribes were expected as the inhabitants of a place and region. Perhaps this could be taken as the root of tribe and non-tribal distinction, which is more of a geographical and political distinction made possible through legislation of the state, rather than a sociological and anthropological category.

Following India's independence, apparently taking a cue from the Government of India Act of 1935, the Bordoloi Committee (formed under the Constituent Assembly of India) report paved way for the insertion of Sixth Schedule[5] in the Constitution of India to safeguard the interests of the tribal populace in the hills of Northeast India. The three hill districts of Khasi, Garo and Jaintia come under the direct purview of this protective layer (under Sixth Schedule).[6] The Khasi, Garo and Jaintia tribes were granted the ST[7] status. Article 366 (25) of Indian constitution defined STs as 'such tribes or tribal communities or parts of or groups within such tribes or tribal communities as are deemed under Article 342 to be Scheduled Tribes for the purposes of this constitution'. According to Article 342 (I) of the Indian constitution, ST is very much a category of population of a specific place that can only be the result of a 'public notification' by president after consultation with Governor of a state or Union Territory.

An important point to be noted here is that a tribe is least known through well-defined socio-economic and cultural traits and characteristics or institutional practices. It is very much a politico-spatial category. It is within this context that we can understand the category of tribe and non-tribes as the corresponding politics of divide. In the following paragraphs, let us explore such categorization as part of the governing practice of state in Meghalaya.

The laws of the state can be broadly classified into the following two domains: (a) regulation of land transfer and trade and (b) protection of 'tribal' customs and institution.

Land, Property and Trade: Defining Tribe and Non-tribe

The Meghalaya Transfer of Land (Regulation) Act, 1971 states that no land (includes immovable property of every descriptions and any rights in or over such property) in Meghalaya can be transferred (means the conveyance of land of one person to another and includes gift, sale, exchange mortgage, lease, surrender or any other mode of transfer) by a tribal to a non-tribal or by a non-tribal to another non-tribal except with the previous sanction of the competent authority, an authority appointed by the Government of Meghalaya through an official notification in the Official Gazette of Meghalaya, Section 3 subsection (1) of the Act. In the Act, a tribal is understood as a person belonging to any of the STs pertaining to Meghalaya and as specified in the Constitution (Scheduled Tribes) Order, 1950, as amended from time to time, and this also includes the Rabhas, Kacharis and Koches who are residents of Meghalaya. This basically means those who are in the list of STs pertaining to the state of Meghalaya are tribes, and this can also implies that those who are not in the list are non-tribal at least in the context of the same state. This further implies that even those STs belonging to other states of India will not be qualified as tribes in the matter of land transfer in Meghalaya. This is an important point, as the distinction of tribe and non-tribe is state- and place-specific, and specific to the issue of land. The land must be registered within 2 years from the commencement of the Act or as stated otherwise by the Government of Meghalaya.

However, there is an exception to this. The transfer of land to a non-tribal does not impinge to the provisions of the Act in case where land is required for a religious purpose such as a place of worship or as a burial or cremation ground or is meant for promoting the interests of the tribal in the field of education or industry. While the distinction between tribe and non-tribe is state- and space-specific, the exceptionality warrants legitimate violation of such distinction on specific purposes. However, what is common to both is that it is the authority that decides when does the exceptionality applies and where. However, the issue is not about who, or when one, decides exceptionality; rather, the issue emerges from the following concern that while distinction between tribes and non-tribes seems to work in favour of the interests of the local people against the so-called non-tribal people, the exceptionality clause or power could be understood as a legal mechanism that allows to break the purpose of distinction. Perhaps this implication of the law explains both the critic of 'non-tribal' and 'tribal'. This also is the basis of the unhappy relationship between the two categories of people. Tribes think such exceptions are used to favour the interests of 'non-tribes'.

According to the Khasi Students' Union (KSU) and Federation of Khasi, Jaintia and Garo People (FKJGP), tribals of the state still continue to be alienated of their land despite the bill being in place. The issue of alienation of land was also an issue between tribes of Meghalaya and other states, not just between tribe and non-tribes. The groups (KSU and FJKGP) wanted to stop land alienation considering the fact that many STs from other parts of India reside in Shillong. One can see that the notion of tribes is strictly limited to three main STs of Meghalaya: Khasi, Garo and Jaintia. Hence, tribe is not just a legal category but also a geographically specific population.

The Meghalaya (Benami Transactions Prohibition) Act, 1980 prohibits benami transactions and the right to recover property held benami for matters (movable or immovable or conducting any business, trade or any transaction by a non-tribal in the name or on behalf of a tribal). The Act states that on and from the commencement of this Act and notwithstanding anything to the contrary contained in any law in force or in any custom or usage benami transaction, in any form, between a tribal and a non-tribal is prohibited and shall be unlawful and void and every person involved in any such transaction shall be deemed to have committed an offence under this Act. However, no transaction in the name of a tribal, which is in favour of or for and on behalf of any tribal organization association or institution, shall be deemed to be benami. Furthermore, no transaction, which occurs between the members of the same family (within a tribe), shall be deemed to be benami (Government of Meghalaya 1980). There had been allegations that 'outsiders' (meaning the non- tribals and, to be precise, those not belonging to non-Khasi, Jaintia and Garo tribes) have been using various loopholes to set up business ventures in the name of local tribal populace. The groups like KSU and FKJGP have been repeatedly making requests to the state government to implement the Act to safeguard the interests of the indigenous people. It has been alleged that outsiders procure land in Meghalaya in the name of local tribal residents to evade the existing land ownership laws (*Telegraph* 2013).

However, loopholes that provide a space for the non-tribals to negotiate often leads to conflicts in the Khasi society. The riot of 1992 that ended with the death of 30 non-tribals and 1 tribal started in the month of August when activists of two student unions, that is, KSU and FKJGP, forced non-tribal traders to close down their shops in the pretext of not owning valid trading licence issued by the Khasi Hills Autonomous District Council (KHADC; Prakash 2008). One dimension of the conflict between the two categories of people with respect to trade is that although the 'non-tribals' are legally restricted to own and transfer land, 'financiers and managers' of trade are actually non-tribals and bulk of the profits goes to them (Nair 1986, 65).

Custom, Culture and Indigeneity: The Khasi as Juridico-political Category

The Khasi Hills Autonomous District (Khasi Social Custom of Lineage) Act, 1997, the act was established to secure the sanctity of Khasi identity that had been followed through customary laws. This

Act was meant to stop those with vested interest in acquiring the ST certificate. However, though this Act was meant to secure the interest of indigenous tribal community, in due process, it also raised questions on identity of the children whose father belonged to non-tribal community; for instance, during my fieldwork, I have encountered that Suzanne Roy Hek who married Joydeep Das, a science teacher in St. Anthony College, faced hurdles in acquiring an ST certificate for her son. It was reported that the Deputy Commissioner's office did not want to provide an ST certificate to a child with a non-tribal father unless he could write his name in Khasi language. This was undoubtedly a big issue for a 3-year-old child.

Although the Act appears to give a legal shield for the Khasi identity, in 2018, a second amendment of the Khasi Hills Autonomous District (Khasi Social Custom of Lineage) Bill was passed in KHADC which stated that children of women who marry non-Khasis will be deemed as non-Khasis. Prior to this, a new clan was created, without losing Khasi status, when a tribal lady gives birth to children with non-Khasi spouse. While introducing the Bill in 2018, KHADC chief executive member, Hispreaching Son Shylla stated, 'It has become necessary to further strengthen the Khasi Social Customs of Lineage by way of codification of Khasi customary laws for effective implementation of the KHAD (Khasi Social Custom of Lineage) Act, 1997 and hence this amendment Bill' (*Shillong Today* 2018).

Shylla stated that anyone who was found violating the provisions of the Bill would lose their Khasi status. The offspring of the Khasi women or Khasi men who violate the Khasi custom of marriage or Khasi custom of lineage shall not be a Khasi. He stated that on commencement of the Act, people who are taking the surname of their father's clan will be given 6 months' time to file an application before the Registration Authority to revert back or change to the matrilineal system of lineage. The Bill makes it mandatory for every Khasi to obtain a Khasi tribe certificate. According to Shylla, furthermore, every chief and headmen shall be the additional Registration Authority and Assistant Registration Authority respectively under the provision of the Act (*Shillong Today* 2018).

The amendment perhaps rose from the fear of losing status (and identity) if laws allow Khasi identity after women marrying non-Khasi man. The objective of the Khasi Hills Autonomous District (Khasi Social Custom of Lineage) Act, 1997 clearly shows such fear and anxiety. The Act states that a large number of people misuse the Khasi Social Lineage for their personal advantages and self-interest. This, under the Act, has disturbed the social and cultural life of the Khasi people. The Act, therefore, emerged as a law for strictly following the 'prevailing Khasi Social Custom of Lineage in order to keep and preserve the traditional matrilineal system of society of the Khasi' and 'for the protection of their interest and at the same time to prevent the claims of Khasi status by unscrupulous persons purely for the benefits, concessions, privilege conferred on the Khasi as a member of the Scheduled Tribe under the Constitution of India' (*The Gazette of Meghalaya* 2015).

At this moment, one should look at the two essential components in the making of identity: concern over misusing Khasi Social Lineage and the laws that seek to address such concern. Despite having established laws meant for protecting the identity of the Khasis, yet unprecedented concern caused by certain elements in the Khasi society creates the notion of insecurity. It can change according to the circumstance and the agent who articulates the concern. Perhaps this is the reason that even after such Act is passed by the state, there is still sense of insecurity on the part of the Khasi organization, particularly the KSU. (We will be dealing more on this organization in later part of the chapter.) The new amendment to derecognize the marriage of Khasi women to non-Khasi men reflects the new concern of losing land and identity. This aspect of customs and their continuous reinterpretation under new circumstances have a serious implication on law that seeks to address the concern. The notion of law as a neutral and a personal constitutional measure then could be a thing that can change whenever an organization in society shows new concern. This is where we would like to say that laws may attempt to address the concern, but they also, directly or indirectly, help in transforming (Khasi) tribe into (Khasi) ethnic identity. This transformation is further consolidated in the institutional structure wherein authority is given power that decides who is and who is not a Khasi.

The Khasi Hills Autonomous District (Village Administration) Bill, 2014 aims to codify, provide and make provision for the administration of villages in the autonomous district of Khasi Hills. It empowers Durbar Shnong to establish the Village Development Council to govern the socio-economic development as per the traditional tribal culture but within the governance structure of democratic India. The functions of Durbar Shnong include protection and conservation of all community lands, maintenance of the population register in the village where the name of each household and its residents is recorded and issuing statutory certificates such as residential certificates, birth and death certificates.

The Village Development Council plans to ensure participation of men, women and youth in welfare and socio-economic development of the village guided by 'Khasi tribal culture'. In addition, the Bill outlines the roles and responsibilities of the traditional chiefs such as Rangbah Shnong and Rangbah Dong, thereby establishing a clear line of accountability in traditional governance structure.

Since its inception, this bill has been marred by controversy. There had been a wide spread protest by the civil society organization over certain clauses of the bill that would delimit the power of the Durbar Shnong with the functioning of the Village Development Council. However, the main contention, as raised by Lambor Malngiang, a Congress MDC from Nongkrem in the winter session of the KHADC, was that the bill would allow other communities to interfere in the traditions and customs of the local tribal community through the membership of Village Development Council.

Further restriction was imposed in 2019 through the Meghalaya Residents Safety and Security Act (MRRSA) of 2016. Under the Act, non-residents including visitors, who stay in the state for more than 24 h are required to undergo registration.

'Children of the Soil': Khasi Students' Union and Federation of Khasi, Jaintia and Garo People

Several young organizations have been at the forefront of mobilization for various issues concerning the 'tribal' community in the state of Meghalaya. However, we shall have an in-depth look at KSU and FKJGP.

Khasi Students' Union

Khasi Students' Union, which is one of the premier organizations in the north-east of India is a group that has an indomitable presence not only in Meghalaya but also on other parts of the Northeast. At present, KSU is considered to be most the foremost civil society organ in Meghalaya with the power to influence government decisions.

Khasi Students' Union was formed on 20 March 1978 in Shillong as a unit of Meghalaya Students' Union (MSU; Freddy 2017, 53). Apparently, motivated by the All Assam Students' Union (AASU) Anti-Foreigner Agitation, KSU was initially started as an amalgamation of students of 12 colleges of Shillong affiliated with the Northeast Hill University at Shillong. This student union, a frontrunner in the 1979 riots[8] perpetrated against 'non-tribals', with the dissolution of MSU, adopted a constitution that clearly witnessed a change of motto from 'For the Welfare of the State and the Community'[9] to 'Mait Shaphrang Khlur Ka Ri' (Strive ahead Children of the Soil). The student union based in Khasi hills spread all over Khasi hills as well as Jaintia Hills. At present, the organization has 25,000 members.[10]

The constitution of KSU embraced on 18 December 1981 highlighted the goals of fostering unity and love among the students of Meghalaya. It also pointed out KSU's firmness to protect fundamental rights and freedom of each of the members of the state. Later on, in 1993, an amendment was made to the constitution that evidently reinforced ethnic preference by providing membership to those individuals only belonging to the Khasi community such as, the Khyriam, Pnar, Bhoi, War and Lyngngam (Freddy 2017). This amendment shifts the language of rights and freedom from 'of each of the members of the state' to 'individuals only belonging to Khasi community'. According to Article 2 of the amended constitution of the KSU (1993; Nongkhlaw 2009), KSU decided to work on the following matters encompassing education, infrastructure, unemployment, safeguarding the interests of the indigenous populace by enacting rules and regulations in business and trade, promotion of dialects and language, unity and peace among tribes, and checking of infiltration of foreigners.

From the above matters, we can see that the notion of indigenous and foreigners is used. The new amendment sought to 'protect and promote' the 'indigenous tribes' of Meghalaya and to stop infiltration of 'foreigners'. There is also a qualification of tribes with indigenous: indigenous tribes. However, what does indigenous mean is least explained except the emphasis of the Khasi tribes of Meghalaya.

Even though in its inception, KSU's main priority was to work for the welfare of student community in Meghalaya, it now shifted to only Khasis. According to Daniel Khyriem, former KSU president and UDP leader, the main objective of KSU was to look into the welfare of Khasi students within and outside the state. This was the reason why under the leadership of Paul Lyndoh (former KSU president), the constitution was amended to make education important for the well-being of the students (Khasis). In 2012, KSU had appealed to the then Education Minister R. C. Laloo for his intervention in controlling the exorbitant rate of school fees enforced by several schools in Meghalaya.

As a proactive union in addressing the concerns of the students in colleges and university, KSU massively protested against the appointment of Dr A. N. Rai, a non-tribal, as the Vice-Chancellor of North Eastern Hill University (NEHU). It was the continuous efforts of KSU that led Dr A. N. Rai to vacate the post of VC in 2013 before the end of his tenure.

Other than student activities, KSU has been vocal in admonishing the policies and works of the government and the local self-governing institutions such as autonomous district councils and the durbars. In 2015, the student union insisted the Khasi District Council to speed up its process of rectifying the controversial Village Administration Bill, 2011[11] for the smooth functioning of the traditional institutions. The district councils opposed the Bill, as they felt contrary to the provisions of the Sixth Schedule and to the prevailing traditional practices, customs and the usages of the tribal communities of the state. KSU has been also proactive in protesting against the uranium mining in uranium-rich Meghalaya by Uranium Corporation of India Limited (UCIL).

Though KSU has been involved in many activities concerning the upliftment of Khasi community, its main agenda revolves around protecting the 'indigenous' community, that is, the Khasi community, from the rising influx of 'non-tribals' in the state of Meghalaya. Since its inception of KSU in 1978, it has been alleged that with most of the government jobs and business in Meghalaya being occupied by the non-tribals, a sense of insecurity loomed large over the Khasi indigenous community. At this juncture, when a minor incident on the day of Durga Puja happened in 1979, KSU immediately led the ethnic violence perpetrated against the Bengalis.

Such politics of preference for the local tribes and violence in 1979[12] pave way for an anti-non-tribal policy of KSU under the lieu of removing the illegal migrants from Bangladesh from the state of Meghalaya. KSU had adopted various propagandas including occasional harassment to propel the non-tribals to move out of the state of Meghalaya. It is interesting to note that though KSU has advocated repeatedly that it is not against the genuine non-tribals of the state, yet there was no exemption in its violent attacks.[13] It has appealed to the government for the inclusion of 1951 as the cut-off year for citizenship of the non-tribals in the state. Following the 1992 riots,[14] KSU almost barred the non-tribal students from getting admission in colleges. Being an advocator for the rights of indigenous community, KSU propelled the government to instil tribal teachers in schools and colleges. Due to this, in 1995, Manas Chaudhuri, the then Education Minister took back his order of appointing two non-tribal faculties for St. Anthony's College. The 1990s era had been the most terrorizing for non-tribals to venture out of their homes due to the unleashed terror of KSU. Even Khasi girls were not free from the diktats of KSU. It was during this period that KSU prohibited girls from wearing salwar kameez, and those who dared to wear them were physically attacked and their clothes torn. KSU also opposed the 1997 Khasi Social Custom of Lineage Bill.[15] It was KSU which was frontal in its opposition against the development of railways in Meghalaya. The student union was fearful that railways would bring in more influx in the state of Meghalaya.

In 2000, KSU launched a movement, which is not a public agitation but an instrument to rejuvenate and awaken the Khasi people to strive ahead with hope and expectation of a brighter future. KSU placed some major demands of this movement before the government. They were:

1. To immediately control influx of people from elsewhere by implementing the Inner Line Regulation System, the Work Permit and the acceptance of 1951 as the cut-off year to remove the names of foreigners.
2. To generate 10,000 jobs in different departments for the unemployed.
3. To reserve employment opportunities in the ratio of 60:40 for the Khasi–Jaintias and Garos.
4. To amend the Land Transfer Act in order to prevent the tribals from other states to acquire lands in Meghalaya and to abolish power of attorney to acquire land.

According to Paul Lyndoh, the then KSU president, the Charter included the 'introduction of Inner Line Permits, Work Permits for non-indigenous labourers and fixation of 1951 as official cut-off year for determination of citizenship status' (*Times of India* 2001). Due to this agitation, the state of Meghalaya was virtually cut off from the rest of the country.

Harassment of non-tribals continued, especially the labourer class. On 20 November 2012, in the name of conducting checking on influx in Mawiong (*Shillong Times* 2012), using a local taxi the members of the union kidnapped and brutally beat up three construction workers from Assam after they failed to produce documents. Among these three workers, Prasanta Dehka died on the spot and Dekanta Bania was seriously injured and admitted to Nongpoh hospital, while third labourer Anand Hajong from Balat was still untraceable.

KSU's anti-non-tribal movement received a new lease of life with the demand for Inner Line Permit (ILP) system in Meghalaya on 2 September 2013. The ILP agitation that garnered the support of almost all the civil society organizations again witnessed KSU-triggered major attacks perpetrated on the non-tribal populace. Along with the Meghalaya Machineries owner Vikash Nandwal, 45-year-old

Bisheshwar Das died during the ILP agitation. Both were allegedly burnt alive by the protestors. The anti-non-tribal policy of KSU still continues to thrive post ILP agitation. Occasional harassment and beatings of non-tribals are at times left unheard. KSU's anti-non-tribal propaganda can be best understood through the words of former KSU president who quoted as follows: 'We remember that it was in 1992 that "outsiders" harassed our people living in Nongmynsong, which was then known as Lal Chand Basti. Our people had to take refuge at Mawlai, Polo and other parts... it was our courage that we could assert ownership of this place, which is a victory for the organization as well as for the entire people' (*Shillong Times* 2017).

Federation of Khasi, Jaintia and Garo People

Another pioneer organization of Meghalaya after KSU, FKJGP was the first successful attempt to unite the so-called indigenous tribes of Meghalaya under one umbrella: Khasi, Garo and Jaintia. This organization, which is scattered in three hills, that is, Khasi, Garo and Jaintia Hills, is considered a prominent civil society organization in Meghalaya.

Structure of Federation

FKJGP was formed on 3 November 1989 at a gathering held at the Khasi National Durbar Hall, Mawkhar. Under the leadership of Sounder Strong Cajee and A. L. Heq,[16] three tribes—Khasi, Garo and Jaintia—formed this federation. Prior to this organization, an effort was made in the mid-1980s by students of Meghalaya to come under the All Meghalaya Students' Union (AMSU), but AMSU could not sustain longer. Unlike the other student organizations, FKJGP usually has members above 18 years of age from different educational background and status. Its main motto, as quoted by Joe Marwin, FKJGP president, is, 'No retreat; no surrender'. Its main objective is to motivate the three tribes to come together for social, economic and political welfare of the tribal society. Activists of FKJGP led by its leader, Sounder S. Cajee toured the length and breadth of the state including Garo Hills to educate the people about the objective of the federation. In the process, people came forward to associate themselves with FKJGP (*Eastern Panorama* 2015). At present, influx is the primary concern of this organization. Although it is not a registered society with a constitution of its own, the organization continues to thrive even with the changing times.

FKJGP has a proper organizational set-up despite lacking a constitution of its own. As three-tier organization comprising the Central Executive Committee (CEC), the General Executive Council (GEC) and the District Executive Committee (DEC) and a number of circles in different districts of the State, FKJGP continues to function with amended by-laws at regular intervals.

CEC of FKJGP is the policy-making body of the organization that comprises of all elected office-bearers. It is presided over by the president who along with elected office-bearers has full authority over the decision-making functions of the organization in all matters except on those that require the general approval of GEC. Another powerful body is GEC, comprising of all the office-bearers of all the circles and units of the organization, which usually deals with general issues including those which the CEC alone cannot decide. This body also looks into the matters related to election of the president and CEC members. The other body, that is, DEC, comprising of office-bearers of the organization in a particular district of the state, functions independently except on issues that need guidance and authorization of CEC (Nongkhlaw 2009). Last but not the least are the circles prevalent in the West Khasi Hills, the East Khasi Hills, the Ri-Bhoi district and the Garo Hills and the Jaintia Hills.

On Development Works

FKJGP has initiated programmes that aim for the development of agriculture in the state; for instance, as part of FKJGP's 25 years of celebration of the Mawryngkneng circle on 19 April 2017, the FKJGP Saisiej Unit held a training programme for farmers. The training programme was organized along with the partnership from the District Agriculture Training Office, Department of Agriculture, Upper Shillong with an aim to uplift farming activities in the region (*The Sentinel* 2017).

The federation has also been frontal in handling educational matters in the state such as re-evaluation of marks obtained in exam at NEHU (2004), demand of giving first preference to local (indigenous) students of the state based on merit in college admission, the lack of teaching and guidance, and administration and upgradation in the Shillong Polytechnic institute. FKJGP has been vocal in its protest against the corruptions in governance system. In 2014, along with the other civil society organizations, the organization demanded the resignation of state urban affairs minister Ampareen Lyngdoh for her alleged involvement in the manipulation of marks during the recruitments for assistant lower primary school teachers in 2010 (Oh Meghalaya 2014).

On 'Non-tribal'

Since its inception as an organization in 1989, FKJGP has been against especially non-tribal businessmen. According to the organization, most of the non-tribal traders did not possess valid non-tribal trading licence from the district council. This was seen as a complete violation of Non-tribal Trading Regulation Act 1954 of the district council. With this issue, FKJGP raked up tensions in the state in 1990, especially in the wake of growing participation of the local (indigenous) people in business and trading activities (Nongkhlaw 2009).

Along with KSU, FKJGP has been vocal in its advocacy against the appointment of non-tribals in important government posts in Meghalaya. In 2016, the organization opposed the inclusion of Abu Taher Mandal as the Meghalaya speaker (*Meghalaya Times* 2016). According to FKJGP, as Meghalaya is essentially a tribal state, the speaker post should be held by an indigenous member of the state only. In this way, they felt, the speaker would be able to respect the local tribal sentiments.

The 2013 ILP movement witnessed a massive unity of civil society organizations. FKJGP was primarily involved in the movement that witnessed the killing of the two non-tribals. FKJGP has been one of the pressure groups in the state demanding implementation of the comprehensive mechanism to check influx and illegal immigration into the state. It was under continuous pressure from the groups like FKJGP that government worked on the entry- and exit-level checkpoints. However, despite garnering massive support in the ILP agitation, fearful of the growing influx of illegal migrants (non-tribal people) in the state, FKJGP has launched a socio-economic movement that would empower the tribals in checking influx in the state.

The student organizations, as mentioned earlier, always have articulated their anti-non-tribal sentiment in lieu of ousting illegal migrants. The Inner Line Permit Agitation that arose in the year 2012 can be seen as one such articulation of the student bodies supported by certain sections of civil societies in Shillong. The aggressive stance of the student bodies during the agitation was extensively reflected when a Marwari businessman, Meghalaya Machineries shop owner in Barabazar and later on a Bihari Tea stall owner in Bishnupur Bazar, Bisheshwar Das, were allegedly burnt alive in their respective workstations. The gruesomeness of these two arson led to widespread protest by the Khasi population in general and yielded to the arrest of four KSU members on charges of murder. However, despite this, due to lack of evidence provided by the state government, these KSU members were acquitted.

Everyday Experience of the 'Non-tribes'

A Khasi trader does not face any hurdle in availing a trading licence from the KHADC, whereas a non-tribal trader has to avail a trading license under the law of the United Khasi-Jaintia Hills District (Trading by Non-Tribals) Regulation, 1954. However, availing this license becomes a tedious task as a No Objection Certificate (NOC) needs to be availed initially from local the traditional institution, that is, the durbars. The durbars which is basically tribal-centric does not easily provide an NOC to non-tribals; for instance, M. A. Sultan, a Muslim Bihari contractor was yet to get a work permit despite having working in Shillong for 32 years. According to him, the KHADC officials demanded ₹0.5 million for issuing a work permit, but, as he could not pay, he had to often face harassment from the officials, propelling him to escape from work at times. Moreover, the Dorbar in Naspati Ghadi where he resides demanded ₹15,000 for issuing an NOC. However, as he could not give the money, no NOC was issued and, thus, he could not seek the permit from the KHADC via a proper channel. It was also informed that M. A. Sultan was not aware of the state government body issuing contract work permit, as he saw overlapping powers of the institutions.

However, despite the adversaries faced by the non-tribals like the above case of M. A. Sultan with respect to the governing institutions, a continuous negotiation is seen between the two broad categories of people. It has been reflected through the interactions with the non-tribals that in order to avail certain licences or NOCs, the non-tribals yield to paying token money to the government officials. Individual non-tribal labourers have to avail a labour licence from the district council to work in different parts of Meghalaya. In Shillong, the licence is provided by East Khasi Hills District Council at a nominal fee of ₹250. However, labour licence is usually not available easily to the non-tribal labour class. It has been alleged that the government authorities generally do not issue labour licence to the non-tribals without extra money.

Kumari Chettri's case may be cited here. Kumari Chettri's husband, a betelnut porter in Barabazar, acquired labour licence only after paying ₹2,000 to the authorities. Similar thoughts were echoed by Kumari Sunar whose husband, a daily wage labourer, had to pay ₹1,500 extra to avail labour licence. Similarly, Shyam Kumar Verma, a Bihari who has a stationary shop in Barabazar initially faced hurdles in acquiring trading licence from KHADC. It was only after he paid an extra a bribery amount of ₹20,000 to the district officials that he could acquire a trading licence for his shop in the year 1990. According to Shyam, presently, the amount of acquiring trading licence through bribe has almost risen to 0.2 million. In 2019, KHADC passed the Khasi Hills Autonomous District (Trading by Non-Tribals) Rules that amended the trading licence fee bringing a major blow to the low-income group of non-tribals who could not afford to pay the money. This often results in harassment by the government officials. Undoubtedly, this also reflects the class dimension in Khasi governance system and non-tribal relationship.

Moreover, it is not an easy task for a non-tribal to acquire permission from durbars or district council without the power of connections or the money. The case of Raju Limbu, a contractor in Shillong is noteworthy in this matter. Since he maintained a good relationship with both the civil society like KSU and government functionaries like KHADC, acquiring a labour licence for workers was a smooth work. Similarly, Mistu Deb, a garment shop owner in Barabazar, acquired trading license through his good connection with Khasi trading officer for a considerable amount of ₹5,000. Along with this, every year, to avail NOCs for the shop, he has to pay ₹750 to Hima Mylliem of Barabazar. Dr Sishir Kumar Sahoo who runs the oldest optical store in the heart of Police Bazar in Shillong also echoed the same views. These Bengali businessmen not only negotiate through money in dealing with the governing bodies, but are also required to pay goonda taxes to the pressure groups, especially KSU on a monthly basis. It is a known fact in Barabazar that non-tribal shop owners would have to pay a considerable amount in the form of taxes every month to pressure groups and are supported by the traditional durbars as well as East KHADC; for instance, Shyam Kumar Verma does not only pay tax to KHADC, but he is also required to pay *Khajana* (token money) to Raja Mylliem yearly along with the entry tax for each carton (per carton ₹10). Despite this, he has to pay yearly ₹2,000 to KSU and FKJGP separately in the name of social welfare. In addition to this he is required to pay the groups whenever they demand money. Undoubtedly, this nexus of student bodies and government machineries highlights the anti-non-tribal sentiments at a large scale.

However, there are instances also where even after paying daily or monthly *Khajana* to Syiem, KSU members occasionally harass the non-tribal traders. Like, Monica Thapa, a street rice shop vendor, pays a *Khajana* of ₹20 per day to the Syiem of Barabazar for her street shop. However, in 2014, a grave situation arose when KSU members tried to take over half of the shop space of non-tribal vendors including hers forcefully in Barabazar area. Santu, a Nepali Christian street garment shop vendor, also faced a similar wrath of KSU harassment. The issue was resolved only after cantonment authorities negotiated the matter.

Unlike tribal organizations like the pressure groups, the non-tribals in Shillong do not have much strong organizational presence in Meghalaya. The dominant power lobby of 'tribal' pressure groups has somewhat stopped the potential growth of non-tribal associations. Moreover, the presence of relevant community organizations is seen to be restricted to economically affluent community members, depriving the lower economical strata. In the case of Nepali community, organizations such as All India Bharatiya Gorkha Parishad, Gorkha Public Panchayat and All Shillong Mahila Samiti were formed for the upliftment of the community. Like Nepali Ekta Samaj, these organizations have been active in providing free courses to the needy students and providing employment also if possible. However, during the 1987 riots, the Gorkha Parishad effectively dealt with KSU through interaction and coordination for the rehabilitation of the displaced Nepali population.[17]

Apart from this, the Central Puja Committee, Ramkrishna Mission, along with non-tribal working entities like Sahayog Multipurpose Co-operative Society, Barabazar Non-Tribal Association, continues to enjoy ample space in the non-tribal society. However, the limitations of the community organization in dealing with pressure groups have restricted the non-tribal populace from exerting their influence in the society. Even in day-to-day issues, non-tribals rather prefer to maintain good relations with tribal politicians rather than approaching the community organizations while dealing with pressure groups. Like for instance, a shop owner like H. Gautam prefers to maintain friendly relations with Paul Lyndoh who, once as KSU president articulated hatred speeches against the non-tribals, was now contesting elections. This to and fro relation brings out the negotiated process that balances relation between both the communities.

To conclude, we would like to state few facts. Tribe is a political unit emerged as result of legislative practices that attempt to give a preferential treatment to the so-called indigenous peoples of Meghalaya. However, over the course of times, tribe has also registered as a political category that needs to be constantly guarded as territorially and culturally specific set of people. This occurs continuously with an invention of another category of population:

'non-tribal'. Under the influence of organizations like KSU and FKJGP, the non-Khasi, Garo and Jaintia people are articulated as 'illegal' immigrants. Constitutional safeguards is said in regard to the existing laws which are unable to address the Khasi insecurity, leading to ILP agitation to check what it being as the outsiders, illegal influx of immigrants. In the process, what is observed of the state is that of entity that has been largely subsumed into the politics of ethnicized civil society groups. Yet, the experiences of people who are excluded as 'non-tribes' also convey interesting everyday negotiating narratives. Both at the individual and roughly organizational capacities, the non-tribes negotiate to live as the others.

Notes

1. The 1961 census of India estimated that approximately 750,000 East Pakistanis had migrated into Assam between 1951 and 1961.
2. A. K. Baruah emphasized on this term while speaking about violent ethnic riots in Meghalaya during an interaction with the interviewer on 12 July 2015 in Shillong.
3. According to Erikson, 'identity formation employs a process of simultaneous reflection and observation, taking place on all levels of mental functioning, by which the individual judges himself in light of what he perceives to be the way in which others judge him in comparison to themselves and to a typology significant to them; while he judges their way of judging him in light of how he perceives himself in comparison to them and to types that have become relevant to him' (Erickson 1959).
4. As seen in the case of Meghalaya, the partially excluded area policy paved way for two types of governance. While the Garo and Jaintia directly came under the purview of British administration, the Khasi were allowed to be governed under the traditional governance system.
5. The Sixth Schedule under the Constitution of India entitles special benefits for the protection and upliftment of the ethnically distinct tribal society of the North East. This law was a step towards the empowerment of the tribals in the region.
6. The colonial administration had identified the three districts, that is, Garo and Khasi-Jaintia Hills, as 'Partially Excluded Areas'.
7. According to the Ministry of Tribal Affairs, the Government of India, the term 'Scheduled Tribes' first appeared in the Constitution of India. See details in, tribal.nic.in/Content/DefinitionpRrofiles.aspx.
8. A minor incident on the day of Durga Puja occurred in 1979, in which, allegedly, KSU led the violence against the Bengalis in Shillong.

9. Conversation with Hamlet Dohling, Former KSU General Secretary, dated 6 February 2012.
10. Conversation with Daniel Khyriem, Former KSU President, dated 7 July 2015.
11. The Village Administration Bill was first introduced in the state when the Ministry of Panchayati Raj, Government of India sent the draft Meghalaya Village Council Act 2011 to the state government with a request for its approval and implementation. Based on lines closer to the Panchayati Raj system, this bill aimed at strengthening the democratic process in the state.
12. The first ethnic riot occurred in Meghalaya between the Khasis and the Bengalis in 1979.
13. Conversation with Daniel Khyriem, Former KSU President, dated 7 July 2015.
14. The Bihari and the Marwari residents were the targets of attack by the Khasis in 1992 ethnic riot.
15. In 1997, KSU opposed the Khasi Social Custom of Lineage Bill passed by the Khasi Hill Autonomous District Council (KHADC) that sought to codify the inheritance system through the female line, stating the matrilineal succession outdated (Baruah 2005).
16. Conversation with Joe Marwin, President of FKJGP, 6 July 2015.
17. B. B. Chettri, retired government employee, is one of the members of All India Bharatiya Gorkha Parishad.

References

Baruah, S. 2003. 'Citizens and Denizens Ethnicity, Homelands, and the Crisis of Displacement in Northeast India.' *Journal of Refugee Studies* 16, no. 1: 44–66.
———. 2005. *Durable Disorder*. Delhi: Oxford University Press.
Eastern Panorama. 2015, March. 'Federation of Khasi-Jaintia and Garo People (FKJGP)'s.' Available at http://www.easternpanorama.in/index.php/other-articles/3122-federation-of-khasi-jaintia-and-garo-people-fkjgp-s (accessed 22 March 2021).
Erickson, E. H. 1959. *Identity and the Life Cycle: Selected Papers*. New York, NY: International University Press.
Ford, R. T. 2005. 'Political Identity as Identity Politics.' *Unbound* 1, no. 53: 53–57.
Freddy, H. J. 2017. *Conflict and Youth Rights in India: Engagement and Identity in the North East*. Singapore: Palgrave McMillan.
Government of Meghalaya. 1980. 'Collection of Meghalaya Acts and Ordinances 1980'. Law Department. Available at http://meglaw.gov.in/Acts/1980 (accessed 23 June 2018).
Hall, S. 1990. 'Cultural Identity and Diaspora.' In *Identity*, edited by J. Rutherford. London: Lawrence and Wishart.
McDuie-Ra, D. 2009. *Civil Society, Democratization and the Search for Human Security: The Politics of the Environment, Gender and Identity in Northeast India*. New Delhi: Nova Science Publishers.

Meetei, N. B. 2014. 'Ethnicity, Colonial Legacy, and Post-Independence Issues of Identity Politics in North-East India.' *Nationalism and Ethnic Politics* 20: 99–115.

Meghalaya Times. 2016, 9 March. 'FKJGP Opposes Mondal as Meghalaya Speaker.' Available at Meghalayatimes.info/index.php/.../18489-fkjgp-opposes-mondal-as-meghalaya-speaker

Nair, M. K. 1986. 'Constraints on the Development of a Land Market in Meghalaya.' *Economic & Political Weekly* 21, no. 30: 65.

Nongkhlaw, Sita. 2009. 'Politics of Pressure Groups in Meghalaya with Special Reference to Student and Youth Organizations' (PhD thesis). North-Eastern Hill University. Available at http://hdl.handle.net/10603/60434 (accessed 22 March 2021).

Oh Meghalaya. 2014, 12 November. 'Ngos threaten to file FIR against CM, demands Ampareen Lyngdoh's resignation'. Oh Meghalaya. Available at http://www.ohmeghalaya.com/ngos-threaten-to-file-fir-against-cm-demands-ampareen-lyngdohs-resignation/ (accessed 22 March 2021).

Prakash, V. 2008. *Terrorism in India's North-East: A Gathering Storm.* New Delhi: Kalpaz Publications.

Shillong Times. 2012, 22 November. 'Two KSU Members, Driver Arrested for Murder and Assault on Labourers.' Available at www.ohmeghalaya.com/two-ksu-members-driver-arrested-for-murder-and-assault-on-labourers/ (accessed 22 March 2021).

———. 2017, 5 April. 'KSU war cry against UCIL, AMD'. *Shillong Times.* Available at http://www.theshillongtimes.com/2017/04/05/ksu-war-cry-against-ucil-amd/ (accessed 22 March 2021).

Shillong Today. 2018, 25 October. 'KHADC introduces Khasi Social Custom of Lineage (Amendment) Bill.' *Shillong Today.*

Tajfel, Henri. 1979. *Social Identity and Intergroup Relations.* Cambridge: Cambridge University Press.

Tajfel, H. 1981. *Human Groups and Social Categories: Studies in Social Psychology.* New York, NY: Cambridge University Press.

Telegraph. 2013, 9 April. 'No Takers for 33-year-old Act.' Available at https://www.telegraphindia.com/1130419/jsp/northeast/story_16801949.jsp (accessed 12 June 2018).

The Sentinel. 2017, 26 April. 'FKJGP's 25 Years of Celebration: Training Programme Held.' Available at https://www.sentinelassam.com/news/fkjgps-25-years-of-celebration-training-programme-held/

Times of India. 2001, 16 August. 'Khasi Leader Warns Against Repressive Measures.' Available at https://timesofindia.indiatimes.com/india/Khasi-leader-warns-against-repressive-measures/articleshow/1428520373.cms (accessed 22 March 2021).

Xaxa, V. 2005, 26 March 26. 'Politics of Language: Religion and Identity: Tribes in India.' *Economic and Political Weekly* 40, no. 13: 1363–1370.

CHAPTER 6

Interrogating the 'Civil Society' in Naga Society

Rashi Bhargava

Empirical studies on civil society are far less in number than theoretical engagements with the concept. This is not surprising, since scholars across the globe have found very little conceptual consensus in its understanding. This can be attributed to the incomplete history of the concept with long disappearances in between and sudden resurgences. Notwithstanding these changes and complementary and conflicting tendencies within it, contemporary understanding of the concept of civil society can be seen as closely tied to that of the 'political' (usually understood as the state), making it more as a sphere of the people and their response to the state and its various institutions. However, such an interrelationship predominantly assumes the existence of the modern state which itself is an historical outcome.

This raises few pertinent questions: Is the concept of civil society, when seen as closely tied to the concept of state, a result of modernity alone, thereby making it a prerogative of modern society? Can it be conceptualized differently when interrogated with reference to different temporal and spatial settings? Numerous historical evidences suggest that one cannot apply the concept of civil society or deploy its language without examining its veracity in a given historical situation. Consequently, there is a need for different theorizations, especially in the context of what is often referred to as the 'Third World' or, more recently, the 'Global South'; for instance, engagement with the concept in India has its own specific history, with scholars highlighting the inadequacy of Western connotations of the same, often arguing that societies showcasing strong ascriptive affiliations need a different theorization of the concept. As the Indian situation has demonstrated, civil society is, thus, not only tied to the 'political' but also to that of the sociocultural sphere. As I argue in this chapter, this sphere can be captured by reconceptualizing the concept of 'civility'.

In such a scenario, questions that we must ask need alteration. Does the concept of civil society allow us to reformulate the relationship between state and society and also explore the changing nature of relationships within the society under study? More so, when the society in question has long been ridden with conflict and violence perpetuated both by state and non-state forces, thereby debunking the dichotomous relationship between society and state, how does one envision the role of culture, history and politics within this (democratic) state–(rebel) society relationship?

Historical Trajectory of Civil Society

Till early 18th century (i.e., classical period, Middle Ages and the Age of Reason), the idea of civil society was based on that of the Greek *Polis* (ancient Greek city-state), followed by medieval town system *burg*. Later articulations posit it as distinct from the state of nature or from the sphere of ecclesiastical matters and, finally, as an establishment of the state based on a legal framework with the 'modern citizen' at its core. Late 18th- and early 19th-century Western intellectual roots of the concept of civil society have been widely discussed[1], highlighting the contribution of political philosophers like John Locke, Thomas Hobbes and Jean-Jacques Rousseau to Scottish Enlightenment thinker Adam Fergusson and to American social and political thinker Alexis De Tocqueville. Each of them saw civil society synonymous to a state of civility either through law, market or democratic organizations and opposed to an already existing sphere of nature. Nineteenth century, which was characterized by the consolidation of capitalism as an economic system and emergence of liberal democratic state, saw civil society as one element in a binary of state–civil society, individual (selfish) interests–collective good, economic life–social life, *gemeinschaft* (community) and *gesellschaft* (civil society). This was most significant in German social and political thought, with G. W. F. Hegel, Karl Marx and Ferdinand Tonnies contributing to the debate and initiating a distinction between (political) state, (economic) market, (social and cultural) family and civil spheres.

By late 19th and early 20th centuries, a sharp distinction between the civil and political spheres was introduced. The 20th century is characterized by collapse of communism and subsequent turbulence in Eastern Europe and emergence of new nationalisms in European countries. Consequently, formulations through the 20th and early 21st century saw quite a few additions to the repertoire of characteristics identified to articulate the concept. This included, civil society as a space for pursuing selfish goals by an individual, as a space to produce discursive reality through communication (Jurgen Habermas) and hegemony (Antonio Gramsci), as a space for mobilization and political participation (theorizations in Global South), as a space for creating social capital (Michael Walzer and Robert Putnam), as the third sector (interest groups, pressure groups, voluntary associations and non-governmental organizations (NGOs) and as a space for performance of power and culture (Jeffrey Alexander).

During the 1980s and 1990s, discomfort with repressive states and unsatisfactory governance led to dissident politics and mobilizations by 'citizens' across different spatial settings to reclaim their space and rights from an ever-interfering and all-encompassing state; for instance, one can look at the Solidarity movement in Poland, the students' movement for civil rights in China and opposition to repressive regimes by intellectuals in Central Asia. Often these mobilizations were understood as located within civil society sphere (see Jayaram 2005) and were articulated in the language of civil society (see Elliott 2003). These political developments across the globe brought into picture, a people-centric and organizational approach in the definition of civil society. Individual rights, egalitarianism and democratic values were foregrounded as the basic foundation of a good society and a healthy democracy redefining 'civility'. As an implication, the concept of civil society was revived even in places where the state may not be as repressive as in the cases mentioned above, making scholars categorize it as an 'overdetermined'[2] concept or as a 'rebound or recovery concept'[3]. Despite scepticism, scholars across disciplinary boundaries and political ideologies have found some merit in the concept leading to numerous theorizations mostly with regard to its (dialectical) relationship with the sphere of politics.

As regards India, most scholars[4] have questioned the adequacy and applicability of the concept in the Indian context, largely looking at it in terms of inhabitants of that sphere instead of focusing only on its role. It is often argued that unlike the European and American contexts where emergence of civil society was facilitated by certain historical processes, beginning from the enlightenment period, advent of private property, consolidation of capitalism and establishment of the liberal states, impetus was provided by historical processes like colonialism and nationalism[5]. These not only created the necessary conditions for mobilization and political participation through associations and organizations, but they also provided the discursive frame and vocabulary for articulating the changes that ensued from the simultaneous processes of colonialism, capitalism and nationalism. It is a space occupied by a small section of the population, thus limiting its scope (the activities of mass participation were categorized as social movements[6]). It may not necessarily be a voluntary sphere and is often constitutive of groups (not individuals) based on ascriptive identities[7]. One of the most prominent intervention was made by Partha Chatterjee (2004) when he introduced the conceptual difference between civil and political society, largely formulated from the point of view of the extent and nature of people's participation in these structures. He defines civil society as that space which is largely occupied by the elites,[8] while political society is looked at as a sphere of the masses or what he calls the 'governed' outlining the 'politics of the governed'. Thus, unlike in the Global North where there were predetermined concepts of 'politics' (defined more in terms of territory [nation state] and scope [institutional]) and 'civility' (often understood in terms of individual entities, i.e., the citizens), theorizations in the Global South had to constantly engage with the changing contours of politics and civility while defining civil society.

Although these above conceptualizations re-establish that finding a consistent definition of 'civil society' is a difficult task, they also point out that 'civil society' needs to be viewed in relation to two concepts of 'political' and 'civil' which are effervescent and, hence, need careful investigation. In the context of the present chapter, I will, thus, attempt to not only look at how civility is perceived but also how people (re-) formulate its relationship to political. Does politics have a role to play in defining this civility or are the two spheres distinct, as it has been usually understood, in most definitions of the civil society? This chapter seeks to address these questions within the context of what is referred to as Nagaland[9] where the (Indian) state–(Naga) society relations have been in conflict over the demand for sovereignty for a long time.

Setting the Context: Civil Societ(ies) in Nagaland

The inclusion of the Naga-inhabited areas within the British administrative territory was gradually achieved between the years 1875 and 1889, although the process began soon after the Treaty of *Yandaboo* in the year 1826.[10] The consolidation of the colonial power in the Naga Hills accompanied by the process of evangelical Christianity gave rise to new social processes. The process which began in the 19th century gained momentum by the second decade of 20th century. It can be argued that gradual exposure to world events, especially the First World War and local histories through various media, particularly through missionary education, service in the labour corps, print media and colonial policies and decisions (especially the Reform Scheme of 1918) left an indelible mark on the Naga social and political history. One such event is the creation of Naga Club in 1918, which is best known for a memorandum submitted to Simon Commission in 1929 outlining 2 courses of action by 20 undersigned Nagas. The first was to remain in direct control of the British (since they were the ones who occupied the Naga 'country' not the Assamese or the Manipuris) and the second, 'not be thrust to the mercy of the people who could never subjugate us, but to leave us alone to determine for ourselves as in the ancient times' (Naga Club Memo to Simon Commission 1929). The Naga Club is, thus, the first formal space where members from different tribes irrespective of their differences joined in to voice out their discomfort with existing state of affairs. It, then, does not come as a surprise that many of the present civil society organizations (CSO) in Nagaland consider Naga Club as the first CSO in the region that stood up against the colonial government and expressed their concerns. A member of Naga Hoho during my field days in Nagaland in 2012–2013 averred that Naga Club was considered the first civil society of the Nagas since it had represented the needs and concerns of the Naga people from a common platform, a thought that was reverberated in other in-depth interviews with some of the members of Naga Peoples Movement for Human Rights (NPMHR).

Noteworthy is that during my study, only one of the respondents recounted the role of Naga Hills District Tribal Council (NHTDC)[11] in creating another platform for articulation of people's concerns. This is astounding since it was NHTDC that gave way to Naga National Council (NNC) comprising 29 members from different Naga tribes. It became the first organization to appoint office-bearers elected from members from various tribal councils. These tribal councils consisted of members from village councils (VCs), thereby making NNC, a supra-tribal entity with a tiered system.[12] The membership of NNC grew by the 1950s when tribal councils from the Tuensang Area[13] and other areas from Manipur joined in. However, neither the British nor the Indian nationalists accepted the authority of NNC on the pretext that it was a self-constituted body comprising a very small section of the missionary school-educated middle class, hence was not representative of the entire Naga population (Baruah 2005). They further claimed that demand for political autonomy is a product of the whims and fancies of a few Nagas only and not the entire Naga population. Despite strong disagreement and stronger attempts to restore their status to that of the 'ancient times' (Naga Club Memo to Simon Commission 1929), Naga-inhabited areas were included within the newly formed Indian (Union) State. This was achieved through signing of the Nine Point agreement—a move that led to the beginning of one of the longest armed conflicts between the Indian state and its (Naga) people. The ambiguity of the last clause in the agreement has been 'the' bone of contention in the relationship between the Indian state and the Naga society. The ideas of 'nation', 'nationalism' and 'sovereignty', which were highly coveted not only in the subcontinent but also across the world, could be seen reverberating in the region and 'the idea of Nagas as a single community of fate became real' (Baruah 2005, 109). This can be identified as an important moment for a society under colonial rule where emphasis came to be levied on a particular kind of state (not colonial) and society (not colonized) where the two were territorially congruent, reminiscent of the European epistemic framework that emerged in the aftermath of the Treaty of Westphalia in 1648. However, like many other parts of the subcontinent that desired to restore their past status, Nagas too saw the British withdrawal as an opportunity to establish their sovereign state, which could not be realized leading to an armed conflict in the region. In the document titled the 'Bedrock of Naga society' published in 2000, it is stated that beginning from the early 1950s, the Naga 'nationalism' gained momentum and was accelerated with the election of A. Z. Phizo as president of the NNC on 11 December 1950. Under Phizo's leadership, the Nagas conducted a plebiscite on 16 May 1951 in which it is claimed 99.9 per cent of the Nagas voted for independence. This plebiscite emotionally integrated various Naga tribes and boosted the morale of the movement. The crackdown of NNC since 1953 and deployment of Armed Forces since 1955[14] is a direct consequence of Indian state's (mis) perception of the root causes of Naga nationalism. It resulted in a standoff between Indian state and Naga nationalist forces claiming many lives and leading to severe loss of property.

Most studies[15] on Northeast India in general and Nagaland in particular have argued that emergence of an organized (civil) sphere is closely linked to growing violence in the region. In the early period of 20th century and more so after India's independence, the region had been gripped in an armed conflict with the state leading to a 'war paradigm' (Oinam 2008). Noteworthy among them are Naga People's Convention[16] and Naga Peace Mission (NPM)[17], but with every negotiation reached between the Indian state and the Naga faction, a subsequent rift within the Naga faction was seen. The fragmentation of the Naga Nationalist sphere into various factions (starting from NNC to People's Independence League to Federal Government of

Nagaland (FGN), to National Socialist Council of Nagaland (NSCN), to Nationalist Socialist Council of *Nagalim* (Isaac-Muivah) NSCN (IM) and NSCN (K) to Nationalist Socialist Council of *Nagalim* (Unification) NSCN (U), to Government of the People's Republic of Nagaland/*Nagalim* (GPRN)/NSCN to name a few) has had serious repercussions not just on the negotiation process between the Indian state and the Nagas but also on the internal dynamics of the Naga Society within the state of Nagaland and the neighbouring areas. Rajagopalan (2008) has argued that the negotiations are inherently problematic since peace negotiations which are founded on compromises and concessions often alienate the excluded group not only from the process but also from those involved in the process. Since each faction claimed to be 'the' representative of the Naga people, continuous attempts were made to put the other one out of the race leading to frequent inter-factional clashes between them. Consequently, the 'internecine rivalry is almost as intense as the conflict with the Indian state' (Rajagopalan 2008, 17). Thus, a number of 'people's initiatives' (informal networks) emerged which addressed the growing concerns of common Naga people. As the situation intensified with conflicts between numerous communities both within a state and those spread over different geopolitical entities (e.g., one can look at the conflict in 2007 between federal states of Nagaland and Manipur), these informal networks not only became more organized, but they also started to expand considerably, sometimes including the already existing structures within its fold. They engaged in the peace and reconciliation process between two or more of the following entities—Indian state, federal state of Nagaland, non-state actors and its numerous factions. One can infer that these organizations and forums were envisioned with the aim to reclaim their space and voice the demands of 'common people'. They came to be referred to as civil society organizations and were theorized[18] as an 'intermediary sphere' with the 'potential for change' attempting to bring about peace and reconciliation in a society wrought with institutionalized political violence.[19] Interestingly, it also the time that one can locate the usage of the new term 'non-state' actors. Kothari had argued that when those wielding power go overboard with their power, there might be countervailing forces that challenge the 'existing paradigms of thought and action' (1986, 210). In view of the above situation, one can locate a new relationship triad—state, non-state and people—each influencing and influenced by the other in myriad ways.

In the geopolitical state of Nagaland, use of the term 'civil society' is not restricted to academic writings; rather, the term 'civil societ(ies)' is very commonly used in public domain (media reports, everyday interaction, etc) as well but with myriad meanings. Although, it is difficult to locate the exact time when the term became popular in Nagaland, one can still locate its entry in the public discourse through media writings in Nagaland between 1990s and 2000s. There was no single term to categorize these organizations, even though most of them were engaged in similar activities. It was here that the print media[20] in Nagaland became an important determinant when it used the term 'civil society' to refer to any group/forum/organization that attempted to address questions of conflict, peace, resolution. Since there was more than one such organization, term 'civil societies' became popular. As noted by a senior journalist during a personal communication in December 2013, 'I do not believe there has been any time that anyone used the word "civil societies" (the plural form, as opposed to the singular 'Civil Society') prior to 2005'.

Noteworthy is that the 1990s[21] was also the period when the concept of civil society had re-entered the global academic scene due to many global political developments. The case of Nagaland allows us to explore how the global resurgence of the term made its way into a society and was appropriated and represented within a specific local context. It is important to refer to Arjun Appadurai (1996) who like many others has argued that European and North American modernity did not enter South Asia in its purest form; instead, the process is much more complex than a mere imitation of the numerous processes within Euro-American contexts. One may then ask, how do Western (Eurocentric and North American) epistemes get translated into local contexts and affect the relationship between the state and society.

Social Politics and Social Power

Following from the above, it can, thus, be said that reference to 'civil societies' in contemporary state of Nagaland indicates varied organizations located within an (exclusive) space where attempt at peacekeeping, reconciliation and unity becomes the qualifying criterion for their inclusion within that space. This further explains why church in Nagaland (Naga Baptist Church Council [NBCC]) was also at one point (and sometimes even now, although it has prima facie left this space to make way for a body made out of different church denominations, namely Forum for Naga Reconciliation) considered to be as much civil as religious. Furthermore, the sphere was extended to include all tribal bodies in the state of Nagaland including students' forum, youth organizations, women organizations and the likes. The inclusion of tribal bodies within the ambit of the term 'civil society' led to further classification of the term, thereby giving rise to terms like 'apex civil societies' and 'civil societies', depending on the coverage area or jurisdiction of the organization. In the state of Nagaland, the term 'apex civil society' is generally used to refer to an organized network of people who claim to represent 'all' Naga Tribes[22] and includes Naga Hoho, Naga Mothers' Association (NMA), Naga Students' Federation (NSF), Eastern Nagaland People's Organization (ENPO), Eastern Naga Students' Federation (ENSF), Eastern Nagaland Women Organisation (ENWO), NBCC, NPMHR and FNR. These are mostly, a four-tiered system, with the state being the highest level, followed by the district, then range and, finally, the village. Thus, at each level, there will be a tribal Hoho, students organization, mothers' association and the Baptist church which represent their respective tribes in the Naga apex bodies. Despite the differences in the year of their emergence, objectives and structures, the civil society organizations in Nagaland have been quite active in dealing with the political impasse in the region. Explicating the role of civil society organizations in contemporary times, a member opined, *Naga Civil Society is caught in the exercise of balancing the two governments for the love of the ordinary citizens.* This could not have been achieved unless CSOs in Nagaland did not create for themselves a formal space. This was done building upon traditional social structures of the Naga society and outlining the contours of what is 'civil'.

'Civil' in Nagaland is a wider concept where engagement with politics is an important characteristic of the civil but not similar to Chatterjee's (1990) articulation of the political. This politics has to be understood at two levels: one, in terms of the engagement with other political entities in the region; two, the way this engagement is understood and experienced by the inhabitants of this sphere—'social politics'—as pointed out by a respondent in the field. The term 'social politics' not only summarizes actors' categorization of their work but also subtly differentiates between political parties and CSOs in the region. It is, thus, significant as it points to some of the main characteristics of the civil society in Nagaland. First and foremost, it is a sphere that is closely tied to politics of the region, especially Naga National Movement, but overtime, it has also become involved in various social, cultural and developmental issues. It is not only different from electoral politics which, as has been pointed out many of my respondents, is 'dirty, power hungry, corrupted and selfish' but also from the non-state politics which thrives on violence, extortion and fear psychosis. It emphasizes the 'neutrality' of the sphere where the entities associated with it are working for the greater good of the Naga people. It is also distinguished from NGOs since NGOs are teens as professional and very often profit-oriented. On the other hand, CSOs are associational (ascriptive identities), voluntary, constitutive of 'true' Nagas and are the watch dogs of the Naga society. One of the members of a CSO in Nagaland during fieldwork opined that unlike NGOs, his organization is *mass based organisation* and it is mandatory for each and every *bonafide* member of the Naga community to be a part of it. He further added that *NGOs can be formed by 5 people and they can start working. But in case of the CSOs, they have mass involvement.* They see themselves as the voice of the voiceless and champions of the downtrodden since they wield 'social power' resulting from a combination of vertical and horizontal alliances located within the cultural bases of collective life of Nagas, improvised in time and space as a result of certain sociopolitical changes. In other words, one can say that in Nagaland, an individual's role in civil society is not determined by his personal capacity or will but within the larger domain of his community ties and relationships. The social organization of the Nagas was made of cross-cutting ties between larger units such as lineages, clans and age-groups,[23] and an individual is born (ascriptive status is important) as a member of a lineage/clan/village/tribe, which becomes an important aspect of her/his self-identity. This identity has now been extended to include the pan-Naga political identity, owing to the various sociopolitical processes.

'Social associations', thus, became a means to not only identify with the community but also give it a formal structure. It not only gave an individual an identity but also provided a support system that drew from traditional structures, intra-tribal affinity and community support.[24] Before the emergence of the modern state system, each tribe within the Naga fold was administered with the help of norms and values of the community which were implemented by the elders in the community.[25] Jacobs et al. (1990) has shown that despite different forms of political organizations (e.g., Angh system for the Konyaks, chieftainship for the Semas and the democratic system for the Angamis), it is the people who wield the final power. Thus, one has to take cognizance of the possibility that the chiefs or the *anghs* do not have absolute power; rather, the political decisions are significantly influenced by the people often represented by their elders. Making a connection between the traditional structures, the role of the elders and contemporary civil societies, a respondent said, 'The term is quite recent just as you have mentioned about the nineties, also the constitution of the bodies but the idea was there all along. To me the first major participation (though debatable looking at the ignorance of the many village elders about the ways of the world outside them, but yes they did represent their folks) was in the late fifties. They were consulted and made a unified stand. The civil societies then comprised of village elders, representatives from group of villages'.

Having established the antecedents of civil society organizations in Nagaland, it can now be argued that although the civil society organizations in Nagaland with their 'in-betweenness' characteristic comprise an intermediary space, a traditional structural support which can be referred to as 'base entity' (Mukherji 2005) has allowed for its widespread usage and acceptance in Nagaland. Thus, the use of the term 'civil society/civil societies has allowed for a reconfiguration of spaces, spheres and planes that have existed for long but were not recognized as such. It has been pointed out in many studies[26] that associationalism based on ascriptive identities is one of the key features of societies like India/elsewhere in South Asia too where communities and not individuals become the primary inhabitant of the civil society sphere. The relationship between the individual and collectivity is, thus, explained through two tendencies—social power through associationalism and opposition to violence of state and non-state actors. There was a need to identify a sphere that was separate from the sphere of political violence either of the state or non-state actors, and none of this was possible unless the state and the non-state were identified as affecting the everyday.

The Missing Pieces

In contemporary Nagaland, 'neutrality' of the Naga civil sphere has come to be contested on various platforms. Conversations with former and senior office-bearers of many CSOs revealed that they carry a sense of nostalgia, often referring to the times when every single person used to support others, worked in cooperation and dealt with situations collectively. This, they opined, is in sharp contrast to present times, when CSOs have become fragmented; people have become opportunist, allowing state and non-state actors to use them as they nurture aspirations for entering electoral politics and, therefore, maintain strong affiliations with one or other political party, thereby compromising the 'social politics' of the CSOs.

In addition, there are a number of people who opine that the phase of 'homogenous Naga' (political) identity is almost over with 'intra-tribal affinity', or what is often referred to as *tribalism* is on the increase. This transformation of the Naga society is also affecting the *civil societies* and their working. Thus, emergence of ENPO, ENSF and ENWO[27] has to be seen in that light. The move was accounted for by the economic and political backwardness of the region which needed special attention. ENPO members do not see it as a typical social organization like other tribal bodies; rather, it is seen as a *socio-economic-political organisation* highlighting social, economic and political problems of the eastern region resulting from continuous neglect by successive state and central governments. Its main objective was outlined as to ensure *political and economic justice* to the people of eastern region. Thus, one can see a diversification of objectives of CSOs in question. The members of the Naga Hoho and the NSF, however, dismissed this split as having a significant effect on social power of the CSOs, as opined by a member of the Naga Hoho who defined ENPO as *Naga brothers who have distanced themselves socially but not politically*. Numerous such splits have emerged in civil society sphere of Nagaland. The Naga Tribal Council (NTC)[28] is a case in point. Such processes highlight not only the fragile but also the fluid nature of this space which is constantly reconstructed with changes within the political realm of the region. Sometimes these changes may be because of state initiatives and polices, while others may be because of certain acts of non-state actors. Notwithstanding these changes, what needs to be remembered is that civil society space in Nagaland allows us to locate major changes in the state–non-state–people triad.

Furthermore, one can locate the gendered nature of this space where women and women's organizations have been sidelined in numerous ways; for instance, women have never occupied major positions within any of the major CSOs. The justification, as shared by one of my respondents, has been that it is difficult for women to meet the rigorous demands of the posts and to fulfil the responsibilities attached to them. Another respondent stated that there is NMA which is exclusively managed by the women. This is interesting because, given the intermediary nature of the CSOs, members of the NMA have always been the first to mediate between the warring factions and have been termed as 'socially sanctioned peacemakers' (Manchanda 2005, viii). It, thus, raises the question that if peacemaking is seen as an important feature of CSOs in Nagaland, then despite their significant role in the process, why do Naga women occupy a secondary position within civil society sphere. The answer is not too difficult to locate. As mentioned earlier, CSOs in Nagaland are built from the traditional structures which also affects the way it is organized in terms of its gender dynamics. The strength of NMA is located in the concept of 'motherhood', understood as a unique responsibility endowed to mothers by God for the making of human society. The idea was to extend a mother's responsibility beyond the domain of her house to combat social evils such as alcoholism, drug addiction, screening of demoralizing video films, economic exploitation and rampant destruction of forests.[29] Since the 1990s, NMA along with NPMHR has adopted the slogan, *Shed no more Blood* and has tirelessly worked towards peace and reconciliation process in Nagaland. Significantly, criticisms that were levied against many of the CSOs were seldom levied against the organizations that were constituted and managed by women. As averred by the members of different women organizations, unlike the *male dominated* organizations, they do not have any *political masters* and *unlike the men folk, they are not obliged to anyone*. The refusal to get influenced (in the opinion of the women) by other institutions/ actors/parties is often articulated by them as the strength of women's organization in Nagaland.

Having said that, it becomes clear that the civil society in Nagaland reflects the socio-spatial arrangement of Naga society, which indicates the simultaneous existence of integration and differentiation. Following this, one can further argue that the civil society in Nagaland is also affected by macro changes; for instance, in contemporary times, many issues such as development of infrastructure and boost in economy, management of natural resources and push in international trade are increasingly becoming significant. Given the ensuing conflict in the region, it is not difficult to see why the state has been falling back on the road to what is currently understood as 'development' and 'progress'. One may also have to look into the role of this domain for a society that is located in the frontier region of the country and, therefore, has come to incorporate certain such issues that have assumed importance due to the changing world scenario.

With its numerous measures, the Indian state has tried to bring about development in the region, which is often seen as their attempts at resolution of the conflict using development as a discourse, a point that I have discussed in detail elsewhere (Bhargava 2011). Some of these measures include establishment of North Eastern Council (NEC) in the year 1971, Ministry of Development of the North Eastern Region (DoNER) in the year 2001, and the Look East policy which began in the year 1992. However, as mentioned earlier, the context of the Nagaland state is not only different because of the years long movement in the region but also because of the constitutional provision of Article 371 (A) that has allowed the state to have its own VCs and village development boards (VDBs) that draw membership mainly from the community (the focus on local as a category). The role of elders is of major significance in the Naga society which manifests itself institutionally through VDBs and VCs. These institutions at the village level along with the community linkages allowed for a possible arena of state–society synergy manifested best in the communitization process that came about through the enactment of the Nagaland Communitisation of Public Institutions and Services Act, 2002. Reviewing the process of communitization, R. S. Pandey in his work *Communitisation: The Third Way of Governance* (2010) talks about how the government in Nagaland has made headway in dealing with lack of development in significant areas such as health, education, power utilities and water supply systems by roping in community representative bodies like VCs and VDBs. He argued that such a move was only possible because of the community structure of the Nagas which allows for a creation of a social capital that derives its strength from the individual's relationship with the community.

Adding on to Pandey's work on governance in Nagaland, this chapter contends that because of their constitution, civil society organizations in Nagaland have become an important determinant in the process of development and governance in the state. The list of issues that various organizations address is a long one covering matters that may be political, cultural, social, religious, economic, developmental or infrastructural. Thus, at one given point, there will not just be a public meeting addressing the issues emerging from Look East Policy (now Act East Policy) of the central government and but also a protest regarding the erratic power and water supply in the state. Equal attention (if not more) will be paid to the perceived issue of illegal immigrants (from Bangladesh) in the region as to the question of safeguarding and promoting Naga history and culture. To address these numerous issues, various organizations conduct numerous activities and organize different events which are in line with their aims and objectives. Protest rallies, seminars and bandhs organized by CSOs are a common sight. In addition, they also serve memoranda and rejoinders to various actors, agencies and sections of the Naga public sphere which mainly engage in issues that relate to the social, cultural, economic and political spheres of the Naga society. Issue of numerous public and press statements is also a common sight in the state. These activities are mostly explained as part of their resistance to both government and underground forces. It is also deemed as an important indicator of the (*neutral*) role they play in the creation of a better Naga society by working hard to eliminate the vices of the Naga society. Is not that what the civil society should look like—bettering the society?

An exploration into organizations beginning from the clan/*khel*/village level to the level of district reveals a comprehensive picture. Thus, during my fieldwork in the region, in the year 2012–2013, it emerged that on one hand, Naga national issue along with questions of reconciliation between different factions (it is after all seen as the pre-requisite for an 'honourable' solution) occupies the centre stage for the organizations at the state (read Naga level), while on the other hand, for organizations at the district/range/village level, it is just one of the issues to be addressed, that too mainly to maintain the peace within their jurisdiction. Thus, these organizations occupy themselves with more immediate concerns; for instance, Angami Youth Organization (AYO) is concerned with environmental and ecological issues and spreads awareness about climate change, biodiversity and resource conservation. Similarly, Chakhesang Mothers' Association (CMA) addresses a variety of issues in addition to women's issues, beginning from surprise checking of educational institutions and healthcare facilities to bursting smuggling rackets to clean election campaign with NBCC, to pressurizing the government to implement its policies, or, for instance, the students union in a village in Mon was more concerned with the cleanliness in the village, ways to control a fire in case one breaks out or how to improve education in the schools in the village. As opposed to the village students' union, Konyak Students' Union engages in activities like ensuring *proper* burial to the dead,[30] ban on opium and liquor, putting a stop to *painful and sometimes gruesome* practice of tattooing, creating awareness about hygiene and directing their attention to education of the community.

Thus, an interrogation into these issues reveals the ways in which civil society organizations in Nagaland relate differentially to the state manifested either in the form of the Indian centre or the federal state of Nagaland. This makes us relook at the concepts of civil society and state, configuring them not as constants, rather as processes (Mitchell 2006) which are affected by various factors of the given social structure. Following from this, the case of Nagaland explicates that civil society is one of the key players affecting the working of the state, sometimes keeping the state in check while at others, working closely to work for the growth of the society.

To conclude, the chapter tried to indicate how the concept of civil society in Nagaland cannot be seen in opposition to the political; rather, it is very closely embedded within the political. In addition, it also draws attention to how 'politics operate in different cultural and historical contexts' (Spencer, 2007: 6). Thus, in the case of the Nagas, the articulation of the civil society cannot be dissociated from the sociocultural organization of the communities that had allowed for various organizations to exist. In addition, one can see significant relations between various terms and processes; hence, the existence of a strong state and nation-building processes (both by the Indian state and by Naga nationals) that came to dominate much of their past and present had a much vital role to play. The existence of this sphere which is ever expanding can be seen as largely emerging from a disillusionment or disenchantment from two entities—state and nationalist forces. Elliot (2003) has stated that civil society 'has assumed mythic proportions as a tool of the social imagination, an ideological construct for a good society' (2003, 3). It is 'an answer to civic estrangement and an emblem of modernisation' (Elliot 2003, 4).

At the end, we may ask how does an investigation of Naga society help us reformulate the concept of 'civil society'? It is in opposition to other forces that are violent and an intermediary space that allows for people's voices and opinions to be articulated to reconstruct their society. Just like institutions of democracy, it has, thus, become about institutions of 'civility' so as to deal with the political violence and situations thereafter that have engulfed the entire society.

Notes

1. For details, see Cohen and Arato (1992), Comaroff and Comaroff (1999), Elliot (2003) and Jayaram (2005).
2. Gellner (2009), who stated 'Civil society was "civil" as opposed to "military" in the Americas (as well as in Bangladesh and Pakistan); it was of the people, not the one party state, in eastern Europe; it was independent of party bias or office seeking in Asia; everywhere it was "civilized" in the sense that it stood for public and democratic negotiation of disagreement and rule of law' (p. 3).

3. Jayaram (2005, 15). He also argues that the 20th and 21st century resurgence of the concept locates it at the intersection of the economic, political and social relations that human beings enter into (p. 18).
4. Jayaram (2005), Oommen (2004), Gupta (2000), Uberoi (2003) and Beteille (2000) to name a few.
5. For details, see Kothari (1986), Chandhoke (1995, 2003, 2007), Mahajan (1999) and Varshney (2001), Kaviraj (2001) who were mainly concerned with the performance of the Indian State post-independence and questions of democracy, citizenship and modern forms of organizations and association
6. See Kothari (1986), Oommen (1990, 2004).
7. For details, see Varshney (2001), Chandhoke (2003), Hann (1996), Oommen (2004), Elliot (2010).
8. The group that Chatterjee calls the elites, is referred to by Kothari (1986) as classes. Despite using different words, it is important to note that both of them argued that civil society is a domain of a small section of the population.
9. In this chapter, Nagaland refers to the geopolitical and administrative unit within the larger geopolitical unit of India. Notwithstanding the many contestations with regard to the use of the term 'Naga', here it is used here to refer to various tribes that have come to identify themselves or are identified by others as 'Naga'. For details, look up Bhargava (2014). Civil Society in Nagaland: A Sociological Analysis, PhD Thesis.
10. For details, see Nag (2002) and Baruah (2005).
11. Elwin (1961) has stated that NHDTC was formed in the aftermath of WW II to facilitate post-war reconstruction and rebuilding of the Naga Society.
12. *Times of Kohima* (September 1946), 1–4 (quoted in Thomas 2010).
13. Now divided into four districts—Tuensang, Mon, Kiphire and Longleng.
14. In the year 1955, Assam rifles were sent to the Naga Hills.
15. For details, see Nag (2002), Misra (2003), Baruah (2005), Oinam (2008).
16. Naga People's Convention comprising 1,765 traditional representatives of the different Naga tribes belonging to Naga Hills and Tuensang Areas and some 2,000 observers met at Kohima from 22 to 26 August 1957 under the chairmanship of Dr Imkongliba.
17. A four-member peace mission (Naga Peace Mission) comprising Jaya Prakash Narayan, then Chief Minister of Assam Bimal Prasad Chaliha, Rev Michael Scott and Shankerrao Deo which was the result of the intervention of the Baptist Church in Nagaland.
18. See Misra (2003), Oinam (2008) and Sharma (2010). This is not to say that there was no literature that included the category of civil society, or that there were no civil society organizations; rather, the point is to highlight the sudden increase in the number of such articles.
19. It refers to the ongoing struggles between the Indian State's nation-building processes and people's refusal to be a part of it. In statist terms, it has been

referred to as insurgency and counter-insurgency, while others have seen it as ethno/subnationalist movements and Indian state's response to it. But most significant development was the growing conflict, sometimes leading to fratricidal killings, between various organizations.
20. It refers to newspapers like *Nagaland Post*, *Nagaland page* and *The Morung Express*, which have been significant in creating/altering the public opinion, especially when they carry numerous press releases from all kinds of organizations. In addition, the writings of public intellectuals in the media too have a significant role to play in this state of affairs.
21. Often traced to the solidarity movement in Poland in the 1980s.
22. Has constantly been problematized since Naga tribes are spread over other adjoining states as well.
23. For details, see Jacobs et al. (1990).
24. However, this needs to be further qualified as the aspect of 'togetherness' and 'tribal affinity' has always been challenged by 'tribalism' which is now seen as being on an increase.
25. For details on the village structures, see Vashum (2000) and for the role of elders in the community look up Haksar and Luithui (1984) and Shimray (2005).
26. See Varshney (2001), Oommen (2004), for instance.
27. These three draw membership from the Tuensang region of the Nagaland state and is inhabited mainly by six tribes—Phom, Yimchunger, Khiamiungan, Konyak, Sangtam and Chang.
28. See *Nagaland Post*, dated 26 May 2013 and *Eastern Mirror* dated 13 October 2013. NTC was formed following the contestation over Nagaland cabinet decision to accord ST status to Rongmei tribe in Nagaland which came about in July 2012. The organization was formally launched on 12 October 2013.
29. *NMA Silver Jubilee souvenir* 2009, 13.
30. According to KSU's (2011) document on achievements and development, Konyaks used to leave their dead on a platform made of bamboo in open spaces, which was seen as a hazardous practice. Consequently, they passed a resolution to discontinue the old practice and bury their dead. One can find mention of the custom in Fürer-Haimendorf's *Naked Nagas*, 1946.

References

Appadurai, A. 1996. *Modernity at Large: Cultural Dimensions of Globalisation*. Minneapolis, MN: University of Minnesota Press.
Baruah, S. 2005. *Durable Disorders: Understanding the Politics of Northeast India*. New Delhi: Oxford University Press.
Bhargava, R. 2011. 'Discourses and Actions: Indian State in North East India.' In *Exploring North East Indian Writings in English*, edited by Indu Swami, 362–384. New Delhi: Sarup Book Publishers.

Beteille, A. 2000. *Antinomies of Society: Essays on Ideologies and Institutions*. New Delhi: Oxford University Press.

Bhargava, Rashi. 2014. *Civil Society in Nagaland: A Sociological Study*. Unpublished doctoral thesis submitted to Center for the Study of Social Systems, school of social sciences, Jawaharlal Nehru University, New Delhi.

Chandhoke, N. 1995. *State and Civil Society: Explorations in Political Theory*. New Delhi: SAGE Publications.

Chandhoke Neera, 2003. 'The "Civil" and the "Political" in Civil Society.' In *Civil Society and Democracy: A Reader* edited by Carolyn M. Elliott, 238–261. New Delhi: Oxford University Press.

Chandhoke, Neera. 2007. 'Is Violence Constitutive of Civil Society'. *Non-Governmental Public Action Working Paper (NGPAWP) Series*. Published on 13th July, 2007. ISBN - 978-0-85328-102-3. Published on http://www.lse.ac.uk/Publicationswww.lse.ac.uk/Publications

Chatterjee, Partha. 2004. *The Politics of the Governed: Reflections on Popular Politics in Most of the World*. Columbia and New York: Columbia University Press.

Cohen, Jean L. and Andrew Arato. 1992. *Civil Society and Political Theory*. Cambridge, Massachusetts and London, England: MIT Press.

Comaroff, John L. And Jean Comaroff. 1999. *Civil Society and Political Imagination in Africa: Critical Perspectives*. Chicago: University of Chicago Press.

Elliott, C. M. 2003. 'Civil Society and Democracy: A Comparative Review Essay.' In *Civil Society and Democracy: A Reader*, edited by C. M. Elliot, 1–39. New Delhi: Oxford University Press.

Elwin, Verrier. 1997 [1961]. *Nagaland*. Guwahati: Spectrum Publications. Indian Reprint.

Gellner, D. 2009. 'Introduction: How Civil are "Communal" and Ethno-Nationalist Movements?' In *Ethnic Activism and Civil Society in South Asia*, edited by David N. Gellner, 1–24. New Delhi: SAGE Publications.

Gupta, D. 2000. *Culture, Space and Nation-state: From Sentiment to Structure*. New Delhi: SAGE Publications.

Haimendorf, Christoph von Fürer. 1946(reprinted 2004). *The Naked Nagas*. Guwahati: Spectrum Publications.

Hann, C. 1996. 'Introduction: Political Society and Civil Anthropology'. In *Civil Society: Challenging Western Models*, edited by Chris Hann and E. Dunn, pp. 1–26. London and New York, NY: Routledge.

Jacobs, J., A. Macfarlane, S. Harrison, and A. Herle. 1990. *Hill Peoples of Northeast India: The Nagas: Society, Culture and the Colonial Encounter*. London: Thames and Hudson.

Jayaram, N. (2005). *On Civil Society: Issues and Perspectives*. New Delhi and Thousand Oaks, Calif.: Sage Publications.

Luingum, L., and Nandita Haksar. 1984. *Nagaland File: A Question of Human Rights*. New Delhi: Lancer International.

Kaviraj, S. 2001. 'In Search of Civil Society.' In *Civil Society: History and Possibilities*, edited by S. Kaviraj and S. Khilnani, 287–323. New Delhi: Cambridge University Press.

Konyak Students' Union. 2011. *The Constitution of Konyak Students' Union*. Mon, Nagaland: KSU. Fourth edition approved by Federal Assembly on September 21, 2011.

Kothari, R. 1986. *State Against Democracy*. Delhi: Ajanta.

Mahajan, Gurpreet. 1999. 'Civil Society and Its Avatars: What Happened to Freedom and Democracy?'. *Economic and Political Weekly* 34(2): 1188–1196.

Manchanda, Rita. 2005. 'Naga women making a difference: peace building in northeastern India.' *Women Waging Peace Policy Commission Series* edited by Sanam Naraghi Anderlini. Cambridge: Hunt Alternative Fund. Accessed 28 April 2014. www.womenwagingpeace.net

Misra, Udayon. 2003. 'Naga Peace Talks High Hopes and Hard Realities'. *Economic and Political Weekly* 38, no. 7: 593–597.

Mitchell, T. 2006. 'Society, Economy and the State Effect.' In *The Anthropology of the State: A Reader*, edited by A. Sharma and A. Gupta, 169–185. Oxford: Blackwell.

Mukherji, P. N. 2005. 'Sociology in South Asia: Indigenisation as Universalising Social Science.' *Sociological Bulletin* 54, no. 3, Special Issue on South Asia: The State of Sociology: Issues of Relevance and Rigour (September–December 2005): 311–324.

Nag, S. 2002. *Contesting Marginality: Ethnicity, Insurgency and Sub-Nationalism in Northeast India*. New Delhi: Manohar Publishing House.

Naga Club Memo to Simon Commission. 1929. Available at https://www.thenagarepublic.com/files/naga-club-memo-to-simon-commission-1929/ (accessed 9 October 2017).

Naga Mothers' Association. 2009. *Naga Mothers' Association (NMA) celebrates 25: 14th February1984–2009*. Kohima: NMA.

Nagaland Pradesh Congress Committee (I). 2000. 'Bedrock of Naga Society'. Available at http://www.nenanews.com/ng10.htm (accessed 4 May 2014).

Oinam, Bhagat. 2008. 'State of the States: Mapping India's Northeast'. *Working Paper No. 12*. Project on *Internal Conflicts and State-Building Challenges in Asia*. Washington DC: East-West Center.

Oommen, T.K. 1990. *State and Society in India: Studies in Nation-Building*. New Delhi: Sage Publications.

Oommen, T. K. 2004. *Nation, Civil Society and Social Movements: Essays in Political Sociology*. New Delhi: SAGE Publications.

Pandey, R. S. 2010. *Communitisation: The Third Way of Governance*. New Delhi: Concept Publishing Company Pvt. Limited.

Rajagopalan, Swarna. 2008. 'Peace Accords in Northeast India: Journey over Milestones Policy studies 46.' Project on *Internal Conflicts and State-Building Challenges in Asia*. Washington DC: East-West Center.

Accessed 29 April 2014 http://www.eastwestcenter.org/publications/peace-accords-northeast-india-journey-over-milestones

Sharma, K. N. 2010. 'Civil Society and Democracy: Absence of the Sovereign in Northeast India.' *Eastern Quarterly* 6, no. 3: 106–115.

Shimray, A. S. Atai. 2005. *Let Freedom Ring: Story of Naga Nationalism.* New Delhi: Promila and Co. Publishers.

Spencer, Jonathan. 2007. *Anthropology, Politics, and the State: Democracy and Violence in South Asia.* Cambridge: Cambridge University Press.

Thomas, John. 2010. *Missionaries, Church and the Formation of Naga Political Identity, 1918–1997* (PhD thesis). Jawaharlal Nehru University, Delhi.

Uberoi, J. P. S. 2003. 'Civil Society.' In *The Oxford Companion to Sociology and Social Anthropology*, edited by Veena Das, Vol. I, 114–135. New Delhi: Oxford University Press.

Varshney, A. 2001. 'Ethnic Conflict and Civil Society: India and Beyond.' *World Politics* 53: 362–398.

Vashum, R. 2000. *Nagas' Right to Self-determination: An Anthropological-Historical Perspective.* Delhi: Mittal Publications.

Part III

Security, Emergency Laws and Protest

CHAPTER 7

Politics of Counter-insurgency and the Expansion of Security Bureaucracy

M. Amarjeet Singh and
R. K. Sanayaima

Ever since insurgency essentially started in the Northeast region of India in the 1950s, the state of India has been engaging with various insurgent groups, but the region is still not able to get rid of insurgency. The root causes of insurgency are varied which differ from case to case in which the resentments over the 'merger' into the Indian Union, fear of Bengali immigration and cultural distinctiveness are the predominant ones. Insurgency continues to spread and has acquired various new meanings and strategies: demand for autonomy, territorial identity, state within state, etc. It is alleged that the increase in the number of insurgent groups in state likes Manipur is because of the state's engineer to split and engage major insurgent groups such as United National Liberation Front (UNLF), United Liberation Front of Asom (ULFA) and NSCN (IM). Living in such a situation, the people have suffered hardships and sufferings. The state's capacity to deliver goods and services and guarantee rule of law and security have not been progressive all these years. On the contrary, the state's response has been largely limited to the use of force, call for peace talks (reconciliation) and providing more development funds, even when one knows that development indicators such as health, poverty and employment are not showing signs of improvement in the region.

The Northeast region is a landlocked and isolated area physically connected to the rest of the country by a narrow strip of land in North Bengal area of the state of West Bengal and is surrounded by at least four countries, namely Bangladesh, Bhutan, Nepal, China and Myanmar. Hence, the region is seen as strategically important for the 'defence of the country' (Ludra 1999, 267). Thus, the region has always been viewed mainly from a national security perspective. The armed forces came to be represented as the unifying force. The North East Division of the Ministry of Home Affairs oversees internal security and law and order situation including insurgency and talks with insurgent groups. The entry of foreign nationals is restricted in several parts of the region. Under the Foreigners (Protected Areas) Order, 1958, whole/parts of Arunachal Pradesh, Manipur, Mizoram, Nagaland and Sikkim are considered as protected area.[1] It was only recently that the restriction was lifted from Manipur, Nagaland and Mizoram for 5 years with effect from 1 April 2018. Even the construction of bridges and roads has military significance. The construction of Bogibeel bridge, a 4.94 km-rail-cum-road bridge, on Brahmaputra River in Assam not only enhances connectivity between Assam and Arunachal Pradesh but also enables faster troop movement.

Under these emerging circumstances, it is imperative to examine the exact nature of state's dealing with insurgents in the region. To briefly state the problematic of our study, the following statements may be taken for consideration: on the one hand, the nature of insurgency has begun to change allegedly from a voice of sovereign state demand to that of ethnicized identity and territoriality politics leading to ethnic conflicts and tension. On the other hand, the measures adopted to tackle insurgency (and ethnic conflict) have mostly led to the expansion of security bureaucracy, not an effective transformation to state of peace on ground in Northeast region. This chapter will look into this state of contradictory affairs in what we call 'counter-insurgency': what counter-insurgency does mean, if insurgency is not merely continuing its presence but also transforming into new meanings and identities, is a central question in this chapter.

State Approach, Crisis of Legitimacy

Broadly, the interventions of state of India to deal with insurgency in its Northeast region may be discussed as follows.

First, the Government of India considers insurgency as a 'law and order' problem (even though various civil society bodies like Coalition of Civil Society Groups based in Manipur argue that insurgency is not a law and order but a political problem), and it enjoys the monopoly of legitimate use of military force under special laws like the Armed Forces (Special Powers) Act (AFSPA), 1958. The counter-insurgency strategies involved the use of divisive tactics to split the insurgents and used one against the other (Sahni and Routray 2001). Although law and order is a state subject, the central government has been assisting the states in the region and also has been involved directly in countering insurgency, which, we argue, has led to the use of vast resources in expanding the administration of security (bureaucracy). These resources include the reimbursement of security-related expenditure to the state governments under the Reimbursement of Security Related Expenditure Scheme, deployment of central armed police forces, assistance for modernization of state police, setting up of India Reserve Battalions, banning insurgent groups under the Unlawful Activities (Prevention) Act, 1967, enforcement of the AFSPA and formation of Unified Command Structure comprising of army, paramilitary forces and police (Rajya Sabha Secretariat 2018).

Second, the government had conducted talks with the insurgents to cease operation against each other leading to the signing of agreements. Some agreements have resulted in the formation of states such as Nagaland and Mizoram out of Assam and autonomous regions such as the Bodoland Territorial Region in Assam,[2] but some agreements could not produce any significant impact. There are several ongoing ceasefires between the insurgent groups and the government. The ongoing Suspension of Operation between the Government of India and Kuki insurgents in Manipur can be cited as an example. There are several attractive monetary as well employment schemes (about which we will deal in little details later in the chapter) for the former insurgents (Rajya Sabha Secretariat 2018).

Third, the central government allocates funds for carrying out development works in the region. In addition to the funds allocated by several central ministries, there is an independent ministry known as the Ministry of Development of North Eastern Region (DoNER) and an autonomous planning body known as the North Eastern Council for the development of the region. Some states have been awarded 'peace bonuses' by the central government for being able to maintain peace; for example, a sum of ₹1,824.5 million was given to Mizoram during 2000–2001 for being a peaceful state after years of insurgency (Government of Mizoram 2001). In 2003, Nagaland was awarded (by converting ₹3,650 million Ways and Means Advance as a one-time Non-Plan grant) (Press Releases 2003). Other states like Sikkim had sought the benefit. Former Sikkim Chief Minister Pawan Chamling once remarked as follows: 'In a meeting of Internal National Security chaired by the Prime Minister..., I have placed a demand for peace bonus for Sikkim for being the most peaceful state in the country. In other parts of the country, crores of rupees are being spent to restore normalcy in strife torn areas. In the same way, I have demanded bonus for the development of the state which maintain peace and amity' (Government of Sikkim 2003, 81). Perhaps, for the Chief Minister, peace means absence of insurgency-based violence. However, if we see the overall state and society relationship, we do not see a peaceful state. One may cite the case of large-scale people movement against the state development projects such as Teesta Hydel power projects that are being criticized for being anti-people, as they lead to displacement of 'indigenous people'. As a result, one can contest the ground on which he claimed Sikkim to be the most peaceful state in the country.

However, in spite of the above measures, the region could not get rid of insurgency. Moving away from old demand of sovereign state, separately from India, different insurgency movements are aiming to achieve various forms of autonomy to independence in many areas of the region. It is reported that the ongoing peace talks between the Government of India and NSCN (IM) would result in some forms of autonomy for the Nagas over culture and resources. Also, the ongoing suspension of operation between Kuki insurgents and the Government of India reported deal with the demand for 'state within state' (meaning, maximum autonomy for the Kukis, even though exact nature of autonomy is yet to be cleared) of Manipur. On the other hand, the insurgents are able to create parastatal institutions in areas of their control where they lay down own rules and have the means and resources to enforce such rules. On such institutions, the Federal Government of Nagaland and the Government of the People's Republic of Nagaland with parliamentary institutions, such as Tatar Hoho, and standing armies such as Naga Home Guards and Naga Army can be cited. Some groups have institutional arrangement to collect funds locally to run their administration. The taxes are collected from state officials, traders, contractors, politicians and common people. They not only monitor the agencies of the state but also administer their own social welfare services to gain public support. In this way, the functions which are ordinarily within the jurisdiction of the state are also exercised by the non-state institutions. In exchange for those services, the insurgent groups receive their share of public support and also taxes. Hence, they even serve as more reliable providers of security, deserving of financial contribution and support and more worthy of loyalty than the state (Baruah 2002).

Several insurgent groups stood to protect and safeguard the communities in which they belong from any threat by other communities; for instance, the Kuki insurgency was founded during the 1990s to defend the Kuki people from the Naga insurgency. The Kuki insurgents oppose the claims of the Naga insurgents over their much publicized 'the Naga inhabited areas' of Manipur. Thus, the demand for the 'homeland' in the 'Kuki areas' in the hills of Manipur got cemented (Kom 2010). Usually, insurgent groups try to play moral guardians and protectors of the communities which they represent; though they operate within a limited space, these campaigns have succeeded in projecting an image of 'protectors' of the lives and traditions of the people which they seek to serve. They have been particularly astute in their choice of issues, such as issuing diktats on cultural matters, punishment to drug users and peddlers, curb on examination malpractices and other forms of corruption. Among multiples instances, the Operation New Kangleipak (Kangleipak is Manipur's historical name) by the Kanglei Yawol Kanna Lup (KYKL), an insurgent group, mainly targeted examination malpractices in Manipur such as copying. Those who violated the moral code were punished (Routray 2005). The overall impact has been the crisis of legitimacy of state (institutions).

Historicizing Violence

When the Nagas of Naga Hills district of Assam rejected the autonomy arrangement under the Sixth Schedule of the Constitution of India, boycotted the first general election of India and declared independence, the government swiftly acted by deploying armed forces in the district in 1955 to counter the separatists. The government insisted that since Naga Hills was an integral part of India, the question of its independence did not arise. The Naga National Council (NNC) was declared unlawful in 1952. It was soon followed by the enforcement of the Assam Maintenance of Public Order (Autonomous Districts) Act, 1953 to impose collective fine and prohibit public gatherings. The district was declared a disturbed area in 1956 under The Assam Disturbed Areas Act, 1955. The situation of the district was mentioned in Report of the State Reorganisation Commission (1955, 193):

> The Naga Hills district presents another special problem. Owing to the activities of the extremist elements, the law and order situation in this area has been unstable in recent years. The Nagas boycotted the elections to the autonomous bodies, with the result that the area had to be administered directly by the Assam government. It has been represented to us that the law and order problem in the Naga Hills district is the same as in the Tuensang area of the NEFA, and that unless the entire area is brought under the authority the situation cannot be effectively dealt with.

Such official understanding of the Naga Hills district of the then Assam as one that 'presents another special problem' and, hence, a 'law and order' problem because of the 'extremist elements' and boycott of elections led to employment of extraordinary laws. The Armed Forces

(Assam and Manipur) Special Powers Regulation, 1958 was enforced in the district and some areas of nearby Manipur (the regulation subsequently became the Armed Forces [Assam and Manipur] Special Powers Act, 1958). This Act authorizes armed forces such as the army, the Assam Rifles and the Rashtriya Rifles to exercise 'special powers' in the 'disturbed areas'. This Act has its origin in India in the colonial-era ordinance—the Armed Forces (Special Powers) Ordinance, 1942, which was enforced during the Quit India movement in order to curb Indians from participating in the freedom movement. It was later rechristened as the Armed Forces (Assam and Manipur) Special Powers Ordinance, 1958, which subsequently became the Armed Forces (Assam and Manipur) Special Powers Act, 1958 in September 1958.

After the union territories of Manipur, Tripura, Mizoram and Arunachal Pradesh became states and bifurcation of Meghalaya from Assam in 1972, the Act was rechristened as the AFSPA to confer power upon the central government to declare an area 'disturbed'. The power was once vested in the Assam government. In due course of time, the Act was gradually extended to other states (Manipur was declared 'disturbed area' in 1980 and Assam in 1990). A version of the same law was introduced in Jammu and Kashmir in 1990. According to this Act (India Code 2020, 2):

> Any commissioned officer, warrant officer, non-commissioned officer or any other person of equivalent rank in the armed forces may, in a disturbed area, (a) if he is of opinion that it is necessary so to do for the maintenance of public order, after giving such due warning as he may consider necessary, fire upon or otherwise use force, even to the causing of death, against any person who is acting in contravention of any law or order for the time being in force in the disturbed area prohibiting the assembly of five or more persons or the carrying of weapons or of things capable of being used as weapons or of fire-arms, ammunition or explosive substances.

Despite the deployment of more armed forces with impunity, protecting state's armed forces for their action against any trial in the court of laws, under AFSPA, insurgency extended to different areas. The Manipuris alleged that the princely state of Manipur had unwillingly joined India after coercing their king. The resentment against the act of state considered to be a 'merger to the Union of India' or 'take over' led to an insurgency movement. Manipur became a state of India in 1972, but it could not get rid of insurgency. Manipur was declared a disturbed area in 1980 and large numbers of armed forces were deployed. The insurgents reportedly took shelter along the border of India and Myanmar. India shares a 1,640-km-long border with Myanmar covering the states of Arunachal Pradesh, Mizoram, Nagaland and Manipur. The two countries have reportedly conducted joint operations against the insurgents in the dense jungles along the border areas. In Manipur, the security forces had launched several anti-insurgent operations including Operation Somtal II in 2007 to clear nearly 1,000 sq. km of Somtal located along the border in Chandel district. Numerous insurgent groups are said to operating in the state.

As the insurgents in Mizo (Lushai) Hills district of Assam declared independence from India in March 1966, armed forces were deployed to establish public order there. The district was declared a disturbed area. Since the insurgent-controlled areas had less population density, hundreds of villages, constituting about 70 per cent of the population of the district were relocated into the larger ones. It was done to isolate the insurgents from the local population. Subsequently, negotiation started between the government and the Mizo National Front (MNF) leading to an agreement in 1986 to elevate the union territory of Mizoram into a state. Mizoram became a state in 1987. This led to the transformation of MNF into a political party and the insurgency came to an end. Mizoram is currently one of the peaceful states in the country. The Act has not been extended after Mizoram attained statehood, but it has not been officially repealed.[3]

Since the 1980s, the insurgency has been no longer confined to Nagaland, Mizoram and Manipur. Assam witnessed the ULFA-led insurgency, which virtually set up a parallel state structure. However, months after the killing of Surendra Paul, a prominent tea planter, in 1990, the state government was dismissed and presidential rule (the central rule) was imposed on the state. Assam was declared a disturbed area and ULFA an unlawful organization. In 1990 itself, the army launched a massive flush-out operation against the insurgents, known as Operation Bajrang, which reportedly arrested about 500 insurgents. The operation was suspended in 1991 in order to hold the state legislature elections. After the elections, Operation Rhino was launched in September leading to the arrest and killing of several insurgent leaders. The operation was suspended in January 1992 after ULFA showed willingness to talk to the government. The talk did not materialize, but ULFA resulted in a serious split which led the surrender of around 4,000 insurgents. However, the split had a negligible effect on ULFA (Sinha 2007, 169–171).

The armed forces have been accused of misusing their discretionary powers. They had been rarely punished for misuse of power against the civilian population.[4] On 11 July 2004, a dozen women protested naked in front of Kangla Fort in Imphal to protest the killing of Manorama, whom the state alleged as an insurgent. The venue chosen for the protest was significant as the fort was then occupied by the Assam Rifles. Earlier in an incident that occurred on 2 November 2000, 10 people were killed at Malom in Imphal by the Assam Rifles. This led to fast unto death by another lady, Irom Sharmila Devi. Allegedly, the incident took place in response to an attack by unknown people on the Assam Rifles in the area. She survived by forced feeding for several years and ended the fast in August 2016. As normal life was paralysed in Manipur after the killing of Manorama, the then Prime Minister Manmohan Singh visited Imphal. A committee was set up to review the Act. The Prime Minister promised to shift the Assam Rifles from the Kangla Fort and conversion of Manipur University into a centrally funded university. The Act was withdrawn from Imphal municipal area. The said committee reportedly submitted a report to the government in 2005. However, nothing had happened.

Recently, the Supreme Court of the country had sought a probe into cases of extrajudicial killings.[5] The local residents were against the imposition of the AFSPA. However, others, particularly armed forces and state leaders, were in favour of the Act to protect the state against internal disturbances, uphold integrity of the country, curb terrorism and insurgency and protect sensitive border areas. They alleged that without the discretionary powers, the security forces would be demoralized and reluctant to carry out counter-insurgency operations (Kamboj 2004). In response to a petition filed by the Naga Peoples Movement for Human Rights (NPMHR) and others, the Supreme Court upheld the constitutional validity of the Act.[6]

In order to coordinate and oversee the counter-insurgency operation in the state of Assam, a three-tier command mechanism of the army, police and other paramilitary forces, known as the Unified Command, was constituted in 1997. The command, headed by the Chief Minister, met regularly to review security situation in the state. Since Assam has a long border with Bhutan, the insurgents could easily infiltrate into the country. Bhutan was also allegedly lending support to the insurgents. Finally, India convinced Bhutan to take action against them and also offered all possible assistance. In 2003, Bhutan launched a military operation against ULFA and other insurgents who were taking shelter in its soil. Following this operation, several insurgents were handed over to India, but the whereabouts of many others is still unknown. India also could persuade Bangladesh to take action to push back the insurgents. However, they have reportedly found shelter in Myanmar.

Insurgency also started in Tripura in the late 1970s which intensified thereafter. Major parts of the state (40 of the 70 police station limits) were declared disturbed areas in 1997. The insurgents were brought under control. As a result, AFSPA was withdrawn from the state in 2015.

Tables 7.1 and 7.2 show the major operations launched by state security forces in the region and some of the major incidents that caused death or injury to the civilian population.

Table 7.1 *Major Operations against Insurgents by the Security Forces*

S. No.	State	Name of the Operation	Year	Main Target
1	Manipur	Operation Bluebird	1987	Naga insurgents
2	Assam	Operation Bajrang	1990	United Liberation Front of Asom
3	Assam	Operation Rhino	1991	United Liberation Front of Asom

S. No.	State	Name of the Operation	Year	Main Target
4	Manipur	Operation Sunnyvale	1993	Manipuri insurgents
5	Manipur	Operation Khengjoi or Somtal-I	2006	United National Liberation Front
6	Manipur	Operation Somtal-II	2007	United National Liberation Front
7	Manipur	Operation Summer Storm	2009	Manipuri insurgents
8	Indo-Myanmar border	Operation Sunrise	2019	Insurgents of Manipur, Nagaland and Assam
9	Manipur	Operation Kekru Naga	2019	Hideout of NSCN-IM (National Socialist Council of Nagaland-Isak Muivah)

Source: Compiled from English-language newspapers published in India, such as *The Telegraph, The Sentinel, The Assam Tribune, The Imphal Free Press* and *The Shillong Times*.
Note: This list is indicative only.

Table 7.2 Major Violent Incidents Causing Death and Injury to the Civilian Population

S. No.	State	Year	Incident
1	Assam	1991	Fourteen officials, including a Russian coalmine expert Sergei Gritchenko, two bureaucrats and eight Oil and Natural Gas Corporation (ONGC) officers/engineers were abducted by United Liberation Front of Asom (ULFA) from different parts of the state on 1 July. The Russian coalmine expert and two ONGC engineers were subsequently killed. The others were released one after another in exchange for the release of several jailed ULFA insurgents.

(Table 7.2 Continued)

(Table 7.2 Continued)

S. No.	State	Year	Incident
2	Assam	1996	Thirty-four train passengers were killed and several others wounded in a powerful bomb explosion on the Delhi-bound Brahmaputra Mail Express at Sesapani in Kokrajhar district on 30 December.
3	Tripura	2002	Insurgents shot dead 20 policemen and wounded many others in a surprise attack in West Tripura district.
4	Nagaland	2004	Twenty-six people, including women and children, were killed and several others wounded in two powerful bomb blasts triggered by unidentified persons at a railway station and a nearby market at Dimapur. The incidents occurred on 2 October.
5	Manipur	2008	A powerful bomb explosion in Imphal on 21 October killed at least 18 persons and left 35 wounded.
6	Assam	2008	Nine near-simultaneous bomb explosions (three each in Guwahati and Kokrajhar, two at Barpeta Road and one in Bongaigaon) on 30 October claimed nearly 90 civilian lives and wounded more than 300 others.
7	Assam	2016	Fourteen people, including an insurgent, were killed in Kokrajhar district.
8	Arunachal Pradesh	2019	Militants shot and killed an Arunachal Pradesh legislator, his son and nine others in Tirap district.

Source: Compiled from English-language newspapers, such as *The Telegraph, The Sentinel, The Assam Tribune, The Imphal Free Press* and *The Shillong Times*.
Note: The list excludes several other operations.

Governing the Affairs of Security

The above section shows the long view of the state and insurgency affairs in the Northeast region of India. In this section, we deal with what we call 'governing security affairs', by which we mean both the nature and scale of extraordinary laws the state has spent and the financial and security-related expenditure of the state in dealing with insurgency. The idea of governing is used to show how the state, which cannot put an end to insurgency, has administered matters (laws, financial schemes and other security-related schemes and expenditure) related with the security measures in the region.

There is a clear demarcation of powers between the central government and the state governments in counter-insurgency measures. The state government is responsible for maintaining public order and policing, but, the central government provides assistance to the states in dealing with terrorism and insurgency. Although the primary responsibility of maintaining public order and policing rests with the state government, the central government has been assisting the states in dealing with 'terrorism, militancy, insurgency and extremism' (Government of India 2019, 7). The Central Armed Police Forces (CAPFs) are deployed to assist the states in counter-insurgency operations and provide security to vulnerable installations. Over 800 Coys (a Coy comprises about 130 personnel) of CAPFs and 18 COBRA teams are deployed for border guarding and counter-insurgency operations. Fifty-one Indian Reserve Battalions (a battalion consists of about 1,000 personnel) have already been functional in the region (Government of India 2018, 24). In addition, there are unspecified numbers of Indian Army personnel deployed in the region to tackle insurgency.

The counter-insurgency strategies also included the use of divisive tactics to split the insurgent groups and used one against the other. Even if the government could not fully solve insurgency, it could nevertheless keep the insurgents under control. In all the talks, the government had succeeded in persuading all the warring parties to accept its terms and conditions and accept solutions within the framework of the law of the country. Thus, peace accords can serve two-fold objectives: uphold the unity and integrity of the country and redress some of the common grievances. The central government has always been part of any peace accord because it gives most of the concessions including the power to form a new state or an autonomous region. It used to be the prerogative of the government to decide on whom to begin negotiations with and whom to exclude. It generally tried to negotiate with the key groups.

The notion of assisting state government (a federal unit of the union of India), however, can be problematized considering the investment the state of India (the central government) makes in counter-insurgency programmes in the region in terms of length and nature of employment extraordinary laws like AFSPA, on the one hand and manpower and financial investment in security-related activities, on the other.

As we have seen in the above section of historicizing violence in the region, laws like AFSPA which are supposed to be exceptional laws have been employed till now even when one knows that insurgency continues to spread and change its strategies and meanings. This means that an exceptional law has become a normal law. In a critically examined work on AFSPA, Bimol Akoijam has shown that AFSPA is an act of 'Disguised war' (Bimol Akoijam 2005, 486–487). AFSPA is presented as an instrument 'in aid of civil power' (Section 3 of the Act) to 'suppress' 'armed revolt' or 'armed insurgency' in the Northeast region. It was supposed to be a 'temporary measure', but the actual operation of the act for over four decades has shown that all stated claims are false. He further argues that the uninterrupted military presence in the region, inaugurated by AFSPA, has in no way brought peace to the area. On the contrary, to him, it can be seen as the instrument of a self-fulfilling prophecy, and it is questionable as to whether AFSPA is a response to, or the progenitor of, the insurgency in the Northeast. Further to him, with regard to civilian government in the state, by legitimizing the use of military force in the internal affairs of the state beyond what is already provided in the Criminal Procedure Code and the provisions of emergency in the constitution, AFSPA seeks to supplant rather than supplement civil authority with military authority in the administration of everyday life. Therefore, the idea of assisting the state, while dealing with insurgency in the region, is in reality an act with greater force both in scale and consequence. Two things come from the above argument: one, AFSPA is questionable because insurgency never ends and peace never comes; two, it is an act that supplants rather than supplements civilian authority.

In fact, the presence of military forces in public space and civilian affairs has become a new normal in the region. There are numerous military outposts in villages and towns. In states such as Manipur, Assam and Nagaland, there would be more military outposts than the police stations. Several government offices, schools and abandoned movie halls have been converted into military outposts. The students of Manipur University have been demanding the shifting of the Assam Rifles to a suitable place (*The Sangai Express* 2020).

Beside the above reading of the laws and act of counter-insurgency juridically, it is important to see the following ways the state invests in counter-insurgency: one, the financial schemes and other security-related financial expenditures under the central government (see, Table 7.3); two, the services that armed forces provide in public affairs. The Ministry of Home Affairs has been implementing 'surrender and rehabilitation' schemes for insurgents since 1998. The benefits include a grant of ₹0.4 million to each surrenderee, which is to be kept as a fixed deposit in a bank for 3 years. There are provisions for payment of a stipend of ₹6,000 per month per surrenderee and vocational training (Government of India 2018, 25). States of the region, affected by insurgency, have also been provided financial assistance under security-related expenditure since 1998. Under this scheme, the expenditure incurred by the states on various items, including raising of Indian Reserve Battalions, logistics provided to the CAPFs/Army deployed in the state, ex-gratia grant and gratuitous relief to the victim of extremist violence, 75 per cent of the expenditure incurred on petrol, oil and lubricants in operations and honorarium paid to village guards/village defence committee/home guards deployed for security purposes, maintenance of designated camps of insurgents who have entered into agreement are reimbursed (Government of India 2004, 34).

The armed forces, apparently to legitimize their role in countering insurgency and longer presence in public, also enter deeply into the civilian space, while they perform non-military 'humane initiatives' such as social services, medical check-ups in villages, assisting of voluntary organizations and blood donation camps; for example, a village in Manipur's Chandel district has been provided with electricity by the Assam Rifles by setting up a solar power plant (Press

Table 7.3 Assistance under Security-related Expenditure (in ₹ Crore)

Year	Assam	Nagaland	Manipur	Tripura	Meghalaya	Arunachal Pradesh	Total
2000-2001	63.97	7.50	14.18	15.00	3.21	1.00	104.86
2005-2006	63.91	24.83	33.65	27.00	13.17	1.35	163.91
2012-2013	112.86	69.36	20.62	11.32	-	50.74	264.90
2013-2014	159.18	42.50	25.01	42.18	16.60	4.53	290.00
2014-2015	106.69	57.88	37.76	27.23	12.61	18.83	261.00
2015-2016	140.07	67.61	45.78	12.98	12.63	0.93	280.00
2016-2017	148.70	61.48	31.86	36.62	9.19	12.15	300.00
2017-2018[a]	221.51	13.16	9.23	16.60	12.60	10.90	284.00

Source: Government of India (2018, 19, 291).
Note: [a]Up to 31 December 2017.

Trust of India 2018). The Assam Rifles is often called the 'friends of the hill people'. The Army undertakes military civic action programmes (see, Table 7.4) in order to win the hearts and minds of the people under operations like Sadbhavana and Samaritan. The focus areas are imparting education (setting up of Army goodwill schools), women empowerment, community and infrastructural development (organizing sports and cultural programmes), health and veterinary care, water supply schemes, electrification, animal husbandry and border area development. The armed forces also actively participate in rescue and relief operations caused by floods, landslides, snowfall and to rescue stranded miners (Government of India 2019, 178–186).

State police, in addition to central forces, constitute an integral part of the security governance, although the police in disturbed areas are not granted special powers. The police also play a crucial role in counter-insurgency. There are special police units to fight the insurgents. Police personnel who fought the insurgents are awarded with the President's Police Medal for Distinguished Service, Police Medal for Meritorious Service and Police Medal for Gallantry on the occasions of the Republic Day and Independence Day celebrations (see, Table 7.5).

Former police officers, Home Secretaries, Army Generals, and intelligence officers were appointed as Governors of the states. Recently, Mr R. N. Ravi, a former intelligence officer, became the Governor of Nagaland. Former Army Generals and police officers became the Governors of Assam during 1997–2008. Presently, more politicians have been appointed as Governors. The Governors play key roles particularly in the sensitive border states in security matters.

The civilian face of the counter-insurgency is represented by the Governor and the Chief Minister of the state. In the matter of policy, civil authority controls the security forces. However, regarding command and control, the power vests exclusively in the security forces. Thus, the relationship between them is based on shared responsibility. The Governor acts as the representative of the central government who is responsible to report on the affairs of the state. He/she serves as a vital link between the central government and the state government.

In fact, the insurgency has subsided significantly over the past few years, with several insurgent groups holding ceasefire with the

Table 7.4 Funds Released to Army/Central Armed Police Forces Deployed in the Northeast under the Civic Action Programme (in ₹ Lakhs)

Organization	2012-2013	2013-2014	2014-2015	2015-2016	2016-2017	2017-2018 (up to 31 December 2017)
Border Security Force	230.00	262.50	50.00	150.00	150.00	150.00
Central Reserve Police Force	150.00	-	27.00	150.00	150.00	150.00
Indo-Tibetan Border Police	100.00	68.00	75.00	100.00	80.00	100.00
Sashastra Seema Bal	150.00	17.76	69.00	70.00	70.00	70.00
Assam Rifles	200.00	350.00	200.00	350.00	350.00	350.00
Indian Army	120.00	150.00	179.00	180.00	180.00	180.00
Total	950.00	848.26	600.00	1,000.00	980.00	1,200.00

Source: Government of India (2018, 291).

Table 7.5 Strength of State Police Force

State	Police Station[a]	Civil Police[a]	Armed Police[a]	Total[a]	Number of Indian Reserve Battalions[b]
Arunachal Pradesh	66	2,987	2,913	5,900	5
Assam	240	22,977	30,946	53,923	9
Manipur	57	4,743	9,241	13,984	9
Meghalaya	26	5,955	2,626	8,581	4
Mizoram	31	2,948	3,852	6,800	5
Nagaland	45	7,367	9,020	16,387	7
Tripura	44	7,786	4,596	12,382	9
Sikkim	26	2,500	1,500	4,000	3
Total	535	57,263	64,694	121,957	51

Sources: [a]Government of India (2004, 33); [b]Government of India (2018, 24).

government. The Ministry of Defence maintained that 'compared to the peak of insurgency in the region in the last two decades since 1997, there has been phenomenal improvement in security situation in the region' (Government of India 2019, 8). Officially, there was no insurgency-related violence in 2017 in Sikkim, Mizoram and Tripura (Government of India 2019). AFSPA has been recently withdrawn from Tripura, Meghalaya and partially from Arunachal Pradesh due to the improvement in the security situations (see, Table 7.6).

Although the above figures show a sign of withdrawal of AFSPA and there are signs of declining insurgency, the Northeast region is still governed through the lens of security and, hence, the importance of administrating the security matters is still the core business of the state in India. This reminds us of the following statement of the Report of the State Reorganisation Commission (1955, 32–33).

> ... another factor relevant from the point of view of national security is the size and resources of the border states. While the primary responsibility for defence arrangements must be that of the Central Government, a considerable burden relating to security

Table 7.6 The Armed Forces (Special Powers) Act in Northeast India

S. No.	Area	Year of Enactment	Year of Withdrawal
1	Naga Hills district/Nagaland	1958	
2	Mizo Hills district/Mizoram	1966	1987
3	Manipur	1980	
4	Tripura	1997	2019
5	Meghalaya	1991	2019
6	Arunachal Pradesh	1991	2019
7	Assam	1990	
8	Sikkim		

Source: Compiled from English-language newspapers.

arrangements must be borne by the State. It is, therefore, important that a border State should be a well-administered, stable and resourceful unit, capable of meeting the emergent problems arising out of military exigencies. This means that normally it would be safer to have on our borders relatively larger and resourceful States rather than small and less resilient units.

Conclusion

In Northeast India, the armed forces may play more crucial roles as the region is projected as a sensitive border area. Thus, if the special powers given to them under the AFSPA are withdrawn, the armed forces will continue to exercise special responsibilities in the region because they are necessary for defending the country from external and internal threats. They are the guardians of the frontiers, security, economic and political system of the country. The novel idea of integrating the Northeast India with Southeast Asia and the rest of India requires a violent-free Northeast for which the security bureaucracy shall play a pivotal role. Recently, the power to arrest anyone and search a place without warrant was granted to the Assam Rifles deployed along the border with Myanmar in Assam, Arunachal Pradesh, Manipur, Nagaland and Mizoram. The rationale behind this is the difficulties the security forces face in making seizures and arrest in Mizoram, but, the notification had to be withdrawn due to local opposition.

Having lived through several years of insurgency and ethnic conflict have contributed in the mushrooming of civil society groups such as the Meira Paibis, NMA and NPMHR, which were founded in the 1970s. Others such as Apunba Lup of Manipur came into existence in response to specific incident of the alleged rape and murder of Manorama Devi, a lady, by the Assam Rifles in 2004. They play diverse roles. Some focus on human rights issues and advocacy, while others focus on upholding the interests of the community which they claim to represent. Some have been also at the forefront of promoting peace.

The enduring experience of the AFSPA gives an indication of the conflict between the local interest and national security interest. Since the border areas are considered sensitive, the armed forces continue to be crucial with or without the discretionary powers. Besides the insurgency, the frequent occurrence of ethnic conflict apparently became the new ground for the deployment of armed forces. This reportedly occurred during the blockade of a crucial highway in Manipur by certain Naga groups, during the violent conflicts between the Kukis and the Nagas in the 1990s, and the Kukis-and the Karbis between 2003 and 2004 in Assam. Taken all the developments together, we argue that measures to tackle insurgency and ethnic conflict led to the expansion of security administration and governance in the region, in which the civilian face of the counter-insurgency is represented by the Governor and the Chief Minister of the state, but command and control vests exclusively in the security forces. This means that the civilian–state democratic relationship is not only suffered but also is supplanted mostly by the security concerns and the security administration. Furthermore, one may say the state is able to control the insurgents to some extent, but the region still cannot get rid of insurgency and newer instances of conflicts are increasingly seen.

Notes

1. See, 'Frequently Asked Questions on Protected Area Permit (PAP)/Restricted Area Permit (RAP) regime', New Delhi: Ministry of External Affairs.

2. The Government of India, Government of Assam and Bodo representatives concluded an agreement in New Delhi on 27 January 2020 with the aim of ending Bodo insurgency. The government promised to grant a special development package of about ₹1,500 crores over 3 years for undertaking development works in the Bodoland Territorial Region of Assam.
3. Reacting to a Ministry of Home Affairs notification to give power to arrest anyone and search a place without warrant to the Assam Rifles deployed along the Myanmar border in Assam, Arunachal Pradesh, Manipur, Nagaland and Mizoram, the Mizo Zirlai Pawl (MZP) has renewed the demand for the repeal of the Act from Mizoram. The said notification has been withdrawn.
4. In January 2020, a lady Indian Police Service officer had complained that a personal of Assam Rifles detained and misbehaved with her and her police escorts at a border check near the India–Myanmar border in Manipur.
5. The Extrajudicial Execution Victim Families Association Manipur placed before the court details of 62 cases from 2007 to 2012 and also a list of 1,528 cases of extrajudicial executions carried out by the police and security forces since 1979. See, *The Hindu* (2012).
6. Supreme Court of India on Armed Forces (Special Powers) Act, 1958. Available at http://www.upr-info.org/IMG/pdf/COHR_IND_UPR_S1_2008anx_Annex_XXIII_Supreme_Court_ruling_on_AFSPA.pdf (accessed 22 July 2012).

References

Baruah, Sanjib. 2002. 'Gulliver's Troubles: State and Militants in North-East India.' *Economic & Political Weekly* 37, no. 41: 4178–4182.

Bimol Akoijam, A. 2005. 'Another 9/11, Another Act of Terror: The "Embedded Disorder" of the AFSPA.' In *Bare Acts*, edited by Monica Narula Shuddhabrata Sengupta, Jeebesh Bagchi, Geert Lovink, and Lawrence Liang, 486–487. New Delhi: CSDS-Sarai.

Government of India. 2004. *Annual Report 2003–2004*. New Delhi: Ministry of Home Affairs.

———. 2018. *Annual Report 2017–18, Annexure IV*. New Delhi: Ministry of Home Affairs.

———. 2019. *Annual Report 2018–19*. New Delhi: Ministry of Defence.

Government of Mizoram. 2001, March 20. *Budget Speech of Pu Zoramthanga, Chief Minister for 2001–2002*. Aizawl: Government of Mizoram.

Government of Sikkim. 2003. *53rd Independence Day', in Sikkim: Perspectives and Vision, Speeches of Chief Minister Pawan Chamling*. Gangtok; New Delhi: Information and Public Relations Department, and Indus Publishing Company.

India Code. 2020. *The Armed Forces (Special Powers) Act, 1958*. New Delhi: Ministry of Law and Justice, Government of India.

Kamboj, Anil. 2004. 'Manipur and Armed Forces (Special Powers) Act 1958', *Strategic Analysis*, 28, 4: 616–620.
Kom, Sekholal, Ch. 2010. 'Ethnic Mobilisation and Militancy in Northeast India: A Case of Manipur.' *The Indian Journal of Political Science* 71, no. 3: 869–879.
Ludra, Kuldip Singh. 1999. *National Security Papers*. Chandigarh: Thakur Strategic Research Centre.
Press Releases. 2003, June 8. 'PM's Statement on Boosting Peace Initiatives in J&K, Nagaland and Mizoram.' New Delhi. Available at https://archivepmo.nic.in/abv/content_print.php?nodeid=1835&nodetype=1 (accessed 11 August 2019).
Press Trust of India. 2018, April 24. 'Assam Rifles Provides Electricity to Interior Manipur Village.' *Business Standard*. Available at https://www.businessstandard.com/article/pti-stories/assam-rifles-provides-electricity-to-interior-manipur-village-118042400214_1.html (accessed 31 March 2021).
Rajya Sabha Secretariat. 2018. *Two Hundred Thirteenth Report Security Situation in the North Eastern States of India*, Report Number 213. New Delhi: Rajya Sabha Secretariat.
Routray, Prasad Bibhu. 2005. *The Militant Moral Police*. Available at https://www.outlookindia.com/website/story/the-militant-moral-police/226217 (accessed 15 July 2019).
Sahni, Ajai, and B. P. Routray. 2001. 'SULFA: Terror by Another Name.' *Faultlines* 9: 1–19.
Sinha, S. P. 2007. *Lost Opportunities: 50 Years of Insurgency in the North-east and India's Response*. New Delhi: Lancer Publishers & Distributors.
State Reorganisation Commission. 1955. *Report of the State Reorganisation Commission*. New Delhi: State Reorganisation Commission.
The Hindu. 2012, 3 October. 'Notice to Centre, Manipur on Extra-judicial Killings.' https://www.thehindu.com/news/national/other-states/Court-notice-to-Centre-Manipur-on-killings/article12542604.ece (accessed 31 March 2021).
The Sangai Express. 2020, 10 January. 'Shift AR Post from MU: MUSU to CM.' Imphal. https://www.thesangaiexpress.com/Encyc/2020/1/10/By-Our-Staff-ReporterIMPHAL-Jan-9-A-team-of-Manipur-University-Students-Union-MUSU-submitted-a-memorandum-to-Chief-Minister-N-Biren-Singh-today-containing-various-demands-ranging-from-shifting.amp.html (accessed 31 March 2021).

CHAPTER 8

Emergency Law in Nagaland and State's Classification of People as Suspect[1]

Chubatila

The debate on the controversial Armed Forces Special Powers Act, 1958 (AFSPA) in India has recently resurged, particularly after two significant developments: the repeal of the AFSPA from the state of Tripura after 18 years of its enforcement, 'in view of the significant taming of terrorism' and 'the decrease of militancy-related incidents in Tripura over the last few years'[2] and the unilateral abrogation of the ceasefire agreement by the National Socialist Council of Nagalim-Khaplang (NSCN-K)[3] with the Government of India after 14 years, on 27 March 2015, before its expiry that was due on 26 April 2015.[4] The end of the ceasefire has already witnessed escalation in violence and mounting tension with security forces being attacked in a series of ambushes at different areas of Nagaland and Manipur (*Business Standard* 2015). Everyday lives of people had been gripped with fear and terror, their mobility had been restricted and their daily activities had been suspended. The horror of ambush combing operations of the 1980s and 1990s in both Manipur and Nagaland where innocent men, women and children were assaulted and tortured on suspicion, revisits peoples' minds.[5] The latest extension of the Act by another 6 months in Nagaland has been vehemently opposed by the current state government as well as the opposition party and prominent social organizations such as the Naga Hoho, the Naga Mothers' Association (NMA), the Naga Students' Federation (NSF) and the Naga Tribes Council (NTC) calling it 'undemocratic', 'terrorising', 'suppressing' and 'inhuman'.[6]

This chapter examines the emergency nature of the AFSPA through a detailed analysis of habeas corpus cases and its dossier from Nagaland, the earliest region where the Act has been implemented and is still in force. The suspension of citizen's rights and privileges under the writ of habeas corpus is taken as a major indicator of an emergency situation in any constitutional democracy. The chapter attempts to go beyond the critique of the Act from the perspective of human rights abuse (although not undermining the same) and questions the exceptionalism that the state enforces through this Act. It emphasizes on the techniques used to classify, mark out and regulate a 'suspect population' or 'suspect community', thereby domesticating wartime practices in the everyday legal discourse, particularly the everyday vocabulary of AFSPA. Illegal detention, torture and custodial death(s) become routine when such exceptionalism is normalized, as I try to show through the case discussed in the end.

AFSPA and its provisions have been brutally assailed by academics, humanitarian activists, policy analysts and various civil society actors mainly for its draconian nature and the terror it proliferates. Following Jacques Derrida, Dolly Kikon critiques the Act by arguing that 'law is not justice', thereby characterizing AFSPA as a political manoeuvre by the state to 'proselytize recalcitrant citizens' (2009, 271). Bimol Akoijam (2011) has argued that AFSPA is a 'diabolical legal fiction' architected on legislative vagueness about intent or scope.[7] This emergency law on terror is in fact a law of terror, or what Bimol Akoijam (2005) calls, a 'disguised war' and an 'embedded disorder' in Indian democracy. Pradip Phanjoubam has also called AFSPA 'a raw instrument of war' (cited in Chadha 2012, 37). Furthermore, the Jeevan Reddy Committee Report characterized AFSPA as 'a symbol of oppression, an object of hate and an instrument of discrimination and high-handedness' (Justice Jeevan Reddy Committee 2005, 75).

Having given these critiques, I attempt to show how the emergency law of the AFSPA constitutes exceptional subjects (in law and politics), thereby producing the figure of the 'suspect' and regulates the 'suspect community'. This is shown through analyses of habeas corpus cases from Nagaland. In such cases, the classificatory practices of the state are clearly manifested as the population is marked as 'suspects', and these suspects are organized on the basis of a triple colour gradation into 'Black', 'Grey' and 'White', moving into the everyday vocabulary of AFSPA. However, the main objective of classifying people has been veiled under maintaining 'standards of surveillance' and to act as a check on 'prejudicial activities' (terms in the parlance of military intelligence that are intentionally intelligible only to the security forces). To examine such classification, I take a close look at the various documents that make up a habeas corpus petition; how a detenue is constituted and defined through these documents and records; and how these documents are used and relied upon and established as the 'truth' without any qualms by the courts to define the legality or illegality of detentions made by the security forces operating under AFSPA. I focus on how the discourse of the army which classifies suspects (insurgents) into the three colour codes intersects with legal discourse on the legality of the detention of those classified as 'insurgents'.

I refer to various documentation processes that go into filing a habeas corpus petition and the production of 'truth'. I ask, 'if papers were to speak for themselves what would the different certificates/annexure included in a *habeas corpus* case file say'? I focus on the relationship between truth, violence and the law and describe how the power of the state manifests through bureaucratic manoeuvres. In doing so, I try to read into the technique by which 'suspects' are officially produced through different illegalities enabled by such official documents.

To understand the technique of marking out and classifying specific sections of the population through 'hyperlegality'[8] in bureaucratization, it is pertinent to flag the work of Ujjwal Kumar Singh who explores the intricate relationship between extraordinary laws and the creation of a 'suspect community' (2007, 58). He details the cases under Prevention of Terrorism Ordinance (POTO) 2001 to show how an entire community is made suspect through enabling 'arrests... prolonged detention without evidence, encouraged shoddy investigation...use of torture and other extra-legal forms of investigation...and ultimately through its arbitrary and selective use' (Singh 2007, 185–186). An important technique by which the state adopts the 'state of exception'[9] on certain geographical areas or community groups within the state is through what Singh terms the 'politics of exclusion' (Singh 2007). This is achieved through extraordinary laws, which become instrumental in maintaining the hegemonic structures of the nation state, thereby legitimizing the exception.

In the following sections, I suggest that such legitimization is carried out through the promulgation of extraordinary laws as AFSPA and imposed upon people for decades at end, all in the name of 'national security' and preservation of 'law and order'. Furthermore, I argue that the application of AFSPA has reinstated an apparatus which includes a vocabulary for classifying suspects as well as bureaucratic apparatus that produces what Emma Tarlo has called 'paper truths' (2003, 9). However, I must first begin with a brief description of the history of habeas corpus in India before I return to the stories of violence and humiliation archived in the paper book of a habeas corpus writ.

Habeas Corpus: The History and Body of the Writ

The literal meaning of the word 'habeas corpus', with its etymological roots in Latin, is 'have the body', 'produce the body', or broadly, 'let the body go free' (Hussain 2003, 36). It is a legal remedy provided for in almost every modern constitution of the world today to its citizens as a safeguard of individual freedom and liberty, particularly from the excesses of state power. This writ is 'a court order commanding that an imprisoned person be personally produced in court and that an explanation be provided as to why that person is detained'

(Wilkes Jr. 2002, 2). It seeks to establish the procedural legality of the detention and is one of the most fundamental legal remedies guaranteeing the right of a person to be free from unlawful detention or custody. Hence, Clark and McCoy (2000) aptly characterized habeas corpus as the most fundamental legal right.

To understand the contemporary exercise of habeas corpus in India, one needs to look into the circumstances that led to its institution. Hussain (2003) traces the legal history of habeas corpus in India to the 17th century during the time of Lord Coke, through the jurisdiction of the Crown Court in Calcutta. The writ originated as a means to facilitate sovereign power over his subjects and his territory and in order to bring the subjects into direct confrontation with the law. However, the writ may be currently understood and used; originally, when it was introduced, it was meant as a 'protection that grew out of a reciprocal subjection and allegiance' (Hussain 2003, 69). This is an insightful thought for nation states such as India where citizens' allegiance to the state is questionable, especially when demands for secession from the state are quite rampant from different groups within the country.

However, what began as a writ of sovereign privilege was converted by Lord Coke and his successors into a subject's right of appeal. Hussain (2003) looks at how habeas corpus was used to legitimize colonial rule in India and how it gradually evolved into a resource of rights for the citizens against the state executive. He notes that the relation of the Crown with his subjects became 'a mode of binding subjects to the law and its economies of power' (2003, 70). As Hussain argues, 'the extent of the King's sovereignty is understood by where the "writ runs", where it can be issued and enforced' (2003, 70). Hence, it also acted as a signifier of administrative control over the same jurisdiction over which it 'ran'. The legal subject, then, is posited as a by-product necessitated and created by power and, as he calls it, 'one of its prime effects' (Hussain 2003, 71). Hussain very aptly states that 'more than the production of a right, new or otherwise, *habeas corpus* indicates a manoeuvre in the production of a new configuration of law and sovereignty' (2003, 72). Taking a cue from Hussain, who looks at the suspension of habeas corpus as a 'marker of emergency', I proceed to viewing at the suspension of the rights and privileges under the writ of habeas corpus as a major indicator of an emergency situation in any constitutional mechanism (2003, 70). Let us look at a typical case of habeas corpus along with its certificates.

The Habeas Paper Book and Its Accompanying Certificates

A typical habeas paper book consists of a writ petition filed by the petitioner on behalf of the detenue(s) through an advocate. The petition consists of all details about the detenue, the date, time and location of arrest and allegations against the security forces if any. A deponent from the armed forces replies to this petition through a counter-affidavit or affidavit-in-reply to the petition answering, defending and/or denying the allegations made in the petition. Besides these documents, various exhibits showing necessary details related to the arrest or detention of the detenue constitute a habeas corpus petition. These could be either included in the affidavit or the counter-affidavit. I now discuss in brief the various certificates accompanying a habeas corpus petition.

The No Claim/Harassment Certificate is a certificate which the detenue is made to sign before his/her handing and taking over takes place between the security forces and the local police. In it, she/he signs in the standardized format stating that during the apprehension, no harassment, ill treatment or beatings had been exerted on him/her by the security forces. In some case, the detenue had been made to sign a blank paper, which is later filled in to suit the case of the security forces. The No Claim/Harassment Certificate also ensures that the detenue does not make any allegation against anybody (read: the security forces) so as to claim any compensation at any later stage through any agency or court of law. However, compensation has been ordered for in most cases by the court despite the detenue signing to such an agreement.

Another significant dossier in a habeas corpus petition is the Medical Fitness Certificate since the court relies on this certificate to ascertain any instances of torture or ill treatment of the detenue while under detention. This is signed by the medical officer examining the detenue at the time of handing over to the local police station, or in his/her absence, a police representative. However, a lot of discrepancies arise when the medical examiner does not enter the right records for reasons convenient to the security forces. This is particularly so when the detenue is hospitalized at military hospitals during the detention; for instance, in the case of *Mr. Mhathung vs. Union of India & Ors* (1996), the detenue, whose medical certificate declared him fit for discharge, was directly admitted to the local civil hospital on being handed over to the local police station, since his condition was still critical, as detailed later in the essay. There are also cases where external injury was clearly mentioned in the medical certificate; yet no further action or proceeding was carried forth in the case nor any mention of torture found in the judgement. This reflects the court's mildness towards the issue of torture.

A First Information Report (FIR) is primarily the document which explains in detail the circumstances occasioning the arrest of the detenue(s). It includes the manner in which the detenue was arrested and for which offence he/she was arrested. It also provides details found out on further interrogation about the person arrested, weapons/items or any incriminating documents found with him either at his residence or on his body during the time of arrest, and also furnishes recommendations made to the local police on how the person should be detained. Gradation of a detenue is generally mentioned in FIR. FIR also states the Act or specific section of it under which the detenue was apprehended or is advised to be booked under.

The Handing/Taking over Certificate keeps record of the date, time and place from where the detenue was apprehended, at which police station he/she is handed over and at what time and date. It specifies the grade—Black, Grey, or White—given to the detenue according to the findings of the interrogation. It also mentions the items/documents if any, from the detenue during the time of arrest and any other details if necessary. This certificate is jointly signed by the local police and the security forces, when the detenue(s) is handed over by the security forces and taken over by the local police or magistrate, whichever is earlier (usually the former).

A Joint Interrogation Report includes the preliminary interrogation report jointly taken by the army, the police and the local administration conducted on the detenue in a much organized manner. In fact, there is a format followed in which everything about the detenue is noted beginning with his/her familial, educational and socio-economic background, and his/her political ideologies. In cases where the detenue happens to be involved with the underground movement, details such as the circumstances leading to his/her joining, the place of his/her training and his/her rank are asked for and recorded. Even details of whether he/she had been involved in activities such as ambushes on any person are clearly recorded to ascertain and establish the illegality and extent of his/her involvement with the underground movement.

Grading of Detenus into 'Black', 'Grey' And 'White'

The security forces use categories of war to classify the body population into different categories of suspicion.[10] The suspect community is divided into three categories by the security forces—categories belonging to the vernacular of war rather than the vocabulary of policing. Evidence of such classification of prisoners has been found in habeas corpus writ petitions filed under AFSPA and some (in fact, 7 out of 77 cases studied) under the National Security Act (NSA), 1980.[11] Detenus under AFSPA comprised of civilians, mostly young men 'suspected' to be 'insurgents' or sympathizers of insurgents. Such classifications of 'suspects' were not remarked in other punitive legislations, and literature on these classificatory practices is very scant in the Indian context. Once a person is apprehended under AFSPA, he/she is interrogated by the security forces. Based on this interrogation and other reports about the person from sources known to the security forces, he/she is classified under a specific category which could be 'Black', 'Grey' or 'White'. It is also determined depending on the nature of his activity, or inactivity, mainly with the underground forces operating in various parts of the state. This classification is mentioned clearly in either the Interrogation Report, the First Information Report or even the Handing and Taking Over Certificate. I provide below a detailed description of the gradation as found in the habeas corpus dossiers filed in the Kohima Bench of the Gauhati High Court between the years 1995 and 1999.[12]

A detenue is graded as 'Black' when there is concrete evidence or proof against him for his involvement in anti-national activities such as his involvement in killings, ambushes, etc. carried out by outfits declared 'illegal' or 'anti-national' by the state. A detenue is also classified as 'Black' for possession of illegal arms or any other ammunition and involvement in such other acts of suspicious nature, which are considered a threat to the security of the state and the people. This evidence is arrived at through the interrogations carried out once the person is arrested as well as through 'incriminating' documents or any other arms recovered from his residence during the search conducted by the security forces. In the cases I collated, there were 44 cases involving 69 detenus graded as 'Black'.[13]

The detenus classified as 'Grey' are apprehended and graded on a suspicious nature, their involvement being of an indirect kind in acts which are seen to be equally threatening to the security of the state. However, for any prolonged detention of such individuals, there should be specific information and evidence against him/her for his/her actions. Some examples of activities which could let a detenue be labelled as 'Grey' are providing shelter or food to people involved in anti-lawful activities and being sympathetic to their actions and providing information to aid unlawful activities which are a threat to the state. Here, one might question the discrepancies in such gradation that might arise in a situation where the security force and the police involved in carrying out the interrogation confuse voluntary provision of shelter, food, information and others to one provided involuntarily, under duress.

Apart from the earlier mentioned case, in another case of 'Grey', nine men were 'apprehended' as 'suspects' by the personnel of 3rd Corps, Rangapahar, during an 'ambush combing operation' from a village named Midzephema, in Nagaland, right after an ambush on a convoy of the security forces. After interrogation, the security forces found out that 'all (other) (*sic*) detenus had assisted the undergrounds in carrying out the ambush on the convoy of security forces. They had not only provided shelter and food to the undergrounds but also assisted them in selecting the ambush site...' (*Atomu Sumi vs. Union of India & Ors* 1997, p. 4 of counter-affidavit). Thereafter, five of them were graded 'Grey', while the other four were graded 'Black'. However, it is not clear as to what criterion had been used to ascertain such categorization in this case since all of them had been involved some way or the other in the said ambush.

When a detenue is labelled 'Grey', it is found that he is defined as someone who was forced to support 'anti-national activity'; for instance, we find that in *Shri. Vikhato Sumi Vs. UoI & Ors* (1996), where the detenue was illegally detained for two days. The reason of him being graded 'Grey' was because of '...his voluntary confession of the activities (of) senior ranking functionaries of anti-national elements. Reveals individual may have been forced to provide lodging etc. He is graded GREY'.[14]

A person described as 'white' is someone 'who either had committed a cognizable offence or against whom reasonable suspicion exists; such persons alone are to be arrested. Innocent persons are not to be arrested and later to give a clean chit to them as being "white"' (*NPMHR vs. UoI* 1997, para 6 (b)). If a detenue is found innocent, without any suspicion against him, he is handed over graded as 'white' to the police for release; for example, in *Lhokeyi Sumi Vs. Union of India & Ors* (1996), two detenus detained for 7 days were graded 'White' with the recommendation that:

> On investigation it was found that both the above mentioned individuals do not belong to any underground organisation nor are they involved in any anti-national activities. However, their relatives are believed to be in the underground organization. However, detailed investigation revealed that they are innocent. They are declared as "WHITE" and handed over to West Police Station to be released.[15]

The other habeas corpus petition in which detenue(s) were graded 'white' was in *Shri H Asheto Vs. Union of India and Ors* (1996) wherein two detenus were detained for 4 and 7 days, respectively. This, again, undoubtedly evokes questions about the manner and the pattern in which the gradation has been done. There were only two cases involving four detenus graded as 'white' from the Kohima Bench petitions in the period I studied. In both cases, no reasons were stated for the delay in handing over the innocent detenus to the local police station.

A conversation with Col (Retd) M. S. Thakur, who had served in the security force stationed in Nagaland during the 1960s as well as the time around 1996 and 1997, helped me to understand the classification of an individual detained by the security forces after interrogation. He explained to me that a joint interrogation team comprising of the intelligence team of security forces and the local police were constituted in Nagaland to carry out any kind of interrogation which were meant to extract information from the detenue(s). In another telephonic interview with the same interviewee,[16] I got to learn how the elders from the villages and towns are used as sources for validating the activity of a person 'suspected' by the army and how it helps the army in preparing the list of suspects from an area. This list is used in conjunction with the information gathered by intelligence sources working with the army in determining whether the person arrested falls under 'Black', 'Grey' or 'White' after the interrogation.

Details of the classification of gradation done are given below:

Classification of Gradation of the Detenus

	Grade	No. of Cases	No. of Detenus
1.	Black	44	69
2.	White	2	4
3.	Grey	2	6

Source: Author.

There were five cases involving seven detenus whose gradation could not be ascertained owing to factors such as missing FIRs and other documents where such specification has been done, although they are highly probable to be 'Black' since they are also categorized as involved in 'anti-national' activities, as indicated by documents such as the counter-affidavit.

Techniques of Torture Used in Extracting 'Confessions'

In this section, I briefly point out the torture techniques used by the army in Nagaland on the detenus, as documented in the dossiers of judgements analysed.[17] It is possible to argue that the vocabulary of war has become so normalized that not only does it inhabit judgements but also the way in which lawyers craft their arguments against custodial torture; for instance, from the interviews I conducted in December 2008 in Kohima among some lawyers from the Kohima Bench, I learnt from a senior lawyer, Shri. Lanu Jamir, who stated that:

> it (referring to the AFSPA) does not give the security forces the right to detain and torture a detenue although he may be graded as "black" since the constitutional provision under the ASFPA, is to hand him over to the local police station with the least possible delay.[18]

The above discussion manifests that the exceptional powers granted to the army have been 'expanded' through the production of suspect communities. The army officials interpret and determine 'degrees' of 'suspicion' by detaining people who they think help and support 'insurgents', for example, by coding such population as 'Grey'. Hence, young Naga men, especially policed by the army are vulnerable to illegal detention. All these are made possible through the instrument of law and its enabling power. Law acts as an instrument of power by providing those acting on behalf of it, empowering them with provisions that create space for a regime of terror, which is then exerted on those found to be in non-conformity to its ideals and principles.

From the 44 cases of 'Black', torture had been alleged clearly in 7 cases. However, the detenus in the two cases of custodial deaths were ungraded. Also, it might be necessary to mention that only three cases where the detenus developed complications after their apprehension and had to be hospitalized in the army hospital were graded 'Black'. This leads us on to the discussion of the various forms of torture mentioned in the habeas corpus petitions from Nagaland.

The following kinds of torture techniques were used on detenus for extracting 'confession' by the security forces: blindfolding the person(s) during apprehension from one's residence in the presence and witnesses of his family members, electric shocks or electrocution, administering drugged injections and thereafter operating upon the person's body, tying the person by hanging him upside down and mocking at him, pouring water through (the) nostrils and beating with blunt objects. These techniques are, however, just a few that are found to have been used through the externally visible marks left on the bodies of the detenus post detention. Mr Ashipri Poumai, another senior lawyer in the Gauhati High Court, Kohima Bench, mentioned 'the systematic way of killing or elimination deployed by the army, which ensures that no externally visible injuries are made on the body of the detenue', and opines that 'the security forces in this way projects itself to the people as a disciplined institution/body, therefore Constitutional'.[19] In this process of ensuring that no externally visible or indelible marks are left on the bodies, recourse could be taken to other more internally effective and externally invisible methods of torture practised by the security forces.

The cases analysed in my study allow us to understand the materiality of documents and the functions certification serves in establishing a category, particularly a 'suspect'. These cases were chosen from the many habeas corpus petitions bearing in mind the certificates they invoked and the paper war in court through the affidavit and counter-affidavits related to the detention. These are cases involving torture, illegal detention and custodial death. Through these, attention is paid to the ways in which both the citizens filing the petition and the security forces negotiate through documents in a court of law. Out of the many, I discuss one case in certificatory detail for the purpose of this chapter and its arguments.

Torture as 'Attempted Suicide': The Case of Lotha[20]

One evening, at a time when there was so much tension and fear, and normal life meant curfews from 6 am to 6 pm, a certain young man of 28 years was apprehended unannounced from his own home at around

6:30 pm. This incident occurred on 15 March 1996 at Dimapur in Nagaland. Mr Lotha was taken away by the security forces in their vehicle without providing any reason for the arrest, as his family members watched helplessly in terror. Since his arrest, the family contacted and enquired the local administration and all other sources likely to be of some help. However, 65 long hours elapsed without hearing anything of the whereabouts of Lotha. Hence, his uncle Mr Mathung approached the Kohima Bench of the Gauhati High Court to file a habeas corpus writ petition under Article 226 of the Indian Constitution, against the illegal and prolonged detention of his nephew.

In the petition, the detenue's lawyer had argued that 'the continued detention of the detenue...for interrogation and torture is absolutely without any authority of law' (*Mr. Mathung vs. Union of India & Ors* 1996). He also invoked Section 5 of the AFSPA which stipulates that there should be no 'unreasonable delay' in handing over a detenue to the nearest police station or a magistrate once he is apprehended. There was a clear violation of this provision in Lotha's case, as the police station happened to be located barely a few kilometres away from the army headquarters. Besides pointing out the motive of the prolonged detention as solely for 'interrogation and torture', the lawyer also added it was to destroy the life and limbs of the detenue in total violation of his fundamental rights guaranteed under Articles 21 and 22 of the Constitution.[21]

Against these allegations made by Lotha's lawyer, the Company Commander of the Headquarter 3rd Corps, responsible for Lotha's arrest, as respondent of the army, filed a counter-affidavit affirming that the apprehension was done 'on suspicion and also on reliable and specific information by the Security Forces ...in accordance to the law' (*Mr. Mathung vs. Union of India & Ors* 1996, p. 4 of affidavit). Similar to all other responses to allegations against detention and delay in handing over a detenue to the police, the respondent cited 'operational commitments' as the reason. The Company Commander also shifted the blame for the delayed detention to the detenue himself alleging that Lotha attempted to commit suicide while in custody with the aid of a broken water bottle, and since then had to be hospitalized at the 165 Military Hospital. Attempt to commit suicide while in custody is normalized as an operational constraint.[22]

The Company Commander's response was then riposted by Lotha's lawyer, who repudiated the claims of the army about Lotha's suicidal attempt. He did this by reproducing a recorded file of Lotha's narration to his uncle, the petitioner, about the detailed manner of his torture during the detention. This statement was taken by Lotha's uncle Mathung, at the Civil hospital Dimapur on 29 March 1996, after Lotha was directly hospitalized once he was handed over to the police by the security forces. Lotha described how he was 'electrocuted all over his body, tied and hung upside down, mocking at him that even Jesus Christ suffered in the similar manner',[23] and that while he was drugged, they had cut his neck and operated his abdomen.

The modality of torture experienced by Lotha operates in the economy of torture where torture is racialized and communalized (Bhuwania 2009; Rao 2001). From this painful account, the 'art of inflicting pain' on the body is directed equally at destroying the world, an inner world where religion provides meaning to live. The torturer destroys both the word and the world of the tortured (Scarry 1985). Drawing upon the work of Scarry, Cover calls torture 'the deliberate infliction of pain in order to destroy the victim's normative world and capacity to create shared realities' (1985, 1603). Cover (1986) points out that interrogation as part of torture is rarely designed to extract information; rather, he argues 'more commonly, the torturer's interrogation is designed to demonstrate the end of the normative world of the victim-the end of what the victim values, the end of the bonds that constitute the community in which the values are grounded' (Cover 1986, 1603). Such torture practices also shed light on how the state treats those citizens located on the geopolitical fringes of the national body politic. FIR of Lotha is discussed in the following section.

First Information Report of Lotha

Lotha's FIR classifies him clearly as 'Black'. As mentioned above, a detenue is graded as 'Black' when there is concrete evidence or proof against him for his involvement in anti-national activities such as his involvement in killings, ambushes etc. carried out by outfits declared 'illegal' or 'anti-national' by the state, possession of illegal arms or any other ammunition and such other acts of suspicious nature, which are considered a threat to the security of the state and the people. Apparently, Lotha was enrolled as a first-year student of BA at a reputed college in Shillong, Meghalaya, when he was approached by one of the underground personnel who happened to belong to his community. He was threatened with dire consequences if he refused to join the National Socialist Council of Nagaland (NSCN). Hence, he became a member in October 1992 and after about 3 years, he deserted the faction on 6 July 1995. His biographical account (as given in FIR) also recorded that Lotha was an officer level cadre of Special Task Force (STF) with a 'high average intelligence'. According to this report, the security forces claimed that Lotha was detained and interrogated for two main offences—his involvement with NSCN and for taking active part in two attacks in 1994, leading to the death of eight people.[24] In this case, we can notice a blurring between secessionism and terrorism, and correspondingly the AFSPA, 1958 and the Unlawful Activities (Prevention) Act, 1967, as the detenue was registered under the latter Act (as revealed through FIR). This is not the first time secessionism and terrorism have been understood to mean the same. The judgement in *Col. Jagmohan and Ors Vs. The State of Manipur and Ors* (1996, para 6) emphasized the use of AFSPA to 'contain the unlawful activities of certain *terrorist organisations* and its members undermining the security and sovereignty of the nation'. The question is, why is the AFSPA, and not the uniform UA(P)A like the rest of India, implemented to contain 'terrorism' in the AFSPA areas. Is it, therefore, a special legislation, a differential legislation for these areas, in maintaining and enforcing India's security and sovereignty?

Arguing against this paper truth, the petitioner's counsel submitted the report of the joint interrogation made by the Investigating Officer (IO) of the case, Special Branch and the Special Investigation Branch (SIB) stating that the detenue was no longer a member of NSCN during the apprehension, as he had already discharged from his duties in 1995 on 'moral grounds'. He argued that the detenue's confessional statement recorded while in custody of the security forces could not be relied upon since it was extracted under duress, after the infliction of torture and injury.

It is important to note that the performance of torture as self-inflicted injury is enacted by the production of several certificatory practices, which function as paper truths. These practices include production of No Claim/Harassment Certificate, extraction of promise or making the detenue sign or write in paper such promise or claim, etc. The army produced a No Claim/Harassment Certificate (*Mr. Mathung vs. Union of India & Ors* 1996) signed by Lotha, which stated that *since he had no allegation against anyone for ill treatment or harassment, he would not claim any compensation in future* (italics mine). While this document was challenged in court later during the habeas hearing, it is pertinent to note that the file produced on any detenue extracts a promise not to claim any compensation for the deprivation of life or liberty in the eventuality of release. While the context of torture and illegal detention diminishes or even nullifies any evidentiary or legal value of this certificate, it fulfils another symbolic function, one that commits the detenue in writing to the 'law' of the army to ensure that the tortured subject is complicit in his own subjection in such paper truths. As Cover says,

> The 'interpretations' or 'conversations' that are the preconditions for violent incarceration are themselves implements of violence. To obscure this fact is precisely analogous to ignoring the background screams or visible instruments of torture in an inquisitor's interrogation. The experience of the prisoner is, from the outset, an experience of being violently dominated, and it is coloured from the beginning by the fear of being violently treated (Cover 1986, 1608).

This 'fear' of violence from the security forces compels a detenue to authenticate false certificates stating as true. The No Claim/Harassment Certificate itself bears a trace of its own lack of authenticity. Here, it was claimed that Lotha had signed the No Claim/Harassment Certificate attesting to the fact that during his detention, he was neither ill-treated nor harassed by anyone, and that he has no allegation against anybody and would not claim any compensation at a later stage through an agency or court of law. This was signed dated 28 March 1996. Lotha was arrested on 15 March 1996 and released on 28 March 1996.

Now I turn to the Discharge Certificate issued by the medical officer of the 165 Military Hospital on 28 March 1996. This certificate is divided into three parts. The first part lists the name and rank of the patient. The second part describes the unit of underground to which the detenue belongs and the date and time of his arrest, followed by the date of discharge, his International Code Number and the diagnosis and recommendation ('fit for discharge' in this case). The medical officer certified that at the time of admission, Lotha had incurred a 'self-inflicted wound (illegible) and injury larynx and abdomen (OPID)' (*sic*), and on 28 March 1996 declared him fit for discharge. Moreover, on 28 March 1996, the medical officer certified that he had examined Lotha who 'has been found to be physically fit and mentally sound', and that 'no sign of torture/harassment was found on the body' of detenue 'while he was under the custody of the security forces'. This is followed by the sentence, 'he was admitted in 165 Military Hospital for treatment (discharge certificate attached)'.

However, the details of the discharge certificate were found to be problematic once it was corroborated by other reports. It was corroborated by the Injury Report, a fully handwritten report, signed by a group of six doctors from the Dimapur Civil Hospital, the Under Surgery Department, Prisoners' Room, Bed No. I (where the detenue was shifted right after he was discharged from the army hospital). The barely legible handwritten report reads as follows:

Cut mark present in front of neck measuring 5-6 inches;

Hoarseness of voice, cannot speak clearly due to injury (illegible word) laryngeal nerve;

Operation seen in abdomen from epigastrium to below umbilicus with a cut mark on left side of abdomen;

Tenderness present on both (two illegible words). (*Mr. Mathung vs. Union of India & Ors* 1996, p. 19)

The next document attached as annexure to the same habeas corpus file (*Mr. Mathung vs. Union of India & Ors* 1996, Annexure) is a newspaper report titled, 'Detenue Tortured', *Nagaland Post* published on 30 March 1996. This news item narrated how the detenue was *'handed over to the police in a critical condition* and had to be immediately shifted to Dimapur Civil Hospital' (italics mine). It further narrated the way in which the detenue was 'tortured through beatings and electric shocks all over his body including his private parts during detention inside the army cantonment'. The newspaper report, citing 'family sources' stated that the detenue was 'tied and hung upside down while the army personnel jeered at him by saying that even Jesus Christ died in similar fashion'. The news report also stated that 'there were two incisions one across the throat—four inches long—while the second across the abdomen some seven inches long, which appeared to be marks by surgery', and that Lotha was 'injected with some drug and became unconscious and…had been operated upon which he discovered only after regaining consciousness' (*Mr. Mathung vs. Union of India & Ors* 1996, p. 20).

This annexure is immediately followed by a rejoinder by the Army in the same newspaper the following day under the paper's 'postmortem' section. The main section of the rejoinder reads:

> On 18 March 1996, he asked a sentry for water to drink, which was provided in a bottle. Richard (name changed) broke the bottle against the wall and with the broken end attempted to commit suicide by inflicting injury to his throat and abdomen. Due to prompt action of the sentry on duty, Richard was prevented from causing further injury to himself and was immediately removed to hospital. Accordingly, a complaint for attempted suicide was lodged with the police. Meanwhile, Richard was given medical attention at the Military Hospital where doctors have to surgically remove a piece of glass embedded in the abdomen of Richard, thus saving his life…
> The reports of torture and ill-treatment are false and malicious.
> (*Mr. Mathung vs. Union of India & Ors* 1996, Annexure-F, p. 21)

This rejoinder had been produced by the army as a cover-up for their excesses by projecting the armed forces as 'saviours' of detenus from inflicting self-harm and rescuing them from ending their lives. In Lotha's case, in the affidavit-in-support of the detenue filed by his petitioner, the latter has prayed to the court for directing the respondents to pay a sum of ₹0.1 million for illegal detention, a sum of ₹0.2

million for torture and harassment during the same and also to pay up all expenses incurred by the detenue for his recovery. Hence, the petitioner states the No Claim Certificate, Discharge Certificate from Military Hospital and the Medical Certificate documents were contradictory and 'fabricated in order to suit the case of the security forces' (*Mr. Mathung vs. Union of India & Ors* 1996, p. 9). In the final order regarding the claim for compensation, the court directed the detenue to refer to the observations made by the apex court in *D.K. Basu* Vs. *State of West Bengal*.[25] The court recognized the violence that the paper truths of the army forged by allowing the claim for compensation as requested by the petitioner.

Conclusion

The chapter strives to understand how impunity and immunity are enabled and established for the security forces through a proliferation of certificates or paper documents (paper truths) and the mechanism of producing (or classifying) a body as 'suspect'. Without these certificates or documents, it would be impossible to make a detenue legible in court or visible to law. At the same time, there is an inbuilt impunity in and through these certificates, which provides a safe passage in legalizing (and covering up) the excesses committed by the security forces. The same legal remedy (habeas corpus) that frees a detenue from custody has the possibility of binding him to the law through various 'paper truths' (of the security forces) accompanying the writ. In other words, though habeas corpus has shifted from a writ of sovereign privilege to a subject's right of appeal in postcolonial India, it is very much a mechanism which can be used to normalize the violent acts enabled through the Act (on the body of the detenue). Hence, the very fact that the filing of a habeas corpus petition for detentions under AFSPA cannot guarantee a citizen's Constitutional right not to be indefinitely detained leads one to question the very essence of a constitutional Act.[26] To reiterate, such embedded illegalities in this extraordinary Act qualify it to be considered as an emergency mechanism of the state in wielding its power over population(s) which it considers as 'suspect'. By forcing the detenus to sign these certificates while under their custody, the security forces become the source of law and violence. Supported by documents, such classification plays a very crucial role in regulating, identifying and even excluding population(s). Following Foucault, Carol Snyder understands classifications as 'social instruments, powerful codes whose frequent function is to exclude, confine, or incarcerate "deviant" types' (1984, 210). It creates the figure of a 'suspect' through a proliferation of documents, laws and a myriad of bureaucratic practices, which are normalized in the politico-juridical system. Also, such practices make way for a discourse of military and war into everyday legal procedures, thereby normalizing an otherwise emergency exercise.

The proliferative case book in a habeas corpus case is indicative of the generation of *hyperlegality* which marks exceptional law. The domestication of categories of war in constitutional law shown clearly by the case law on habeas corpus suggests the importance of looking at the processes of certification deployed by the security state to normalize the brutal violence authorized by emergency law in the Northeast. Thus, Hussain is right in saying that habeas corpus is one legal provision in which the state 'claims sovereign immunity by law' (2007 83). Through the suspension of this writ, the sovereign power of the state is continuously reasserted and exercised upon the people of the 'disturbed areas'.

Notes

1. I would like to thank my MPhil/PhD supervisor, Dr Pratiksha Baxi, Associate Professor at the Centre for the Study of Law and Governance, Jawaharlal Nehru University, for her critical comments and insights on the chapter.
2. In the words of the Chief Minister of Tripura, Mr Manik Sarkar, himself. Available in a report on http://www.firstpost.com/india/afspa-removed-in-tripura-after-18-years-heres-why-it-was-enforced-and-why-its-gone-now-2266770.html (accessed 19 June 2015).
3. One of the major underground factions of Nagaland, formed out of the splinter within NSCN in 1988 and based out of Myanmar. Currently, it has joined hands with other 'separatist outfits' from the North East. See, http://indianexpress.com/article/opinion/editorials/end-of-the-limbo/
4. It should be noted, however, that the Act was extended by another 6 months in the states of Manipur (w.e.f. 06 January, 2020), Nagaland (w.e.f. 30 June, 2020), and Assam (w.e.f. 28 August, 2020) and in three districts and four police stations of Arunachal Pradesh (w.e.f. 01 October, 2020).

See, https://www.mha.gov.in/commoncontent/armed-forces-special-power-act-1958 (accessed 12 November 2020).
And, https://timesofindia.indiatimes.com/india/afspa-extended-in-assam-for-6-more-months/articleshow/77746984.cms (accessed 12 November 2020).

5. From the very outset, I want to categorically state that the aim of the chapter is to analyse AFSPA. The author equally condemns the brutal ambushes carried out by the underground factions on the security forces as much as the violence and torture inflicted by the army personnel on innocent men, women and children on mere suspicion, in the name of maintaining law and order shielded by the Act.
6. See, https://www.thehindu.com/news/national/other-states/civil-society-groups-officials-opposition-decry-afspa-extension-in-nagaland/article30476798.ece (accessed 30 October 2020).
7. See http://kanglaonline.com/2011/09/afspa-tragedy-of-delinking-its-political-premise/ (accessed 12 May 2012).
8. Defined by Hussain as "the proliferation of regulations and administrative procedures that mark the daily management of contemporary crisis" (Hussain 2007, 740).
9. Agamben describes the state of exception as a technique 'that allows for the physical elimination, not only of political adversaries, but of entire categories of citizens who for some reasons cannot be integrated into the political system' (Agamben 2005, 2).
10. Earliest classification of 'suspects' into categories of 'Black', 'White' and 'Grey' by the state as an emergency wartime measure has been found to be practised during the Second World War when civilian 'suspects' entering or returning to India, seen as threats 'prejudicial' to the security of the nation, were interrogated at so-called forward camps and categorised (Chubatila 2014).
11. These findings were part of my research at the Gauhati High Court, Kohima Bench.
12. Post-1999, there is hardly any case of detention that comes to the court, perhaps mainly due to the ceasefire agreement between the Government of India and various factions of the underground movement beginning 1997 with the National Socialist Council of Nagalim (NSCN)-Isak-Muivah faction followed by the NSCN-Khaplang group in 2001.
13. I cite some of the cases of 'Blacks' here: *Mr. Mhathung vs. UoI & Ors* (1996); *Theimila vs. UoI & Ors* (1996); *Mr. Lhokeyi Yepthomi vs. State of Nagaland* (1996); *Mr. James Poumai vs. UoI & Ors* (1996); *Shri Y. Patton vs. UoI & Ors* (1996); *Keheilhoubeiu Solo vs. UoI & Ors* (1997).
14. *Shri. H. Asheto vs. UoI & Ors* mentioned in Handing and Taking over Certificate.
15. *Lhokeyi Sumi vs. UoI & Ors*, mentioned in the FIR.
16. Telephonic conversation on 30 June 2009.
17. Cases from the study where torture of detenus by the security forces had been alleged in the petition were: *Benjamin Marin vs. Union of India* (1996);

Mr. Mathung vs. Union of India & Ors (1996); *Mr. Apam Singmai vs. Union of India & Ors* (1996); *Mr. Lhokeyi Yepthomi vs. State of Nagaland* (1996); *Smti. Aseu Tase vs. Union of India & Ors* (1996); *Keheilhoubeiu Solo vs. Union of India & Ors* (1997); *N. A. Shishak vs. Union of India & Ors* (1997); and *Shri. Viselie Pochury vs. Union of India & Ors* (1997). These are exclusive of cases where the security forces alleged detenus to have developed various ailments during custody, who had to be admitted to the army hospital for number of days before being released. I argue that through such malingering, the security forces portray the detenue as someone who is physically or mentally unfit prior to the detention, and the detention centre provides care to such a detenue who lacks access to medical facility or food and nutrition.

18. Personal Interview held on 15 December 2008 at the Gauhati High Court, Kohima Bench.
19. Personal interview held on 17 December 2008 at the residence of Mr Ashipri Poumai at Kohima.
20. See *Mr. Mathung vs. Union of India & Ors* (1996).
21. While Article 21 guarantees that no person shall be deprived of his life or personal liberty except according to the procedure established by law, Article 22 broadly lays down protection against arrest and detention of a person without being informed, and if arrested and detained to be produced before the nearest magistrate within a period of 24 h, unless the person detained is an 'enemy alien' or is arrested or detained under any law providing for preventive detention.
22. Lotha's is not a stray case wherein the army blamed the detenue and his disease or self-infliction for delayed or prolonged detention. There were other cases from the study where detenus were accused of feigning their illnesses or self-injury, whereby they had to be hospitalized in the army hospital. These cases indicate the medicalization of torture by which I mean the representation of torture or the impact of illegal detention on the health of the detenue is converted into a natural illness or self-inflicted injury. In this particular case, the detenue is portrayed as someone who feigns injury to defame the army.
23. This section stipulates that once a person is detained and taken into custody by the armed forces, he should be handed over to the nearest police station 'with the least possible delay' (Section 5 of AFSPA).
24. This is also reflected in the detenue's confessional statement made to the SF and given in Annexure A, *Mr. Mathung vs. Union of India & Ors* (1996), p. 15.
25. *D.K. Basu vs. State of West Bengal*; this is a very significant case on custodial deaths and compensation heard in the Supreme Court after the matter was raised by the then Executive Chairman, Legal Services Aid, West Bengal, to the then Chief Justice of India, as a writ petition under the Public Interest Litigation category. This case has been cited as a precedent in cases of illegal

detention and custodial violence exercised by the state agencies, and its rectification.
26. The constitutionality and legality of the AFSPA, 1958 was questioned in the landmark NPMHR vs. Union of India case in 1997 *(NPMHR vs. UoI, INDLAW SC 1720)* at the Supreme Court of India which was however upheld.

References

Agamben, Giorgio. 2005. *State of Exception*. Translated by Kevin Attell. Chicago, USA: The University of Chicago Press.
Atomu Sumi vs. Union of India & Ors. 1997. Writ Petition No. 76 (K). Gauhati High Court, Kohima Bench (p. 4 of counter-affidavit).
Benjamin Marin vs. Union of India. 1996. Writ Petition No. 12 (K). Gauhati High Court.
Bhuwania, Anuj. 2009, June. '"Very Wicked Children": "Indian *Torture*" and the Madras *Torture* Commission Report of 1855'. *Sur: International Journal on Human Rights* 6, no. 10: 6–27.
Bimol Akoijam, A. 2005. 'Another 9/11, Another Act of Terror: The Embedded Disorder of the AFSPA'. In *Bare Acts*, edited by Monica Narula, 481–491. New Delhi: Sarai Reader.
———. 2011, 10 September. 'AFSPA: Tragedy of Delinking Its Political Premise'. *Kangla Online*. Available at http://kanglaonline.com/2011/09/afspa-tragedy-of-delinking-its-political-premise/ (accessed 12 May 2012).
Business Standard. 2015, 29 May. 'NSCN-K Ambushes Assam Rifles Once Again'. Available at http://www.business-standard.com/article/news-ians/nscn-k-ambush-assam-rifles-again-one-injured-115052901732_1.html (accessed on 22 March 2021).
Chadha, Vivek, ed. 2012, November. *Armed Forces Special Powers Act: The Debate*. IDSA Monograph Series No. 7. New Delhi: Lancers Books.
Chubatila. 2014. 'Everyday Life of Emergency Law in Nagaland'. Unpublished PhD thesis. New Delhi: Jawaharlal Nehru University.
Clark, David and Gerard McCoy. 2000. *The Most Fundamental Legal Right: Habeas Corpus in the Commonwealth*. New York, NY: Oxford University Press.
Col. Jagmohan Singh and Ors. vs. The State of Manipur and Ors. 2005. MANU/GH/0185/2005.
Cover, Robert M. 1986. *Violence and the Word*. Faculty Scholarship Series, Paper 2708. Available at http://digitalcommons.law.yale.edu/fss_papers/2708 (accessed on 24 May 2014).
D.K. Basu vs. State of West Bengal. 1997. 1 SCC 416.
Hussain, Nasser. 2003. *The Jurisprudence of Emergency: Colonialism and the Rule of Law*. Ann Arbor, MI: The University of Michigan Press.

Hussain, Nasser. 2007. 'Hyperlegality', *New Criminal Law Review*, 10, 4: 514–531.
Justice Jeevan Reddy Committee. 2005. Report of the Committee headed by Justice (Retd) B. P. Jeevan Reddy to Review the Armed Forces (Special Powers) Act, 1958. http://www.hindu.com/nic/afa/ (accessed 20 March 2012).
Keheilhoubeiu Solo vs. Union of India & Ors. 1997. Writ Petition No. 36 (K). Gauhati High Court.
Kikon, Dolly. 2009. 'The Predicament of Justice: 50 Years of AFSPA'. *Contemporary South Asia* 17, no. 3: 271–282.
Lhokeyi Sumi vs. UoI & Ors. 1996. Writ Petition No. 125 (K). Gauhati High Court.
Mr. Apam Singmai vs. Union of India & Ors. 1996. Writ Petition No. 44(K). Gauhati High Court.
Mr. James Poumai vs. UoI & Ors. 1996. Writ Petition No. 72 (K). Gauhati High Court.
Mr. Lhokeyi Yepthomi vs. State of Nagaland. 1996. Writ Petition No. 66(K). Gauhati High Court.
Mr. Mhathung vs. Union of India & Ors. 1996. Writ Petition No. 30 (K). Gauhati High Court, Kohima Bench.
N. A. Shishak vs. Union of India & Ors. 1997. Writ Petition No. 90 (K). Gauhati High Court.
NPMHR vs. UoI. 1997. INDLAW SC 1720.
Rao, Anupama. 2001, 27 October. 'Problems of Violence, States of Terror: Torture in Colonial India'. *Economic & Political Weekly* 36, no. 43: 4125–4133.
Scarry, Elaine. 1985. *The Body in Pain.* New York, NY: Oxford University Press.
Shri Y. Patton vs. UoI & Ors. 1996. Writ Petition No. 86 (K). Gauhati High Court.
Shri. H. Asheto vs. UoI & Ors. 1996. Writ Petition No. 37 (K). Gauhati High Court.
Shri. Viselie Pochury vs. Union of India & Ors. 1997. Writ Petition No. 134(K). Gauhati High Court.
Singh, Ujjwal Kumar. 2007. *The State, Democracy and Anti-terror Laws in India.* New Delhi: SAGE Publications.
Smti. Aseu Tase vs. Union of India & Ors. 1996. Writ Petition No. 97(K). Gauhati High Court.
Snyder, Carol. 1984, May. 'Analyzing Classifications: Foucault for Advanced Writing'. *College Composition and Communication* 35, no. 2: 209–216.
Tarlo, Emma. 2003. *Unsettling Memories: Narratives of India's 'Emergency'.* New Delhi: Permanent Black.
Theimila vs. UoI & Ors. 1996. Writ Petition No. 38 (K). Gauhati High Court.
Wilkes Jr., Donald E. 2002. *The Writ of Habeas Corpus, Scholarly Works.* University of Georgia School of Law. http://digitalcommons.law.uga.edu/fac_artchop/182 (accessed 29 May 2011).

CHAPTER 9

Encountering the State in Manipur
A Political History of Women in Public Space

L. Basanti Devi

In this chapter we analyse the relationship between a specific category of women and the state in the political history of Manipur. Historically, the state has witnessed the women's protest movement—directed not at the society but at the perceived and experienced 'wrongs done' by the state. In a work by Rajeswari Sundar Rajan (2003), she refers to the 'terms of engagement' between the state and women in India while discussing women, laws and citizenship in post-colonial India. She basically deals with gendered laws in post-colonial India that lead to organize women's response, thereby questioning the idea of citizenship in India with respect to the laws that directly impinge on the life of women. Rajan argues that women and the state constitute each other. This engagement is between the actors considered as 'legitimate adversaries' in a democratic society: women and the state. However, women and the state in the context of Manipur have, at most times, not been engaged as legitimate adversaries; there is the state that lays claim to exercise monopoly over legitimate use of violence, on the one hand, and women who challenge the laws and actions of the state, on the other hand. The state categorizes women participating in protests as those 'linked with insurgents'. However, to the women, their movement is a legitimate exercise that they are compelled to participate in to establish societies free from torture, inequality and state violence. Such engagement compels one to explore the specific meaning of women and the space in which they operate in such history. As a result, this study is intended to discuss the following question: what specific understandings of space and category of women emerged in the course of engagement between women and the state in the political history of Manipur?

This chapter is organized broadly under the following two themes: the women and the state in colonial times; and the women and the state in post-colonial times. It is based on a survey of archival literature, as well as fieldwork carried out largely in Imphal in Manipur.

Colonial State, 'Unruly' Women and *Lan*

The 1891 Anglo-Manipur War that led to the defeat of Manipur state heralded a new era in the history of Manipur. The nature of Manipur as a native state changed as a result of this defeat. The British asserted the moral right to annex Manipur; yet, in an act of clemency by the British Crown, it was re-granted the status of a state ruled by the native ruler. Direct annexation was not done; instead, the native ruler governed Manipur as per the dictates of the Government of British India. Chura Chand, grandson of Raja Nara Singh, was selected as the new raja. Maxwell was appointed as the Political Agent and Superintendent of the state of Manipur. The state had to pay tributes to the British Raj. However, one exception was made regarding the control of the state of Manipur. A policy of least interference was adopted with regard to the customs, traditions and institutions of Manipur. British dominion hence made a distinction between the state and society, that is, social customs/traditions.

Women's response against the colonial state took place in a more or less organized fashion during the colonial rule in Manipur in 1904, 1939 and 1940. Such encounters with the colonial state are called

'Nupi Lan'. The first Nupi Lan occurred in 1904, largely because of the use of male labour by the state, and the second Nupi Lan was the result of the issue of scarcity of rice. However, we feel that the idea of women confronting the state can be traced more to the second Nupi Lan than the earlier one, as far as the records are concerned. Before we actually deal with the encounter between the women and the colonial state, it is important to locate the spaces of women—public and private.

The public presence of women was not necessarily a by-product of agitations against the colonial state. The fact that the involvement of women in agriculture was integrated, from the time of transplantation up to the sale of the produce in the markets, played an important role in marking such presence in the market space of the largely agrarian Meitei society. Such public presence is also considered as an extension of the women's private presence in the familial domain, in which women had to take up roles for the upkeep of the family and economic security (Yambem 1976). Presence of women historically in public is also being interpreted as the historic Burmese-Manipuri of 1817 and the followed up seven years devastation of Manipur which, Yambem (1976) argued, led to declining male population as it was the duties of menfolks to go the war and as a result larger responsibility of women in maintaining the family. In the earlier pre-colonial structure of the Meitei society, the mandate on males to provide their service to the state also led to a situation where women took the role of running the family. In brief, the public presence of women is an extension of the patriarchal structure that divides roles on the basis of gender: war for men and family maintenance for women. It can be stated that the public space of women was very much still an extension of their private space, as the division of roles on the basis of gender was not contested.

However, this presence of women in public, although reinforcing the patriarchal structure of the Meitei society, turned out to be a space of resistance against the colonial state dealing with rice exports. For instance, the boycott of the market during the agitation of the 1930s in opposition to the Marwaris' monopoly over rice exports was an effective one—'a virtual hartal of the whole bazaar, affecting the economy' (Yambem 1976, 825). Perhaps, one may also argue that the collective response of the women to the state arose from the necessity to confront an organized state structure that had a greater impact on the society than the earlier pre-colonial state structure.

The issue of rice scarcity was a serious one. The area under rice cultivation in Manipur between 1921 and 1939 increased by little (18,838 acres) compared to the volume of rice exports (292,174 maunds). The export was raised to the high volume of 372,174 maunds in 1938, just a year before the infamous women's agitation. In addition, excess rainfall also caused the possibility of low harvest of rice. Sensing the scarcity of rice, the Manipur State Darbar passed resolutions (on 13 September 1939) for stopping the export of rice outside Manipur, but it was stopped only for 40 days (from 14 September to 21 November 1939) (Ibid, 327). The women's agitation of 1939 raised the following demands: (a) ban on the export of rice; (b) disabling of rice mills; (c) control of the market; and (d) tackling of the issue of the atrocities committed against women during the agitation. These issues constituted the core of the women's response to the state, which included the Maharaja of Manipur, the Darbar and the Political Agent.

Major protests by women took place in Imphal during 11–15 December 1939. A large number of women came out in front of the telegraph office on 12 December to demand stoppage of rice exports. On 13 December, these women demanded closure of rice mills owned by the Marwaris and some Meiteis. The women marched to rice mills, stopped rice carts from rural areas from reaching the bazaar for sale and stopped Marwari traders from buying the rice. In the process of these agitations, women were injured in a bayonet charge. By 1940, the issue of the agitations moved beyond the economic demands to the demand for the trial of those police personnel responsible for injuring women, and the Darbar and the Raja of Manipur were asked to constitute a tribunal.

On the part of the colonial state, what concerned the colonial officials was the continuity of the agitations even after the Darbar stopped the export of rice and disabled the rice mills. Mr Gimson, the Political Agent, held the view that the women did not understand what they were doing. This was perhaps because of his assumption that the movement was basically about economic concerns and once they were addressed the agitations would end. The colonial officials defended the police's bayonet attack on the female agitators. Army official Major Bulfield, who was present at the telegraph office during the incident, observed that the women were an 'unruly mob' during the agitation. The women who stopped the carts bringing rice to the bazaar were charged with 'unlawful assembly' under Section 143 of the Indian Penal Code (IPC). Under this section, those women were taken as unlawful women.

The emergence of the popular leader Irabot, however, not only gave a new direction to the women's agitation of 1939 but also gave it the new meaning of a people's movement (for details see, Singh, 1989: 103–139). A mention must be made of the public speech Irabot gave on 7 January 1940, in which he spoke about the oncoming famine due to rise in rice price, flooding of paddy fields and export of rice from Manipur. He spoke of the state that worked to end starvation due to famine and protect the citizens, rather than collecting taxes from people. He said, 'state is the people and that of the two-Food and Tax-food is by far the more essential one. If the people of Manipur die of starvation the state itself will be nowhere. Where then comes the question of taxation?' Next, he argued that the rice mills had contributed to the loss of jobs among people who had lived by husking rice previously and to the rise of unemployment, because of the export of rice outside Manipur. He said: 'Thus the mills have exported what is due to the hungry millions. The mill is an effective weapon for the millionaire to extort the morsel from the mouth of the ill-fed men'. Irabot further spoke of the women who took the lead in the agitation. He was of the opinion that the women's demands for ending the export of rice and disabling the mills were made for the welfare of those with hungry stomachs. Instead, the women had been injured by bayonets.

What is so striking is the difference in the reading of the women's agitation between the colonial officials and Irabot. While the officials interpreted the agitation as that of 'unruly women' and considered the cause to be merely economic, not political, Irabot felt that the agitation of the women was a movement of the 'people'; to Irabot, the women did what they did for the welfare of the people. This emphasis on people can be noticed in the charter of demands passed during the same public meeting on 7 January 1940 where Irabot gave his speech; 11 demands were included in the charter, which had already been submitted to the Darbar and the Maharaja of Manipur. These demands were as follows: to stop the export of rice till the next harvest; to stop rice mills completely; to decide the case of the bayonet charge that had severely injured five women; to remove the sitting Darbar members and replace them with new ones through elections; to remove state servants in the police department; to establish a legislative council; to decide the case of a woman who was kicked on her chest by a policeman; to decide the case of 10 women charged with picketing; to decide the case of a woman who was assaulted by being kicked on her private parts by a policeman; to decide the case of assault on the crowd on 14 January 1940; and lastly to decide the case of nine leaders of Manipur Praja Sanmeloni arrested and detained in police custody without being informed of the charges against them.

From the above discussion, a few things have to be re-emphasized before we proceed to the next section. An active public space for women, although not contesting the gender-based division of roles (war for men, family and economic security for women), was seen while they encountered the state. The encounter brings up the meanings of unruly women. The notion of unruliness is almost equal to illegality or illegitimacy in the eyes of the colonial state. On the other hand, in the interpretation of Hijam Irabot, unruly women are legitimate/rightful women resisting for the welfare of the people. While the notions of public space, women and people are importance to discuss, the issue of legitimate and illegitimate protests/movements continuously shape encounters between women and the state, even in contemporary times.

Women's Post-colonial Writings: The Space of Women

In the August issue (1969) of *Lamyanba* journal published in Imphal, Manipur, issues of women were raised. Some of the key issues found in women's writings in the late 1960s were those of polygamy, 'forced' elopement of women, domestic violence against women, unequal treatment of women before and after marriage, as far as job and career were concerned, etc. One Rammabai Yenkhoibi writing in *Lamyanba* journal (first issue, August 1969, 11–15) on the 'Burden of Manipuri Women' contradicted stories circulated on Manipuri women as liberated ones in the old times by citing empirical experiences of women in the 1960s. She wrote that there was a possibility of women belonging to royal lineages having enjoyed some sort of high status, but empirically, common women did not enjoy an equal status as men. Even the sort of freedom possibly enjoyed by women of royal lineages was no more seen. Interestingly, Yenkhoibi quoted Hindu philosopher Manu who said that freedom for women is not possible.

Another issue brought up in this writing was the issue of forced elopement—forced because it was done without the consent of women. It was a practice among menfolk, who helped one of them force a woman to elope with him. The last issue Yenkhoibi brought up was the issue of domestication of married women. This was a situation in which a woman, after her marriage, would not be given a chance to take a public job outside her household or utilize her innate talents, if any.

However, these issues perhaps lost their importance or failed to occupy their place in the public discourse of 20th-century Manipur. This has to do with the increasing importance given to the idea of Manipur and its unique historical and cultural identity at this time. In the process, the possibility of questioning the social and customary control over women was ruled out; rather, the society/culture was defended as being different from the rest of Indian societies. This is also seen in the women's writings, which compare Manipuri women with the rest of Indian women.

Unlike Yenkhoibi's piece, in a piece by another woman Sabita (1 November 1969, 11–13), we find a different understanding of women in the history of Manipur. Sabita argued that the place of women had been respectable and dignified since historical times. The identity of Manipuri women was undisturbed. This piece is more a defence of the historical identity of Manipur's women—that their identity does not discriminate against them. The first king of the Meitei kingdom who ruled in 33 AD, Meidungu Pakhangba, is understood to have given women their due place in society and not discriminated against them; rather, a separate department that took care of women, called 'Macha Loishang', was established by the state.

When it comes to the status of women, that this historical consciousness comes as part of defending the uniqueness of Manipur is the point that needs to be emphasized. Such a historical consciousness was manifested in the women's writing through their comparisons with the rest of Indian society. This also brings up the point that the construction of dignified Manipuri women emerged alongside the construction of images of 'other women'. The identity of the 'other' as a society that kept its women under a *purdah* system is visible in this writing. The assumption is that women under the *purdah* system did not have the chance to participate in the struggle for the betterment of society. However, Manipuri women were unlike those under the *purdah* system, instead actively participating in the struggle for the betterment of society (Sabita 1969, 11).

In the writing of Sabita (1969), there is the construction of the 'feminine' nature of Manipuri women as consisting of both sober and courageous behaviours. Unlike the previous writings, it provides a defence of the folk traditions that fundamentally decide the nature of women and are used as a yardstick for the evaluation of the behaviours of 'modern' women. Interestingly, the idea of modernity is questioned. Also, the idea of women being public people not domesticated all the time is the picture that is projected. In a way, the hold of patriarchy is interpreted as not so strong, such that women's presence in public was understood as the prominent feature of Manipur.

The images of women struggling for their daily livelihood, female vendors catching fish from Waithou Lake outside Imphal city and later bringing it to the main market in Imphal, women collecting firewood from the hills, etc. are the prominent faces of women that are emphasized. Not comparing with the rest of societies in India, this imagery of women was also questioning apparently the middle-class women in Manipuri society at that point of time. The piece of writing cited here depicts the struggling woman as the real identity of the

Manipuri women. However, at the same time, these struggling women are also depicted as those who gave equal importance to beautification of their body; the idea of beauty here consists, for instance, of combing one's hair. Sabita (1969) located such women in the marketplace of Manipur. Women were understood to be experts in various walks of life, including agriculture and weaving.

Some writings also identified that there was an unresolved issue of women—around the connection between their private and public life. Sneha Sagolsem's piece (1 December 1969: 19–24) on issues of Manipuri women dives into three spheres of women's life: individual (*lannai*), household (*imung manung*) and public (*mayamgi*). The distinction of the world of individual (*lannai*), though without much explanation in the above writing, is something that appears to help to enquire/intervene the other two spheres. The world of the individual was the world where Sagolshembi (1969) did not find any male–female distinction, because it was the world where everyone, as individual beings, has similar desires, expectations, pains and pleasures. The world of the household was where the burdens of women were found to be rooted. Looking after the nitty-gritty of the household was understood as the duty of women; a gender-based division of roles was prevalent. A married woman performed multiple roles within the confines of the family; in addition to the domestic chores, a married woman had to maintain balance her time between these chores to satisfy her in-laws, children and husband. Sagolshembi (1969) also spoke about those classes of women who were educated, employed or specialized in a profession. For these women, their professional tasks had to be managed alongside their household chores. In the 1960s, Macha Leima, an organization formed by women, emerged to address issues faced by women as a result of social transformation in the period 1950–1970. An ex-president of Macha Leima described the period 1960–1970 as a period of social contradiction—women making history as a collective force and being confined within their individual households.

While the above writings speak of a consciousness of the emerging history in the middle of the 20th century, they nevertheless show the absence of an organized movement either to address the specific concerns of the women or to channelize the responsibility of women for the larger interests of Manipur as a nation. There had been an apparent tension so far in the women's consciousness, between their personal world and public world. Did the rise of the Manipuri nation as a new consciousness resolve this seeming tension or contradiction? Perhaps not, but the idea of Manipur did successfully drive a new identity of women later in the history of Manipur. What appear as contradictions around the space and identity of women in the post-colonial writings cited above seem to resolve into strength in the sphere of the movement that the women began in the 1980s to address the issue of human rights violation. This means that the women's public identity, though an extension of their private sphere and norms, became a political resource to challenge the state. We discuss this aspect later in the chapter. In the following two sections, we discuss the rise of Manipur as a nation, the political history of insurgency and the state intervention to deal with insurgency. These developments formed the backdrop for the rise of the political mother, which we discuss later.

Manipur: Nation, Insurgency and Resistance

For an idea of Manipur as a nation in the 1960s, the idea of history (and time) was brought in as central to the new historical consciousness and responsibility in the first issue of the monthly journal called *Lamyanba* (published on 13 August 1969). This journal was later known for its close association with (or rather as a mouthpiece of) the Pan Manipur Youth League (PANMYL). History was understood as the 'wave of times' wherein many *jatis* (nations) were drowned and many others emerged and changed their faces. History was also understood as the sphere of war (*chainabung*) wherein the weak *jatis* lost and many won. The 20th century was understood as the historical time for young Manipur, whose responsibility was sought to be borne by youths. Further it was stated that the nation prioritizes the roots of cultural identity, nurturing of the mother tongue, quality education, economic growth, unity between the hill and valley people and unity among Manipuris living outside and inside Manipur. For such planning of the young nation, a need was felt for an agency or organization, a key for an 'organised political life' that would inform the above elements in a 'uniform and progressive nation'.

In 1968, a group of educated Manipuris met at Guwahati University, with the meeting organized by the Guwahati Manipuri Student Union. Manipuris from Manipur, Assam and Tripura were represented. The young Manipur as it emerged through this meeting was a hope of early Manipuris. A noted educationist of early Manipur, Chingamkham Pishak Singh, who was a principal of a school at that time, commented that it was difficult for older-generation Manipuris like him to lay down their life, as it was difficult to imagine the fate of Manipur after their passing. However, a group of young Manipuris took the responsibility to work towards a new nation called Manipur.

In a column written in the 1960s, it was stated that if mother Manipur had a voice, she would have cried aloud on seeing the state of affairs in Manipur in the middle of the 20th century. Almost after more than 10 years, the idea of Manipur as a motherland that needed to be protected and nurtured was formed. A new wave of Manipuri nationalist consciousness spread among the generation of educated Manipuris. Among the above-mentioned affairs affecting Manipur in the middle of the 20th century, the merger of Manipur with India was a crucial one.

Manipur's existence as a sovereign kingdom for many centuries came to an end when the British defeated her in the Anglo-Manipur War of 1891 (Jhaljit 1968, 5). Thereafter, the Queen of Britain assumed suzerainty over the kingdom until British paramountcy in India lapsed on 14 August 1947 (Ibungohal Singh 1987, 155). Through a general election in June 1948, under the Manipur Constitution of 1947, popular sovereignty was enforced (Sanajaoba 1998, 254). The first ever assembly sitting on 18 October 1948 heralded Manipur as a constitutional monarchy. The Maharaja of Manipur signed the Standstill Agreement and Instrument of Accession with India on 11 August 1947. A movement for democratic governance in the state was initiated, and the Maharaja of

Manipur framed the Manipur State Constitution Act, 1947. This democratic government continued to function till the enforcement of the Manipur Merger Agreement, 1949. After the signing of the Merger Agreement, Manipur joined the Indian Union on 15 October 1949. The elected legislative assembly was dissolved, and the Council of Ministers was disbanded.

The Constitution of India was enforced on 26 January 1950. It gave Manipur the status of a Part C state. An Advisory Council for Manipur, whose members were appointed by the president of India in consultation with the chief commissioner of Manipur, was formed. Manipur was upgraded to the status of a union territory in 1956. A provision was also made for a Territorial Council that consisted of 30 elected and two nominated members, but it did not enjoy law-making, financial and judicial powers. After the second general election of 1957, the Territorial Council came into existence and started functioning, but the council failed to attract popular sentiment. Voices were raised demanding a responsible government. In this respect, the leftist parties took the initiative and launched a mass movement in order to press the government to concede to the demand.

In 1962, the third general election was held in Manipur. The Union Territories Act, 1963 (the 14th Amendment to the Constitution) provided a Legislative Assembly of 30 elected members and a Council of Ministers for Manipur. The territorial government failed to arouse any enthusiasm in Manipur. The territorial status deprived the MLAs (Members of Legislative Assembly) of Manipur of the chance to take part in the elections for the president, who was directly responsible for the administration of the territory. The members of the Legislative Assembly of Manipur territory and their electors realized that they did not enjoy equal rights as their counterparts in other states. The conferment of statehood to Nagaland in 1962 further disheartened the people of Manipur. All the political parties, including the Congress, joined hands and demanded statehood for Manipur. The years 1968–1970 in Manipur proved to be a period of frequent *hartals*, relay-hunger strikes, arrests, lathi charges and firings. Normal activities remained paralysed most of the time. In January 1972, Manipur was awarded the status of a state.

The origin of the Manipur–India conflict lay in the merger agreement, former vice president of the United Committee Manipur (UCM) Y. Nabachandra has stated.[1] Prominent civil society leaders like him hold the view that the merger agreement was forced upon the King of Manipur and did not take due consent from the elected people representatives in the then Manipur State Assembly (under Manipur Constitution, 1947). This sentiment was reflected in the public meeting. During the National Convention on Merger Issue held on 28–29 October 1993 in Imphal, it was declared that the agreement was 'lacking constitutional validity and having no legality' and was an act of 'Annexation' (Manipur Government 1993). The genesis of political unrest and subsequent armed conflicts between the state and armed opposition groups (AOGs) (termed insurgent organizations from the state's perspective) has been largely traced in this argument. The relationship between Manipur and India has been defined as antagonistic. AOGs, such as the United National Liberation Front (UNLF; in 1964), People's Revolutionary Party of Kangleipak (PREPAK; in 1977), People's Liberation Army (PLA; in 1978), Kangleipak Communist Party (KCP; in 1980) and Kanglei Yawon Kanna Lup (KYKL; in 1994), were formed.[2]

In an interview with the author, a civil society leader (Dhanabir Laishram) gave his opinion (Laishram, 'Resolution of Armed-conflict in Manipur') that the AOGs, their conception and their demand for self-determination were historically rooted and juxtaposed against the nation building enterprise (the merger, for instance) of the Indian state (Laishram, 'Resolution of Armed-conflict in Manipur'). However, insurgency in Manipur existed prior to the merger of Manipur with India. The communists under the leadership of Hijam Irabot were anti-Congress and anti-merger. In 1950, they issued a warning against cooperation with the administration. The communists sought social reforms, including rights for women, landownership for peasants and workers and adequate food and clothing for all. The difference between this insurgent action and the one that emerged after the 1960s is that the latter was primarily based on the self-determination right of Manipur as a sovereign state. For other scholars, insurgency is linked to the 'hurt sentiment' of Manipuris because of the treatment of Manipur as a Part C state. For instance, to Paratt (2005), the focus of the opposition after such treatment inevitably shifted to the 'underground armed resistance movements' (John 2005, 119).

The usage of the term 'insurgency', mostly because of the above terms of self-determination, hurt sentiments and resistance, becomes problematic. For those left-leaning non-state actors, it was sometimes understood as a 'class struggle'[3] between the oppressed and the oppressor. For them, India was a 'foreign oppressor' that took away Manipur's sovereignty.[4] Their national territory was under the control of the 'occupying Indian forces', and the natives were oppressed. To them, it was not a case of waging war against the Indian government. This was a war of resistance against the hidden war initiated by the 'foreign oppressor'.[5] They also clarified that theirs was not a separatist movement; all they wanted was that Government of India (GoI) and its security forces leave the 'occupied land'.[6] They also, as a result, rejected peace talks proposed by both the state and the central government.

State's Violence: 'Disturbed Area' and the Armed Forces Special Powers Act

GoI legislated the Armed Forces Special Powers Act, 1958 (AFSPA) in Manipur much before the insurgency began or armed opposition groups started to resist. The act was extended and implemented throughout Manipur in 1980. As per this act (notification of Disturbed Areas), the security forces have been given extraordinary powers to operate against the 'insurgents in the disturbed areas'. The power to declare an area 'disturbed' lies with the governor or the central government, which has to form an opinion that the use of armed forces 'in the aid of civil power' is essential and then notify the area as a 'disturbed area'.

Section 3 of the AFSPA, as amended in 1972, states as follows:

> If in relation to any state or Union Territory to which this act extends, the Governor of that State or the administrator of that Union Territory or the Central Government, in either case, if of the opinion that the whole or any part of such State of Union

territory, as the case may be, is in such a disturbed or dangerous condition that the use of armed forces in aid of the civil power is necessary, the Governor of that State or the Administrator of that Union Territory or the Central Government, as the case may be, may by notification in the Official Gazette, declare the whole or such part of such State or Union territory to be a disturbed area (Asian Centre for Human Rights 2005).

The special powers granted to the security forces under the act are arbitrary powers over life and death.[7] The following powers show such arbitrary power. Section 4 permits anyone of or above the rank of a non-commissioned officer, or an equivalent rank, to fire upon or otherwise use force, even to cause death, against any person who acts in contravention of any law or order. Section 4(a) permits power to shoot even to the cause of death for the maintenance of public order, after giving such due warning as he may consider necessary, fire upon or otherwise use force, even to the causing of death, against any person who is acting in contravention of any law or order for the time being in force in the disturbed area prohibiting the assembly of five or more persons or the carrying of weapons or of things capable of being used as weapons or of firearms, ammunition or explosive substances. Section 4(c) permits the arrest, without warrant, of any person who has committed a cognizable offence or against whom a reasonable suspicion exists that he has committed or is about to commit a cognizable offence, and on such a person such force as may be necessary may be used to effect the arrest. Section 4(d) permits to enter and search without warrant any premises to make any such arrest as aforesaid or to recover any person believed to be wrongfully restrained or confined or any property reasonably suspected to be stolen property or any arms, ammunition or explosive substances believed to be unlawfully kept in such premises, and may for that purpose use such force as may be necessary. Section 5 states that any person arrested and taken into custody under this act shall be made over to the officer in charge of the nearest police station with the least possible delay, together with a report of the circumstances warranting the arrest.

The arbitrary power over 'life and death' of persons cannot be challenged in a court of law. Section 6 states that no prosecution, lawsuit or other legal proceeding shall be instituted, except with the previous sanction of the central government, against any person in respect of anything done or purported to be done in exercise of the powers conferred by this act.

It is alleged that security forces have destroyed homes and other structures, presuming them to be used by insurgents, acting under the provisions of Section 4(b) of the AFSPA. People of Manipur feel that an arrest without warrant is a serious encroachment on the right to liberty of a person. The power of search and seizure under Section 4(d) has been extensively used by the armed forces in cordon and search operations, leading to widespread violations of fundamental rights of citizens, and the forces have detained arrested persons (Section 5) for several days in their custody. Due to the protection under Section 6 of the act, some security personnel have even violated the human rights of people and left the victims without any effective remedy. The failure to identify those responsible for human rights violations and to bring them to justice has meant that some members of the security force continue to believe that they are above the law and can violate human rights with impunity.

Political Mother: Meira Paibis as the State's Adversary

Where does the women's movement that emerged in the 1980s figure in the above development? This section deals with this issue. Historically, Meira Paibi is considered to have emerged as a mass movement, known as Nupi Kanglup in the 1980s. However, two moments in the past are important for understanding the rise of Meira Paibis as the state's adversary.

On 26 April 1980, at around 9:15 am, unidentified gunmen allegedly fired upon the Central Reserve Police Force (CRPF) personnel stationed at Langjing Camp, Imphal West, killing two CRPF personnel. After the gunmen left, the CRPF personnel turned on local innocent people and tortured them. People were dragged out of their houses, and a search operation was conducted to catch those identified as members of the cadres of the PREPAK. The menfolk from each family were called out to stand with their hands up for the entire day.

Women of the area and nearby areas began an agitation against the alleged atrocities of the security personnel. A protest rally was held on 28 May 1980, in which reportedly more than 10,000 women participated, gathering at Mapal Kangjeibung, Imphal. The security personnel picked up protesters in trucks and took them to an army camp at Khurai, Imphal East. On the way, a pregnant woman named Piyari fell from the truck and lost her life. Her death was followed by women's mobilizations and protests at various places in Imphal. In remembrance of this particular incident, the Meira Paibi Observation Committee, constituted by the Poirei Leimarol Meira Paibi Apunba Manipur (PLMPAM), has been observing Meira Paibi Numit (Meira Paibi Day) on 28 May each year.

In another incident, on 29 December 1980, army personnel arrested three young boys on the allegation of their planting a bomb. Lourembam Ibomcha was cleaning his house in Maibam Leikai when the Jammu and Kashmir Army personnel arrested him. Some local female activists of the area immediately informed leaders of the popular organizations like the Nupi Samaj, including Momon Devi, Chaobi Devi and Rani Devi. They went to the army camp at Canchipur, Imphal, pleaded Ibomcha's innocence and demanded his immediate release. Ibomcha, tortured in custody, was released later. However, the army personnel then unleashed an operation in the same Maibam Leikai, and menfolk were harassed whenever they ventured out of their homes. Subsequently, women took on the task of patrolling the locality at night with torches in their hands to protect the people. Since this incident, 29 December has been regarded as the day women began to launch the movement to 'save innocent sons' from the 'brutal army'. Every year, the Nupi Samaj observes 29 December as Meira Paibi Houdokhiba Numit. In an interview, Ima Ramani, a leader of the Nupi Samaj, expressed that they struggled because the boy was innocent.

The two incidents narrated above, though different in their immediate cause, suggest that Meira Paibis came into existence to stop atrocities of the security forces committed against innocent civilians.

The movement acquired the structure of an organization, although not strictly. Looking at its social networking and activities since the 1990s, the expansion of the organization of Meira Paibis increased not only in Manipur but beyond the state borders as well, such as in Hozai, Assam. The grassroots form of the organization brought many informal local women's groups into the relatively more organized network. There is a strong historical presence of informal women's bodies in Manipuri society. These informal organizations have catered mainly to social and economic needs. For instance, Manipuri women have a long history of informal credit associations. Though some still remain traditional, others have registered for welfare purposes and as credit-based organizations under the Manipur Society Registration Act, 1989, of the state government.

In due course of time, the movement acquired an organizational structure. Two leading women-led organizations based in Imphal began to lead the movement: the Nupi Samaj and the PLMPAM. The Nupi Samaj was registered in 1978 under the Societies Registration Act, 1860 (as published in the Gazette of India, 1960), while the PLMPAM was registered in 1986 under the Manipur Co-operative Societies Act, 1976.

The mode of communication is a vital element for the organization of the Meira Paibis. Here, mutual trust depends on constant meetings at the state and local levels. The PLMPAM, for instance, has regular meetings (weekly, monthly and yearly), yet the frequency of these meetings varies according to the leaders' perception of the level of tension. At times, the women at the local, district and state levels encounter difficulties in keeping everyone informed. However, a significant feature of the Meira Paibi organization is the manner in which the women get together. Here, again, the traditional ways of communication among the women are retained. Historically, in times of need, all one has needed to do is pick up a stone or a pebble and hit the nearest electric pole with it. The message is then loud and clear—that a meeting is being called—and all the women in that particular *leikai* (locality) gather together in the premises of the local club. If at all the situation requires the attention and cooperation of adjoining neighbouring bodies, then the message is sent across in the same manner. In times of acute social or political crises, at least one woman from every household participates. With the entry of mobile phones, communication among the Meira Paibi 'imas' (mothers) became much easier than before. Most of the Meira Paibi leaders use cell phones to communicate with each other.

Leaders are selected on the basis of their experience and the trust they have developed with the rest of the members of their group. The most active member is elected to act as the office-bearer. Mandated by peer pressure and community status, membership is universal, but the extent of participation varies with the women's own inclination and the severity of the situation at hand. Most of the time, female activists are busy with organizational activities, including sit-in demonstrations and street meetings. They also attend meetings and seminars of other civil society organizations.

Meira Paibis, an Ideology to Counter De-politicization

A leader of the Nupi Samaj, Ramani, stated that various local bodies, clubs and women's associations have been swayed by corruption and selfish motives during elections (see *Imphal Free Press* 2010; *The Sangai Express* 2009). It was also stated that no one has made any conscious effort to understand the true image of the Meira Paibis and the essence behind their movement. Instead, many people have started looking upon the Meira Paibis as some groups of women who can be easily used by politicians as vote banks during elections. Thus, an effort has been made to engage state appropriation of Meira Paibi.

The PLMPAM distinguishes between Meira Paibi activities and government-sponsored programmes. It uses pamphlets to refine the boundary of the activities and ideology of the Meira Paibis: a Meira Paibi should only focus on the issues of violation of human rights by the army, repeal of repressive laws and the AFSPA. Anything beyond these activities is not part of the duties of Meira Paibis. Observation days (28 May and 29 December—observation of Meira Paibi Numit) offer a space to discuss the ups and downs of Meira Paibi activities, their successes and failures.[8]

A key strategy of the Meira Paibi organization has been to counter what it calls 'state-sponsored Meira Paibis' and their increasing numbers in society. The PLMPAM has asserted that the state-sponsored Meira Paibis are the women's groups that formed and organized in relation to governmental policies and programmes, such as the Civic Action Programme (CAP), National Rural Employment Guarantee Act (NREGA) and the public distribution system (PDS), and those that are also associated with or have formed as the women's wing of any political party. These, they consider, attempt to divide the movement and create factions among the women to de-politicize the Meira Paibis. De-politicizing would mean that the issue of accessibility to various government schemes and benefits would supplant the issue of human rights violations.

The leaders of the PLMPAM also raise the issue of state appropriation of women through the building of Meira Sanghs. A Meira Sangh is a small hut, traditionally used by women as a space for social and political activities. This space is also considered the local site of the Meira Paibi movement. It is said that there are about 2,000 Meira Sanghs in the valley. In recent years, around 800 Meira Sanghs and 100 community halls have been reportedly built under the Civic Action Programme of the state army personnel. In fact, the report of the Ministry of Home Affairs (MHA; 2007–2008) states that in the north-eastern states of India, in order to take the local population into confidence and boost the image of the armed forces among the common people, the army and paramilitary forces conduct Civic Action Programme activities. Under this programme, various welfare/developmental activities are undertaken, such as holding of medical camps, sanitation drives and sports meets, distribution of study material to children, minor repairs of school buildings, roads, bridges, etc., running of adult education centres, etc.[9] These efforts and the support of political parties and army personnel are considered to be among the sources of division in the collective Meira Paibi movement. The perception of the PLMPAM is that these government-supported Meira Sanghs have stopped working for the issues like human rights violations at the hands of state forces but instead have begun to be the defenders of the lives and properties of a class of people that includes bureaucrats and members of the Manipur Legislative Assembly.

In an interview, Memchoubi, the then PLMPAM president, was especially concerned about the changing face of the Meira Sangh. She felt that Meira Sanghs had become more like credit-based associations, not relating with issues concerning political rights of the common people (meaning the right to life). She also felt that they had become sites of petty politics over local issues, through engaging in electoral politics, competing for funds and loans through developing networks with the local politicians, competing for getting a big share of the money from the distribution of essential items under the PDS, etc. She was also concerned about the future of the local Meira Sanghs because of their increasing participation in the self-help group (SHG) programme of the government. Her argument was that certain policies and programmes, like the above programme, are counterproductive to the Meira Paibi movement. This is the reason why new efforts are being made by the PLMPAM to restrict and refine the sphere of activities and identity of the Meira Paibi. In this regard, the pamphlets circulated on the memorial days of the earlier-mentioned historical incidents in 1980 (29 December and 28 May) project the state and its apparatus as anti-people; for instance, in one of the documents printed in the *Meira Paibi* journal, the state is understood as an 'instrument of torture', and the politician as the 'nurturer of army and police rule'.[10]

To conclude, the above discussion shows that the political history of encounters between women and the state is grounded on the specific notions of the space and category of women, on the one hand, and the intersection of the politics of Manipur as a nation, insurgency movements and the state's monopoly over violence, on the other. The discussion on encounters between women and the colonial state brings up the importance of the spaces and categories of women that emerged under the colonial conditions. An active public space, although not contesting the gender-based division of roles (war for men, family and economic security for women), was seen when the women encountered the state. The encounter brought up the meanings of unruly women. Such a notion of unruliness is almost equal to illegality or illegitimacy in the eyes of the colonial state. On the other hand, in the interpretation of a public leader, Hijam Irabot, unruly women were legitimate/rightful women resisting for the welfare of the people.

Post-colonial politics is determined by a complex relationship among three factors: Manipuri nationalism, insurgency and state violence. The spaces and categories of women continue to determine the nature of politics in the public domain. In post-colonial politics, the state and insurgency movements shaped the specific idea of the space and category of women called Meira Paibis. Meira Paibis, as political mothers, emerged to deal with the situation of the state dealing with insurgency through violations of human rights in the public domain. Although the public space for women does not specifically deal with women-specific issues, as shown in the 1960s, state and non-state insurgent conflicts developed a public space and meaning for women. However, women, in the eyes of the state, are illegitimate, illegal mothers, for they are accused of being linked with insurgents. However, for the women, it is their right to protect the rights of citizens.

Notes

1. *The Sangai Express*, April 2, Imphal.
2. Human Rights Initiatives an indigenous advancement and conflict resolution. http://www.hrimanipur.org/index.php/human-rights-in-manipur
3. In socialist revolutions, class struggles occur between the proletariat and the bourgeois, but in liberation struggles, class struggles occur between the oppressed people and the oppressor. For example, in the Cuban revolution, the forces that fought were workers, peasants, petty bourgeois, students, employees in offices, etc. (quoted from Laishram, 'Resolution of Armed-conflict in Manipur'.)
4. Sovereignty is the word that defines self-rule over a well-defined geographical area having fixed boundaries.
5. Here, 'hidden war' means the snatching away of sovereignty, operation of occupying forces on the native soil to maintain the status quo, violation of human rights, etc. (quoted From Laishram, 'Resolution of Armed-conflict in Manipur'.)
6. Memorandum submitted by the Revolutionary People's Front (Manipur) to the Chairman of Decolonization Committee, United Nations, December 11, 1996, p. xv. (quoted from Laishram, 'Resolution of Armed-conflict in Manipur'.)

7. Details of the sections given below are quoted from the report Asian Centre for Human Rights (2005).
8. Pamphlet circulated by the Meira Paibi Observation Committee on 28 May 2007.
9. Government of India, Ministry of Home Affairs, *Annual Report 2017–18*.
10. See, for details, document printed in *Meira Paibi* 1, no. 2 (2006): 59–60.

References

Asian Centre for Human Rights. 2005. *The AFSPA, Lawless Law Enforcement According to the Law, A Representation to the Committee to Review the Armed Forces Special Power Act, 1958*. New Delhi: Asian Centre for Human Rights.

Ibungohal Singh, L. 1987. *Introduction to Manipur*. Imphal: Shri S. Babudhan Singh.

Imphal Free Press. 2010. 'Meira Paibi Founding Day Remembered'. Available at http://kanglaonline.com/2010/12/meira-paibi-founding-day-remembered (accessed on 22 March 2021).

Jhaljit, R. K. 1968. *A Short History of Manipur*. Imphal: J. M. Printing Works.

John, Parrat. 2005. *Wounded Land, Politics of Identity in Modern Manipur*. New Delhi: Mittal Publications.

Manipur Government. 1993, 28–29 October. 'National Convention on Merger Agreement'. G.M. Hall, Imphal, Manipur: People's Democratic Movement.

Rajan, Rajeswari Sunder. 2008 (first published in 2003). *The Scandal of the State: Women, Law, and Citizenship in Postcolonial India*. Ranikhet: Permanent Black.

Sabita. 1969, 1 November. 'Manipuri Chanuragi Saktam.' *Lamyanba*, 4: 11–13.

Sagolshembi, Snehaprabha. 1969, 1 December. 'Manipuri Nupisinghi Wafam.' *Lamyanba*, 5: 19–24.

Sanajaoba, Naorem. 1998. *Manipur: Past and Present*, Vol. I. New Delhi: Mittal Publication.

Singh, Karam Manimohan. 1989. *Hijam Irabot Singh and Political Movements in Manipur*. Delhi: B.R. Publishing Corporation.

The Sangai Express. 2009, 12 April. 'Meira Paibi Martyrs' Day'. http://www.e-pao.net/GP.asp?src=9..130409.apr09

Yambem, Sanamani. 1976, 21 February. 'Nupi Lan: Manipur Women's Agitation, 1939.' *Economic and Political Weekly*, 11, 8: 325–331.

Part IV

Development, Trans-nationality and Accessibility

part IV

The Trajectory of Development, Transnationality and Accessibility

CHAPTER 10

The Trajectory of 'Development' in a Resource Frontier

G. Amarjit Sharma

Seeing Like 'Development'

Roughly since the year 2009–2010, in which I travelled through the hills of Manipur in Northeast India, there has been a strong concern among scholars and activists over the unfolding plights of people on the ground as a result of developmental projects financed by the state of India, international financial institutions (IFIs), like Asian Development Bank (ADB) and Japan International Cooperation Agency (JICA), and rich donor countries, like Japan, particularly in the sectors such as mining, road and railway infrastructure, oil and gas and hydel power. We heard of a Netherlands-based private company, Jubilant Energy, coming to Tamenglong district of Manipur to conduct a survey of oil and gas. Following this, there was an Indian private company, Oil India Limited (OIL), engaging in similar works in the same district. Soon, we came to know about the Asian Highway road building project financed by ADB along the Imphal–Jiribam and

Imphal–Moreh road, and then JICA's involvement in the water supply and irrigation sector.

Equally, there were increased public concerns over the development projects in the above sectors. I was travelling with a research advocacy centre based in Imphal, Centre for Research and Advocacy, Manipur (CRAM), across the hills of Manipur to witness a number of public meetings organized by this centre along with civil society bodies, like Zeliangrong Baudi, and various local clubs and organizations. Arrival of big companies and financing institutions in lands marked by ethnic conflicts, insurgency and unstable governance is always a matter of concern for the local people. This is primarily because the people are hardly aware of what the arrival of the companies and financial institutions means to their lands and resources. Although the state government of Manipur sees this new development as hope for the growth of the state, a hope equally shared by sections of the society on the ground, there are also equally serious concerns over the direction of this development.

A brief discussion on an emerging transnational developmental discourse within which a region like Northeast India is located would be worthwhile (for more details, see my earlier study, Amarjit Sharma 2020). This discourse has to do with India's new economic policy that welcomes external development assistance to various developmental projects on the sectors like road infrastructure and energy. The post-2003–2004 budget announcement of Government of India is significant, because unlike before, India began to set the priority areas for attracting development assistance. As per the new guidelines, India accepts bilateral assistance routed through or co-financed with multilateral agencies. In 2016, India was one of the highest recipients of development assistance from OECD Development Assistant Committee (DAC) members like Germany and Japan. It was the third highest recipient of Germany's Official Development Assistance (ODA) in the world. In 2016, Germany's ODA was mainly targeted at social infrastructure and services, including education, health and population policies, water and sanitation, government and civil society, etc. India was the highest recipient of Japanese ODA in 2016. Japanese ODA has been mostly targeted at economic infrastructure and services, amounting to 51 per cent of the total ODA. In India, ODA is mostly targeted at connectivity projects, including railways and roadways.

Compared to other donor countries, Japan is the largest bilateral donor in India. Japanese ODA in the form of loan assistance, grant aid and technical assistance is received through JICA. The cumulative commitment of the Japanese ODA to India reached JPY 5,244.005 billion as of December 2017 (Ministry of Finance, Government of India 2018, 43). Japan also provides grant aid to India under the following criteria: development impacts, utilization of Japanese technology/know-how and the likelihood of dissemination to other areas. The grant aid is provided to the following sectors: transport (including projects that use information and communications technology and road projects with slope protection measures) and power (including small-scale hydropower projects and solar power projects). The priority areas under the technical cooperation with JICA are public health and medical care, agriculture and rural development, environmental conservation and protection and improvement of economic infrastructure. Under this technical cooperation, the main components include dispatch of experts, a Japanese overseas-cooperation volunteer programme and a training programme involving personnel from different countries who are in India. There are 11 ongoing projects under the technical cooperation (Ministry of Finance, Government of India 2018, 43). Under the technical programme, there are collaborations among non-governmental organizations (NGOs), universities, local governments and public interest corporations in both countries.

When it comes to multilateral assistance to India, there has been an enormous shift. ADB assistance to India has increased from $586 million in 1986–1996 to more than $2.0 billion in 2013–2017. As of December 2017, there were 84 ongoing sovereign loans amounting to $13.467 billion (Ministry of Finance, Government of India 2018, 31). It is reported that the ADB has assured that it would enhance its assistance to India from $2 billion per year to $3 billion per year over the period 2018–2022 (Ministry of Finance, Government of India 2018, 32). The ADB shares the vision of the government of India on regional cooperation and integration: the South Asia Subregional Economic Cooperation (SASEC) programme that brings together Bangladesh, Bhutan, India, Maldives, Myanmar, Nepal and Sri Lanka in a project-based partnership. It has been working with SASEC member countries for over 13 years to build cross-border lines, introduce policy measures to facilitate regional trade and connect roads for the movement of goods and people. In addition, it has been assisting in building the capacity of various executive agencies and has been involved in a technical assistance programme (Ministry of Finance, Government of India 2018, 32).

In Northeast India, on the other hand, bilateral and multilateral agencies are increasingly involved in financing key developmental projects, such as road infrastructure, rural livelihood and biodiversity projects. Bilateral development finance institutions (DFIs), such as Agence Française de Développement (AFD) of France, German Development Bank/KfW of Germany and JICA, are involved in the 'development' of Northeast India, supporting the private sector mainly through equity investments, long-term loans and guarantees. The ADB, European Investment Bank (EIB), International Finance Corporation (IFC) and Islamic Development Bank (IDB) are some of the multilateral DFIs financing projects across Northeast India (Yumnam 2019a).

Over the last few years, however, people's mobilization against these development projects has raised issues over environmental degradation, land acquisition, displacement, rehabilitation and compensation. My extensive field trips to Manipur's hills brought up multiple sets of problems of the people on the ground. Some of the sectors we covered were the Asian Highway road infrastructure project, oil and gas exploration survey works and hydel power projects. Four concerned areas where such projects are currently ongoing are Tamenglong, Chandel, Thoubal and Ukhrul districts in Manipur. The people affected (or likely to be affected) by these are mobilizing to stop the projects, while the regional states, administrative authorities, local elected authorities and security forces are trying to stifle them. In the course of my field visits, I have come across civil society bodies, like CRAM and Zeliangrong Baudi, holding series of public meetings. In these meetings, decisions are taken to oppose the development projects, like the oil and gas survey works initiated by

Netherlands-based Jubilant Energy and OIL. The task of the public meeting organized by CRAM, along with other public organizations, was primarily to make people aware of the fact that lands and resources are not to be exploited without prior informed consent and participation of the people. Largely developmental projects are understood to plan on the top and there is least space for the people to know what do they mean for the land. The activities of Jubilant Energy and OIL, for instance, were actively opposed by the concerned local organization in the above district. CRAM came up with a report on the impacts of the ADB-financed ring road project in Manipur. The report shows that about 500 families and 1,000 acres of agricultural lands would be affected (Yumnam 2019b).

On the other hand, people do not have enough legal safeguards and resources to stop the projects and strengthen their struggle. They are also likely to be caught and charged based on the National Security Act (NSA) and are reportedly followed and tracked by the state government's intelligence personnel. Yet, vital moral support comes from customary heads and bodies, civic organizations and communities that equally share the projects' impact. The regional elected state governments and local grassroots institutions do not necessarily represent the people's discontentment with the projects. Decisions and policies are primarily centralized. The state and local institutions are mostly involved as the implementing agencies of the development projects. In my field experience at the project site of Thoubal multipurpose hydel power project in Manipur, I have seen people using legal means to challenge the construction of a dam without obtaining prior environmental clearance from the National Green Tribunal.

Broader experience in the field compels activists and scholars to indulge in these worlds at two levels: one is immediate, which manifests in writings and public awareness campaigns; and the other is through networking with people's bodies across the globe which share a similar experience and work towards global campaigns against developmental projects. On the one hand, my concern has been the neglect of such developments in the existing post-colonial development studies in universities and colleges, and less mention and analysis of these concerns in the current development studies on Northeast

India. However, along with big developmental projects, there has been a rise in organizational mobilization involving experts, journalists and communities. These activists also produce a large number of studies that expose the problems of the developmental state.

There is also another world that concerns us—society, including civic bodies, against the developmental state. It is an issue of resistance. We have seen series of civil society mobilization to resist and fight development projects at local, regional, national and global levels. While legitimizing development projects per the nation's needs, the state indulges in acts that create divisions in society. We have seen that the entry of railways infrastructure projects and oil and gas survey works in the district of Tamenglong (Manipur) have led to both people mobilization against them and divisions within the society. Companies are reportedly bribing sections of society and a few armed groups to make their work easy. Various groups of the district reportedly take a significant share of the compensation for land acquisition and villages' displacement. While some protest, some others secretly develop monetary interests and collude with companies and the district administration. It does not mean that there is entirely no genuine debate on the benefits and losses due to development projects among various groups of people. We do come across people debating on resource extraction's benefits for underdeveloped societies. Our only concern is that such debates also often hinder meaningful people mobilization against the harms done by development projects.

These experiences/worlds also compel activists and scholars to provoke further thought. How do we conceptualize governance and resistance? Under the new context of developmental projects of a greater magnitude, 'governance' has more to do with manipulation, appropriation and creation of divisions in society. It is less democratic in the eyes of the people. 'Less democratic' is closely linked to the notions of consent and ownership which people have evolved through their encounters with developmental projects. These notions are not legal and constitutional in the national context—the state does not grant any rights to prior consent taken before initiating projects and ownership over community lands. Yet, these notions draw inspiration from international jurisprudence and have become a new source of 'ecological' citizenship. It is ecological because to say that 'land belongs to us and our consent is essential' is not just a moral statement of a sort of natural right but also a system of re-establishing people's relationship with nature and the environment. In the process, people work across ethnic boundaries and territories.

However, it is also true that the projects are located in a society in which people are poor, unemployment is high and there is minimal availability of necessities and poor connectivity with towns and cities. The trajectory of developmental projects under such circumstances is a huge challenge for society—people like 'development' but not the development projects that displace them. This statement raises the notion of 'development' again. People would say, 'we are not against development—we need roads, water supply, electricity, etc.' Post-structuralist thinkers would suggest complete abandonment of the concept of development and look for post-development ideas. They may ask: if 'development' is the problem, why seek a solution within it? However, the challenge before us as activists and scholars is that we have not found enough practices that show us alternative ways of sustaining life and articulation against the might of the developmental state. It would be wrong to interpret such a lack of sufficient alternative practices as an acceptance of the existing model of development. Instead, our concern is, why could people not find alternatives? How do we see such a situation of looking to the same state for development?

Resistance for sure is seen within such spaces of poverty and marginality. Searching for a complete alternative requires developing a new understanding of the ways people choose to engage with the state. For instance, at the site of the Mapithel dam (Thoubal Multipurpose Project) in Manipur, people sought relief for the families suffering due to the curtailment of their source of livelihood because of dams submerging large areas of agricultural land and forestland. As the dam was never de-commissioned, people adopted different strategies to survive. They also sought relief measures from the government as a form of compensation. However, as the people struggled to protest against the projects for a long time, a new, complex set of politics emerged. Local politics involving sections of political leaders, civil society groups and armed groups became part of the state's engagement to dissolve the anti-dam movement. As a result, much of the people's struggle was also about fighting 'internal enemies'. This emerging complex world compels us to rethink resistance overall, not just that of society against the state. Resistance could also be understood as the varied ways of negotiation for relief measures and/or compensation through public meetings with local political leaders and civil society leaders to raise awareness of such projects' impacts. However, this understanding should not be forgetful of the official power that could shape the course of resistance.

With this brief discussion, in the following sections I engage closely with the historical trajectory of 'development' at national, regional, global and local levels.

The State in 'Development'

A question that strikes us often is why development projects involve mostly a 'non-negotiable' activity and an act or policy that does not require consultation with the people? By looking at development as a conscious act and strategy of the state and (global) capital, not just as an idea, we hope to answer this. Perhaps, the argument of 'development aggression', instead of hoping for change for meaningful lives, could also be understood through the following discussions. In the post-colonial Indian context, development has been looked at as a historically evolved thought and a specific response to the structural constraints such as lack of accumulation of capital stock, lack of productivity, rural backwardness, unemployment, etc. Development as a thought and action is a product of the anti-colonial nationalist history of economic planning and objectives. Simultaneously, development is an exercise conditioned by the representative form of a government based on universal adult franchise.

An interesting criticism against such reading of development (planning) in India comes from neo-Marxist scholars. To Chatterjee (2012), development under India's development planning took a linear path, directed towards a goal or a series of goals separated by stages. It implied fixing priorities between long-term and short-term objectives and making a conscious choice between alternative paths. It was premised upon rational consciousness and will. As 'development' was thought of as a process affecting the whole society, it was also premised upon one consciousness and will—that of the whole. Particulars needed to be subsumed within the whole and made consistent with the general interest. For Chatterjee, such a developmental ideology—that making use of rational thought, conscious choice, one consciousness and one will—was a constituent of the 'self-definition of the post-colonial state'. The state represents the universal, the whole within which 'parts' need to be subsumed.

The state connects to the people–nation not merely through the procedural forms of a representative government but also through the direction of a programme of economic development on behalf of the nation. As in any liberal form of government, the former connects the state's legal–political sovereignty with the sovereignty of the people. The latter connects the sovereign power of the state directly with the economic well-being of the people (Chatterjee 2012, 246–247). However, the two connections do not necessarily have the same implications for a state (Chatterjee 2012, 247). That the people can express through the representative mechanisms of the political process, as their will is not essentially what is right for their economic well-being. What the state thinks is essential for the nation's economic development is not necessarily what would be ratified through the representative mechanisms. The two criteria of representation and legitimacy could well produce contradictory implications for state policy. The contradiction is because of the fact that a development ideology is needed to cling to the state as the principal vehicle for its historical mission (Chatterjee 2012, 247).

The relation between state and nation (people) has been discussed in detail in at least three essential works in India (Chakravarty 1987; Chatterjee 2012; Zachariah 2014). Planning for the development of India was part of the Indian nationalist movement. Formation of the National Planning Committee (NPC) and that of the Bombay Plan (BP), 1944, were crucial moments in the planning history. These initiatives were not merely historical moments but also moments that lay the foundation for post-colonial India, providing the essential linkage between development as the state's primary responsibility and the people as the receivers of that development. In both the NPC and BP processes, an explicit connection was made between economic regeneration projects and development and the broader process of 'nation building' (Zachariah 2014). In the process, the nation was defined as a sort of unified personality and spirit, despite the diversity. This is an essential point for us not merely to understand the politics of planning in India but also to stress the point that a similar logic of the state in developing India as a nation continues to inform the current development projects of India.

A few essential points result from this brief discussion. First, the state is a vital vehicle for development. Second, what the state thinks is necessary for the nation's economic growth is not necessarily what would be ratified through the representative mechanisms (through which people elect the government). Three, there is an explicit connection between economic development and the process of nation building. There are a few important implications of this understanding of the state. 'Development' is what the state thinks of as the right economic action or policy or programme. According to this logic, one can see the real problem—that development is essentially a non-negotiable thought (and act) for the people who would receive it. There is already a presumption that society cannot be trusted as a partner or originator of development. Another implication is that development does not need a consultation with the people on the ground. In this sense, development is primarily what the sovereign decides. This logic leaves practically no space from the beginning for the society to either negotiate or reject economic policies or programmes. Now, let us see how such a logic of the state unfolds in India's 'sensitive' region.

Developing a Region: Security and Welfare

Development as a thought and practice in post-colonial Northeast India acted not merely as an appendage but also as a necessary condition for nation building. The bureaucracy on the ground and the political executives at the top see development as a vehicle for nation building. In other words, development is the pretext on which the state governs a region. Three aspects require our critical attention are as follows: first, the nation expresses as a security state, making development a mode of governing power; second, the expression of the nation as the extractive machine with the apparatus of the security state and third, the security and extractive state uses development to express as a 'compassionate entity' on the ground that state is there to bring welfare to the people. Perhaps for many decades, the development trajectory in Northeast India has manifested the interplay of these three aspects. Let us see briefly how such interplay is manifest.

Studies by Verrier Elwin (1961) show the specific state making processes (not just military presence and establishment of an administrative apparatus to govern the subjects but also the balancing act between security concerns and welfare schemes) that took place in border societies. The Naga Hills and North-East Frontier Agency (NEFA), for instance, were part of what used to be called the colonial state's Excluded Area, yet they were a constant source of anxiety for the independent Indian state. Official concerns partly emerged out of the partial, if not complete, ways in which life here was autonomous from the core provincial administration of British India, and partly from the people's racial and cultural affinity with neighbouring countries. As such, in the early years of independence, state making only through military presence was found insufficient. Development was necessary as a means to colour the state in 'compassionate' terms. Elwin (1961, republished in 1997), writing in the context of Nagaland, pointed out that the plans for developing the hill and forest people in the 1960s, on whom Government of India was spending substantial sums of money, were essentially 'adventures in friendship'. The development of agriculture and animal husbandry, opening of schools, building of hospitals and roads and irrigation schemes were 'tokens of that friendship'. The necessity of the state as 'a compassionate' agency, to Elwin, lies in the rationale that integrating 'long-isolated people with the rest of India' emotionally and psychologically required development to be carried out in the right way to create a sense of friendliness and unity. To Elwin, further, 'the vital thing was that tribal people should feel at home, with a full realization that India is their country, the Government is their Government, that they belong to it, and it belongs to them' (Elwin 1961, 90). This clearly shows development's task to compel people at the border to see India as their state. As discussed in the previous section, the state's logic is that it is a more significant whole within which people and societies considered to be parts are supposed to be subsumed.

In understanding the task of developing Nagaland and its people, two things mattered in the 1960s. One was the perception of the general backwardness of the place and people because of isolation and the history of conflicts within the society and with outsiders in colonial times; the other was what Elwin called the extremist Naga attitude. In Elwin's (Elwin 1961, 32) narrative of the Nagas, there is a construction of a history, of a past of Nagas' living in isolation from the outside, yet internally in 'their hills they fought each other and the menace of headhunting cast a shadow on their lives'. The isolation was occasionally ruptured when their society was encroached by the outside civilization—the tea planters, merchants and police—leading them to raid the plains civilization. In the description, the colonial state is presented as the agency that 'brought order into their lives and helped to banish ignorance', and missionaries as those who 'brought an ideal of gentleness and forgiveness'. However, according to Elwin, a new concept of 'welfare state' arrived at the land of the Nagas only after independence. In brief, although the colonial state and missionaries brought order and 'gentleness' among the Nagas, the idea of the welfare state only came with India's independence (Elwin 1961, 33).

What mattered to Elwin was not merely the idea of isolated people but also 'the Naga attitude'. The Naga attitude, for him, resulted from three propositions (Elwin 1961, 73): (a) Nagas were not Indians and did not want to become Indians; (b) Naga territory was not and had never been part of the Indian territory; and (c) Nagaland was never conquered by India. However, Elwin's engagement with such attitude marks the post-colonial state's peculiar attitude that only the newly independent state could bring progress and change to such a society. One can understand this aspect from Elwin's (1961, 73) following observation:

> India with her great plans for development, spread over periods of five years at a time, was confident that she could help the Nagas to progress in every way without interference with their customs and

along the lines of their own genius. She had already made provision to protect Naga rights in land and forests, to give every Naga complete freedom to practice his own religion or to change it if he so desired, and to enjoy all the privileges of citizenship.

In brief, this idea of development of the Nagas' society went along with an order that could only be assured by the state. Elwin observed that among a people 'who had so recently abandoned headhunting and where there were still inter-tribal and inter-village rivalries and feuds, India felt that the maintenance of law and order, which only she could ensure, was vital for the happiness of the common man'. There is an externality of development and security working to ensure the state's presence in society, for the latter to look up to the former as a source of order and welfare. Nevertheless, this works along with constructing a secular developmental state that ensures the autonomy of the Nagas' customary rights over land and forests and practice of one's own religion.

However, there is a need to unpack the 'secular' further. The word secular means more than toleration of customary rights over land and resources. The utilitarian principle that development works in the interest of a nation as a whole guides the secular developmental state. It works in such a way that the benefits of manipulating natural resources have the least share at the local level. Cederlöf and Sivaramakrishnan (2012), in their introduction to a volume on ecological nationalism, observe that ecological nationalism is expressed in two ways. One way involves the metropolitan secular view of nature and its economic and material uses for the nation. The other is an indigenous, or regionalist, reaction to the expansion of the high-modern nation state in its imperial or post-independence form or to globalization forces that intervene outside the nation state's realm. At the moment, I am not discussing the second way of looking at nature and resources. What should interest us at the moment is the point that the 'secular' works in a fashion that not only favours benefits for the nation as a whole but also allows the forces of globalization to work in favour of the same nation's interests.

What is a 'nation' in the nation's interests? So far, our concern has been that the discourse of development is primarily in the nation's interests, for which the locals' interests have to be subsumed. This means that for the nation's broader economic growth, the concerns of the people directly affected by the investment or developmental projects are secondary. The nation as a broader geopolitical entity comes first, and then come the real interests of people. In other words, the nation could be displacing the notions of 'public good' and 'public trust' under the state's secular metropolitan approach. For instance, we can take a look at the following national laws on resources: Railways Act, 1989, Mines and Minerals (Development and Regulation) Act, 1957, and Open Acreage Licensing Policy (OALP), 2017. During our field visits to Manipur's hill districts, we learnt that these are significant laws that pose considerable challenges to the people on the ground. These laws are 'national' laws, yet people find themselves completely outside of any consultation or participation mechanism. Under the Railways Act, 1989, land is acquired for a 'public purpose' (Section 20[A]). However, what is contestable is the notion of 'public purpose'. At Oinamlong village, Tamenglong, when the land survey for railway construction began in 2009, the villagers found it difficult to understand the project. They were not aware of the laws under which the lands were acquired for the railway project. The villagers alleged that the railway construction had destroyed 'residential plots, agricultural land, forestland, and other livelihood and water resources without the people's prior knowledge and consent' (Nabakumar et al. 2017, 35).

Another serious concern is that national laws largely allow private companies a stronger hand than public voice. Under the new OALP, 2017, any oil company can express interest in an oil block (like the two in Tamenglong and Churachandpur districts of Manipur). This policy opposes the earlier system of a periodic auction of oil blocks by the government under the previous New Exploration and Licensing Policy (NELP). OALP also permits companies to study and specialize in specific geographies if they wish, making the entire country open for exploration and production, with a ready data repository at the Directorate of Hydrocarbons (under the Ministry of Oil and Natural Gas, Government of India). Companies can also extend their block boundaries if they find that the hydrocarbon channels in their designated blocks extend to nearby underground rock layers and the adjoining areas are open. In brief, OALP has empowered oil companies (like

Jubilant Energy in a state like Manipur) to undertake oil and gas works without the government's prior bidding and identification of oil blocks.

This brief exploration means that the notion of public purpose or national interest under secular developmental projects is largely anti-people. In the following section, we discuss how such a secular developmental state transforms a region into a unit within a resource frontier.

The Region in a Resource Frontier

Periphery indeed has acquired a new meaning, notably since India adopted liberalization, privatization and globalization (LPG) in the 1990s. The Look East policy of India (now Act East policy) came into being in the 1990s during Prime Minister Narasimha Rao's term. If one sees India's orientation post 2000, particularly, the perception of Northeast India has shifted dramatically from a violent and insurgency-affected region to a resource-rich region. The Secretary (East) in the Ministry of External Affairs (MEA), Government of India, during the 1990s, Lakhan Mehrotra (2012), observed that since his assumption of charge in May 2004, the then Prime Minister of India Manmohan Singh repetitively stressed the huge benefits likely to accrue to India, in general, and to Northeast India, in particular, through intensification of ties with the Association of Southeast Asian Nations (ASEAN) and its member countries, especially in the areas of trade and commerce. Further, according to him (the secretary), 'there was a growing realization in India of the geo-economic potential of the northeastern region as India's gateway to South East Asia and its value as a bridgehead' (Mehrotra 2012, 76).

In brief, the post-2000 period marks a new phase in which India's vision as a nation whose needs and priorities in extracting resources in the area has become more forceful. Not just political leaders, bureaucrats and policy analysts but also many academic scholars employ a macroeconomic framework to look at the region as a resource-rich yet unexploited region. This understanding is precisely the reason for defining Northeast India as a new resource frontier—an unexploited area. A macroeconomic framework's key concern is the inability to convert rich resources into national benefits for a bigger market. A principal scientist (economics) working at the National Centre for Agricultural Economics and Policy Research (NCAP), New Delhi, argues that the ongoing economic reform process has thrown up several opportunities and challenges. It is a matter of concern that the 'abundant resources, a gamut of crop production possibilities, and rich biodiversity' in Northeast India have remained an unexploited storehouse of natural resources (Barah 2007). The traditional agricultural practices, lack of proper technology interventions and ineffective state policies inhibit the agricultural growth, resulting in an apparent 'developmental divide' between the region and the rest of the country. To capture the advantages of the 'untapped potential in the region of North East India', the states need to reorient their development strategy towards the overall macroeconomic framework. This framework is essential to achieve broader developmental goals (Barah 2007, 14–15).

Moreover, according to such a macroeconomic framework, a subsistence economy based on the customary-land tenure system is always an object of anxiety for the state (global capital), because subsistence is seen as unproductive as per the market's logic. For instance, according to a World Bank consultant, the agricultural practices and land system in Northeast India, although making people self-reliant, cannot be an integral part of the market economy. As a result, developmental interventions in the region are based on the principle of utilitarianism—that the people's resources and lives should be productive mainly through their connection with a competitive market economy, attracting investments through and on the state (Brunner and Global Development Solutions 2010). The macroeconomic framework, however, lacks the essential element of a democratic society: consent. A few things are important here. The macroeconomic framework requires national attention, because, according to the above argument, states in the region are ineffective and unable to turn potential into benefits.

On the one hand, it has a further implication that consolidates the centralizing tendency in the policymaking and national planning and the need for national unity in exploiting the resources. The need for a transparent, accountable and participatory democratic process involving people and states at various levels is completely ruled out. For a macroeconomic framework, such democratic involvement becomes a factor that delays or creates hurdles for the extraction and exploitation of resources. This tendency also leads to continuous tensions between the nation and the region and between the nation and the people on the ground.

Nevertheless, northeastern state's political heads also begin to produce a local imaginary that location of Northeast India as a 'gateway' or 'bridgehead' (of the India's economic linkages with southeast Asia) is the 'opportunity' for local economic development and, thereby, an integral part of globalization for the regional states. It shows that the shifting national vision has active local stakeholders as well. In an interview with a reporter, the chief minister of Manipur, N. Biren Singh, said that Manipur was at the centre of the 20,557-km Asian Highway 1 from Tokyo to Istanbul (*Hindustan Times* 2017). The statement was made around the time of the North East Development Summit held in Imphal in 2017 (21–22 November). If one looks back at the mood in Manipur around the time of this summit, there was sort of a local celebration around Manipur's global image. In a local TV debate ('Manung Hutna' programme of Impact TV, Imphal), for instance, the general secretary of the Manipur Chamber of Commerce (MCC) urged local businessmen and entrepreneurs to register with MCC and be prepared to take the 'opportunities' given to Manipur. An equally large amount of interest, in the mood of celebrating Manipur as 'the gateway of India to South East Asia', is seen in a number of seminars and conferences on themes related to India's (Look East) Act East policy. Manipur is passing through a global moment in which the financial capital (of global financial institutions and agencies, with the support of powerful Western states and emerging powerful Southeast Asian nation states) and India's state together visualize and transform regions within and beyond the state border. Manipur has become part of such visualization and transformation. The idea of Manipur's being at the centre of the Asian Highway is a product of this process.

However, a crucial event that requires serious discussion is the entry of global capital in the nation's needs and priorities. While for the nation global capital is a necessary part of the state's growth, for the people, this global moment is a structural transformation of their subsistence economy, land and agricultural practices and institutional system. It means that land and economy are pressed to undergo an unequal change to suit the global market. The relationship between the nation and global capital deserves a brief discussion. Global capital's entry does not lead to the loosening of a nation's control and sovereign power to decide its priorities. What requires our attention is how the nation (state) continues to be a predominant factor. A major structural economic transformation was seen roughly in the 1990s when the logic of the market economy for the region expanded to accommodate global financial capital, even though the volume of the flow of financial capital (and trade) has increased only over the last few years. We now see a market economy that shows international financial institutions' involvement and foreign countries' interests. Although safeguarding its sovereignty under the new conditions, the state of India is facilitating global capital investment. Northeast India is now imagined as a 'new economic engine of India's growth' (Prime Minister Narendra Modi's speech in Imphal on 16 March 2018), and global capital investment is being welcomed to fulfil this. The increasing Japanese or ADB investment in Northeast India's infrastructure projects is an example of such development.

It is further essential to discuss in this context the current shift in global geopolitics towards the Asia-Pacific region. Chinese economic and military expansion towards the Asia-Pacific region has compelled Japan to look for partner countries to check China's growth. Much of the recent growth in the Indo-ASEAN relationship can also be understood in this context. The increasing development cooperation between India and Japan (particularly in infrastructure development) must also be read in terms of geopolitical (and geo-economic) interests. The importance of Manipur is also primarily derived from this shift. Japan has been investing in Manipur in the Loktak downstream project, irrigation projects and sericulture projects, among others. Netherlands-based oil company Jubilant Energy is investing in Manipur. ADB is investing in Manipur's road infrastructure. In brief, the new-found feeling of being located at the centre between Tokyo and Istanbul, on the one hand, and the feeling of being the gateway of India's connection to Southeast Asia, on the other, are part of this broader, historically evolved development discourse. Because of this development, Manipur is witnessing a new age of neoliberal economic empire directly or indirectly facilitated by powerful nation states.

Ranabir Samaddar (2010) rightly observes that regions and borders are internal borders and the neoliberal empire's lines. Even though the post-colonial imagination of the present states in Northeast India emerged as a region strictly under India's development strategy within the border, today, this idea of the region transcends borders. The region is very much part of the global empire. Manipur's importance as a part of the global imagination of border and people is not merely what India thinks only of Manipur. It is the result of what India thinks of the economic and geo-strategic advantages through linking with the ASEAN. Manipur (Northeast India) emerges as the 'resource-rich' area in acquiring that advantage. Commentaries on the state as the hub or gateway or corridor or new engine of growth all fall under a new empire. President of India Ram Nath Kovind's inaugural speech (21 November 2017) at the North East Development Summit in Imphal reflected such an image of a developed state and a destination of investment within the neoliberal state (and empire).

This above discussion raises the issues of governance and resistance. We deal with these issues in the following section.

Governmentality and the Question of Resistance

How does a state govern a society that has become a resource frontier and has seen several protests against development projects? Governance cannot be a mere act of policy execution and administration. The objectives would also include dealing with dissenting voices. One way of looking at 'governing' is adopting Kalyan Sanyal's argument on capital and governmentality (Sanyal, 2014). There are two phases in developmental projects. One is the capital phase that attempts to extract resources. The other is the governmentality phase, in which the government formulates targeted policies to deal with poverty and deprivation. Extraction or exploitation of the resources like oil and gas or hydel power through development projects happens in the phase of capital investment, which involves land grabbing and displacement of people from their needs-based economy. The claims of the affected people at the sites of developmental projects, like the people at the hydel power project sites in Manipur, Arunachal Pradesh, Sikkim, etc., are that they had a needs-based, if not a wholly self-sufficient, agricultural economy before the projects. However, once the dams submerged large areas of agricultural lands, they were forced to look for new occupations and struggle for their livelihood. This phase is the time when the act of governmentality begins. In this phase, various official attempts are made to instil hope about and highlight the benefits of the developmental projects. Perhaps this is what makes development not only a delusion in the eyes of the public but also something that has negotiable benefits. It is through this illusion that 'development' attempts to act as a rational and legitimate activity.

Thus, governmentality as a modality of power objectifies targeted groups of populations. Such groups would seek and contest with each other for compensation. Governmentality is also a form of power that allows people the ability to seek relief and compensation but not the right to demand a needs-based economy. People are meaningful only as a population group seeking relief and compensation, not as right-bearing persons who can contest the lack of accountability and transparency of developmental projects. Capital operates as the force that does the task of land grabbing and displacement and reduces people to being dependent on welfare services and needs. On the other hand, projects do indeed help diversion of money to non-state actors and cornering of a large share of compensation money by sections of people who illegally access the local administration and government at others' cost.

Another way of looking at the relationship between capital and governmentality is how capital (development financing for the project) is made attractive and legitimate in people's eyes. The most noticeable official (government's and experts') rationale for development projects is that these interventions would generate employment, energy supply and overall revenue. If one does a quick survey of the existing projects, one would find that these objectives are either wholly failed or minimally achieved. The concerned agencies, however, give technical reasons for such failures. What such developmental interventions do is the question. What they do is militarize the areas around such projects, encouraging directly or indirectly inter-community and intra-community divides along the lines of ethnicity, clan, village and ethnic organization and encouraging youth organizations and factions or sections of insurgents to benefit themselves and benefit the company and administration, etc. Then, the promises and objectives of the projects stated in public are merely a legitimization exercise for some lofty goals while dirty politics are allowed to prosper on the ground. Such dirty politics also mean that individuals are not right-bearing citizens who can question but are subjects who can be manipulated. Let us briefly consider an example through the case of oil exploration.

Jubilant Energy's annual report indicates that the two major oil blocks located in Jiribam, Tamenglong and Chuarchandpur have prospective oil resources of volume ranging from 380 billion cubic feet to 1.43 trillion cubic feet (*Business Standard* 2017). In May 2017, Sumit Mahajan, the project manager of the Manipur State Level Convention on Oil Exploration team, said that if it succeeds, oil exploration in Manipur would bring in quite 'a lot of opportunities for the development of both the state and nation as a whole' and that there would be 'a surge in the employment sector paving the way for Manipur's economic prosperity' (*Business Standard* 2017).

However, it is imprudent to believe that the employment of a few skilled labourers and administrative staff would either resolve the unemployment problem or bring development to the state (except for some share of oil revenue). Even if there is opportunity for Manipur's development in terms of employment, I wonder if the same would be what Mahajan described as 'a lot of opportunities'. The project may provide some employment to a few skilled labourers and administrative staff. One needs to know that the objective of an oil project is not precisely to solve the employment problem in a state. In reality, the need for oil exploration arises not from the employment in local areas or state government, or what one may like to assume, from the 'developmental need' of the state, not people.

A study has found that India's per capita oil consumption has increased due to the motorization of the economy. The Indian government's target of increasing the manufacturing sector's share in the gross domestic product (GDP) to 25 per cent by the beginning of the next decade could lead to higher oil consumption in manufacturing. The programme for infrastructure construction (roads and national highways) partly funded through revenues from the higher taxation of oil and oil products is also likely to cause oil demand growth (Sen and Sen 2016). Further, demand for higher oil production would promote 'a free market', promote competitive players and a service economy and ensure oil security for the country, keeping in view strategic and defence considerations. (India Hydrocarbon Vision 2025). The OIL Draft Strategic and Corporate Plan 2011–2020 also urges to 'maintain and enhance reserves and production from North Eastern assets by improving output. Thus, the profitability of OIL would enhance by fully exploiting the potentials of NE assets' (CAG 2015).

If increasing manufacturing's share in India's GDP, financing big national highways, ensuring oil security for strategic considerations and promoting a competitive market economy and profits for companies are the key guiding factors of the oil economy, then it is difficult to justify what Sumit Mahajan meant by 'a lot of opportunities for development' of the state or a 'surge in the employment sector' in Manipur. For India, as a post-colonial state, the nation's needs are not necessarily the needs of the people. Given this aspect of developmental interventions, it is difficult to imagine such interventions as opportunities for developing people.

However, we also need to introspect on the question of resistance. How do we see resistance in the context of the above developments? While there is active engagement from concerned civic bodies against development policies, there are increasing instances in which development projects are negotiated and implemented in surreptitious, horrible and violent manners. Reportedly, leaders, organizations, fictitious insurgent parties, etc. often arrive at an informal agreement to suit their private interests. Interestingly, since these people and groups have already acquired informally coercive power and control over areas of a self-invented sphere of jurisdiction, companies and administrative agencies are found to negotiate first with these classes of people instead of democratically responding to the community. During my field visits and interactions in the district of Tamenglong (Manipur) (in the course of the government's move to welcome oil survey and exploration works), I recorded both the mass movement against the development projects and the alleged counter-popular actions of armed groups of people who had developed, either by consent or by coercion, a relationship with the company and local administration.

Broadly, in the above discussion, we see two emerging trends: one is the reduction of people into a dependent targeted population who would seek compensation and relief; and the other is the emergence of what I referred to as counter-popular acts. If this is the emerging context, one can rethink resistance. One way to understand resistance is to be aware of the state's capacity and technology, both of which use force to stifle protest movements and make people solely dependent on compensations and relief measures. Another way of understanding resistance is the people's willingness to accept that there are internal divisions among them during their movement against development projects. Such divisions could be along the lines of contesting ethnicities and tribes, on the one hand, and approaches (pro- or anti-development) to the development activity. To ignore this fact of divisions and the alleged reports of counter-popular activity by sections of armed groups and local leaders is to miss the possibility of understanding not just the power operating within society but also the expanding areas of resistance studies.

Gledhill (2014), an anthropologist working among South America's lowland indigenous population, observed that collective subjects engaged in acts that might be described as 'resistance' are seldom internally homogenous. That the resisting collective subjects are rarely internally homogenous implies two things. One is that society is not completely insulated from interventions by the dominant power. We have seen this in the above discussion. The state would not only attempt to legitimize developmental projects but also create stakeholders in favour of its visions and objectives. This would lead to internally violent relationships among sections of the people. The society also manifests divisions internally in terms of the perception of the benefits of 'development', because people are poor and marginalized to the extent that they have little sources of livelihood to sustain the momentum of such movements. Nevertheless, I would agree with Gledhill's argument that ignoring divisions among the collective subjects is politically and ethically problematic, particularly if it silences movements against new kinds of domination within the subaltern population itself which are engineered through new interventions by the state or private capital in response to the gains produced by subaltern activism.

References

Amarjit Sharma, G. 2020. 'Development Assistance in Conflict-Affected and Fragile Areas of India'. In Policy Research on Development Cooperation in Situations of Conflict and Fragility. Quezon City: CSO Partnership for Development Effectiveness Working Group on Conflict and Fragility and the International Indigenous Peoples Movement for Self-Determination and Liberation with support from the European Commission and the Swedish International Development Cooperation Agency.

Barah, B. C. 2007. 'Strategies for Agricultural Development in the North-East India: Challenges and Emerging Opportunities'. *Indian Journal of Agricultural Economics* 61, no. 1 (January–March): 13–31.

Brunner, Hans-Peter and Global Development Solutions. 2010. 'The North East India Economy: Resource Base and Constrained Productive Activities'. In *North East India: Local Economic Development and Global Markets*, edited by Hans-Peter Brunner, 30. New Delhi: SAGE Publications.

Business Standard. 2017, 16 May. 'Oil Exploration Underway in Manipur'. Available at https://www.business-standard.com/article/news-ani/oil-exploration-underway-in-manipur-117051600565_1.html#:~:text=Oil%20India%20Limited%2C%20has%20commenced,presence%20of%20hydrocarbons%20in%20Manipur.&text=The%20contracts%20were%20awarded%20under,of%20the%20Government%20of%20India (accessed on 22 March 2021).

CAG. 2015, 9 December. Comptroller and Auditor General of India Report No. 42. Performance Audit on Hydrocarbon Exploration Efforts of Oil India Limited, Union Government, Ministry of Petroleum and Natural Gas.

Cederlöf, Gunnel and K. Sivaramakrishnan. 2012. *Ecological Nationalism*. Ranikhet: Permanent Black.

Chakravarty, Sukhamoy. 1987. *Development Planning: The Indian Experience*. Oxford: Clarendon Press.

Chatterjee, Partha. 2012. *Empire and Nation: Essential Writings 1985–2005*. Ranikhet: Permanent Black.

Elwin, Verrier. 1961. *Nagaland*. Guwahati; Delhi: Spectrum Publications.

Gledhill, John. 2014. 'Indigenous Autonomy, Delinquent States, and the Limits of Resistance'. *History and Anthropology* 25, no. 4: 507–529.

Hindustan Times. 2017, 26 November. 'Manipur Needs Image Makeover to Be India's Act East Hub, Says CM N. Biren'. Available at https://www.hindustantimes.com/brand-stories/flaunt-your-nights-oppo-f19-pro-5g-to-revolutionize-smartphone-videography-101614687826214.html (accessed on 22 March 2021).

India Hydrocarbon Vision 2025, Ministry of Petroleum and Natural Gas, Government of India, http://petroleum.nic.in/sites/default/files/vision.pdf.

Mehrotra, Lakhan. 2012, January–March. 'India's Look East Policy: Its Origin and Development'. *Indian Foreign Affairs Journal* 7, no. 1: 75–85.

Ministry of Finance, Government of India. 2018. *Annual Report, 2017–18.* New Delhi: Government of India.

Nabakumar, W., Jiten Yumnam and Anina Kamei. 2017. *Contestation for Control Over Land and Natural Resources in Manipur in the Wake of Modern Laws.* Guwahati: ActionAid India.

Samaddar, Ranabir. 2010. *Emergence of the Political Subject.* New Delhi: SAGE Publications.

Sanyal, Kalyan. 2014. *Rethinking Capitalist Development: Primitive Accumulation, Governmentality and Post-Colonial Capitalism.* London: Routledge.

Sen, Amrita and Anupama Sen. 2016, March. 'India's Oil Demand: On the Verge of "Take-Off"?' OIES Paper: WPM 65. Oxford: Oxford Institute for Energy Studies.

Yumnam, Jiten. 2019a. 'International Finance Institutions: A Focus on the Private Sector in North East India's Development Challenges'. Available at https://www.realityofaid.org/wp-content/uploads/2019/08/8.-IFIs.pdf (accessed on 20 June 2020).

———. 2019b. 'ADB Road Projects and Concerns in Manipur'. Available at http://www.realityofaid.org/wp-content/uploads/2016/05/RC-1.pdf (accessed on 3 November 2019).

Zachariah, Benjamin. 2014. *Developing India: An Intellectual and Social History, c. 1930–50.* New Delhi: Oxford University Press.

CHAPTER 11

Development Schemes and How People Engage with the State in Manipur

Tanmoy Das

Studies on state–society relationships, especially in the field of 'development', have shown that a state that has enormous stocks of economic resources in the form of development schemes and programmes often finds itself unable to manage and contain those resources (Jayal 2001). The implementation of those resources in the form of development schemes and programmes, as Akhil Gupta notes, forms a key arena where representations of the state are constituted and where its legitimacy is contested (Gupta 2006). This contestation by various demand groups challenge the legitimacy and diminish the independence of the state, reducing it to a state that is weak–strong (Rudolph and Rudolph 1987).

The attempt of this chapter is to see the actual working of the state on the ground through cases of development schemes. The chapter specifically looks into the working of the state by focusing on the relationship between the state (district officials and authority) and the local stakeholders (community elites, local youth organizations, insurgent organizations) in the planning and implementation of development schemes. Though various development schemes are kept in mind in general to understand the working of the state, two schemes—the Mahatma Gandhi National Rural Employment Guarantee Act (MGNREGA) and the Pradhan Mantri Awaas Yojana (PMAY)—remain the primary focus of the chapter.

Though development schemes and programmes are for uplifting the socio-economic conditions of a populace, they are however not immune to the influences of local politics (Dev 2015; Singh 2016). The different hues of influences, by the community elites, local political leaders, insurgent groups, etc., appropriate development schemes for the personal interests of people who are at close proximity to the state or of people of influence and power. This challenges the legitimacy of the state at the ground level. Distribution of schemes is influenced by clientelist motives too. This chronically hampers the motive of development schemes, resulting in the mismanagement of economic resources in the form of funds for schemes.

The general argument against MGNREGA is that, even with the ever-increasing job-card holders and budget, works largely remain incomplete (Bhattacharjee 2017; Ranaware et al. 2015). This chapter, adding to the existing literature, tries to explore and uncover why works remain incomplete. It also brings forward how works are distributed among the beneficiaries, as the different hues of influences affect who gets what work. The other scheme that the chapter looks at is PMAY. The distribution and implementation of this relatively new scheme also bring out new panoramas of politics around it. The influences of non-official intermediaries, like youth organizations, the Church, etc., help individuals in securing a scheme. Conceptualizing this as a patron–client relationship (Scott 1972) helps explore the everyday politics surrounding the schemes. The frontline state that the average villager encounters is the Village Authority (VA) and the officials of the block development office, though mostly this encounter happens through non-official intermediaries, which bestows a certain power on them. This power results in reinforcing their influencing capacity, thus completing the circle of power. The other way in which villagers come across the state is through teachers, doctors, nurses of government schools and community health centres (CHCs), etc., apart from the massive militarization of the region.

An ethnographic study was conducted in two villages: Mongjarong Khunou (Reangpang) and Nungba of Tamenglong district in Manipur. The chapter first focuses on the village as the site of fieldwork, introducing the basic profiles of the village to the reader, such as the educational, occupational and landholding profiles of the village. Following that, it dwells on the two centrally sponsored schemes (MGNREGA and PMAY) and their planning and implementation in the village. Finally, it focuses on locating the state in the village.

This chapter tries to bring out the everyday strategies that people employ to have their share of development. It brings out the complexities that come with the influence of non-state organizations, like insurgent groups.

Developing Villages

In order to see what actually development of villages is, I looked into a sample group of people in the Mongjarong Khunou and Nungba villages of Tamenglong district. A total of 115 sample heads were taken using purposive and snowball sampling. In addition to that, key-informant interviews were conducted with officials, such as the district commissioner of Tamenglong, officials of the District Rural

Table 11.1 *Composition of the Sample Population*

S. No.	Panchayat	Village	Habitation	Population
1	Mongjarong Khunou	Mongjarong Khunou	Reangpang-1 and Reangpang-2	68
2	Nungba	Nungba	Nungba-1	47
			Total Population	115

Source: Fieldwork (2018, May).

Development Agency (DRDA), officials of the chief medical officer (CMO) of Tamenglong, etc.

Out of the total sample population of 115, as shown in Table 11.1, it was found that 23 per cent had received primary education and education below standard 10th, 26 per cent had received secondary education (up to standard 10th). The percentage of the sample population that had received higher secondary education (up to standard 12th) and had graduated were 37 per cent and 14 per cent, respectively.

It would be important here to note that respondents with only primary education had received their education in nearby urban areas. This is because the selected villages do not have proper high-school facilities. Therefore, people send their children to the nearby urban areas for education. Out of the selected villages, the village 'Nungba' touches National Highway 37. Due to this, the village is witnessing socio-economic transformation at a very low scale and is emerging as a small town.

Nungba houses the office of the block development officer (BDO), the CHC and also a high school. Therefore, it attracts students with educational requirements till high school (standard 10th). However, for higher secondary and higher studies, people move to Imphal, Silchar (a border city in Assam) or other parts of the country.

A stable source of income is a major factor in determining a household's condition. In this study, based on their occupation, the sample population were divided into five categories: farmer, government employee, self-employed, student and others. It was found that out of the total sample, 46 per cent were farmers and 30 per cent were self-employed. Government employees and students accounted for only 3 per cent and 14 per cent, respectively.

The 'others' category accounted for 7 per cent, which included people in non-governmental organizations (NGOs), youth organizations, etc. Out of the student respondents (eight in total), two were graduates, four had cleared higher secondary education and the remaining two were in standard 11th, having cleared high school. The self-employed in the sample population included people working as contractors and owning businesses, like hotels (eateries), rice mills, etc.

Most of the villagers are absorbed in agriculture, and farming is done on own agricultural lands and community farming lands (*jhum* cultivation lands). It was found that the villagers mostly had marginal and small lands as own cultivable lands, with 26 per cent having marginal and 63 per cent having small landholdings.[1] Semi-medium and medium landholdings were accounted for by 7 per cent and 4 per cent of the sample population, respectively. People with medium landholdings often refer to their lands as farms, which in most cases are away from their place of residence. In the context of Northeast India, the community landholding or common property resource regime needs clear understanding, that is, 'landless' and 'landholding' have certain implied meanings. For example, a person may not have his/her own land; however, this does not deprive him/her of activities on community land, like *jhum* cultivation, where his/her own labour is applied and the produce is shared among the community, including with him/her.

If we refer to development schemes on paper, they are basically divided into three categories: central-sector schemes, centrally sponsored schemes and state schemes. Centrally sponsored schemes are, as the name suggests, schemes that are largely funded by the central government. These are implemented by the state government. These are further divided into two types of schemes, namely Core of the Core Schemes and Core Schemes. This chapter studies one Core of the Core Scheme (MGNREGA) and one Core Scheme (PMAY).

MGNREGA has an important role in the development of a rural set-up. As the name suggests, it is supposed to provide employment to people for 100 days in a year. On not being employed for 100 days, a beneficiary can claim an amount of monetary compensation from the district administration. This guarantee of employment is ensured through a job card that is issued by the gram panchayat/VA after registration. The registration is valid for 5 years and is renewed from time to time. The job card therefore reflects how many people are enrolled as beneficiaries of the employment scheme. MGNREGA as a scheme is interesting, because it also incorporates the works of other schemes. For example, works that needs to be done under other schemes, such as works relating to horticulture, construction of inter-village roads (IVRs), construction of water reservoirs, etc., are conducted under this scheme. This is further explained later.

As of 2017–2018, there were a total of 31,260 job-card holders in the district of Tamenglong. The two subdivisions, Tamenglong and Nungba, had 10,986 and 3,992 job-card holders, respectively.[2] Table 11.2 provides some basic information, such as the number of job-card holders, number of works to be done and the budget from 2009–2010 to 2017–2018. It is evident from the data that with each passing year, the number of job-card holders is increasing.

Every year, people are registering for 100 days of guaranteed employment, which indicates that less people are joining conventional work and more are relying on MGNREGA for employment.[3] In the same light, the number of works to be done in the district also went up, and so did the total budget. Employment under MGNREGA includes a wide range of works, like horticulture-related works, like clearing of lands, plantation of bananas, oranges, passion fruits, king chillies, teak pineapples, ginger, etc. Other works include drought proofing, afforestation, rural sanitation, solid and liquid waste management, etc. Construction of infrastructure, such as motorable IVRs, slab culverts, water tanks and water reservoirs, renovation of traditional water bodies, roadside drains, river embankments, etc. are also included.

From the expenditure data of 2017–2018, it was found that agriculture-related works (including plantation for afforestation), land development works (like land levelling and filling) and rural connectivity works (building of IVRs, etc.) take up a major share of the allocated budget.[4]

The number of works which unsurprisingly increases every year, to a large extent, include spillover works.[5] These are works that could not be completed within the set time frame and allocated budget and hence need to be revisited with a new budget allocation. The reasons for incomplete works are many, such as bad weather conditions, leading to landslides, *bandhs* and blockades, non-availability of resources, like funds to pay the workers on time, etc. However, due to such reasons, the works keep piling up and the budget allocated keeps rising with each financial year. Another issue related with MGNREGA involves durable asset building. Durable asset building is a far cry due to corruption in the sanctioning of funds, use of materials for building the assets and delay in many other layers/phases of works.

Table 11.2 Overview of Mahatma Gandhi National Rural Employment Guarantee Act in Tamenglong Headquarters and Nungba Subdivisions

S. No	Year	No. of Job-card Holders		No. of Works		Total Budget (in ₹ Lakh)	
		Tamenglong Headquarters	Nungba	Tamenglong Headquarters	Nunbga	Tamenglong Headquarters	Nungba
1	2009–2010	8,862	3,005	216	157	1,173.23	431.78
2	2010–2011	10,014	3,047	281	200	1,358.89	413.47
3	2011–2012	10,437	3,228	544	149	2,191.77	677.88
4	2012–2013	9,748	3,305	534	120	2,047.08	694.05
5	2013–2014	9,631	3,620	1,321	125	1,293.19	871.42
6	2014–2015	9,996	3,751	789	128	2,548.98	956.50
7	2015–2016	10,771	3,923	1,187	1,074	3,145.13	1,145.51
8	2016–2017	10,986	3,992	2,789	1,295	3,481.22	1,265.46
9	2017–2018	10,986	3,992	2,788	399,200	3,478.16	1,264.14

Source: Calculated from the information provided by the office of the District Rural Development Agency (DRDA), Tamenglong.

PMAY is a housing scheme. Under this scheme, the government plans to ensure housing for all by the year 2022, through providing low-cost housing (pukka houses) to the people residing in the rural areas of the country.[6] Households belonging to low-income groups and the Economically Weaker Section are targeted for the scheme. According to data from the Ministry of Rural Development, Government of India, PMAY in the state of Manipur is lagging behind the target it was set to achieve. The year-wise house completion report of 2016–2017 shows that 1,506 houses were built in the year under PMAY across the whole of Manipur. Imphal West, Tamenglong and Ukhrul were the three districts where the housing scheme's performance was lower than the Manipur state average. Imphal West had only 20 houses built (completed), and Ukhrul only 29.

According to Table 11.3, there were only 44 houses built (completed) in Tamenglong district in the year 2016–2017. These figures provoke questions regarding the small number of houses built (completed). Further, looking at the data for the five blocks of Tamenglong district, it is clear that the housing scheme did not achieve the target it was set to achieve.

Khoupum, Nungba headquarters authority (panchayat), Tamenglong and Tousem are the subdivisions were the houses were built. Tamei subdivision surprisingly had no houses built (completed) under the housing scheme. Table 11.4 shows the number of families targeted and registered for the scheme in the five blocks of Tamenglong district as of July 2018.

As Table 11.4 suggests, the sanctioned money for the construction of houses under the scheme is being paid through instalments. The housing scheme process, being lengthy, takes time, as the work is divided in phases.[7] After the registration of people, the beneficiary list is made. Thereafter, the physical location where the house is to be built is geo-tagged, and then the funds are sanctioned to the beneficiaries. The funds are sanctioned in instalments after the beneficiary accounts are verified. Table 11.4 shows data relating to the completed houses and not those under construction.

Table 11.3 Number of Houses Completed under PMAY-G till 2018 (Tamenglong, Block Wise)

S. No.	Block Name	Houses Completed in 2013-2014	Houses Completed in 2015-2016	Houses Completed in 2016-2017	Houses Completed in 2017-2018	Houses Completed in 2018-2019	Total Houses Completed in 2017-2019
1	Khoupum	0	0	1	0	0	1
2	Nungba	0	0	4	0	0	4
3	Tamei	0	0	0	0	0	0
4	Tamenglong	0	0	14	0	0	14
5	Tousem	0	0	25	0	0	25
	Total	0	0	44	0	0	44

Source: Compiled from the data provided on number of houses completed under PMAY-G in Tamenglong, Manipur, 2018 by Ministry of Rural Development, Government of India. (accessed November 2018).

Table 11.4 Physical Progress of the Housing Scheme under Pradhan Mantri Gramin Awaas Yojana till 2018 (Tamenglong)

S. No.	Block Name	Target Fixed by Districts	Registered	Geo-tagged Out of Registered	Sanctioned Out of Geo-tagged	Sanctioned with Verified Accounts	Instalments				Completed
							1st	2nd	3rd	4th	
1	Khoupum	85	110	106	85	83	82	74	26	0	1
2	Nungba	246	305	287	221	221	221	221	203	0	4
3	Tamei	217	319	228	212	192	199	147	97	0	0
4	Tamenglong	171	209	155	127	127	127	123	76	0	14
5	Tousem	349	425	415	349	349	349	349	333	0	25
	Total	1,068	1,572	1,269	1,063	1,041	1,047	982	760	0	44

Source: Compiled from the data provided on physical progress of the Housing scheme under PMAY-G in Tamenglong, Manipur 2018 by Ministry of Rural Development, Government of India. (accessed November 2018).

Apart from the gaps in the above-mentioned schemes, which are intended to bring about development in the rural areas of Manipur, the study identifies other gaps as well, relating to health, education, drinking-water supply, critical linkages, like rural roads or IVRs, banking facilities, markets, etc. In various districts of Manipur, the Comptroller and Auditor General (CAG) of India reports point out, funds for MGNREGA have been diverted for civil works, which is a contravention of MGNREGA.[8] The reasons for the diversion of funds were not accepted by the Ministry of Rural Development, Government of India, as MGNREGA does not contain any instruction for such diversion of funds. Irregularities, like diversion and blockage of funds and irregular transfer of funds to bank accounts (of the beneficiaries), have been documented in the CAG reports, adding to the question of whether development schemes are actually helping the targeted population.[9]

CAG reports also bring forward the issues of excess expenditure incurred due to preparation of estimates of works at rates higher than those admissible under MGNREGA. They also throw light on the issue of payments disbursed in cash to the executing agencies as refunds after completion of works, resulting in excess payment.[10] These issues raise questions on the actual working of the state on the ground and also about how the general populace perceives the state and development schemes.

The district report of Baseline Survey of Minority Concentrated Districts, Tamenglong, indicates that awareness relating to development schemes are uniform across the district; however, the proportion of beneficiaries is less when compared to the level of awareness. The report also points out that employment and livelihood opportunities and access to drinking water, health and education remain the major concerns of the villagers of Tamenglong district.[11] This subsequently makes it important to understand how the developments schemes are perceived and understood by the common people in the grassroots. This in return is expected to paint a holistic picture of the development status of the district and blocks, in general, and that of villages, in particular. The following section discusses how people engage with the state through implementation of the development schemes.

Schemes and How People Engage with the State

During my fieldwork in Tamenglong district (Manipur), I witnessed two ways of people's perception of the state. First, the state is seen through the people's ease or difficulty in accessing the authority for seeking various kinds of legitimate benefits. Second, the state is seen through how it monitors and is accountable for the developmental works on the ground. Lack of monitoring of development schemes on the ground leaves on the locals the impression of an absentee state in daily life.

On the other hand, a strong presence of the state is also seen through the security lens. To the understanding of people, several state security forces' camps and number of big infrastructural projects on oil and gas survey works, dams and road infrastructure increasingly seen in the district have aggregated to a resource extractive and militarized state. In Tamenglong district, the Assam Rifles (AR) has one battalion (23rd AR) with several (4–5) companies (small troops) dispatched all over the area. Likewise, a battalion of the Central Reserve Police Force (CRPF) and its several companies, along with the Manipur Rifles, are camped. These companies are situated in the areas like the bridges crossing the rivers of Irang and Barak, etc.

Apart from militarization, the strong presence of the state is also visible and experienced in the district through infrastructure projects, like construction of dams, railway bridges and tunnels and broadening of highways. For instance, a 141-m-tall railway bridge is under construction in Noney district (bifurcated from Tamenglong), which shall become one of the highest railway bridges in the world. A total of 45 tunnels have been bored into the hills for laying the railway lines. These rising infrastructure development works and militarization of the area go in parallel to each other. The field offices of the development projects are inside the military camps. From interviews of the villagers, it was learnt that there were a number of seismic surveys done for oil exploration too. A Netherlands-based company, Jubilant Energy, and the Indian company Oil India Limited have shown active interest in exploring the gas and oil mineral resources in the district since around 2010. These projects have been protested against by the villages chiefs and masses. People allege that they have 'indigenous' right over the resources around them and that they were not informed prior to the initiation of these projects.

Against the backdrop of such presence of the state (through militarization and big infrastructure projects), it is significant to see how people engage with the development schemes meant for them directly. It becomes more concerning for the people in the district that while the state has a strong presence through the security forces and various developmental projects, like construction of roads, dams, etc., they daily encounter a minimal state in terms of delivering development schemes related to village roads, rural employment and housing. This engagement, however, cannot be seen through only the binary of state–society confrontation. In the context of protests against developmental projects, like anti-dam and anti–oil and gas exploration movements, one may see the state and society as relatively organized binary units. However, in the developmental schemes, such binary is loosened up to more internally heterogenous units. We shall look into this heterogeneity through looking at the interests and politics of local stakeholders in the schemes, citing various interviews and engagements. In brief, our study of the developmental schemes indicates multiple ways of seeing the state. The state has become very much part of society, such that multiple stakeholders have emerged in society. Not only is the state configured while implementing schemes, but society also manifests more than one way of engaging the state. It would be wrong to see the state and society as singular and watertight entities.

In the following discussion, we try to understand such a state and society. The district primarily being agrarian, life in Tamenglong, in general, and Reangpang and Nungba, in particular, basically revolves around the *jhum* fields, orange plantation fields and everyday chores of households and small businesses (shops). The development schemes, projects and militarization of the area are a few means through which most of the villagers see the state from a distance and at the same time experience and understand it when the need arises. A few people have regular and frequent interactions with the authorities of the state. These authorities include people who are former or present members of the VA and those close to the local Member of Legislative Assembly (MLA) and working as social workers. They are usually the go-to people for gathering all sorts of information, ranging from information relating to new schemes launched by the government to the upcoming *bandhs* that are to be called by the insurgent groups. The villagers' interactions with any form of the state or state institutions start with them.

One of the most popular development schemes in the study area is MGNREGA. However, the study found that at the most, MGNREGA provides less than 50 days of employment and, many a time, even less through the entire year. The fieldwork interactions with the villagers revealed their dissatisfaction relating to the distribution and implementation of the scheme, as they believed that the authorities were corrupt.[12]

An account of such corruption practice was shared by one of the villagers, whose identity shall remain anonymous:

> The money (wages) for the employment scheme is not paid fairly. Since the job cards are usually kept with the village authority, it becomes difficult to know how many villagers (job card holders) have actually gotten the job. Not all registered for jobs get work. You must not be surprised if you learn that the wife of the village chief also has her name registered for work under MGNREGA. Why does she need to work? In her name the village authority withdraws the payment. And when it comes to payment, a lump-sum amount is paid to the workers and the large part of the money is divided between the BDO office workers, village authority and the contractor.[13]

With the introduction of direct benefit transfer (DBT), the funds that are directly transferred to a beneficiary's bank account are also far from safe. There are some instances where a beneficiary agrees to the VA's demand to keep half of their payment and only receives the other half. Even for people to withdraw money from their respective beneficiary accounts, a person (mostly from the VA) has to collect all the bank passbooks and travel all the way to Noney town, as it hosts the nearest banking facility. The understanding of receiving half payments can be out of fear, out of compulsion and/or out of patronage.

The villagers' understanding of the state and its agencies are however not limited to the VA. The teachers at government schools, doctors at CHCs and officers at the nearest BDO are also points through which the state is engaged and experienced by them. However, taking into account absenteeism (Wouters 2018; of teachers and doctors in schools and CHCs), the villagers tend to perceive that the state is not able to provide basic services to its citizens, such as health, education, drinking water, etc. In response to this, they use the community and its strength to provide services to itself.

The following account supports my argument, showing how the villagers respond to the gaps that are supposed to be filled by the state. During my second visit to the site in May 2018, I discovered that the villagers of Reangpang-1 had decided to build a water reservoir, as they were tired waiting for the state to take action on this matter. Previously, a survey had been conducted for finding the optimal location for extraction of water from the Irang River. Arei Malangmai, one of the villagers, excited like several others, shared:

> They shall be using German technology to bring water up in the hills. After that our village shall at least get rid of the water scarcity problem. We have been pushing every government office starting from the block office, to the DC office. However, as government offices are deaf to our requests. They take it for granted, but water is necessity, water is life. But now we shall finally have it.[14]

With their excitement fading, the village community, with the patronage of the local MLA, contributed and started building a water reservoir next to the church. As the church has the largest corrugated tin roof and is located at a high altitude, much water can be collected through rainwater harvesting. The altitude also makes it easy for the water to flow down the pipes for the villagers to use. The usage of the water is however only limited to village functions, such as marriages, village celebrations and festivals, like Christmas. Apart from this, the village faces problems relating to the lack of IVRs, improper functioning of the schools and health centres, etc. Not all problems are collectively solved by the community, and wherever possible, the patronage of village elites and political parties becomes necessary to fill the gaps. This further reinforces the patron–client relationship and works in favour of the elites. However, not always are the gaps and poor functioning of the state challenged and managed by the community. As shown later, people try to address the issues by participating in the VA elections, sometimes being unsuccessful and sometimes re-electing the entire VA body.

Paul Kamei was approached by the villagers to contest for the post of village secretary, as they believed that Paul, being educated, young and enthusiastic, would do good work for the village. Paul was elected and took the responsibility as village secretary. However, within a year, he resigned from the post. Upon being interviewed, Paul revealed that due to the dishonest behaviour among other VA members, an uncordial relationship started brewing, which acted as a barrier to any honest endeavour for the village. He added that it was better to step down from the post rather have an unhealthy relationship with people of power and influence.

The newly elected VA members are influenced by the existing VA members on decision-making relating to crucial issues of the village, such as development planning and implementation, family disputes, land disputes, etc. 'The VA seems hijacked by the former VA members', Paul added. This further engulfs them in deeds of corruption too. Paul decided that he alone could do no good and hence resigned from the post. He now plans to leave for work to Bengaluru and hopes to do good there. One might as well see this as a classic example of brain drain; however, viewing this through the lens of social relations makes better sense. That is, social relations and the social fabric of harmony gets heavily affected further fueling distrust and dislike among the different clans and tribes of the village. Paul's resignation from the post of village secretary points to the loss of social capital that he could have harnessed and maintained for the well-being of the village. Paul responded to the poor functioning of the state by departing from the state machinery—the VA in this case.

However, there were other instances where the poor functioning of the VA was questioned and the whole VA was re-elected. Augustine Malangmei, a resident of Reangpang village, recalled and shared that several years ago, the whole VA had been changed before the completion of its tenure.[15] This had to be done through approaching the sub-divisional office and the office of the deputy commissioner of the district. The reasons for the change and re-elections were many, including absenteeism, bias towards the people of the same clan, re-channelization of funds for personal benefits, etc.[16] This rather small instance shows how the people collectively responded to the VA and ended up re-electing its members for its fresh functioning.

In brief, the state is perceived and understood mostly in accordance with the interaction that happens at the VA level. Within this level, people negotiate with, respond to and experience the state. Thus, the state is seen with hope as an entity that would do good for the people; however, at the same time, with its inability to deliver services to the people, it is perceived—often rightly—to be corrupt.

The State and the Villagers: The Bittersweet Relationship

For most villagers, an encounter with the state other than at the VA level is not an everyday phenomenon. However, when the state calls for a collective village meeting for introducing programmes, like 'Go to Village', the people get to encounter the different levels of the state.[17] Go to Village is a mission launched in Manipur to 'identify eligible and deserving beneficiaries for development schemes and deliver government services at their doorstep'. At gatherings such as these, where the ministers, local MLA and bureaucrats all gather and promises are made, the state usually takes the form of an enchanting entity. With its promises on the development of the people and announcements of various schemes, the state takes the form of an entity of prosperity. Similarly, the Assam Rifles' social outreach programme, which offers social services, like distributing computers, water tanks, solar/electric lamps, etc., is seen as a confidence building measure by the villagers.

The villagers are glad to receive such services. However, at other instances, the state no longer remains an enchanting entity and rather gets transformed into a repulsive entity (for all the right reasons). With massive militarization of the region, the patrolling troops are disliked. The villagers try their best to avoid interaction with the troops, especially at times of patrolling. It therefore becomes clear that people critique the state; however, they need and welcome it too. This indicates the bittersweet relationship of the state and society; the way the latter sees the state as an enchanting entity and good, on the one hand, and critiques and resists it, on the other hand, is perhaps the way the state is perceived and understood in everyday life.

A similar bittersweet relationship is also seen at institutional levels, like at the level of the DRDA and Autonomous District Council (ADC), when it comes to the planning and implementation of schemes. Both, being district-level institutions, are seen as implementing agencies. However, the DRDA, being directly controlled by the district administration, has relatively more control over the centrally sponsored schemes (their planning, implementation and monitoring). Though development works in the district are largely conceived, planned and implemented by the DRDA, the ADC too is involved in various ways, like through proposing works and recommending beneficiaries for several schemes. Works such as construction, repair, maintenance of roads, bridges, channels and buildings are even transferred to the district council by the district administration for their implementation—that is, sometimes, the ADC is entrusted with the implementation of certain development schemes. However, especially considering centrally sponsored schemes, like MGNREGA, the district administration directly works with the VA, and the wages also are distributed by the district administration through DBT. The district council and the district administration are therefore sometimes found to be caught in this bittersweet relationship.

Nexuses, Corruption and the Patron–Client Relationship

With the ever-degrading condition of the roads (especially the IVRs), the never-used shopping complex that is left abandoned in Nungba and the delay of payments for works under MGNREGA, one is compelled to think: will development ever set foot? The members of the Nungba Youth Association (NYA) expressed their tiredness when discussing development. Blessing, a member of the NYA, shared:

> Let me tell you, when any funds arrive for any works, negotiations start at every level. The village authority, the contractors, the BDO, the insurgents, everyone negotiates for the share of the money. It largely impacts the development works as the quality of work is low which degrades over time. I wonder why a patch of land needs to be blacked topped every year in the winter season?[18]

The budget for the works under the employment schemes only increases year after year, as shown in Table 11.2. The blacktopping of roads too happens every year. Many of the works are left incomplete, as the funds are all spent in completing the previous year's leftover works. This creates a spillover of works, and funds are siphoned off through showing that the previous year's works were done in the current year with the funds allocated for the latter. The works like clearing of shrubs and levelling of land for construction of water reservoirs, roads, etc. are done with materials of low quality and standard. This results in the need for renovation or reconstruction within 2 years. The renovation and reconstruction then go through the same process, and the vicious cycle of corruption remains unbroken.

Discussing at length, another member (who is kept anonymous), shared:

> An unavoidable thing is the percentage of share that is to be given to the insurgent groups. I don't know what will happen to the fate of our Naga struggle. But it seems a very distant dream if not impossible. Anyway, the leaders and commanders of the groups are being incapable of handling a Naga homeland. They are divided among themselves. Now they sustain from the contributions, donations and even extortion. The Army, DC, ADC, ministers, all know about it. It is an open secret.[19]

The interviews shed light that the insurgents gain knowledge relating to the amount of funds sanctioned for a particular work, and then the percentage is decided upon. The demand for this share of funds is then made known to the contractor through the workers working at the site or communicated through other means. This chronically hampers the development works. It was also learnt that some contractors have an understanding with the insurgent groups and share the profit. This indicates a nexus (Baruah 2005) between the contractors, insurgent groups and, sometimes, even state officials.

Interviewing a local contractor did not yield any significant information. The local contractor blamed the state for not providing funds for the works taken up. In addition, he expressed grievance relating to the insurgent group's demand for a percentage share:

> It is a sleepy place. No prospects for job, no healthcare, no education facility, but it is our land so we love it and live here. Payments for our works get delayed and works never finish in time. And phases of works never get completed. Authorities do not release monies on time. The demands of percentage share from IM and ZUF is also taxing. They demand huge sums of money and give us deadline for payment. Sometimes, we have to pay from our pockets. But somehow, we manage.[20]

Basically, the entities in the nexus (contractors, insurgent groups, state officials and villagers) keep blaming one another for the underdevelopment. The blame usually stops at the insurgent groups. It was learnt from other villagers that the local contractor was building a new house in Tamenglong town, which leads one to question his narrative. On spillover of works, one such visible instance relates to one of the habitations of Reangpang-1 village. This habitation is situated at the hilltop, and there are two ways to reach it. One is a narrow trail through the dense forest. The other path is from the other side of the hill, wide enough for a vehicle to travel. However, this trail, just cleared of trees and bushes, is equally difficult to navigate. At the start of the stretch of road from the national highway stands a board displaying information regarding the road to be constructed.[21] However, no road has been built in years. This poses a major problem for the people in accessing facilities, such as banks, markets, health centres, schools, etc., and during monsoon, the trail becomes slippery, adding to the difficulties of the villagers. During the course of the fieldwork in May 2018, when enquired about the incomplete construction of the road to the village, the respondents stated that the *thekadar* (contractor) was responsible for the incomplete work; as the *thekadar* had left the work after clearing the bushes and trees.

On the contrary, people see the contractor also as a patron who helps the villagers in various forms, like through lending money to the needy and helping people get a share of the work when they can secure tenders for any works. I club them as the elites.[22] The relationship that some of the villagers have with the village elites or people in power can be understood through the patron–client relationship. Various studies show that clientelism is much ubiquitous when it comes to the analysis of politics and is based on the exchange of goods and/or services (access to schemes and programmes) between political parties, elites and common people (Hicken 2011; Kitschelt and Wilkinson 2007; Stokes et al. 2013; Tillin, Deshpande, and Kailash 2015).

The patron–client relationship is a concept that can be used to understand the dynamics of the distribution of development schemes in Reangpang and Nungba. However, interviewing the VA members and the officials of the state on improper implementation of development schemes largely brings out the insurgency issue. It seems that the officials try to hide their deeds under the banner of insurgent groups and their percentage demands (of funds). The siphoning off and re-channelization of the development funds and inadequate monitoring and accountability of the state officials in matters related to implementation of the development schemes can be easily understood as acts of corruption and misgovernment. However, the villagers have their own sense of engagement with the state, its resources and officials, as shown in the previous sections.

It was also learnt through the interviews that many a time, state officials and the village chairman have an informal understanding about the way the funds should be used. National Highway 53 touches Nungba village; as a result, there mushroomed shops taking the shape of a market. The area also serves as a *haat* for the village. There also lies an abandoned multi-storey building. This building was built some 4–5 years ago by the VA and the then BDO. It was built with the expectation of setting up a new marketplace, as that region in the village was witnessing market expansion and a boost in its economic activities. However, it lay abandoned when the study was conducted. When enquiries were made about the reason for the same, a few interesting dimensions came up.

The multi-storey building had been built under the village development programme to establish a thriving economy, which was then at its infant stage. Travellers from Jiribam and Silchar, when travelling to Imphal, use National Highway 53.[23] Since Nungba relatively falls in between the two destinations, it gradually became a place for travellers to rest and have meals in between the journey. This is also one of the reasons why Nungba is a growing economy. The building was supposed to cater to such needs. However, there was a dispute regarding where the building should be constructed. The villagers wanted it to be at the heart of the marketplace, as it would well serve the purpose. However, much against the collective will of the villagers, the VA chairman (also the village chief) selected a site closer to his home, which is located at the end of the market site. The contract for the building's construction too was given to a *thekadar* who was well associated with the then BDO. Likewise, the materials for the construction were bought from vendors known to them. The building developed a crack in one of its walls due to an earthquake, resulting in its abandonment by the people, who are scared to set up a market there and are angry. One respondent wondered how a newly built building could develop such a crack. It is not very hard to understand that the materials used for the construction of the building were of very low quality. The village chairman, the secretary and the BDO are blamed for this incident.[24]

These actions subsequently divided the village into camps. The building till date stays abandoned, and the daily market found its place near the Nungba bus stand, adjacent to the entrance leading to the CHC. In the case of PMAY, a financial assistance of ₹75,000–130,000 is supposed to be provided to the beneficiaries in phases and instalments.[25] From the field observations and responses from the villagers, it was learnt that the amount for one beneficiary is distributed among two–three people by the VA. As Pantipou Kamei, a respondent, shared, this was done by the VA to gain popularity among the villagers as a good leader who works for the benefit of all and not only his clan. Further, this would earn him a good name and help him with his future political aspirations.[26]

The list of beneficiaries usually includes the people or families that support the VA members in their interests. This patronage helps them in ensuring and securing the development schemes as beneficiaries. Insights from the interviews reveal that some of the beneficiaries only get the lowest-quality corrugated tin roof as assistance, whereas the scheme promises a pukka house. Though there are some pukka houses built in Reangpang-2 village, the blueprint and instructions to build houses under the scheme were however not followed. Walls of the houses were built no wider than 5 inches and were built with poor workmanship and using poorer materials. The works were not supervised by the junior engineers and technical assistant available at the block level. This left the villagers in a helpless condition, with no place to voice their grievances.

Conclusion

It is quite difficult to simply conclude on the nature of the workings of the state and society, especially in the hills of Manipur. The state that the villagers encounter on an everyday basis is the VA. This forefront state has the authority for and major responsibility of the effective implementation of development schemes. However, the VA, through the development schemes, regulates and controls the politics of the village. Who gets what then becomes a result of who knows whom well and how cordial their relationship is. The clandestine relationship that the villagers have with the people in power and authority decides how well they can secure a scheme for themselves. The influence of the insurgents holds a major stake in the local politics quite about everything. The question then is: what is the role of the state in these conditions? Do the higher levels of the state, those at the district and Manipur state, not know of the ground realities? One would firmly assume that the latter are not alien to the higher authorities' knowledge. If so, then why does the state let things be the way they are even when its legitimacy is challenged? There are various other schemes (which the study did not dwell upon) through which the nexus can be understood. Studying these would only enrich our knowledge on the workings of the state and the politics of schemes, eventually opening up new vistas of research and knowledge production.

Notes

1. Department of Agriculture and cooperation, Agriculture Census Division, categorizes landholding sizes as marginal (less than 1 hectare), small (1–2 hectares), semi-medium (2–4 hectares), medium (4–10 hectares) and large (above 10 hectares).
2. The villages for the study come under Nungba subdivision; however, I have included Tamenglong subdivision too, for the sake of comparison between the subdivisions.
3. In the rural and remote places, in general, and in the rural villages where this study was conducted, in particular, conventional work would basically mean engaging in agriculture, owning small businesses, like a shop or a roadside hotel, and having a salaried government job.
4. The budget for the Mahatma Gandhi National Rural Employment Guarantee Act (MGNREGA)—a Core of the Core Scheme—basically gets sanctioned in the yearly government budget, which then flows through the implementation and monitoring agencies, like the district commissioner and the Block Development Officer (BDO), to the villagers through direct benefit transfer.
5. However, the data provided by the office of the district commissioner do not show any spillover of works, though another section of works proposed to be done in the next year is provided. Spillover of works is discussed in a later section.
6. Pradhan Mantri Awaas Yojana (PMAY) is a revised housing scheme launched in June 2015. Prior to 2015, this housing scheme existed under the name of Indira Awaas Yojana (IAY). With the revision of the scheme, the targets were also revised.
7. However, there are no defined phases of work relating to the construction of houses under PMAY. The progress of work depends on the availability of funds, materials and masons, etc.
8. Report of the Comptroller and Auditor General of India, Government of Manipur, Report no. 1 of 2016. Six per cent of the total budget for MGNREGA can be used for administrative expenses. However, funds

amounting to ₹42.65 lakh were used for the construction of a new building for dedicated staff and for repair works in the DRDA quarters. This instance is of Thoubal district.
9. Report of the Comptroller and Auditor General of India on Social and General Sectors, Government of Manipur Report no. 2 of 2018.
10. Report of the Comptroller and Auditor General of India on Social and General Sectors, Government of Manipur Report no. 1 of 2017. Excess expenditure in Bishnupur's Moirang block and excess payment in Chandel district.
11. The Baseline Survey of Minority Concentrated Districts; District Report Tamenglong. Study commissioned by Ministry of Minority Affairs, GoI. Study conducted by Omeo Kumar Das Institute of Social Change and Development: Guwahati.
12. In some cases of corruption, as indicated by the villagers, it was learnt that the contractor to whom the tender of the job is given negotiates with the Village Authority (VA) and siphon offs a large share of the fund for the work. The negotiation depends on the understanding the VA and the contractor have with each other relating to the factors like material cost and duration of work.
13. Interviewed and discussed over the month of March 2018.
14. I interviewed Arei on 12 May 2018, at his residence in Reangpang. By 'they', Arei meant the district administration and the NGOs (non-governmental organizations) overlooking the work.
15. The term of a VA is 3 years starting from the date of the first meeting (https://indiacode.nic.in/handle/123456789/1666?locale=en).
16. The members of the VA are required to attend its meetings every single time. Some instances of a member missing a meeting are overlooked; however, if a member misses six consecutive meetings, then that member has to resign.
17. By collective village meetings, I mean meetings of the kind where people of several villages meet in an agreed-upon place (usually a pivotal village). For details of the 'Go to Village' programme under the government of Manipur, see http://gotovillage.in/
18. I interviewed Blessing and members of the Nungba Youth Association (NYA) on 15 May 2018.
19. A percentage share is claimed by the insurgent groups (National Socialist Council of Nagaland–Isak Muivah [NSCN-IM], National Socialist Council of Nagaland–Khaplang [NSCN-K] and Zeliangrong United Front [ZUF]) as a contribution to and donation for the Naga cause (fight for liberty and self-rule against the Indian state and its forces). Interviewed on 15 April 2018.
20. I interviewed the local contractor of Nungba at his residency on 1 May 2018.
21. Information regarding the kilometres of road to be constructed, the phases in which they are to be constructed, the estimated budget and other such

details were displayed on the board. It is now well past the year of the start of this project.
22. For my study, I define elites as people with political and economic power—people who can influence decisions using their power in the political ladder/hierarchy and/or economic power. I identify elites as VA members, economically well-to-do families and the MLA and their allies in the village.
23. Jiribam is a district in Manipur, and Silchar is a district in Assam's Barak Valley. Both, being border districts of their respective states, see a constant flow of people for various purposes.
24. I interviewed Blessing on 15 May 2018.
25. See https://pmayg.nic.in/netiay/about-us.aspx
26. I interviewed Pangtipou Kamei on 29 May 2018.

References

Baruah, S. 2005. *Durable Disorder: Understanding the Politics of Northeast India.* New Delhi: Oxford University Press.
Bhattacharjee, G. 2017, 24 June). 'MGNREGA as Distribution of Dole.' *Economic and Political Weekly* 52, nos. 25–26: 29–33.
Dev, R. 2015. 'Institutionalizing Social Policies in the Margins: A Comparative Study of "NAREGA" in Meghalaya and Jharkhand.' In *Politics of Welfare: Comparisons Across Indian States*, edited by L. Tillin, R. Deshpande, and K. K. Kailash, 146. New Delhi: Oxford University Press.
Gupta, A. 2006. 'Blurred Boundaries: The Discourse of Corruption, the Culture of Politics, and the Imagined State.' In *The Anthropology of the State: A Reader*, edited by A. Sharma and A. Gupta, 219. Malden, MA: Blackwell Publishing.
Hicken, A. 2011. 'Clientelism.' *Annual Review of Political Science* 14, no. 1: 289–310.
Jayal, N. G. 2001. 'The State and Democracy in India or What Happened to Welfare, Secularism, and Development.' In *Themes in Politics: Democracy in India*, edited by N. G. Jayal, 194. New Delhi: Oxford University Press.
Kitschelt, H., and S. I. Wilkinson. 2007. *Patrons, Clients and Policies: Patterns of Democratic Accountability and Political Competition.* Cambridge: Cambridge University Press.
Ranaware, K., U. Das, A. Kulkarni, and S. Narayanan. 2015, 28 March. 'MGNREGA Works and Their Impacts A Study of Maharashtra.' *Economic & Political Weekly* 50, no. 13: 53–61.
Rudolph, L. I., and S. H. Rudolph. 1987. *The Pursuit of Lakshmi: The Political Economy of the Indian State.* New Delhi: Orient Longman Limited.
Scott, J. C. 1972. 'Patron-Client Politics and Political Change in Southeast Asia.' *The American Political Science Review* 66, no. 1: 91–113.
Singh, S. 2016. *The Local in Governance; Politics, Decentralization and Environment.* New Delhi: Oxford.

Stokes, S. C., T. Dunning, M. Nazareno, and V. Brusco. 2013. *Brokers, Voters, and Clientelism: The Puzzle of Distributive Politics.* London: Cambridge University Press.

Tillin, L., R. Deshpande, and K. K. Kailash. 2015. 'Introduction: Comparing the Politics of Welfare across Indian States.' In *Politics of Welfare: Comparisons Across Indian States*, edited by R. D. Louise Tillin, 8. New Delhi: Oxford University Press.

Wouters, J. J. 2018. *In the Shadows of Naga Insurgency: Tribes, State, and Violence in Northeast India.* New Delhi: Oxford.

CHAPTER 12

Informal Political Networks, *Dalals* and Local Governance in Assam

Amiya Kumar Das

It is by now a substantial reality that in any kind of transaction, social networks play a significant role. Regardless of whether it is a material or non-material transaction, social networks play a determining role in defining different social relations. Granovetter puts it as 'strength of weak ties', which is attributed as a key element of social relations. In the cases of productivity, market, innovation and profit, social networks play a key role in achieving the expected outcomes. People having larger social networks and more interactions with other people have greater possibilities of acquiring services and resources. It is the social network of an individual which determines his/her location in the competitive world of market (Granovetter 1973, 1995). Thus, informal or formal ways of connecting different people of society can be regarded as important aspects of the distribution of public resources and benefits.

Usually, public- or private-sector resources and schemes are distributed in a structured and formal manner. However, in practice, a contrasting picture appears which brings to light some untold stories of public administration in India (Gupta 2012). How people try to acquire maximum benefits surpassing those of others, by jeopardizing the integrity of public sector institutions, is an important and emerging issue in the everyday practice of public governance in India. How people are trapped in the quagmire of red tape and nepotism and how they try to find alternative ways to get rid of this quagmire are the key concerns of various social scientists. How people use their personal connections to acquire maximum benefits, how certain relations of people get precedence over other relations, how vulnerable and marginalized people leave no stone unturned to acquire benefits and how public resources are distributed among the common people are important aspects of public administration in a neoliberal economy (Das and Poole 2004).

In a developing country like India, citizens, to a large extent, have to depend on the state for their basic requirements to maintain a minimum standard of living. Under such circumstances, the state plays an important role, as the elected representatives and public officials hold central positions in governance and also in the delivery of public services. In this context, proper conceptualization of the state in an informal set-up is crucial in order to understand different aspects of the latter and its politics. The state should be understood anthropologically, instead of being understood as having a discrete or singular identity; following the analysis of Foucault, the state should be regarded as a bundle of everyday institutions and forms of rules (Corbridge et al. 2012). In this context, it is not possible to offer a comprehensive review and survey of the nature of the state here. Rather, the aim of this chapter is to demonstrate the fluid interrelationships between the organs of the state and marginalized people.

It is by now well understood that the rich and affluent do not always need to engage with the state machinery in direct ways on a day-to-day basis; on the other hand, poor people do need this engagement more. For their sustenance, they are dependent on the state. They consider the state as their guardian. Inequitable distribution of public resources and inequities based on ethnicity, community and also regional differences have a huge impact on the overall development of a society. Meanwhile, corruption too adds several pathways that hinder progress.

In India, the government is present in some way or the other, mostly in the form of soft power trying to keep an eye on every move an individual makes at an individual level—be it a common citizen or a government employee. Yet, commodities and services are not equally distributed among all the people in a society. This has led to people engaging informal ways to reach the concerned authorities or department of the government.

These informal ways have helped people get their work done within a limited period of time. Networks are being created on the basis of religion, ethnicity and community alliance and also through paid intermediaries (*dalals*) that take bribes to get one access to welfare services and also to government documentations. How networks are becoming a crucial factor in the acquisition of benefits has been discussed by various scholars. The social capital of an individual which the individual acquires through social interactions and hereditary positions has multiple roles in the distribution and accumulation of resources (Bourdieu 1984). In a nutshell, social networks, in the form of social interactions, social capital, cultural capital or a complex assimilation of these elements, have a deciding role in the process of the distribution of public resources and benefits. People who do not have large social networks or cultural capital have to find other ways to reach government officials or concerned authorities. Here comes the role of the intermediaries. As put forward by Tocqueville, 'intermediary bodies stand between the isolated individual and the tyrannical potential of the majority or the state' (Galnoor 1975). This chapter tries to elucidate the role of the intermediaries and social networks, how through petty corruption people get benefits, how the state operates within this sphere, how religion, community and ethnicity networks are built and how, like through relying on intermediaries, people evolve alternative ways to reach out to officials for availing their benefits.

The Field

The survey for the present study was conducted in Napam panchayat of Sonitpur district in Assam. The demographic structure of Napam panchayat is heterogeneous, comprising the communities such as the ex–tea garden community, the tea-garden tribes known as *adivasis* in

Assam, the Bengali-speaking (Mymensingha) Hindus and Muslims, Nepalis, Boros, Kacharis, Biharis and Assamese caste Hindus. Most of the people are involved in agricultural activities, while poor sections of the population depend on wage labour at construction sites besides agricultural activities. Among the villages under study, which are located in Napam panchayat, one village is also called Napam, which is located adjacent to Tezpur University, and another village, Amolapam, is located on the other side of the university. Bhitor Parowa and Noorbari tea estates are located near Tezpur town.

The above-mentioned villages are mostly dependent on mono crops. Very few cultivators opt for double-crop cultivation. The River Jia Bharali flows near these villages. There is no forest located around these villages. Collection of forest products is out of the question. From March to August, these areas receive a heavy amount of rain. Most of the time, villagers face the problem of flood.

Governance processes lead to people's interaction with various state-level institutions. In order to understand these processes, a sample was drawn from the voter list. Through random sampling procedure, the list of respondents was selected from the voter lists of these villages. The people from the panchayat claim that it is one of the biggest panchayats in Assam in terms of population size. The objective of this survey was to understand the various nuances of the governance and people's perception about the same. The main objectives were to know the status and affordability of and accessibility to such services as education, health and various social welfare schemes.

People do various kinds of jobs to sustain themselves and their families. Sometimes, it is difficult for them to get a job or earn, due to lack of enough working opportunities. People often go to Tezpur town to work as daily wage labourers. A few also work in stationery or grocery shops as helpers. A majority of landless men and women work on agricultural lands. However, local landowners often complain that they are not able to generate any earnings from agriculture. They do not get people to work on their lands. They attribute this to two main factors. One is the Mahatma Gandhi National Rural Employment Guarantee Act (MGNREGA), which gives temporary employment to many people. The landowners claim that since it is a government project, there is much laxity. Doing less work, the labourers can earn a full day's wage. Hence, people do not want to come and work on the agricultural fields, where they have to do a certain amount of work in the presence of the landowner. It is also seen that in the study area, many people, even if they have a substantial amount of land, do not prefer to cultivate it. They have started leasing it out to other professional farmers who cultivate cash crops or vegetables with a high amount of investment and the use of chemicals.

Another factor the locals attribute to for the lack of labour force to work on the agricultural fields is the presence of brick kilns. A lot of manual labour is needed to work in the kiln. Mostly, the owners in this industry pay a good amount of money in advance to the labourers. Thus, the latter prefer to work in this sector though it demands a lot of hard work. The labour force cannot leave the work half-done, as they have to enter into an agreement before starting the work. The brick kiln industry uses an exploitative system to contractually employ whole families to work in the kiln, including children. In the Napam panchayat area, many new brick kilns have come up. The other categories of services in the area include teaching and other forms of employment in governmental and non-governmental sectors. There are people who are engaged in small business, owning petty shops in front of the university area. The main business centres in this locality are Napam centre and Panchmile centre. A market area in this locality is called as the centre. The market area here needs a special mention. In Tezpur town, most of the shops close by 7.30 pm, but these centres are mostly open until 11 pm. In these two market centres, people discuss various things, from religion to governance, politics and economic activities.

Out of the surveyed households, the majority residents have primary-level education, followed by those with no education. Very few come under the category of 'graduate and above'. People with higher-secondary education formed just 18 per cent of the surveyed population. During the survey and interview, it was found that though people are interested in education, they cannot afford it. The present generation has started sending their children to school because of the Mid-day Meal Scheme (MDM) of the government and free elementary education. Most of them feel that though their children get free food in the schools, the quality of education is not good in government-run schools. They feel that private schools are better than government schools, though they are more expensive than the government schools.

Napam panchayat is inhibited mostly by people adhering to Hinduism and Islam. They are Bengali-speaking Muslims and Hindus. The Nepalis, tea tribes, Assamese, Biharis and others follow Hinduism. They constitute the majority in the Napam area. Parts of the population of India belong to different categories on the basis of their socio-economic status, making them eligible for different kinds of social, economic and political benefits under the affirmative action of the Government of India. These categories are Scheduled Tribes (ST), Scheduled Castes (SC) and Other Backward Classes (OBC). Those who are considered socially advanced are classified under the 'General' category, and these people are not eligible for availing any benefit under the affirmative-action policy of the government.

This study examines how such groups of people in the Napam area have accessed welfare schemes. Of the sampled population, 54 per cent informed that they belong to the General category, and 33 per cent are OBCs, whereas SCs and STs constitute 12 per cent each. However, most of the people state their category as 'General', as they do not know their category exactly. Another reason for this is that they have never used their social category for acquiring any kind of service or scheme.

The study was conducted between 2014 and 2019. To understand different aspects of local-level governance and the role of social network in it, our survey explored ways of distribution of resources, how people interact to acquire benefits, how the officials accommodate with different situations to accomplish their tasks and how people try to acquire benefits in an informal way even after dealing with the rigid structure and formal rules and regulations, the researcher has to rely on both the primary and secondary data. To understand the different dynamics of interactions, the role of intermediaries (*dalals*), etc., we reviewed much literature, such as journals, books, newspaper articles, etc., to understand the distribution of resources at the grassroots level. To ascertain what mechanisms are employed by people to receive the benefits that they are entitled to, the researcher observed the functioning of the gram panchayat office in Napam.

The study's attempt was to understand how the different identities of caste, creed and religion are being actualized and translated in the process of the distribution of government resources. Personal affiliation to different groups and communities and social networks plays a crucial role in the process of mobilization of public resources and schemes. To determine how people find alternative ways to reach out to the government or how government policies reach the people through different ways and how resources are distributed through social networks, in this study, we have observed the processes of the distribution of goods and services.

'Sarkar': Government in Reality

What is 'sarkar', and who is the 'sarkar'? In everyday parlance, sarkar conveys more than one meaning and denotes many things that concern people directly. While sarkar means political parties, many view sarkar as a governing body formed through the electoral democratic system of voting and election of representatives. Some equate it to power and security for people—an instrument that has power to control (e.g., there is a mention of sarkar as an authority that controls the price of everyday essential items in the market and provides security to people). These people feel the necessity of such a sarkar. However, for many, sarkar signifies corruption that is irredeemable.[1] As a result, they would say that they do not need government and can survive without it. There is also another meaning given to sarkar, perhaps as a result of 'not needing government', in everyday life—that sarkar is people (which sounds as an assertion of popular sovereignty). One elderly woman, during my interview, replied, *amiei sarkar* ('We are the government').

A significant percentage of the people, during my fieldwork, expressed that the government was corrupt—it was busy with 'unnecessary things' not useful for citizens. The idea of power without responsibility and accountability is also observed: the government has the power to rule over the general masses; yet, powerful people having vested interests misuse the power for their own benefit. Many respondents accuse *dalals* for the misgovernment of their society. This also implies, for some, the absence of effective implementation of 'rules and laws' (e.g., this is seen as a factor leading to corruption). Many respondents stated that they need a 'powerful and corruption-free government' to bring changes in and development to the country. One of the respondents said that only during the elections would several political parties come to different villages and request people to vote for their respective parties. The latter give hope for the people's development through providing various facilities. However, after the elections, they become invisible. The following opinions from the respondents would substantiate the perception about government in the grassroots level.

A middle-aged man who belongs to a Nepali community narrates that for him the government is meaningless.[2] He feels that to become successful in life, we must not depend on the government. The political parties use the people for their own self-interests, as most of the people in his locality and even in many other rural parts of India are illiterate. However, to bring about any change in the government, people must be aware about the true worth of the political parties— their positive and negative intents. A young woman from the same community maintains that the government possesses both good and bad qualities. She says that the government provides full financial support to the people for development purposes. However, in the process of money distribution, some groups with vested interests, generally known by the term 'syndicates',[3] take away the resources meant for the poor people, causing the latter serious sufferings. She emphasizes the need for 'good leaders' who can take the country along the path of 'progress and development'. It is mainly responsible for corruption and price hikes. Many people feel that the sarkar should work for the poor people, as rich people can do things on their own.

However, some people in this locality opine that all political parties are corrupt. They equate 'sarkar' with the political parties. Though the Congress ruled the state for 15 years, it was not able to achieve the main target of development. Thus, one respondent felt that the Asom Gana Parishad (AGP) sarkar would be a better sarkar than the Congress. A man ranted that the Congress was a corrupt party, and that was why the country was not developing. He said that the officials, bureaucrats and politicians were embroiled in severe corruption. It adversely affected the common people, especially the ones who lived below the poverty line. He also mentioned that corruption was the main reason why the gap between the poor and the rich was increasing day by day.

People of Napam have a tendency to equate the government with political parties, such as the Congress, AGP, BJP, etc. For them, the government is a 'necessary evil'. Society takes care of their everyday needs, while the government creates trouble for them. Most women feel that the government does not do anything for their uplift. According to them, the political parties constitute an important part of the government. They are quite concerned about the present political situation. Mainly, they point out that the government does not give any importance to the development of backward areas.

While defining 'sarkar', a woman of around 45 years of age from Bhitor Parowa articulates that the public are the government.[4] This is because the public have the power to select and elect ministers, so that the latter can work for the citizens. However, after attaining power, the ministers assume themselves to be the government and utilize the power wrongly. Another respondent feels that the government is the office where people of a high status work and control everything, which is not for common people. Some of the respondents said that they did not understand all these (politics, government, etc.) things, because they were illiterate. They also felt that there was no need to know about them either, since they had spent half their life without knowing about them. Another old lady, who was a tea-garden labourer, identified ministers with the government. Many respondents feel that the government is something beyond their reach. This is why in villages people do not consider Panchayati Raj Institutions (PRIs) as the 'sarkar' or government. For them, 'sarkar' is an entity that holds a high position, is very powerful and is out of the reach of the common people.

A woman in her late 30s, from a Bengali Hindu community from Napam village, said that the government provided facilities to people[5] and was necessary for a country, especially for one like India where poor people live in large numbers. She opined that the government was everything—the most important thing in any country. She asked: is there a country that runs without a government? Without a government, a country would become instable. Thus, for her, the government is important for controlling our society.

On the side of officials who formed part of the bureaucracy, the issue of governance is implementation. During the interview, issues were raised in the context of e-governance and development schemes. It is believed that the e-governance system is an efficient form of governance. Most of the government officials, including the district informatics officer, feel that the e-governance system helps in reducing red tape and corruption in governance. The district informatics officer, for example, pointed out that issuing passports is much easier today in comparison to earlier days. Similarly, in court cases, judges get cases on the basis of a computerized shuffling system. In earlier days, there was a possibility that an individual judge might choose his/her cases based on some personal interest. However, now, computer programmes decide which judge gets which case.

Napam is part of the Balipara development block. The block development officer (BDO) of the Balipara development block said that MGNREGA was a very good poverty alleviation programme but was not working properly.[6] He said that the workers generally did not work according to the wages they got. Further, according to him, many MGNREGA workers, men and women, sit idle at the work site. If officials tell them to work, they retort that their money is for them and nobody can take away their money from them. They even threaten to go on a *dharna* (protest). The district informatics officer felt that people did only half the work but got full wages. They did not do quality work. He narrated that too much political intervention was also a problem in India. He had been reading an Assamese newspaper and had found a news item citing Michelle Obama, who was then the United States' First Lady, urging students to go to China and study the kind of development it had initiated. Then, he opined that in a country like India, where many people are still illiterate, democracy would not work. He said, 'Look at China, even if it is an authoritarian country, it is developing much faster and is going to be a super power very soon'. He also mentioned that though India had some wonderful social welfare programmes, the implementation and execution of these programmes were miserable. There are various reasons for this. The intervention of politicians is the biggest hurdle, whereby all kinds of programmes, even those with very good intentions, end up in disaster.

From the views gathered from various respondents, it appears that many understand that a government or sarkar is formed by their votes. The government is formed by the support of common people. According to them, the government is an important part of the country, because it implements laws and regulations. However, the government has become a necessary evil. Nevertheless, there is a second meaning to government that perhaps represents the thoughts of the deprived section of people, (e.g., those deprived of the benefits of welfare schemes which they are entitled to): the government is not a necessary entity, and one can survive without the government. Being dependent on the government, according to this section, is like wasting one's life without any meaning or achievement.

The Panchayat

In the Napam panchayat office, around 1:30 p.m., there was nobody except the *chowkidar*, and there was a man outside the office making some noise and abusing the *chowkidar*. When the latter was asked about what had happened, the man replied in anger that he had been coming to the office for many days to get a 'road pass'[7] but had not found anybody in the office except the chowkidar, who does not have the authority to issue this pass. The man, Abdul Hasim, shouted, '*kono nathake office ot...kiman dinor pora ahi aso mor eko kam howa nai, heiya sauk, president or chaki...khali hoi ase*' ('Nobody is present in the office...I have been coming here for so many days but none of my work has been done yet... look at that president's empty chair').

When the chowkidar was asked whether the president would come to the office that day or not, he replied in the negative—because of some personal work, the president would not come that day. He said that it was the time of panchayat elections, and the president was busy with several party meetings; therefore, it would be hard to meet him.

An old man who was waiting outside the panchayat house for the president stated, '*school or head master e mok koisil kone kone BPL card pabo tar list bonabo, kintu xeiya koribo golei manuhe muk bea pabo*' ('The headmaster of the school asked me to make a list of people who need to get a BPL card, but people will hate me if I do so'). He implied that there was much corruption in the selection of beneficiaries of the BPL (below poverty line) card. He even said that officials took bribes to provide any official document.

He narrated:

ami sorkaror prapyo nohoy, sorkar amar prapyo...jiman sakorial manuh ase ei bharotot, sob congressi manuh. Sonia Gandhi, Indira Gandhi bhal manuh, xeiya amar ma-deuta hoteu koi amiu kou.... Kintu ji eibur step by step (he means bureaucrats) manuh jene member, president, councilor, xeibilak beiman, dalal.... Ami congress ok support koru karon ma deuta e koi 'haat'[8] nohole kamei nohoy. kintu congress e aji amak eiya dise.... congress e amak diya nai, beleg sorkar howa hole dile heten.... ami Muslim holeu Bangladeshi nohoy...Muslim holei konob Bangladeshi hoi najai.

(Government is our right; it is not the other way around.... All the people engaged in government services are Congress party supporters.... Our parents said that Sonia Gandhi and Indira Gandhi are good people and I also agree. But these 'step by step' people (bureaucrats) like member, president, councilor etc. are actually corrupt and become *dalal*.... We supported Congress because our parents said that nothing can be done without a 'Hand'. You look today, what Congress has given us. We would definitely be benefited if there were another party in rule.... We are Muslims...we are not Bangladeshis, one does not become a Bangladeshi being a Muslim.)

He continued that the fee of a lawyer was ₹120, but if one went to court, a lawyer would demand ₹500 for the initiation of a case. If one went to the police station, the police would charge ₹50 for registering a case. So many wine shops, opium businesses and gambling operations were operating in Puniyani village.... These things are known to Panchmile police station, Goroimari police station, Tezpur main police station and even the deputy commissioner (DC) and the MLA. According to the man, people could not provide money, but they could provide a more valuable thing than money—their vote ('We give our vote to make them win'). In the conversation, he was frequently talking about '*dalals*'. He does not blame the Congress party or the state as a whole but merely these *dalals*, or power-hungry bureaucrats and officials, who exercise power over the masses.

People's Experiences at the Government Office

In their everyday life, most people visit the court and the government offices such as the agriculture office, block development office, panchayat office, DC's office, post office, revenue office, district transport office, etc. The officials there ask for bribes even for routine work. The problem is especially severe in the offices of the panchayat, Circle and DC and at the court and the police station. For a caste certificate, one has to pay at least ₹50 at the panchayat office, which is a very difficult prospect for poor people. Similarly, to get any work done at the Circle or DC office, one has to bribe officials directly or indirectly. Government officials behave well with people who bribe them and do their work but ignore people who do not bribe them. State-government officials do not come to office on time, do not give people vital information and take a lot of time to do even a small job. There is a problem of communication in terms of the language of governance, and often, people have intermediaries do their paperwork. However, government officials say that people are illiterate and ignorant about paperwork and do not understand official procedures despite the officials' best efforts to help.

The president of the panchayat claimed that it had implemented many developmental schemes and programmes, like Indira Awaas Yojana (IAY) and MGNREGA, from which 82 per cent of the population of Napam panchayat have benefitted. Panchayat members said that the panchayat had transferred all central- and state-government funds and benefits to the people, but the people said that only a few benefitted from panchayat activities and that the panchayat officials asked one IAY applicant to pay ₹10,000.

Interestingly, when people from rural areas visit the court, they try to contact an advocate from their own neighbourhood, religion or community, or one who speaks their language. They feel that they can trust only someone who speaks their language, which is one of the biggest obstacles in smooth governance. When people understand both the language of governance and everyday life, they prefer to visit the advocate who belongs to their own community.

The post-73rd Amendment phase is vital for the village society in India. As an institution of local self-government, the panchayat got a legal status with this amendment. However, the amendment also had a vast impact on the community life of the people apart from giving legal status to the panchayats. The caste system constitutes one of the most important components of Indian village society. The complex nature of the village society and the factions formed on the basis of caste are seen as impediments to the implementation of the 73rd amendment. In Assam, even though the practice of the caste system is not as rigid as it is in northern and southern India, it still exists in a very subtle form. The Brahmins and other high-caste Hindu groups in Assam downplay caste as a dominant social category. However, people belonging to lower caste groups, including Dalits, assert that caste still plays a great role in high-level politics, be it in the legislative arena or in the bureaucracy sphere. It is interesting to note that although caste and various other affiliations play an important role in the working of the panchayat, there are some effects of the panchayat also on the life of the people in the village. The influence of the community on the working of the panchayat ranges from selection of the beneficiaries and giving effect on various decision-making process. On the other hand, the effect of panchayat on community life is reflected in terms of group formation on the basis of different political parties.

From a sociological perspective, it is very interesting to look at the issue of community life and its changing patterns with the advent of panchayats. In Assam, the institution of Namghar used to work as the mobilizing force for the communities in a village. It not only worked as a cultural institution but also was a place for villagers' bonding, a means of identity and a place for decision-making. The importance of Namghar in Assam also lies in another context. Assam does not have Gram Sabhas in the modern sense of the term. The Namghar would perform the function of the Gram Sabha in the Assamese Hindu villages of the Brahmaputra Valley, because people used to gather in the Namghar to discuss various matters of social importance, including village development activities. Besides, small conflicts were also resolved in the Namghar.

It is observed that the introduction of the panchayat with the 73rd Amendment became a point of conflict within the community life based on Namghar. There is a visible shift in the group identity of the village, from a community based on Namghar to a faction based on political parties. Clashes in the village along party lines are becoming common nowadays. The situation has reached a stage where people have even started performing various religious activities with people from the same political parties.

While electioneering acts as a periodic occasion for the mobilization of people, the association of villagers with panchayats is a regular phenomenon. The people complained that the panchayat had brought the menace of corruption to the village. Some people stated that those who were in power in the panchayat did not even feel ashamed to indulge in corruption. They did it to fulfil their narrow interests. The beneficiaries of the various schemes are selected mainly along party lines, as well as on the basis of community and kinship ties. In the process, the actual needy persons are deprived of the benefits of the welfare schemes. Panchayat members have to oblige the party leaders and workers, as well as members from their community. The ultimate objectives of electioneering and institutionalization of panchayats, as discussed earlier, are eventually to ensure transparent and good governance. It is expected that such processes would lead to decentralization of power. On the contrary, however, what seems to have occurred at the ground level is that some corrupt and dishonest individuals with unholy alliances with higher-level political leaders and administrative officials have disrupted and derailed these objectives.

The Janus-Faced *Dalals*

In a socially and politically unstable society, people tend to form a community network, so that the person in power can help them at times of need. As Brinkerhoff and Goldsmith argue,

> [U]nder competitive conditions, political bosses need criteria to single out and reward followers and to exclude non-supporters. Even as such benefits dry up, there is logic to voting for politicians from one's own tribal or linguistic group, on the grounds that such a politician will tend to defend the interests of the group as a whole. (Brinkerhoff and Goldsmith 2002, 20).

A widow from Noorbari narrated a terrible story about intermediaries, whom she hates as they are very greedy and unreliable. She mentioned that a few years after her husband had died, since she had been facing troubles meeting her family's basic needs, she paid a *dalal* ₹30,000 to get her son a job and voted as he told her to, but her son did not get a job and the *dalal* never contacted her after that. She said she regretted her mistake.

From the respondents in Napam area, it was found that there are fixed rates to be paid to the *dalal*s for getting the benefits of various government schemes that are supposed to be distributed for free. People therefore demand prevention of corruption in the *gaon* panchayat. During this fieldwork, the villagers also informed us about many instances of discrepancies at the *gaon*-panchayat level. The brokers have fixed rates—pay ₹10,000 for the IAY, ₹1,000–₹1,500 for a latrine from the WASH (Water, Sanitation and Hygiene) scheme and ₹300–₹500 for a tin roof—but the price may be discounted for a person loyal to the political party in power.

Among the people interviewed in October 2018, there was one post office peon on contract.[9] He said that there were rules and regulations—if one does not get one's rightful benefits, then one could write an application to the panchayat president and get the same. Another person replied strongly, '*Belege jodi nilikhi pai, ami kyo likhibo lage*' ('If somebody get something without writing any application, then why should we write').

Some people who are keen to keep themselves updated politically are well aware about the situation and know the legality of the PRIs. People complain that hardly any developmental work has been done by the Congress government—that the latter is totally corrupt and does not understand anything except money. The *dalal* is the biggest object of hatred for the people. When it came to the question of governance, they started abusing the *dalal*, and when they were asked why they contacted him always if they hated him that much, they replied that there was a *mazboori* (compulsion), and because of the *mazboori* they had to contact a *dalal*. One respondent argued in front of the gathering that poor people did not get job cards and jobs through MGNREGA—only the rich ones did. He claimed that he could show how rich people got job cards and money. He said, '*konu din hatar kud eta dhara nai, si pai paisa*' meaning that he had never held a shovel or spade but got money from the MGNREGA scheme.

A man at the Napam centre spoke about the government and the governed in the context of the elections and their leader and explained the election mechanism. He said that the brokers know whom, how and when to contact. The night before the elections, they pay anyone who might get them a few votes for ₹500 or ₹1,000. The money may not last more than a couple of days but is enough to fool people for 5 years. 'Everybody is playing with one another', he said. 'There are strings attached to us; we are like *khilonas* (puppets) in the hands of political leaders, and we dance the way they want us to'. While he was narrating this, the owner of a paan shop voiced the same concern as him. They together emphasized how their village, especially the rural areas, was in a very difficult situation.

A male primary-school teacher from the Nepali community of Napam village had collected money from around 25 elderly persons—₹200 per head—saying that he would get them old-age pension. He told them that he knew officials in the block office to get this done. Till now, however, these people have not received any pension. A Muslim woman aged 30 from Rupkuria village, who was an *anganwadi* worker, took ₹1,000 each from around 30 persons, promising them old-age pension, various loans, ration card, etc. She told the people that their names would not be included in the list of beneficiaries if they did not pay a bribe to the government officials at the block office. However, till now, only six persons have received old-age pension. It was also found that the husband of an *anganwadi* worker from the Muslim community in Bhalukjharan village collected around ₹5,000 each from around 15 persons, promising them jobs in *anganwadi* centres. Only two have been provided with jobs.

Conclusion

Interactions between the state and poor people often happen on a regular basis; however, the rich and the affluent do not need to engage with the state as much as the poor do. The intermediaries like the *dalals* facilitate the transactions or engagements between the affluent class and the state. The *dalals* are influenced by ethnicity, community and, to an extent, regional differences. The *dalals* are just one example of the many informal ways to reach and avail the benefits of the state. The formal way of putting this can be, having a good 'social capital', which is again not isolated to ethnicity, community and religion. Much research is therefore needed at different times (government regimes) and in different spaces (places) to understand the ever-evolving and complex nature of people's engagement with the state.

In a country like India, it is not possible to have a governance system that is totally based on formal mechanisms. Most people who belong to the poorer sections of society do not always know the language of governance. In this context, the *dalal* becomes important in helping them and takes some incentives for the same. This involvement of intermediaries creates difficult conditions for both the governed and the state. It was believed that due to digitalization and e-governance the role of intermediaries would become insignificant. However, it is seen from the study that most of those who do not know how to handle digital processes depend on the customer-support point. These customer-support points are believed to act as intermediaries between the people and the government. Thus, one needs to look at the complex process of interaction between the people and the state which is mediated through *dalals* to understand the nature and process of governance in the margins.

Notes

1. India recently witnessed the 'India Against Corruption' movement led by Anna Hazare. This anti-corruption movement caught people's imagination. Capitalizing on this campaign, Arvind Kejriwal, with his supporters, formed a party called the Aam Aadmi Party, which formed the government in Delhi for 49 days. Electronic media and print media equally carried live coverage and news stories of the anti-corruption movement. These events had an all-India impact due to the continuous electronic media coverage. Even the rural masses who were hardly concerned about the big corruption at the national level came to understand some of the issues. They were concerned about the immediate livelihood issues and challenges they faced in everyday life. It appears that in the context of our study, such anti-corruption discourse has influenced many people, even in rural areas, who have started stating that corruption is the root cause of all sorts of problems in governance.
2. Interviewed on March 2018 at Napam Village.
3. In Assam, people generally refer to a 'syndicate' as an organized group of individuals formed to do some illegal activities. The term denotes the racketeers responsible for hoarding money, collecting illegal tax money and hiking the price of essential commodities.
4. Interviewed on April 2018 at Bhitor Parowa.
5. Interviewed on April 2018 at Napam village.
6. The interview was conducted in the month of March 2018 at the office of the block development officer (BDO), Balipara.
7. To enter the army cantonment area in Solamar region, one requires a permit. An outburst by a person is observed in the following.
8. *Haat* means hand, which is the electoral symbol of the Indian National Congress party.
9. Many people were interviewed, and non-participant observations were collected in October 2018 in and around the panchayat office in relation to their complaints and frustrations.

References

Bourdieu, P., ed. 1984. *Distinction: A Social Critique of the Judgement of Taste*. Cambridge, MA: Harvard University Press.

Brinkerhoff, D. W. and A. A. Goldsmith. 2002. *Clientelism, Patrimonialism and Democratic Governance: An Overview and Framework for Assessment and Programming*. Washington: United States Agency of International Development (USAID).

Corbridge, S., M. Williams and R. Véron. 2012. 'Politics of Middleman and Political Society'. In *Re-framing Democracy and Agency in India*, edited by Ajay Gudavarthy, 172–198. London: Anthem Press.

Corbridge, Stuart, Glyn Williams, Manoj Srivastava and René Véron. 2005. *Seeing the State: Governance and Governmentality in India.* New York, NY: Cambridge University Press.

Das, V. and D. Poole. ed. 2004. *Anthropology in the Margins of the State.* New Delhi: Oxford University Press.

Galnoor, Itzhak. 1975. 'Government Secrecy: Exchanges, Intermediaries, and Middlemen'. *American Society for Public Administration* 35, no. 1: 32–42. Available at https://www.jstor.org/stable/975199 (accessed on 22 March 2021).

Granovetter, Mark. 1973. 'The Strength of Weak Ties'. *American Journal of Sociology* 78, no. 6: 1360–1380.

———. 1995. *Getting a Job: A Study of Contacts and Careers*, 2nd ed. Chicago, IL: University of Chicago Press.

Gupta, Akhil. 2012. *Red Tape: Bureaucracy, Structural Violence and Poverty in India.* Durham: Duke University Press.

About the Editor and the Contributors

Editor

G. Amarjit Sharma is an Assistant Professor at the Special Centre for the Study of North East India (SCSNEI), Jawaharlal Nehru University (JNU), Delhi, India. He has previously taught political studies at Nambol L. Sanoi College, Bishnupur District, Manipur (2009–2013). He has been associated with a summer institute on Critical Global Humanities at the Brown International Advanced Research Institutes (BIARI), Brown University, USA (2011). He was associated with the Peace Research Institute Oslo, Norway, and collaborated on a project titled 'Making Women Count for Peace'. He has published papers in the journals such as *Economic & Political Weekly*, *The Eastern Anthropologist*, *The Oriental Anthropologist* and *Man in India*. He has also contributed chapters in edited volumes on critical studies in politics, modernity and ethnic processes, cultural practices, identity politics and other subjects. He is primarily interested in the political economy of development, tribal and ethnic studies and anthropology of state and society.

Contributors

Sherin Ajin is a doctoral student at the National Institute of Advanced Studies, Bengaluru. Registered at the Manipal Academy of Higher Education, her doctoral thesis engages with spatialization and processes of legitimation of nation state at the borderland of Tawang through the popular discourses of security and development. Her areas of interest include critical border studies, processes of identity formation and political philosophy. Her recently published work is 'Situating the Sino-Indian Border of Tawang in the Border Studies

Discourse' in *Tawang, Monpas and Tibetan Buddhism in Transition*, edited by M. Mayilvaganan, N. Khatoon and S. Bej (2020).

Rashi Bhargava is an Assistant Professor at the Department of Sociology, Maitreyi College, University of Delhi. She recently published a co-edited book with Achla Pritam Tandon and Gopi Tripathy titled *Social Scientist in South Asia: Personal Narratives, Social Forces and Negotiations* (2020). Her upcoming publications include a co-edited volume with Tiplut Nongbri titled *Materiality and Visuality in North East India: An Interdisciplinary Perspective*.

Anup Shekhar Chakraborty is an Assistant Professor, Department of Political Science and Political Studies, Netaji Institute for Asian Studies, Kolkata, and a member of the Mahanirban Calcutta Research Group, Kolkata. He was the recipient of the International Development Research Centre, DEF and IDF 'India Social Science Research Award 2009'. He was the C. R. Parekh Fellow (2011–2012) at Asia Research Centre, London School of Economics and Political Science. He has authored *Hegemonies, Hyphenations, Hybridisations: Braided Entanglements of Identities, Religion and Politics in Mizoram* (2020), *Religion and Politics in Mizoram* (2020), *Politics of Autonomy and Ethnic Cocooning in Mizoram* (2015) and *Hegemony to Hyphenation: Hybridization of Identities and Politics in Mizoram* (2015). He has also co-edited (with Padam Nepal) *Politics of Culture, Identity, and Protest in North-east India* (2012, Vols 1 and 2) and *Politics of Exclusions and Inclusions in India: Construing Commonalities and Complexities* (2016).

Oyindrila Chattopadhyay is a research associate at Institute for Conflict Management in New Delhi. She received her PhD degree from SCSNEI, JNU. She is interested in South Asia, India's internal security, conflict studies, migration and ethnicity. She is currently working on conflict scenarios, including militant activities in Northeast India.

Chubatila teaches political science at the master's level at St. Joseph University, Dimapur, Nagaland. She completed her MPhil/PhD programme from the Centre for the Study of Law and Governance, JNU. Her research interests include violence and the state, extraordinary laws, classificatory practices of the state, 'suspect' populations and governance and its legal aspects.

Amiya Kumar Das is an Associate Professor at the Department of Sociology, and coordinator of Centre for Public Policy and Governance at Tezpur University, Assam. He has co-edited a book with Sadan Jha, and Dev Nath Pathak titled *Neighbourhoods in Urban India: In Between Home and the City* (2021) and with Dev Nath Pathak, *Investigating Developmentalism: Notions of Development in the Social Sphere* (2019). He has also recently contributed six entries on the topics related to 'Governance and Government' in the *Global Encyclopedia of Public Administration, Public Policy, and Governance*, edited by A. Farazmand (2020).

Tanmoy Das is a doctoral student at SCSNEI, JNU, Delhi. He works on state capacities and development schemes in Northeast India.

L. Basanti Devi completed her PhD from the Centre for the Study of Social Systems, JNU, Delhi. She was associated with Omeo Kumar Das Institute of Social Change and Development, Guwahati, and Peace Research Institute Oslo, Norway, for a project, 'Women Count for Peace: Gender, Empowerment and Conflict in South Asia', funded by the Research Council, Norway. She was associated with a summer institute on Humanitarian Response and Post-conflict Reconstruction under BIARI, Brown University, USA, in 2015. Her recent publication is 'Meira Paibis: Forms of Activism and Representation of Women in Manipur,' in *Women, Peace and Security in Northeast India*, edited by Ashild Kolas (2017).

Jangkhomang Guite is an Associate Professor at the Department of History, Manipur University, Manipur. Earlier, he was assistant professor at the Centre for Historical Studies, JNU, Delhi, and at the Department of History, Assam University, Silchar, Assam. He is the author of the book *Against State, against History: Freedom,*

Resistance and Statelessness in Upland Northeast India (2018). Some of his recently published articles in journals are 'Colonialism and Its Unruly? The Colonial State and Kuki Raids in Nineteenth Century Northeast India', *Modern Asian Studies* (2014, vol. 48, no. 5, 1188–232); 'Civilisation and Its Malcontents: The Politics of Kuki Raid in Nineteenth Century Northeast India', *The Indian Economic & Social History Review* (2011, vol. 48, no. 3, 339–376); and 'Representing Local Participation in INA–Japanese Imphal Campaign: The Case of Kukis in Manipur, 1943–45', *Indian Historical Review* (2010, vol. 37, no. 2, 291–310).

Santosh Hasnu is an Assistant Professor teaching undergraduate history courses at Hansraj College, University of Delhi. Recently, he has published on labour mobilization for road construction in colonial India: 'Disciplining the Hill Tribes into *Coolie* Labour for Road Construction', in *The Palgrave Handbook of Bondage and Human Rights in Africa and Asia*, edited by Gwyn Campbell and Alessandro Stanziani (2020) and 'Inception of Aviation Routes between India and China' (*Economic & Political Weekly*, 2017). His forthcoming works include 'Coolie Labour, Tea Planters and Transport in Colonial India' for an ITH volume, *Global Commodity Chains and Labour Relations* (2021).

R. K. Sanayaima is a doctoral student at the Centre for North East Studies and Policy Research, Jamia Millia Islamia (A Central University), New Delhi. Earlier, he was a research assistant at the Nehru Memorial Museum and Library, Delhi.

M. Amarjeet Singh is a Professor and Hon. Director at the Centre for North East Studies and Policy Research, Jamia Millia Islamia (A Central University), New Delhi, where he teaches courses on social conflict and society and politics of India's Northeast. He has previously worked with Institute for Defence Studies and Analyses, New Delhi, and National Institute of Advanced Studies, Indian Institute of Science Campus, Bengaluru. He has written on conflict studies, identity politics and migration studies in widely circulated journals, such as *Journal* of *Asian Public Policy*, *Small Wars & Insurgencies*, *Commonwealth & Comparative Politics* and *Economic & Political Weekly*. He has edited several books, including *Identity, Contestation and Development in Northeast India* (2016), *Northeast India and India's Act East Policy: Identifying the Priorities* (2019) and *Understanding Urbanisation in Northeast India: Issues and Challenges* (2020).

Index

Aam Aadmi Party, 293
Act East Policy (earlier Look East Policy), 139, 237
Ahom Dynasty, 3–4
Ahom-Sanskritic culture of Brahmaputra Valley and Barak Valley, 4
aliens in big Indian cities, northeasterners feeling as, 9
All Assam Students' Union (AASU), 14, 110
All Bodo Students' Union (ABSU), 14
All India Bharatiya Gorkha Parishad, 120
All Meghalaya Students' Union (AMSU), 114
All Shillong Mahila Samiti, 120
Angami Youth Organization (AYO), 140
Anglo-Burmese War in 1826, 27
Anglo-Garo War 1872–1873, 79
Anglo-Khasi War 1829–1833, 79
Anglo-Manipur War 1891, 79, 86, 198, 207
Ao, Imkongliba, 76
Armed Forces (Assam and Manipur) Special Powers Act, 1958, 155
Armed Forces (Assam and Manipur) Special Powers Ordinance, 1958, 155
Armed Forces (Assam and Manipur) Special Powers Regulation, 1958, 155
Armed Forces Special Powers Act (AFSPA), 1958, 151, 155, 158, 172–75, 179, 183

Armed Forces (Special Powers) Ordinance, 1942, 155
armed opposition groups (AOG), 209
Arunachal Pradesh, 5, 50–53
  timber extraction in, 62
Asian Development Bank (ADB), 223, 226, 240
Assam, 17
Assam Movement (1979–1985), 77, 79
  British control over, 5
  experience of people at government offices, 287–89
  Napam panchayat, 285–87
  Napam panchayat of Sonitpur, fieldwork in, 277–81
  paid intermediaries (*dalals*) in, 290–92
  sarkar (government) in reality, 281–85
Assam Disturbed Areas Act, 1955, 154
Assam Maintenance of Public Order (Autonomous Districts) Act, 1953, 154
Assam Rifles, 155
Association of Southeast Asian Nations (ASEAN), 237

Barphookan, Lachit, 77
Berger, John, 53
Bhagabati, Ananda, 6
Bhasa Sahid (language martyrs) 1961, 89
bilateral development finance institutions (DFIs), 226
BJP, 283

Bombay Plan (BP), 1944, 231
Border Area Development
  Programme (BADP), 61
borders
  defined, 49
  mental representation of, 49
Bordoloi Committee, 103
Brahma, Rupnath, 79
British East India Company (EIC), 25
British policy of Partially Excluded
  and Excluded of 1874, 102
British rule in Northeast, 4
Buddhism, 60
Bum La, 57
Burmese aggression, 4

Cachar, 43–45
  and British Raj ideology, 31–38
  and laws of succession, 31–38
  as British protectorate, 29–31
  military establishment by British,
    38–43
  pre-colonial political condition of,
    26–29
Central Reserve Police Force
  (CRPF), 212
Centre for Research Advocacy
  Manipur (CRAM), 226
Chakhesang Mothers' Association
  (CMA), 140
Chambers, O. A., 11
Chamling, Pawan, 152
Chand, Chura, 198
Chandra, Govind, 25, 29, 31, 43
Chandra, Krishna, 27
Chaube, S. K., 4
Chettri, N. S., 15
China, 50
  occupation of Tibet, 58
Chin Hills Regulations, 1896, 12
Civic Action Programme (CAP), 216
civil society(ies), concept of
  defined, 127–28
  historical trajectory of, 125–28

Coalition of Civil Society Groups,
  Manipur, 151
Cold War, 49
commemoration in public spaces, of
  Northeast states, 74–85
  and contested memories, 95–97
  counter-memory, 87–92
  kinship memory and activism,
    86–87
  remembrance to silent
    communities, 92, 94–95
Comptroller and Auditor General
  (CAG), 258
Conferment of Equal Facilities to
  the Permanent Gorkha Settlers of
  Mizoram, 15
Congress, 283
Congress (I), 15
Constitution (Scheduled Tribes)
  Order, 1950, 104
corporate social responsibility (CSR),
  62
cosmetic federalism, 5

Dalai Lama
  14th, 50
  fifth, 51
  sixth, 51
Daulatram, Jairamdas, 58
Department of Karmik and
  Adhyatmik Affairs (DoKAA), 63
detenus, grading of, 179–82
developmental ideology—rational
  thought, 231
developmental projects, 230–32
Devi, Irom Sharmila, 157
diffusionist modernizing, 6
Downs, F. S., 3

Eagleton, Terry, 53–57
Eastern Nagaland People
  Organization (ENPO), 133
Eastern Nagaland Women
  Organisation (ENWO), 133, 136

Eastern Naga's Public Organization (ENPO), 136
Eastern Naga Students' Federation (ENSF), 133, 136
East Khasi Hills Autonomous District Council, 119
Elwin, Verrier, 59
emotional integration, 59
ethnic boundaries, 102
ethnic conflicts, between Nepali Gorkha and local populations, 13–19
ethnonationalism, 95
Extent of Local Laws Act of 1874, 103
extrajudicial killings, 157

Federation of Khasi, Jaintia and Garo People (FKJGP), 105–06, 114–17
fei-ization, 9
Fergusson, Adam, 125
First Information Report (FIR), 178–79
FNR, 133

Galden Namgyal Lhatse monastery, Tawang, 59
Gallawalahs, 11
Garo Hills Regulation of 1876, 103
Garo tribe, 101, 103
gemeinschaft (civil society), 126
gemeinschaft (community), 126
geo-ethnic character, 6
geographical location, of Northeast region, 150
Ghising, Subash, 18
globalization, 49
Gorkha, 11
Gorkhaland movement, 17–19
Gorkha Public Panchayat, 120
Gorkhas
    Indian Nepalis called, 13
    permanent settlement in Mizoram, 10–12
Gorkhey identity, 18

governmentality of developments projects, 241–46
Government of India Act, 1935, 52, 103
Gramsci, Antonio, 126
Great Assam earthquake of 1950, 58
Gurung, Bimal, 18
Guwahati Manipuri Student Union, 207
gye tongpa, 51

haat, 293
habeas corpus, 185, 191–92
    defined, 175–77
    history of, 175–77
    in India, 176
    writ of sovereign privilege, 177
habeas paper book, 177–79
Habermas, Jurgen, 126
Haryana, 17
Hazare, Anna, 293
Hegel, G. W. F., 126
Hindi-Chini bhai bhai, 50
Hobbes, Thomas, 125
homogenous Naga (political) identity, 136

India Against Corruption, 293
Indo-China war of 1962, 54
Inner Line Permit (ILP) movement, 2013, 12, 52, 114, 116
insurgency in Northeast region
    governance of security affairs, 160–68
    historicizing violence, 154–58
    interventions of state of India to deal with, 151–54
    operations against insurgents, 158
    origin of, 150
    reasons for, 150
    violent incidents, impact on civilian, 160
intermediary bodies, 277
Islamic Development Bank (IDB), 226

Jaintia tribe, 101, 103
Jaintia Uprising 1860–1862, 79
Japan International Cooperation Agency (JICA), 223
Jaswantgarh, 56–57
Joint Interrogation Report, 179

Kangleipak Communist Party (KCP), 209
Kanglei Yawon Kanna Lup (KYKL), 154, 209
Kejriwal, Arvind, 293
Khandu, Pema, 64
Khasi Hills Autonomous District Council (KHADC), 106, 117, 119
Khasi Hills Autonomous District (Khasi Social Custom of Lineage) Act, 1997, 106–07
Khasi Hills Autonomous District (Khasi Social Custom of Lineage) Bill, 107
Khasi Hills Autonomous District (Trading by Non-Tribals) Rules 2019, 118
Khasi Hills Autonomous District (Village Administration) Bill, 2014, 108
Khasi Students' Union (KSU), 14, 105–06, 108, 110–14, 119, 121
Khasi tribe, 8, 103
Khonoma Fort, 82
Kingdom of Manipur, 3
Kingdom of Tripura, 4
Kristian Thalai Pawl (KTP), 17
Kuki-Chin-Lushai tribes, 10

Laldenga, Pu (Fahter of Mizo Nation), 82
Lamaic mysticism, 50
Lamyanba journal, 202, 203, 206
legal modernity, Henry Maine's theory of, 43
Leviathan (Thomas Hobbes), 48
Lewin, T. H., 11

liberal democratic state, 126
liberalization, privatization and globalization (LPG) in 1990, 237
Limbu, M. K., 15
Locke, John, 125

Macha Loishang, 204
Mahatma Gandhi National Rural Employment Guarantee Act (MGNREGA), 249
Mandal Commission Report, 17
Manipur
AFSPA in, 210–12
and postcolonial writings by women, 202–06
and space of women, 202–06
and women response against colonial state, 198–202
as nation, 206–10
Burmese annexation in 1817, 43
corruption in developmental projects, 270
developing villages of, 250–55
government schemes and engagement of people, 259–64
insurgency in, 206–10
Manipur Constitution of 1947, 207
Manipur Merger Agreement, 1949, 208
Meira Paibis (known as Nupi Kanglup) mass-based movement to counter depoliticization, 217–18
MGNREGA in, 254
patron–client relationship, 270
PMAY-G in, 255–58
relationship between state and villagers, 264–65
resistance in, 206–10
Manipur Chamber of Commerce (MCC), 239
Marx, Karl, 126
McMahon Line, 52

Meghalaya, 5, 17
  anti-colonial movements in, 79–82
  discourse of tribal and non-tribal, 101
  Khasi tribe as juridico-political category, 106–09
  land rights in, 104–06
  non-tribes, everyday experience of, 117–21
  property rights in, 104–06
  trading in, 104–06
Meghalaya (Benami Transactions Prohibition) Act, 1980, 105–06
Meghalaya Residents Safety and Security Bill (MRRSA) of 2016, 109
Meghalaya Students' Union (MSU), 110
Meghalaya Transfer of Land (Regulation) Act, 1971, 104
memorialization process, 73
Mid-day Meal (MDM) Scheme, 279
migration, 4
  among new frontiers, 9–13
  of Bengali Hindus from East Bengal, 10
Mines and Minerals (Development and Regulation) Act, 1957, 236
Ministry of Development of the North Eastern Region (DoNER), 61, 138, 152
misrepresentation of tribes, in non-tribal states, 75
Mizo Accord in 1986, 76
Mizo National Front (MNF), 15, 76, 82, 156
Mizoram Gorkha Youth Association (MGYA), 16
Mizoram Muslim Welfare Society (MMWS), 17
Mizo Zirlai Pawl (MZP), 16
Modi, Narendra, 240
monogamy of tribes, 76
Monpa folklore, 51
Mysore Tibetan Settlement, 63

Naga Baptist Church Council (NBCC), 133
Naga civil society, 133
Naga Club, 129
Naga Hills, British annexation of, 5
Naga Hills District Tribal Council (NHTDC), 129
Naga Hoho, 133, 136
Naga Labour Corps, 82
Nagaland, 5, 17
  civil society organizations in, 128–32
  extortion money used to terrorise Nepali/Gorkha, 15
  missing pieces in civil society, 136–41
  Nagaland Communitisation of Public Institutions and Services Act, 2002, 139
  Nepalis burnt in, 13
  social politics and power, 132–36
Naga Mothers' Association (NMA), 173, 133
Naga National Council (NNC), 77, 82, 129–30, 154
Naga People's Council, 76
Naga People's Movement for Human Rights (NPMHR), 129, 133, 157, 169
Naga Students' Federation (NSF), 133, 173
Naga Tribal Council (NTC), 137
Naga Tribes Council (NTC), 173
Nangbah, U. Kiang, 76, 79
Nathu La, 56
National Centre for Agricultural Economics and Policy Research (NCAP), 238
National Green Tribunal (NGT), 64
National Hydro Power Corporation's (NHPC) Gurez model, 62
National Planning Committee (NPC), 231
National Register of Citizens of India (NRC), 5

National Rural Employment
　Guarantee Act (NREGA), 216
National Security Act (NSA), 1980,
　179
National Socialist Council of
　Nagaland (NSCN), 131
National Socialist Council of Nagalim-
　Khaplang (NSCN-K), 131
Nehru Park, 77
Nepamul, 13
nepotism, 276
New Exploration and Licensing
　Policy (NELP), 236
NITI Forum for North East, 61
North-East Border Defence
　Committee (Himmatsinghji
　Committee) 1951, 58
North Eastern Council (NEC), 7,
　61, 138
North-Eastern Frontier, British
　acknowledge strategic significance
　of, 4
North Eastern Hill University
　(NEHU), 111
Northeastern territorial zones and
　spaces, 6
Northeast Experts, 8
North-East Frontier Agency
　(NEFA), 50, 52, 54, 60
North-East Frontier Tract, 52
North East Students Organization, 10
NSCN (IM), 131, 149
NSCN (U), 131
Nungba Youth Association (NYA),
　266
Nupi Lan, 199
Nupi Samaj, 214–15
Nyukmádong, Chinese aggression
　at, 55
Nyukmadong War Memorial, 56

Obama, Michelle, 284
OECD Development Assistant
　Committee (DAC), 224

Open Acreage Licensing Policy
　(OALP), 2017, 236
Operation Bajrang, 156
Operation Somtal II in 2007, 156
ostensible homogeneities, 7–9

Panchayati Raj Institutions (PRIs), 283
Pan Manipur Youth League
　(PANMYL), 206
Patel, Sardar, 58
People's Independence League, 130
People's Liberation Army (PLA), 209
People's Revolutionary Party of
　Kangleipak (PREPAK), 209, 212
Phizo, A. Z. (Father of the [Naga]
　Nation), 82
Phodrang, Ganden, 50
politics of exclusion, 175
politics of remembering, 74
post-colonial administration in the
　Northeast, 6
postcolonial period/moment, in
　ex-colonies, 72–74
Pradhan Mantri Awaas Yojana
　(PMAY), 249
Prevention of Terrorism Ordinance
　(POTO) 2001, 175
public distribution system (PDS),
　216
Punjab, 17
Putnam, Robert, 126

Railways Act, 1989, 236
Ram, Tula, 26–27, 31
Rao, Narasimha, 237
Rashtriya Rifles, 155
Rawat, Nain Singh, 52
red tape, 276
Reimbursement of Security Related
　Expenditure Scheme, 151
resistance in region, due
　developments projects, 241–46
resource frontier, 237–41
Rousseau, Jean-Jacques, 125

Samaddar, Ranabir, 4
Sangma, Pa Togan, 79
Sangma, Togan, 76
Sankerdev Park, 77
Save Mon Region Federation (SMRF), 64
Scheduled Districts Act, 103
security of state, 232–37
Sharma, R. K., 13
Simon Commission, 128
Singh, Chourjeet, 27, 29
Singh, Gambhir, 26–27, 29, 31, 38–43
Singh, Lakshman, 60
Singh, Manmohan, 157
Singh, Marjeet, 27–29
Singh, N. Biren, 239
Singh, Raja Nara, 198
Sing, Tirot, 76
Sing, U. Tirot, 79
social associations, 135–36
social capital, 277
social identity (theory of), 102
South Asia Sub-regional Economic Cooperation (SASEC) programme, 225
Sradhanjalee Park, 77
St. Bartholomew's Day massacre (1572), Paris, 48
subnationalism, 95

Tawang
  and Indo-China relations, 50–53
  anti-dam agitations on hydropower MoUs, 63–64
  firing incident in 2016, 63
  militarized development in, 58–62
  production of nationalist visual regime, 53–57
  twin name boards for tourist and pilgrim sites, 64
Tawang Monpa community, 64
terms of engagement, 197

Thapa, B. K., 15
Thapa, J. P., 15
The Union Territories Act, 1963, 208
Tibet Autonomous Region, 50
Tirot Sing Memorial, 79
Tocqueville, De Alexis, 125
Togan Sangma Memorial Park, 79
Tonnies, Ferdinand, 126
Topeng La, 57
torture
  attempted suicide attempt by Lotha, case study, 184–91
  techniques used in extracting confessions, 183–84
transnational developmental discourse, 224–30
Treaty of Badarpur (1824), 30–31, 37
Treaty of Westphalia in 1648, 130
Treaty of *Yandaboo* 1826, 128
tribalism, 136
tribalogy, 75, 76
tribe(s)
  and identity politics, 100–03
  as politico-spatial category, 103–04
  versus hill tribes, 102
  versus plains, 102

U. Kiang Nangbah Memorial Park, 79
Unified Command, 158
United Committee Manipur (UCM) Y, 209
United Khasi-Jaintia Hills District (Trading by Non-Tribals) Regulation, 1954, 117
United Liberation Front of Asom (ULFA), 149, 156–58
United National Liberation Front (UNLF), 149, 209
Unlawful Activities (Prevention) Act, 1967, 151, 187
Uranium Corporation of India Limited (UCIL), 111

Vaishnavite culture of Manipur valley, 4
variegated heterogeneities, 7–9
village councils (VCs), 138
village development boards (VDBs), 138

Walzer, Michael, 126
Weiner, Myron, 5
welfare of state, 232–37

Young Mizo Association (YMA), 17
Yul Mandrelgang, 51

Zeliangrong Baudi civil society group, 224, 226
Zemithang, 57
Zo Hills, 11
Zo/Mizo tribes, 4, 8, 19